STRICTLY PERSONAL

John S. D. Eisenhower

STRICTLY PERSONAL

1974

DOUBLEDAY & COMPANY, INC.
GARDEN CITY, NEW YORK

PHOTOGRAPH CREDITS

4 and 5. Harris and Ewing, Washington, D.C.   16. Wide World Photos   17. United States Army Photograph   19. United States Navy Photograph   25. United States Army Photograph   26. United States Army, Special Corps   28. United States Army Photograph   30. United Press Photo   32 and 33. Wide World Photos   34. United Press Photo   35. United Press Photo   37. Wide World Photos   38. United States Army Photograph   39. Wide World Photos   40. Paul Schutzer, Time-Life Picture Agency   43. United States Information Service, India   44. French Embassy, Press and Information Division   45. Wide World Photos   46. Wide World Photos   48. George Cserna, New York City   49. The White House, Official Photograph   50 and 53. United States Information Service, Brussels, Belgium   51. Institut Belge d'Information et de Documentation

Library of Congress Cataloging in Publication Data

Eisenhower, John S. D., 1922–
  Strictly personal.

  Autobiographical.
  1. Eisenhower, John S. D., 1922– I. Title.
E748.E29A37   327′.2′0924 [B]
ISBN 0-385-07071-3
Library of Congress Catalog Card Number 73-20510

To my Mother, Mamie Doud Eisenhower

ACKNOWLEDGMENTS

A book of this type is pretty much of a one-man job, but not quite. Other people make their contributions, some of them indispensable.

When I began writing, I had very little idea where I was going. Within a couple of days of getting off the plane from Brussels, I was beginning dictation, beginning with the last chapter, the Brussels experience. But even six months later, with many chapters drafted—some of which do not appear between these covers—the text constituted a rather formless mass, far from orderly, and with its final form a complete mystery.

It is here that I am deeply indebted to Bill Henderson of Doubleday. Seeing some possibilities in the morass, he encouraged me to send him chapter after chapter, as drafted, rendering suggestions and encouragement long before any contract had been signed.

The mainstay of the writing effort was my loyal secretary of six years, Mrs. Judith Horvath Tegethoff. Not only did she slug out draft after draft; she also took care of my personal business affairs as she had done in Brussels, leaving me free to "think book" as much as possible. Also, since she had been witness to the experience from the period described in "The Writing Game," she was able to offer valuable suggestions.

I am also indebted to those who took the time to refresh my memory on important facts. Such individuals include Edwin Crowley, William Buell, Michael Conlin, and George Moffitt of the State Department, all staff officers of the Brussels Embassy during my tenure as ambassador. My wife, Barbara, my Mother, my son, David, Colonel Roger Nye, Colonel Charles Tyson, and others contributed information and perspective in selected portions.

I am grateful to such persons as Admiral Arleigh Burke, The Honorable John J. McCloy, Brigadier General Frank McCarthy, and General Anthony McAuliffe for their permission to reproduce portions of their correspondence to lend credence and spice to the text. The cooperation of Dr. John Wickman, Don Wilson, and the staff of the Eisenhower Library at Abilene, Kansas, were also invaluable. Miss Bettie Sprigg, of the Directorate for Defense Information, Department of Defense, assisted in obtaining photographs from the Army Photo Library, as she had done with *The Bitter Woods* five years earlier.

Finally, I am highly indebted to my present secretary, Mrs. Walter E. (Ruth) Capper, who took over competently and without a hitch during the last several months after circumstances forced Judy's departure. Our final deadline would never have been made without the back-up help of Mrs. Oscar E. (Joyce) Mehring (formerly McGough), Mrs. Jerrold D. (Joan) Tyler, and Miss Judy Michlo, all of whom aided in the rush of typing the final manuscript.

Contents

Introduction

I have long been conscious that mine has been a privileged life. By the sheer circumstance of being the son of a prominent public figure, I have been thrust into situations and witnessed events that have deeply affected my life and outlook. With this consciousness, I have long harbored an ambition to share some of these experiences with others, realizing that anything I have to say of interest pertains to what I have seen rather than what I have done. As time has gone on and my appetite for writing as a profession has been whetted, this ambition has gradually approached the proportions of an obsession.

This desire to put certain impressions on paper is not completely altruistic. The fact of having lived for periods of my life in an atmosphere where contact was common with such world figures as Stalin, Churchill, De Gaulle, Adenauer, Khrushchev, Dulles, Patton, and Marshall—to name a few—has given me a certain loneliness and difficulty in making small talk. One does not drop such names in casual conversation except among intimates. But in a book of this type—recognizing it for what it is—one can do so freely.

Furthermore with age, memory does not improve. We all, from time to time, feel absolutely confident that a given event happened on a specified date in a certain way. Then, on checking the records, one finds that memory has done him a disservice. This point was driven home to me in the process of writing *The Bitter Woods,* a book on the Battle of the Bulge in World War II. The champagne of that work was the interviewing of prominent military commanders. Without variation, the commanders who had recorded their experiences and viewpoints had little new to supplement their writings. And those who had not recorded the events of their lives were often subject to distinct errors in fact. For example, one general told me of a meeting he had held with Field Marshal Montgomery at St. Vith, Belgium, on December 21, 1944. On double checking, it turned out that Montgomery had never been to that spot. Another officer told of an encounter with General Matthew Ridgway on December 19, 1944, near Stoumont, Belgium. As it turned out, Ridgway had not yet arrived in the vicinity on that day. These I cite merely as examples of the fallibility of the human memory. And as time goes on, I find that my own becomes less and less accurate.

As a boy I enjoyed reading about certain segments of history. My interest centered to a large extent on ancient times, particularly Roman. As I recall, my school grades in the subject were never spectacular, but I learned later that a feel for history cannot be achieved through formal studies, at least until one can specialize after finishing his undergraduate years. I was intrigued, however, by the adventures of Pausanias, a Greek traveler, geographer, historian, and reporter who, in the second century A.D., wrote his famous book, *Description of Greece*. Pausanias traveled from the Jordan River to Rome, and as the result of his vivid descriptions of fortifications, buildings, works of art, and nature, history has been much enriched. His writings regarding the ruins of Mycenae led to its discovery by archaeologists in modern times. Yet what fascinated me about this early reporter were not the details of what he wrote so much as the satisfaction he must have felt in creating these records.

My military career as such was undistinguished. For my seventeen years active duty I did my best; but a large portion of the time was spent in rather routine assignments which could have been filled by anyone. This is not the least abnormal. Most career officers, I think, share the feeling that over the course of the years they have spent most of their time preparing themselves for only a couple of significant tours of duty. In my case the two truly worthwhile, strictly military assignments consisted of instructing English at West Point (where I furthered my education) and the year with the 3d Infantry Division in Korea. And even these tours were rather commonplace.

In only a few areas has my experience been the least bit unique:

as a witness to the activities of the Allied high command in World War II; as a White House staff officer from 1958 to 1961; as United States ambassador to Belgium from 1969 to 1971; and in a few other sporadic episodes.

In recording certain events I have been forced to be selective. I have also attempted to avoid material that has already been reported. For example, I have purposely omitted descriptions of my father's presidential visits to India, South America, and the Far East in 1959–60, absorbing as they were at the time. (After all, one definition of a bore is a person with total recall.) In addition, I have attempted to avoid editorializing as much as possible, although not with complete success.

I decided to write these reminiscences while planning departure from my post as United States ambassador to Belgium in the late summer of 1971. I began work on the text within a few days of arrival home. Nevertheless, circumstances have not allowed me to concentrate on them exclusively. I have represented President Nixon on two ceremonial occasions, at the funeral of King Frederick IX of Denmark in January 1972 and at the fifth Inauguration of President Chiang Kai-shek in May 1972. I have served as Consultant to the President as chairman of the Interagency Classification Review Committee, charged with supervising the downgrading of secret materials in the hands of the Government; I have become immersed once more in the Army Reserve; and I have of necessity been involved in a couple of business enterprises to pay the bills. Nevertheless, none of these activities would make particularly interesting reading; more important, one has to select an arbitrary cut-off time if he is ever going to finish a book. I selected our departure from Brussels in late September 1971. My viewpoints as portrayed in this book belong to that period, no effort having been made to revise them with the swift passage of events since.

All in all, it has been an interesting life to date, full of events and only rarely dull. I am sometimes asked whether I would have preferred it otherwise—to have been a completely private citizen or, if my father had not gone into the White House, to have continued as an Army officer. I find it difficult to answer because things simply happened the way they did. On balance, I believe I prefer it this way. For this trail has taken me through events worth reporting.

However, once these first fifty years are recorded on paper they can be put to bed. In my own mind, then I will feel free, I hope, without living in the past, to go on to other things, whatever they may be.

STRICTLY PERSONAL

1

The Raising of an Army Brat

I am certain that I was born standing at attention. Perhaps I was something like the top sergeant who was not born, but issued. With a few lapses of minor rebellion throughout my life, I am inclined to think that I remained in that posture, figuratively, for many years, until I was nearly forty. Certain factors contributed to this: a Spartan upbringing; West Point training; and the circumstance of my father's meteoric rise to prominence during my early twenties. His unusual success, while exhilarating to us all, made me feel that among strangers I was always some sort of curiosity. And it affected the normal relations between a father and son, making it doubly difficult for me to establish my own identity.

During the last decade—indeed, beginning with my father's departure from the White House in January 1961—I believe I have been successful in doing this, and the natural mutual respect and affection that existed between Dad and me during the last years of his life were rewarding indeed. But essentially this book is the story of a son living in the shadow of a great man, undergoing unusual experiences but at the same time struggling to attain a normal degree of independence.

I remember little of my early childhood, but certain unrelated and insignificant impressions stick up like peaks above the clouds: a new tricycle at Fort Leavenworth (age three) . . . an impressive pile of lumber stacked on the second floor of Otis Hall . . . Louise Kahle, wife of one of Dad's classmates, counting the dimples on the backs of my pudgy hands . . . Mother singing to me in the car. But most vivid of all was the night I invaded Dad's attic study, normally off limits. He and his friend Leonard T. ("Gee") Gerow,

both students at the Command and General Staff School, Fort
Leavenworth, Kansas, were poring intensely over a large table,
eyeshades protecting them from the glare of a brilliant, low-hung
lamp. I was too small to see what was on the table but stared in
wonderment at the huge maps tacked on the wall. The two young
officers were going over the next day's tactical problem. Dad and
Gee welcomed me with a laugh and shoved me out the door in
the course of perhaps half a minute.

The years during which I was four and five years old are for
some reason almost completely blank in my memory, although a
long letter from Dad to Great-Aunt Eda indicates that my enthusiasm for Christmas was normal for a five-year-old. During
this period, after completing the course at the Command and General Staff School at Leavenworth, Dad was assigned first to Fort
Benning, Georgia and then for a year at the Army War College in
Washington, D.C.

My first clear, continuing recollection begins with a moment in
1928 behind the Wyoming Apartments at Columbia Road and
Connecticut Avenue, where an equestrian statue of General
George B. McClellan gazes austerely downtown toward Dupont
Circle and the White House. One day, as my mother and I were
out on the small grass plot behind the building, two or three people
joined us. Among them was a boy, the same age as I, named
George A. Horkan, Jr.; our parents were friends. "Bo" Horkan
and I got together to play a few times, little realizing that the two
of us, twins except for the color of our hair, would be lifelong
friends, brothers in every respect except that we had different sets
of parents. Soon, however, Dad was ordered to Paris to serve on
the Battle Monuments Commission under General John J. Pershing. My sixth birthday occurred aboard ship, and my recollection
of the large birthday cake in the ornate dining room of the *S.S.
America* remains strong.

The trip to Europe in 1928 somehow seems to have stimulated
my memory, for I remember many details, of staying in a French
hotel (where breakfast was limited to orange juice and croissants)
and then of moving to a small ground-floor apartment on the
Right Bank of the Seine, about a mile and a half downstream from
the Trocadero and the Eiffel Tower. The apartment was small but

boasted a stone courtyard of perhaps eight by ten feet, adequate space for a six-year-old to play. (I was able to find the apartment, near Pont Mirabeau on a visit nearly nineteen years later.) While in Paris I attended the McJanet School for American children. The first day, when my mother dropped me off, I howled and screamed; but when she came by to pick me up that evening, I refused for a while to go home.

Within a span of a few months—perhaps weeks—we were joined in Paris by the Horkans and the then Captain George A. Horkan was assigned, like Dad, to the Battle Monuments Commission. At this point the friendship between Bo and me, which has grown through the years, began to take real root.

Dad was engaged in ghost-writing an official guide book, *The American Battlefields in France*. This task required a great deal of travel to all the World War I sites. Quite often Bo would accompany us to places like Reims, Compiègne, Château-Thierry, and the Argonne Forest. The Argonne, a forbidding patch of woods, had been the scene of one of the controversial American battles of the war. To Bo and me the place was enchanting: dense, almost impenetrable. We were fascinated with stories of American military valor. In the Argonne we had lunch at the location of Major Charles W. Whittlesey's "Lost Battalion." Sergeant Alvin York, the foremost American hero of World War I, whose exploits occurred in this special spot, became someone very special to Bo and me.

Most of the battlefields of France were flat, pleasant farming areas. On the other hand, Verdun was a forbidding place. A large portion of the town still lay in ruins from the war, only ten years before. Its most frightening place was a strong point named Fort Douaumont. As we approached the door to this grim, squat monster, a human skull—with one tooth—grinned at us from a recess. Without hesitation Bo and I decided that this was the time to leave and go to the bathroom. Dad, his mind on his business, was annoyed. Somehow our natural needs were taken care of, and we stumbled our way through some of the eerie, dank passageways, with occasional dim lights to guide our way. Nearby we visited the Trench of Bayonets, where perhaps a squad of Frenchmen, preparing to go over the top, had been buried alive by the impact of a nearby German shell. By some miracle the bayonets had remained sticking out of the ground, and the bodies of the victims had been left unmolested by the French as a national monument.

On these trips Bo and I picked up readily available souvenirs—helmets, bayonets, and other bits of leftover hardware. (We later sandpapered the helmets to the point where light shone through.) At one point I became interested in an object that resembled a pineapple and started to give it a kick. The driver, horrified, grabbed me just in time. Instances of French farmers being blown to bits by ten-year-old grenades and shells were still common.

Back in Paris, Bo and I made full use of our souvenirs to play war continually. We alternately pretended we were Sergeant York or General Pershing. We had both met Pershing at least once. (The Germans, in our war games, rarely received fair treatment.) Our mutual interest in military history, particularly that of Western Europe, was thus kindled at an early age.

Dad's tour in Paris lasted only a year and two months. In late 1929 we found ourselves back in Washington, living once more in the Wyoming Apartments. Upstairs on the seventh floor were Gee Gerow, from Leavenworth days, and his wife, Katie, whom I admired particularly since she had been a nurse in the World War. Within a few months after our arrival home, a brand-new school, John Quincy Adams, was completed on Nineteenth Street, with its large playground just across the alley from the Wyoming. I was to spend practically my entire grade school life at JQA. Within a couple of years the Horkans also returned; Bo now had a baby sister, Kay.

Growing up in Washington through my grade school years made life a little different from that of the "typical" Army brat.[1] Most Army families lived on posts and moved every three or four years. The various posts were, by and large, ideal places for children, with athletic facilities, including horses, abounding. Afternoon parades, Sunday polo games, and standing at attention when the flag went down at dusk created an atmosphere far different from that of the city. The fact that one third of the youngsters would

[1] For some reason, sons of Army families are dubbed "brats." The Navy, more dignified, call their children "Navy juniors."

come and go every year made the Army brat generally a sociable type of person, easy to make friends with, and gregarious. Since the Army in those days resembled a large family, a youngster arriving on a new post would in all likelihood find a couple of friends he had known on a previous assignment. And he would find himself readily and uncritically accepted into the gang immediately on arrival.

Life was wholesome, and the parents often banded together and made rules to ensure that privileges among the children were reasonably uniform. Since the gates of the posts were guarded and automobile speed limits were exceedingly slow and strictly enforced, parents worried little about the safety of their children, and little restriction was placed on their movements. On the other hand, Army officers tended to be strict disciplinarians in the home. A standard story has it that one Army brat, in danger of being "found" (expelled) from West Point because of academic deficiency, was instructed to telegraph his parents "Yes" if he passed the all-important final examinations and "No" if he failed. Having passed, he dutifully wired YES. The parents, meanwhile, having forgotten the code, wired back, YES WHAT? The cadet's reply was obvious: YES, SIR.

All of this atmosphere tended to make the Army brat a rather different kind of youngster, adaptability being his most noticeable quality. But I personally missed out on a great deal of this atmosphere living in Washington, except that the family had done a good deal of moving in my earliest years and, of course, the fact that my father was as strict a disciplinarian as any.

But there were distinct advantages in the fact that our family remained in Washington for so long. JQA, it turned out, was an excellent school; therefore my education in my earlier years was uninterrupted, and I was not subjected to the disadvantages, academically, that so many Army brats suffered because of attending so many different schools. And there was something to be said for being exposed to the heterogeneous group of youngsters I knew at JQA. One of my best friends, "Jakie" Silver, was the son of a delicatessen owner—I remember that because the two of us occasionally ate at his father's place. I was unaware of the backgrounds of any of the others—Cowan, Robinson, Plitman, Neff, Mitchell.

And always, though he was a grade or so behind me at first because he had attended a French school in Paris, Bo and I remained close, spending nights together and broadening our military perspective to include the air war. *G-8 and His Battle Aces,* Eddie Ricken-backer, and Baron Manfred von Richtofen, with his red tri-winged Fokker, now took their places beside Sergeant York.

Duty with troops on a post was generally considered the most desirable life for an Army officer, and Dad writhed in frustration in Washington during our seven-year stay. He worked like a slave in the old State-War-Navy Building (now the Executive Office Building of the White House) and longed for line duty. Neverthe-less, his time in Washington under Secretary of War Patrick J. Hurley, his successor, George Dern, and Chief of Staff General Douglas MacArthur set him apart from many run-of-the-mill Army officers and gave him a feel for the Washington scene and the processes of government that he could be thankful for in later years.

Life in the Wyoming Apartments followed a strict regimen. Dad and I rose about the same time, just before eight. We shared a bathroom—sometimes shared a bathtub—and the time was spent constructively. In those morning sessions I was grilled without mercy on the multiplication tables, so that I was always weeks ahead of my class. And no errors were tolerated. But the morning bathroom sessions were not all devoted to schoolwork. We had time to talk about things in general and we had our laughs. For some reason, possibly to save time, Dad and I often shared a tub of bath water. Usually I would bathe first while Dad was shaving, and Dad would then climb in after me. One morning Dad decided to dispense with this usual ritual, but I was insistent. My determina-tion that he bathe that day must have puzzled him, but finally he gave way. The result was rewarding. Dad stuck his foot in the water and let out a howl that must have been heard throughout the Wyoming Apartments. Blue, shivering, but delighted, I leaped out of the freezing water and charged laughing into the bedroom to tell Mother of the success of my prank.

After school I always reported home and then went out to play on nearby Dean's Hill, where the Washington Hilton now stands, until dinner at exactly 6 P.M. After dinner I did my homework, and it seemed that every night Dad would work in the living room, scratching on a pad, long after I went to bed. By and large, I stayed back in the room that Dad and I shared for dressing. We did little as a family except for occasional outings to Haines Point or a monthly dinner at the Sun Restaurant, where the only superior Chinese food has ever been made.

During these years I was being raised among a group of remarkable Army officers. Undesirable duty as it may have seemed, officers with a real future in the Army spent a large proportion of their time in Washington. Troop units were scarce, and an incredible amount of work, considering it was peace time, was being done in the War Department by military officers wearing civilian clothes. Since an officer's pay was scant—and I was almost the only child of the group—my parents' friends gathered frequently at the apartment (nicknamed "Club Eisenhower"). Three of the men, Gerow, Walton Walker, and Wade Haislip, had been lieutenants together in the 19th Infantry in 1916; they all later attained four stars in World War II. But the group also included the Everett S. Hugheses, the P. A. Hodgsons,[2] and the Sam Beaches. Occasionally Dad's youngest brother, Milton, and his wife, Helen, would join the crowd. I came to know all these men well, but of course I had no yardstick with which to measure their collective potential greatness.

When the "Club" gathered, I stayed in my room like all youngsters but would come out and join in for short stretches of time. Occasionally, one or two of Dad's friends might saunter back to converse seriously. Of all these, perhaps Dad's deepest admirer was Everett Hughes, who later became Inspector General in the European Theater and still later Chief of Ordnance. "Uncle Everett" used to tell me at great length of my Dad's virtues. "Your father is a man to watch!" he admonished me one evening. I agreed, but in the light of the Old Man's disciplinary policies, I probably interpreted the statement a little differently from the way it was intended.

The extent to which I was the mascot of this group of affection-

---

[2] Dad's roommate in West Point. A magnificent football player but plagued all his life by rheumatism and arthritis. Without this handicap, "P.A." would undoubtedly have later become an outstanding combat leader.

ate men—whose humanity has rarely been appreciated by the general public—is illustrated by the way they joined an organization I concocted as a child about nine or ten years of age. Somewhere I had read a novel involving medieval comrades who considered themselves "blood brothers." The ceremony that solemnified the association was that members of this intimate organization should prick their respective fingers, mixing their blood together in a glass of water.

One by one the members of Club Eisenhower would undergo the ordeal, along with a ritual the format of which has escaped me. Gee Gerow, Everett Hughes, P. A. Hodgson, Sam Beach, and "Ham" Haislip—probably more—became blood brothers. This initiation procedure could hardly have been pleasant for the adults, administered by a child, but it created in me—and I know in them also—an unusual feeling of affinity. For years thereafter they referred to me as "Blood Brother John." In my own adult years this reference made me a little uncomfortable, as if I had imposed on them in times past. But when they finally passed away, one by one, I always felt a grief similar to that of losing a second father.

Occasionally, on Sundays Mother, Dad, and I would drive around town, and the two would pay the formal social calls prescribed by the rigid Washington protocol. This was a chore that Dad detested and he made little secret of it. We would travel from one apartment house to another in our 1927 Buick and the folks, Dad in derby hat and striped pants, would drop in at each place for a few minutes while I waited in the car. On rare Sundays Dad would play golf at the Old Soldiers' Home with Colonel Jimmy Ulio, then Adjutant General of the Army. Though Dad had played little, he went after the game with the same intensity as in later years. The golf tees consisted of small, wet piles of sand, molded to desired height. Dad had a powerful swing but a horrendous slice to go with it. He seemed to wind up in the alfalfa an inordinate amount of the time, the air punctuated with certain expletives that I had thought were unknown to adults—only to kids.

A few times we went out to Fort Myer to visit Dad's old friend George S. Patton, Jr. I always held the Pattons in considerable awe, because of their obvious wealth and the fact that Patton was a lieutenant colonel while Dad was a major. Silver horsemanship trophies covered a complete wall in the living room of their quarters. Patton was a good-humored man who loved to joke. His language was full of the purple expressions for which he later became famous. I was astonished that he not only swore profusely around ladies but also encouraged all three of his children to do the same. When young George, a fine boy slightly younger than I, would come out with an appropriate piece of blasphemy, Patton would roar with pleasure. These visits, though rare, were always pleasant.

Viewed from the perspective of having raised four children, I can recognize that Mother and Dad were good parents, although very strict. They had not been infected in the 1930s with the permissiveness that has become fashionable in more recent years. Dad himself was a terrifying figure to a small boy. He was powerfully built—in West Point he could chin himself five times with his right hand and three times with his left—and in his youth had literally lived for athletics. I could never measure up to these standards, try as I might. I participated in all sports available at JQA and suppose that I was probably of average caliber. But Dad could never understand why I was not a star. The fact is that I was always painfully thin; Dad wrote from the Philippines when I was fourteen that I had to reach the weight of ninety-two pounds before I could play football. I stuffed myself on bananas and drank about a gallon of water one night before weighing in.

Dad had a policy that I think was a mistake: he never laid a hand on me. Perhaps this stemmed from a fear that, strong as he was, he might inflict serious bodily harm when his temper was aroused. Instead, he conducted discipline largely in a West Point manner. I was dressed down smartly on many occasions but never given a whack. Only once did his policy break down. Having put my elbows on the dinner table after several warnings, I found myself being taken into the bedroom. The grip of Dad's thumb and middle finger on the back of my neck led me to think, almost dispassionately, "Well, John, your time has come; you're finished."

The family—Mother, Dad, and I—lived comfortably but far from lavishly in the Wyoming Apartments. An Army officer, as I have said, was paid poorly in those days, and our spacious three-bedroom apartment was far from cheap. In addition, Dad's job required that his wardrobe include both civilian clothes and uniforms. My Grandfather Doud provided Mother with a full-time maid (for $50 a month) but that was a luxury item. Dad continually pounded into me that we were not wealthy people.

Although Mother was always frail—she had suffered from a rheumatic heart condition since childhood—she had plenty of nervous energy. She managed the household single-handedly and efficiently. Every penny counted. My loss once of a $10 coat—which actually was not my fault—literally shattered her. Though only weighing about 106 pounds at five feet four inches, Mother would take a taxi every week to buy food at the commissary at Fort McNair.[3] To save a few cents of the taxi fare, she and Katie Gerow would stop at Florida Avenue and carry their large sacks of groceries up the hill to the Wyoming, a distance of over a quarter of a mile.

In many ways, Mother remained somewhat in the background, especially in matters where Dad was concerned. She felt her role was to push him forward and to give him all the emotional support he needed, although they would never talk about his business at home. She did everything possible to promote a close relationship between Dad and me and took a great deal of pleasure from hearing about our conversations and study drills in the morning bathroom sessions. Toward me she was exceedingly affectionate, almost smothering me with concern. As a youngster I was subject to violent leg aches, due probably to so much running around on concrete sidewalks and alleys. Many was the time that I would call out in the middle of the night, and Mother, bleary-eyed, would come into my room and rub my shins. With all her maternal manifestations of affection, this rubbing of leg aches in the wee hours of the morning I remember with the greatest feeling of warmth.

Mother and Dad doubtlessly had their quarrels, as both were strong personalities. As Mother has written since Dad's death, some of these quarrels were severe; but it seemed that the Old Man's views nearly always prevailed. But one thing the two of them were careful of: they never quarreled in front of me. I have memories of catching the devil from both of them singly or to-

[3] Named Fort Lesley J. McNair after World War II. It was then simply the Army War College.

gether; but I have no memories of the two of them arguing between themselves, other than an occasional complaint on Mother's part regarding Dad's habit of bringing work home from the office.

Doubtless because of several family tragedies—two of her three sisters and my older brother had died in the course of a few years —Mother tended to be a worrier. When I headed for school every morning, I was bundled up in a muffler, gloves, and other accouterments which would cause mirth among my friends. Like any other youngster, however, I had the geography of the Wyoming Apartments well figured out and knew exactly the point where I would disappear from the sight of her window. Then off would come the gloves, the muffler, and the hat; and I would join my friends for a game of "work-up" baseball.

Every summer between 1929 and 1935 I was sent to Denver to stay with my maternal grandparents, Mr. and Mrs. John S. Doud. After the first year or so I was allowed to go alone on the train, taking the Pennsylvania Railroad to Englewood, a suburb of Chicago, where I would be met by a redcap and put on the Rock Island Line. This experience of traveling alone made me feel quite important, especially since I was given a certain amount of expense money and allowed to pocket the change. With this pecuniary incentive I naturally ate lightly en route.

My grandparents, the Douds, were exceedingly good to me, but along with my Great-Aunt Eda Carlson, they were extremely protective. It was years before I became a free agent to ride my bicycle around Denver. But I had friends and we constructed a tree house in the neighbor's yard across the alley. The family had a pool table in the basement and every evening all would engage in a very serious game. My grandfather Doud ("Pupah") was always acknowledged to be the champion, but I became fairly good. When I entered the Army some years later, some of my new friends believed that I had enjoyed a misspent youth.

I never consciously felt sorry for myself when sent to Denver, although I always made plain my preference to remain in Washington. Since most of my friends stayed behind playing tennis at the S Street Playground, I felt somewhat as if I were going into exile. Furthermore, a certain gloom prevailed in the Doud household at times. My grandparents had never recovered from the shock of losing their nearly grown daughters Eleanor and Buster; and the death of my older brother "Icky," before I was born, hit them hard. Every Sunday the family would go to Fairmont Cemetery to change the flowers on the three graves and then sit silently for what seemed to a small boy an interminable length of time. That ceremony over, however, Sunday became a happier day, with a big meal at noon. The house at 750 Lafayette Street was done in Tudor style, dark and rather cheerless. The bright spot of course was the pool room, a congenial place with pictures and certificates on the wall. It was also the coolest room in the house. What time I spent indoors was normally invested down there.

I was fortunate in that I knew all four of my grandparents reasonably well; none of them died until I was in my twenties. The one I wish I had gotten to know better in particular was Pupah, who had apparently been quite a man in his day. Pupah used to tell me stories of hopping freight trains—Uncle Charlie was killed doing this—and of walking forty miles in a single day, measuring the distance by counting telephone poles. He had gone into the stockyards business and had run an immense establishment in Boone, Iowa, where I presume he met my grandmother. Dad used to wonder at the expertise with which Mr. Doud could tell a good quality hog from a poor one by a few touches of the ears and the snout. As a small boy I had visited these stockyards once and the primitive existence Pupah led there was a source of amazement. His living, sleeping, and dining room contained hardly more than a cot, a table, an old-fashioned telephone, and a single light bulb hanging by a wire from the ceiling. By the time I was really aware of Pupah, however, he was retired, and the Doud family divided their time between San Antonio in the winters and Denver in the summers. This was an unfortunate circumstance, I think, because he seemed to spend the last twenty or so years of his life bored. Except for the times he would be teaching me Civil War songs (accompanied by chords on the piano), telling stories, or playing pool, he seemed a rather detached, gloomy individual. But when he laughed, it was a great belly laugh. His one pleasure every day was to take the streetcar downtown to visit his favorite haunts. He was a great eater; when he visited Fort Lewis in 1940, he pointed out to me after only a few days the "best cherry pie joint in town." He could eat a whole pie without difficulty in one sitting.

In common with the customs of the time, Mr. Doud was inclined to display his prosperity. He wore a diamond in his necktie and allowed himself to grow a huge paunch, not the least embarrassed to have his picture taken in profile—all the way down. His white hair stuck up in a couple of mounds with a clean bald pate in between—all of which made him look distinguished. He was an interesting man, and, as I have mentioned, I really wish that I had known him better in my adult years.

My Grandmother Doud—"Nana" to all of us—was a remarkable person, an odd mixture of Victorian propriety and outgoing friendliness. She might insist that my underwear be mended for fear of "being in an accident," but she was by nature a lot of fun. She loved people. During these summers, for example, when Pupah spent a good deal of time with the family doctor in Pueblo, Nana knew the names of every elevator boy and every waitress in the Whitman Hotel. She had been something of a tomboy as a youngster, and even in her late fifties she loved to play catch with a tennis ball out in the back yard. She prided herself on her fast ball. She was an avid baseball fan, and what little I know about the game I learned from her. When I had the measles one time, in 1933, she sat at my bedside and the two of us followed the World Series with passionate intensity.[4] Joe Cronin was the manager of the Washington Senators at the time, and Nana taught me the names of all the members of the team—"Buddy" Myer, "Ossie" Bluege, and the rest.

Nana was married at an early age and had had all her four children by the time she was in her mid-twenties. She and Dad belied the standing joke regarding the relationship between a man and his mother-in-law. The two constituted a truly mutual admiration society and each took the other's part whenever a family disagreement would arise.

In my quiet resistance against Victorian propriety I had encouragement from my Aunt Frances "Mike" Doud, Mother's younger sister. Full of zip and rebellion, Mike had been quite a handful when Dad was courting Mother in 1916. A true product

---

[4] Unfortunately, our team, the Washington Senators, lost to the New York Giants, four games to one.

of the flapper age, she had an impish sense of humor and a certain abandon; the two of us were close buddies. (In Prohibition days, Mother tells me, Mike and her boy friend emptied Pupah's carefully stored supply of gin, replacing it with water.) When Mike eloped with a Texas entrepreneur—I was the only witness, age three—the Doud family did little to conceal their unhappiness. But Mike went her merry way, and I always loved it when I could be off on a jaunt with Mike and her husband. One time the three of us sneaked off together—I was probably seven years old—and went to the mountains. After we had driven some distance, perhaps as far as either Central City or Leadville, they called back to 750 Lafayette Street. The family—Mother was there at the time— thought that I had been kidnaped, and Mother had taken to her bed. We returned in haste to Denver, chastened.

The atmosphere among the Doud family grew emotional at times. The ladies, particularly Nana, Mike, and Great-Aunt Eda, possessed a remarkable capacity for weeping and screaming at each other and then falling on each other's necks, making up, an hour later. In the absence of Dad, Mother played the role of peacemaker. At the time I viewed these family outbursts with amusement, but in my adult years I seem always to have gone out of my way to avoid a scene.

With it all, we had fun at 750 Lafayette Street, with the pool games, baseball, tree houses, and my precious bicycle. I am inclined to think that the Doud family was hardly atypical for that time, and I look back on those days with pleasure.

Several summers I was able also to visit my Dad's home in Abilene, Kansas. Here the atmosphere was completely different. In this small, quiet town I underwent little or no supervision and loved to wander the streets that "Wild Bill" Hickok had tamed years before. There was no danger to a youngster in Abilene—no fast-moving cars and no crime. Furthermore, Grandmother Eisenhower, the patron saint of Dad's side of the family, was one of the best-humored people I ever met. Both she and Granddad Eisenhower were amused by the delight I felt in my unaccustomed freedom. Sometimes I would help Grandma in the kitchen. We would go out to the chicken yard, grab a fryer, and Grandma would whack its head off while I held it. We would then throw the twitching bird into the bushes, wait a while, and then clean and fry it. I was allowed to sit in the front yard in my undershirt and chew on a drumstick.

During these sojourns Grandma would talk about her life as a little girl and delight me with stories of her six high-spirited sons, each of whom sounded like something out of Mark Twain. Arthur, the oldest, was the least known to me. He left home at age fifteen and made his way to Kansas City, where he got a job in the Commerce Trust Bank as a janitor, later rising to be vice president. Ed, the second son, had been Dad's closest friend among the brothers. To hear the tales told, one would think that they spent their entire time in fist fights, either between the two of them or allied against outsiders. Ed and Dad had devised a scheme for putting each other through college. Dad worked for two years at the Bell Springs Creamery to help put Ed through the University of Michigan before Dad himself went off to West Point. Ed became a successful lawyer in Tacoma, Washington. Always somewhere to the right of Ivan the Terrible in his political thinking, he was a strong, tough man but possessed, underneath it all, of a very affectionate disposition. Dwight, the third child, was, according to Grandma Eisenhower, the most difficult of all. From an early age he had exhibited a mind of his own and a terrible temper. More than once he bloodied his head by beating it up against a tree when things failed to go his own way. He was also the history bug of the family. Grandma was a pacifist as a result of her childhood experiences in Virginia during the Civil War, and she objected to Dad's obsession with things military. Despite her admonitions, Dad would smuggle home books on Napoleon and the Civil War and read them hiding under a bed. Roy, the fourth, lived in nearby Junction City, where he ran a large drugstore. On these visits we would spend a good deal of time with Roy and his three children. His son Bud was a little younger than I, but we were companionable. Earl, the fifth, had become an electrical engineer. He had lost the sight of one eye in an accident during his youth but it had never hampered him. He was a rough-hewn character and great fun. (He and Ed were very much alike in this respect.) The youngest son, Milton, came along ten years after Dad. Having attended Kansas State College, he had gone into the Department of Agriculture where he remained until 1940 and then switched to a prominent career in education. A seventh son, Paul, died in infancy. I listened to the tales of these six hellions with fascination.

I am inclined to think that I was one of David Jacob Eisenhower's favorite grandsons in a way, as I was the only one trained to obey in the manner that he insisted on. When it was bedtime, for example, I would snap to and march off at the first word. Such crisp obedience apparently was not characteristic of all the other grandsons that visited him. Granddad had been a tough bird, a disciplinarian as only a Pennsylvania Dutchman can be. He was also well educated and industrious. He and Grandma Eisenhower, graduates of Lane University, Lecompton, Kansas, could read Greek. When arguing at night about the Bible, they would sometimes pick up the Greek version to settle their disagreements. He had lost his money through the Depression and the absconding of a partner; and in his later years Granddad was in a glum state of mind.

Granddad Eisenhower was a man of few words and no foolishness. In his correspondence he came right to the point. One day while the family was in the Philippines, Dad received a post card from him. The post card was sent from home, Abilene, Kansas, and the message was one simple word: "Hot."

On one of my later visits to Abilene, I undertook a piece of construction, a hen coop out in the chicken yard. I photographed it proudly from every angle and was hurt when, years later, it was dismantled.

Such then were my summers during my grade school years. As they constituted one quarter of my life during that time, they had a distinct influence in forming my outlook on many things in life.

When September rolled around I would head back for Washington. My return would be scheduled so that I would have a week or ten days home before school began—and of course, every year there was the problem, as with all children, of breaking in a new teacher.

My grades in school were good. Usually, as I recall, I stood about second or third in every section of forty. This doubtless was attributable largely to my Dad's insistence that I study. Not only did he drill me in the early mornings on things like multiplication tables but he also demanded that I put out every effort to do well. And my position as an only child, leaving me alone in the back room to study, made academics relatively easy. Thus by the time I reached the eighth grade I was elected president of my class of 120 (three sections). Though our prime interests lay in athletics— my greatest pride was the attainment of an athletic achievement award—youngsters in school tended to look on those with the best grades as the ones to elect class presidents. When Dad was assigned to the Philippines with General MacArthur in 1935, Mother stayed on for a year in the Wyoming Apartment to allow me to finish up my eighth grade schooling.

Strange to say, my prestige as president of the senior class seemed to mean very little to me. Just before graduation I organized a group of four or five boys in French class. We pushed our desks to a row and called ourselves the "Hindenburg Line." Whenever the teacher's back was turned, we would let go on the class with a barrage of chalk. Unfortunately, one day a shell fragment hit the teacher. A great deal of consternation ensued among the authorities of the school as to whether, with a couple of weeks to go, I should be dethroned as class president. However, the time was short and I made the graduation address as previously planned.

Entrenched as I was in Washington, I hated to move away. Above all else I wanted to attend Western High School. However, such a destiny was obviously not in the cards. Mother had given up one year of her family life for me to complete school, and in October of 1936—I was fourteen—the two of us departed from a fog-ridden San Francisco Bay aboard an Army transport, the *U. S. Grant,* bound for the Philippines.

The trip to the Philippines in those days required an entire month. It was a pleasant voyage and not the least bit boring. There were many Army youngsters of my age aboard, and there always seemed to be plenty to do—climbing around the ship, reading, indulging in mild flirtations with the girls. Since we were all going to a small American community, many of those shipboard friendships endured.

When we settled down in the Manila Hotel, I tried to avoid going away to school as long as possible. At the time I was intensely interested in the 1936 political campaign and the effort of Governor Alf M. Landon of Kansas to unseat President Roosevelt. The propaganda and the polls at that time showed Landon well ahead. Somehow I induced the folks to let me stay in Manila long enough to watch the election returns at the Army-Navy Club. As they posted the sad news on the great board in the sweltering heat, I was aghast to witness the drubbing my candidate received. When the election was over my excuses for staying in Manila had run out, and I was whisked off to Baguio, in the mountains of north-central Luzon. There, in Brent School, an Episcopalian mission, I was to remain for the next three and one half years.

My years in the Philippines I look back on as among the happiest of my life. I arrived there having hardly reached the age of puberty and had, as always, protested being away from home. But the atmosphere was hospitable and the youngsters, coming about equally from service families and civilian families living in the Philippines,[5] made all newcomers feel at home. My friendships were warm at Brent, and the school was small. Its students numbered about one hundred, from toddlers in first grade through seniors in high school. The classes often comprised only about five or six; on rare occasions a class would be held for one student.

Baguio is recognized as one of the most delightful spots in the world. The Philippines, of course, are tropical, but Baguio, at a five-thousand-foot elevation, is covered with pine trees and boasts a steady, year-round temperature of about seventy degrees. To say it has an even climate is slightly misleading, because I have been informed that it has the second highest rainfall of any spot on earth. However, the season which corresponds roughly to our winter is dry and slightly cool. And during the rainy season the water comes down in sheets rather than drops—twenty-five inches in twenty-four hours at one time—but for only a couple of hours a day. All runs off the mountains. Thus, even during the rainy season, with the authoritative tropical sun, concrete tennis courts dry

[5] There were 7,000 American civilians living in the Philippines at that time, very largely from sugar plantations and American business enterprises.

off in a half hour. Life in Baguio was rarely inhibited by the season itself.

Strangely, I found academics in Brent School, compared to JQA, remarkably easy. Perhaps this was the result of the smaller classes, for it seemed at the time that everything the books were trying to explain was utterly understandable. Geometry was my best subject. Before even beginning the course I determined that I was going to be the first man in history ever to trisect an angle, something that Euclid had failed to do. I made valiant efforts and even convinced the teacher for a while that I had the master scheme. Though my method turned out to be fallacious, the subject of geometry, both linear and solid, came naturally. In history and English, which required more study, I did less well.

Athletically, I decided to specialize. Having discovered early that my talents in both baseball and basketball were limited—there was no football in the Philippines—I determined that my sport was tennis, a game I had learned from Bo Horkan at the S Street Playground in Washington. Therefore I concentrated on that sport, going by myself in the evenings to serve twenty worn-out tennis balls from court to court, working and slaving on my game continually. I was skinny but wiry and had good reactions. Moreover, I was somewhat lazy, and the idea of dashing around the basketball court in hopes that somebody might throw the ball to me I found not the least enchanting. But I concluded that in tennis, if your techniques are good, you can keep the other fellow running. I was also a strong competitor. As a sophomore I played tennis many times with a good friend, a senior, who had beaten me every time we had played informally on Corregidor and in Baguio. Nevertheless, in the tournaments I managed to win out.

During my sophomore year my tennis game took a turn for the worse, however, and for a strange reason. The famed "Big Bill" Tilden, perhaps the greatest tennis player of them all, played bridge with my Dad in the Manila Hotel while on tennis tour in Manila. He offered to give me a lesson. Dad checked with the authorities up in Baguio and found that the students had a couple of free days between semesters and I could come down to Manila.

Tilden was as good as his word, but hardly known for either his tact or his teaching ability. When we got out on the courts and hit a couple of balls, he immediately sneered, "Now let's see that funny-looking service." In the course of an hour's lesson, Tilden changed my entire service, my forehand (from top spin to flat), and my backhand. He then sent me back to Baguio determined to implement all of his radical changes. Unfortunately, Tilden's style was his own, hardly suited for the average player, but in my zeal to follow the directions of the great man, I completely confused my own game. I frankly think that, although I held my top position in Brent for my entire stay and later played at West Point, my game has probably never been as good as it was when I was a sophomore in high school.

As always, it seems, despite my academic standing and serious nature, I ran into certain difficulties with the authorities. This time it was over what I considered unreasonably stringent rules segregating the boys and the girls. My flame from sophomore year on was a Navy junior named Nancy, to whom I was quite attached. She was a natural athlete and I drilled her and drilled her in tennis until she became good enough to win the girls' championship. The authorities, however, were restrictive and old-maidish in their close supervision of dances and outside activities. We were extremely trustworthy youngsters, and no harm was ever going to result from letting us be alone on occasion. One evening I let my views be known and was confined to the campus for a couple of weeks. Nothing could have bothered me less, so long as I had my $1.00 a week allowance with which my friends could buy my tennis balls. I simply spent my entire life around the tennis courts.

During our last summer in the Philippines the folks were living in the air-conditioned portion of the Manila Hotel, where General MacArthur resided in the penthouse. I was preparing to return to Brent. Mother, who had become a close friend of Jean Mac-Arthur's, insisted that I take the elevator up to the top floor to say good-by. I expected to meet only Mrs. MacArthur, but on my arrival at the penthouse she exclaimed that the general would be terribly sorry if he missed me. She led me out to the roof garden where MacArthur was pacing up and down, hands clasped behind his back. Immediately his theatrical impulses manifested themselves. He walked over and shook hands—in his typical fashion with his left hand on my right shoulder—and recited in detail the positions I had been elected to for my senior year. I was to be president of the class, president of the student body, editor-in-chief of the magazine, editor-in-chief of the yearbook. We both completely ignored the fact that the senior class would consist of five pupils, only two of whom were boys; and all these jobs were reserved for seniors. But the general's memory, his charm and his ability to show interest in an inconsequential boy always impressed me and explained to a large degree how he was able to mesmerize any individual he wanted, even including my recalcitrant Old Man.

The Philippines at this time were in the process of being groomed for independence. By the Tydings-McDuffie Act, which set up the Philippine Commonwealth, the Islands were to enjoy a semi-autonomous status between 1935 and July 4, 1946. General Mac-Arthur, having retired as Army Chief of Staff, had come to the Philippines with a mission to organize an effective Philippine army. A complete government had been set up with Manuel Quezon as "President." The atmosphere was good, but sensitive Americans were aware of the growing feeling of independence among the Filipinos. On the other hand, the new republic was being fashioned in almost slavish imitation of the United States. I was amused, for example, when visiting the Philippine Military Academy, only a few hundred yards from Brent, to observe the extent to which their military school emulated West Point. Their uniforms were almost identical and in their yearbook they employed West Point slang, including such terms as "femmes" to denote ladies. The Filipino cadets, nevertheless, marched and conducted themselves well. This was doubtless the work of such West Point graduates as Captain (later Colonel) Pastor Martelino,[6] the first superintendent of the Philippine Military Academy.

By and large the Philippines were prospering. They were developing an army, including a small air corps equipped with Stearman trainers. They drilled in tropical uniform and worked hard at their tasks. The Philippine Constabulary was at the time a separate entity. Its greatest difficulty seemed to be the maintenance of order in the Southern Islands, where the Moros retained a degree of unrecognized independence. When the United States took over

[6] Colonel Martelino was captured on Bataan. Later released, he joined the underground. Captured once again, he was executed by the Japanese in January 1945.

the Philippines from Spain in 1898, we tacitly promised the Moros that when the Philippines should become independent—always planned—the Moros would receive autonomy as a separate state. From that time until the late 1930s everybody had forgotten this pledge except the Moros themselves. Thus, when it came time to collect taxes either in Mindanao or in the Sulu Archipelago—locations of two different branches of the Moro sect—the authorities would habitually run into trouble. Despite its tribulations, the Constabulary was in the process of being integrated into the regular Philippine Army while we were there, but I am not certain whether this process was complete before 1941.

In the meantime, Dad had taken up an interest in flying. He would arise at an ungodly hour in the morning and drive out to Camp Murphy, where the Philippine Air Corps was being trained under the direction of Lieutenants Bill Lee and "Lefty" Parker. He would then take an hour's flying instruction before going to work in the Walled City of Manila. Dad was a good student, despite his advanced age of forty-six years, and did snap rolls, loops, and perhaps even Immelmann turns with the best of them. He never made solo cross-country flights to the best of my knowledge. He did, however, come to Baguio to pick me up a couple of times along with Lee or Parker. One time I was allowed to handle the controls. I could see Mount Arayat in Pampanga ahead of me. Mount Arayat was only about two thousand feet high, but my instinct was to keep pulling back on the steering wheel to be sure to miss it. Eventually we reached an altitude of eleven thousand feet. On our descent at Camp Murphy Dad developed a severe earache, due to clogging in one of his Eustachian tubes. He was in pain for several hours thereafter.

During our stay in the Philippines we made several trips to the Southern Islands. Once a friend and I were allowed to go by ourselves aboard the motor ship *Legazpi*. In Mindanao a Philippine Army officer, possibly currying favor, presented me with a white cockatoo with a poorly healed broken wing. I was delighted with the bird, whom I named "Oswald." His entire vocabulary consisted of the word *agop*, of which I never learned the translation. I had also planned to pick up a monkey, but failed to find one. On docking in Manila, I took Dad aboard and introduced Oswald to him.

Real outbursts of temper were rare with Dad—and he almost always recovered immediately—but when he did become angry, he was spectacular. This time he outdid himself. "There's nothing I hate worse than parrots and monkeys!" he roared. I thought this a little illogical but was at least relieved that I hadn't found my monkey.

The incident created a temporary family crisis. Dad refused to sit in the same room with Oswald, but the door between our bedrooms was open. And every time Oswald said "Agop," I could see Dad wince, even from the rear. In short order Oswald was relegated to a small room where the hotel elevator boys congregated; Mother saved the situation by calling a friend at Fort McKinley, who had both the facilities and the zest for giving Oswald a good home. The whole matter turned out happily.

On another occasion I went with the folks to Zamboanga for a few days. The Southern Islands were pretty much all the same—coconut trees, banana trees, and hard-working people on the sugar plantations. We saw the monument on Mactan Island where Ferdinand Magellan had been killed by the Philippine natives in 1521. We threw pennies to the divers in Zamboanga and saw the ramshackle tomb of the Sultan of Sulu.

There were two elements in the Philippine experience that added a little excitement to an otherwise routine life. A minor one was the prevalence of earthquakes. In the summer of 1937 I was visiting a friend, Jack Cook, at Fort Stotsenburg (now Clark Field), when one of them hit. I was walking my bicycle out to the garage at the time and noticed nothing peculiar. When I returned to the house, Jack yelled, "John, you just missed an earthquake!" I looked at the walls and noticed that a number of the pictures were askew. I paid little attention—I think I was coming down with a case of dengue fever—but when I returned to Manila a couple of weeks later I heard the frightening details. The quake had hit the island of Luzon in an intensity more severe than that of the 1906 earthquake in San Francisco. The folks had been out at a party at the time; but on their return they discovered that a giant *apparador* (movable clothes closet) had fallen flat across the bed where Dad would have been sleeping. Had he been in bed, the crash might have killed him. That night, I was told, thousands of people slept on the Luneta, a large park between the Manila Hotel and the Army-Navy Club. I was amused that the next-door neighbors in the hotel, a rather convivial couple, had lost $100 worth of liquor in the quake. Downtown in Manila a new department store, Heacocks, supposedly earthquake-proof, had to be condemned. Various times in the next couple of years we experienced quakes in Baguio. Without exception I slept through all of them while everyone else cleared out of the dormitories and stood in the open. I was a sound sleeper in those days.

A more major source of excitement was the series of war scares between the United States and the Japanese. In 1937, it will be recalled, the Japanese pushed their invasion of China into Nanking. At about the same time, they attacked a United States gunboat, the *U.S.S. Panay,* on the Yangtze River. These incidents resulted in the evacuation of all military dependents from China to the Philippines. Thus the student body of Brent School was swelled to include former residents of Shanghai, Tientsin, Tsingtau, and other places on the Chinese mainland. Opinions of the students were varied regarding the Chinese situation, including the stature of its President Chiang Kai-shek. Thus Brent School became an even more stimulating international community.

The difficulties our country had with the Japanese continued throughout the rest of our stay. Admiral Harry Yarnell, at one point, was forbidden by the Japanese to sail a destroyer from the Asiatic Fleet into Swatow, a rather minor city on the Chinese coast. Yarnell, apparently acting on his own, defied the order and went in anyway. The Japanese backed down, and this courageous act created a swell of pride in the hearts of Americans. War scares continued throughout Dad's tour of duty, but it always seemed that the Japanese would back down when engaged in direct confrontation. While scary at times, even to the students up in Baguio, they tended to create an artificial cockiness and sense of American superiority.

During all this, my attachment for the United States Navy increased, probably because the Asiatic Fleet was the most visible sign of American power in the Far East. True, on the one night of the year when all service people would gather at the Army-Navy Club to watch a little button on a string indicate the position of the ball in the Army-Navy football game, the rivalry was intense as ever. But when the fleet would pull in to Manila Bay, the sight would always give me a thrill. This paltry force consisted of the heavy cruiser *Augusta,* the light cruiser *Marblehead,* perhaps a dozen four-stacker "tin can" destroyers from World War I, the submarine tender *Canopus,* and a small antisubmarine warfare aircraft carrier. When returning to the United States for Dad's leave in 1938, I was able to take real close-up pictures of the majestic *Augusta,* sitting off the Bund in Shanghai.

In Shanghai the economic situation was running wild. The Japanese were issuing local yen in great amounts, backing them up with their home currency. Thus, the exchange rate with the dollar in China had run all out of proportion. As a result, visitors such as our family could attend a luxurious movie, sitting in plush armchairs, for about four cents. A haircut cost between two and three cents. Other prices in Shanghai were comparable. Before the Japanese discovered and remedied the situation, astute profiteers could make enormous gains by purchasing yen in Shanghai for sale in Japan.

One high moment occurred when the liner *President Coolidge* pulled into Yokohama on that same trip home in the summer of 1938. Arrogant Japanese officials boarding the ship were pointedly harassing passengers desiring to go ashore. Knowing ahead of time of Dad's background and position, they gave him special attention in their interrogations. Finally Dad lost his temper and said, "I want nothing here; only to spend a few damned yen in your country!" Immediately the immigration officials cleared him. At lunch that day all the passengers were irritated and feeling superpatriotic. The ship's orchestra struck up the "American Patrol" in the course of the meal. Everyone present let up a howl of applause—rebel yells and all.

Our visits to Tokyo and Yokohama were uneventful except for the speed with which the taxi driver took us from one city to the next. The two cities even then were combined into one, but the way this madman ducked in and out of the traffic caused Mother to pull out smelling salts and declare that she had many things yet to do in this world and had no inclination to terminate her stay at this point. While traveling around Yokohama, however, we found it remarkable that several individuals turned up and offered to act as guides. True, they managed to secure excellent bargains in our shopping expeditions, but their knowledge of America led us to suspect that they were Japanese agents. Then one, in fact, made a slip and indicated knowledge of Dad's background. So we knew we were being followed. In Kobe the same thing occurred. The city was undergoing heavy rains and landslides at the time, and our taxi driver volunteered without extra charge to take us on circuitous routes to reach the places we intended to go to. Dad had no objection to these services on the part of the Japanese Government. They were convenient and he in truth had no espionage in mind.

On September 3, 1939, Dad, Mother, and I sat with our ears glued to an antiquated radio in the Manila apartment of Colonel Howard Smith and his wife, Kitty. We were listening to Neville Chamberlain's announcement that Great Britain was at war with Germany. France followed suit. Shortly thereafter we learned of the torpedoing of the British liner *Athenia,* reminiscent of the *Lusitania* in World War I and its effect on American public opinion.

For two days prior to this declaration, German forces had been invading Poland and local Army officers with whom Dad played bridge were taking the matter lightly and going about their business as usual.

Dad viewed the situation with no such detachment. The European war that he had been expecting for years was now upon the country; and since the Japanese were at the moment showing no signs of aggressive action, Dad's thoughts were now turning toward rejoining the Army in the United States, in hopes of an eventual field command. Besides his desire to get back with active troops, there were other factors pointing toward a decision to leave. One of these was a falling out with General MacArthur which, while it never came to a breaking point, resulted in a cooling off of their formerly warm relationship.

Naturally, I was not a witness to the incident but Dad reported it in his book *At Ease* and referred to it occasionally in informal conversation. The incident revolved around an idea that General

MacArthur had apparently originated himself, that morale of the Philippine population might be given a boost by means of a somewhat elaborate display of military might. He had asked Dad and his colleague, Colonel Jimmy Ord, to look into the possibility of bringing units of the Philippine Army to parade in Manila. Dad and Ord protested to the general but understood, correctly or incorrectly, that MacArthur had given the order to begin planning anyway. When President Quezon learned of preparations for such an affair, he became highly incensed and protested to MacArthur. At this point MacArthur denied ever having given any such orders—a complete repudiation of both Dad and Jimmy Ord. Naturally, the project had been canceled forthwith, but Dad and Ord believed that MacArthur had not been square about the matter. Who was right MacArthur on the one hand or Dad and Ord on the other—is immaterial, but the fact that the two younger officers believed their chief had let them down and run for cover was important because it removed much of Dad's enthusiasm for his job. This zest was almost completely destroyed when shortly thereafter Jimmy Ord was killed in an airplane crash in the mountains of Baguio.[7]

For practically the only time in my recollection we held a family council, called, without a doubt, to enable Dad to clarify his own thoughts. I could tell from our conversation that Dad's mind was really made up. "The only reason left for me to stay in this place," he said as he paced the floor of our living room, "is the extra money the Philippine Government is giving me. Other than that, there's not much to keep me here." Dad did almost all the talking. Mother, I knew, would be delighted to go home; she detested the tropics. For my part, I wanted to finish school at Brent. But neither one of us said much. It took little time for Dad to decide to ask for relief from duty with MacArthur and return to the States.

Accordingly, I was uprooted in mid-year from Brent School and with a heavy heart departed for Manila. At the pier to send us off to the United States were General and Mrs. MacArthur, the general carrying a bottle of whiskey as a going-away present. The general and the lieutenant colonel still held a sort of peculiar

[7] See *At Ease*, pp. 225–26.

mutual admiration, despite their differences, and such a gesture was uncommon for this normally thoughtless and egocentric man.

On our arrival back in San Francisco aboard the *President Coolidge,* Dad received immediate orders to remain temporarily at the Presidio of San Francisco to engage in some sort of planning activity. Fortunately Fort Lewis, our next station was located near Tacoma, Washington, where Uncle Ed lived. I was sent to stay with Ed and his daughter Janice until Dad and Mother could come up and get settled on the post.

During this time Ed and I became good friends. Ed considered President Roosevelt a work of the devil, and I, being pro-Republican but far less violent, sometimes took the other side. Though I was only seventeen years old at the time, Ed treated me as an equal, especially during our long evening discussions. He loved an argument above anything else in the world. In the course of our conversations, he declared that I should forego any ideas of becoming a "professional killer" and go to law school at his expense, later to join his law office. It was easy to demur. "I can argue with you, Ed, and love it. But," I said, "I could never work for you." Despite the fact that I sometimes wondered about this decision in later years, I believe it was right, as Ed and I always remained warm friends.

Fort Lewis was an exciting post in those days. Dad's first assignment there was to the 3d Division. He loved everything about it. After all the years of high-level duty with its political intrigues, he was ecstatic to be assigned to troops. He held two jobs; he commanded the 1st Battalion, 15th Infantry, and also held the position of regimental executive under Colonel Jesse Ladd. It seemed to me that this arrangement would result in a certain favoritism toward the 1st Battalion, but I detected no resentment along these lines.

In April 1940 I joined Dad while the division was on maneuvers at Fort Ord and occupied the other cot in his wall tent. Here we witnessed the beginnings of a growing army—new tanks, the new 81-mm mortar, and night firing by machine guns, using tracer ammunition. The 15th Infantry had its officers' mess in a modest temporary building. Colonel Ladd's son Fred and I sat down at the end of the table next to a couple of lieutenants who were on the receiving end of Dad's relaxed but peremptory orders. One day a demonstration of the 81-mm mortar had been conducted by a Lieutenant White. White had spent hours adjusting his weapons with great results. After the appropriate accolades, the Old Man had said, "Now Lieutenant White will move the mortars three hundred yards to the rear and fire again." The result had been a disaster. Lieutenant White groused all through the evening meal about the affair, seeming, apparently, to hold me somehow partially responsible. I viewed his problems with a certain detachment.

The 15th Infantry—I believe it was really Dad's doing—was enamored of the "Beer Barrel Polka." The regiment, it was claimed, would march only to that piece of music. Thus, when the 3d Division would pass in review, the band would stop when the first elements of the 15th reached the line and burst into the "Polka." Trivial as this matter may seem, it was the stuff of which morale was made.

From first grade through high school, every school seemed to become easier. Academic standards at Stadium High, Tacoma, were low because of the lack of motivation on the part of the students. Thus it was little problem to obtain high grades with a minimum of effort. But one subject I put a great deal of effort into: English composition. The reason, no doubt, lay in the fact that, having lived in a distant land, I thought I had something to write about. I was encouraged by an otherwise irascible teacher named Mr. B. K. Daniels, who was proud that he himself had traveled a good deal. Stimulated by my success in the classroom, I began to write as a hobby. At home I would write articles on the Far East, emulating reporters such as Demaree Bess and Pete Martin. I would then put them away, only to be lost.

One day at Fort Lewis—in 1940, I believe—Dad showed me a remarkable letter from General MacArthur, telling of a communication MacArthur had received from President Roosevelt. In the event of another world war, Roosevelt had notified him, he (MacArthur) would lead the American Forces in Europe. I recall one specific sentence: "Naturally this pleases me very much."

The astounding thing about this communication, as I gaped at it, was not that General MacArthur had received such a promise. The prospects of United States participation in the war still seemed remote, and few if any at that time expected it to erupt in the Pacific. Roosevelt's promise was vague and MacArthur seemed to be the logical choice. (Dad was still a lieutenant colonel.) What surprised me, however, was MacArthur's candor. Apparently he and Dad, despite past events, were still communicating, at least occasionally, on a friendly, confidential basis.

That summer I drove Mother from Fort Lewis to Boise, Idaho, where Dad joined us. Later in Denver I served as best man, making all the arrangements, for Aunt Mike's second wedding, to George Gordon Moore.

My final destination on the trip was Washington, D.C., where I was to attend a West Point preparatory school at 1918 N Street, run by Homer B. Millard. Mr. Millard's middle name was Behne, from which he derived the somewhat affectionate nickname of "Beanie." He was quite a character—short, spare, sun-tanned, mean, and arbitrary. His objective, wise indeed, was to make his preparatory school more difficult than plebe year at West Point; and he did a good job. West Point in those days had an artificially rigid entrance examination. In geometry, for example, it had not succumbed to the easier modern courses.[8] In the course of the year Beanie drove us through the geometry book, the algebra book, an American history book, and an ancient history book, three times each. We also memorized English authors, works, and quotes from Beanie's ingenious pamphlets. If anyone missed a question in math, he was given a second chance. If he failed the second time, he was required to write out the problem twenty-five times for submission the next day, in addition to his other studies. Two errors in history required copying the chapter, word for word. The English teacher had a list of a thousand often-misspelled words. If a student missed a couple of them on an English theme, he was directed to copy the entire list several times.

[8] There was, for example, a long problem, which took two pages, to construct and prove, dividing a circle into ten equal parts, using only a compass and a straight edge.

On our introduction to the school, Beanie Millard stood before us, swaying from foot to foot, with a long pointer between his hands. Softly he began, "You know, gentlemen, you don't need to do a thing I say here; it's completely up to you. You're on your own; you don't have to listen to a word I say." Then raising his voice in a crescendo, Beanie shouted, "BUT IF YOU DON'T, YOU CAN PACK UP YOUR BAGS AND GO HOME TOMORROW MORNING!" He looked searchingly around the room and asked for questions. There were none. "Well," Beanie said, swaying with a slight smirk on his face, "we understand each other, gentlemen. I have you where I want you and there is not a goddam thing you can do about it."

Beanie meant what he said. Every night we were sealed in our rooms by a small wire placed through an eye hook on the outside of our bedroom doors. If a student needed to go to the bathroom, he would have to break the seal and report himself immediately to Beanie. His word would be honored. However, any infraction of Beanie's rigid honor system caused immediate dismissal. His powerful public address system worked two ways; it allowed him to listen in on any conversation in any room. In modern parlance, every room was bugged. Nobody was authorized to visit anybody else's room, even outside of study hours. Once when a group were visiting illegally, someone said, "Don't worry; he can't hear us." Immediately the public address system roared out, "The hell I can't!"

One night, when Beanie had been partying, he caught me studying late. On the spot I was sentenced to indefinite confinement to my room. The next morning he released me.

And yet Beanie had a certain sense of humor. As he was given a bit to drinking, this sense of humor was sometimes inconsistent. One night he caught a couple of students sleeping on the roof. He immediately called them down and directed them to jog all the way to the Washington Monument and back in their pajamas. Beanie followed along behind them, sticking his head out of the window of his car, yelling, "Faster, faster!"

Needless to say, Beanie Millard's system was effective. He guaranteed that if a student could survive his course throughout the year, he would have a 90 per cent chance of passing the West

Point examinations. The catch was, of course, that Beanie eliminated students periodically, so that by the time the year was over, only those he was sure would pass still remained in school. Strange to say, despite the stern regimen, the students enjoyed this bizarre atmosphere, congenially laughing at and with Beanie —but sure that, if successful, they would be able to achieve their goal of entering West Point.

When in later years West Point relaxed its entrance examinations, accepting standard college boards, the need for a Millard School as we knew it disappeared. Beanie went into the Service during World War II and later set up another school, doubtless with much milder rules, on the West Coast.

As the son of a Regular Army officer, I was entitled by law to compete for a presidential appointment to West Point in March 1941. However, as a resident of Kansas, I was also eligible for a senatorial or congressional appointment. If possible to attain, the political appointment would be preferable, not only because it would involve an easier entrance examination but also, if successful, it would open another vacancy for one of my fellow Army brats via the presidential route. Therefore Dad, with the assistance of his youngest brother, Milton, began the usual procedure of requesting an appointment from Senator Arthur Capper of Kansas, together with what political influence the two could muster. Senator Capper, in common with most members of Congress, allowed any West Point hopeful to take the standard competitive examination administered by the Civil Service, in October 1940. This device was logical for a politician; by allowing a candidate to take the competitive he could do a favor for all who applied. By making one arbitrary appointment, he could consolidate one friend but alienate fifty others. The competitive, in other words, let him off the hook. Since only about five of Capper's candidates had attended any school like Beanie's, I was really competing against perhaps four others. Those who had not attended "cram" school could practically be discounted. Thus I wound up first on Senator Capper's list as the result of the examination and thereby received the senator's principal appointment to enter West Point on July 1, 1941, in the class of 1945.[9]

[9] Although the vast majority of senators and congressmen based their appointments on the results of the competitive, they were not obligated to do so. In my

Having received this news, I determined that I should return home to Fort Lewis. I had certain physical problems to contend with, and I deemed it best to go back and take care of them. Most important, I was underweight: 138 pounds at six feet one inch was the minimum requirement and I was below it. Furthermore, the intensive studying was beginning to tell on my eyesight, which had to be 20/20 in those days. Since the "validating" academic examination, an abbreviated test for high school graduates, was simple and noncompetitive, I was unworried on that score. Accordingly, for the last few weeks of 1940 I sat up at night and illegally copied the essentials of Beanie's invaluable English pamphlets. All this had to be done under cover of a blanket draped over my bunk to avoid detection. When at Christmas I broke the news of my departure to Beanie, he was unhappy but could do nothing to stop me. (The timing saved my parents from paying the spring tuition.) And Beanie, while disappointed to lose a student who would in all probability improve his statistics, really understood. He remained a good friend in our later contacts during his life.

I was home for Christmas 1940. The carols seemed a bit ironic in proclaiming, "Peace on Earth, Good Will to Men." When I frowned, the Old Man looked at me and murmured, "Be glad for peace while you've still got it."

In March 1941 a group of about thirty candidates at Fort Lewis took the validating examination, both physical and academic, for entrance to West Point. Though the academic test was fairly easy, the physical had me a little concerned, as my vision was only a fuzzy 20/20 and I had a marked touch of color blindness. The eye tests were not too searching, however, and my good friend "Doc" Plugh may have been slightly charitable. My weight had risen above the 138 pound mark. Therefore, in a few weeks I received orders to report to West Point as a "new cadet" some time during the morning of July 1, between the hours of eight and noon.

case, I also took the competitive of Congressman Edward Rees, 4th District of Kansas. When I won in the whole state, I assumed that the appointment from 4th District was mine also. Not true; Rees had already promised the appointment to someone else and his insincerity was disclosed only by the coincidence that I, from his district, had won Senator Capper's appointment.

From that time on I relaxed, sleeping in and playing tennis all day, making the most of my last few weeks of freedom. But with it all, I was restive. Despite the fact that I was nearly nineteen years old, had been away from home for years, and was soon to leave for good, my parents, as long as I remained under their roof, remained protective. I looked forward to the day when my life, though restricted by normal collegiate standards, would be governed by the same rules as those of my fellows.

By coincidence, Dad and Mother were to report to Fort Sam Houston, Texas, on the same day I was to enter West Point. Thus we were all beginning new lives. From that time on I would be on my own.

2

A Tanglefoot Goes to West Point

On July 1, 1941, some five hundred and fifty bewildered young-sters between ages seventeen and twenty-one converged from all parts of the country on the oldest post in the U. S. Army—West Point, New York. They came in all shapes and sizes—within West Point's physical standards—from all walks of life, from all types of backgrounds, and with varying notions of what lay ahead. The motley mob, most of whom struggled up the hill from the East Shore Railroad station to Central Barracks, were alike, how ever, in two respects: they were, by and large, highly motivated—and they were, with one exception, solidly Caucasian.

A number of these young men had been soldiers in the Army; most were political appointees; some were college graduates; and a sizable number were Army brats, who had dreamed throughout their youths of this day. Douglas MacArthur had been among this last group on a June day of 1899; during his later years he termed his entrance as a cadet to West Point his "highest honor."

Forty-two years after MacArthur, I was entering West Point under similar circumstances, as an Army brat. But my emotions, as the hour approached, were somewhat more mixed than the way MacArthur in his old age described the hour. My feeling, so well-remembered, was one of controlled, determined trepidation.

Throughout my younger years I had been bombarded from all sides by the subject of West Point. Generally, Dad and his Army friends had, wittingly or not, romanticized it. The sight of the Old Man pacing the floor, ear glued to the radio, alternately cheer-ing and cursing as the tide turned during the annual Army-Navy football game, was enough to convince me of the passionate devo-tion he held for the place. In private Dad would tell me of his own cadet career, normally in light terms, depicting the institution as the greatest and toughest in the world—and himself as the one rugged individual who could rise above it all. Through the years he claimed that I was under no obligation whatsoever to attend myself. But even as a youngster I could detect a certain note of his protesting too much. Further, his insistence that I do exercises to ensure passing the physical—just in case I wanted to go—indicated his anxiety that I at least keep my options open.

Actually, the Old Man did not browbeat me. Of my own volition, when visiting Denver in the summers, I had gone through the West Point 1915 year book, the *Howitzer,* in detail. True, I focused on the members of the 1915 football team—P. A. Hodgson was one of the big stars—but I memorized the faces of all, to the extent that even today I can identify nearly a half of the class by their pictures. It was not Dad's influence completely that sent me to West Point; it was largely my own romantic view of the place, born partly from my idolization of the Old Man but also, perhaps, from the contrast depicted in the *Howitzer* with the Victorian propriety of the Doud family.

By the time I attended Brent School in the Philippines, I had more or less presumed in my own mind that, if qualified, I would go to West Point. In the Philippines I could see what Dad was doing with the Philippine Army and I liked the atmosphere of the military. When we returned to the States and Dad joined the 3d Division at Fort Lewis, I refined my ambitions; not only would I go to West Point but I would also select the Infantry, as the only branch of the service.

I was well aware of what an ordeal plebe year at West Point would be. The system, I knew, was strict, the purpose being (1) to reduce the individual to a subhuman status, susceptible to indoctrination, and (2) to weed out those who lacked the necessary determination.

Much ado was made in those days regarding the exact time to report on the morning of July 1. The hours of reporting, as I have said, were between 8 A.M., and noon. I was advised not to arrive too early, as the first "new cadets"[1] to enter would be given spe-

---

[1] During "beast barracks" new plebes were not considered members of the Corps until a formal ceremony at the end of the first month. Hence the term "new cadet" in lieu of "cadet."

cial attention by the "Beast Detail," those selected members of the first class (i.e., seniors, class of 1942) responsible for the reception of the newcomers. On the other hand, it was well to arrive early enough to avoid being too rushed in the course of the first morning's activities. Looking back from a span of many years, the exact hour of the day to report to duty seems a triviality; it was a paramount consideration at that time.

I reported as directed to the East Academic Building on Thayer Road at about 10 A.M. A sergeant at a desk directed me into one of the classrooms, where each new cadet was given a final physical examination—a quick check-up, mostly to detect communicable disease—and then sent me with my suitcase into the brilliant sunlight of the Central Area of barracks. Another sergeant, checking the roster, directed me to the 1st Division of barracks, where to my disappointment I was to be assigned to 1st Company, which meant that I would eventually wind up either in A or B Company, probably A because of my height. I would much have preferred the more easy-going M Company, at the opposite end of the twelve-company regiment. M Company was the descendant of Dad's old beloved F Company. However, there was no time to give the matter a thought and the assignment was by no means negotiable.

Within seconds a large, heavy-set, blond-haired first class cadet, immaculately dressed out, seemed to pounce. The cadet sergeant, Charles W. Ryder, Jr., was the son of a classmate of my Dad's, an inconsequential fact. Immediately he began barking a series of abrupt orders, fired off like a machine gun: "Drop your bag! Pick it up! I didn't say set your bag down; I said drop it! Pick it up! Now drop it! Pull those shoulders back! Suck in that horrible gut! Front those slimy green eyes! You want to buy the place? Clamp in those wings; do you think you're going to fly?"

My reaction was strange; I nearly burst out laughing with relief. After all the anticipation, I was finally there. The ball game had started.

Most West Pointers say they can hardly remember their four weeks. Such was my experience. As "beasts" we were kept so busy double-timing to the Cadet Store, drilling, and being instructed in military subjects that only specific, inconsequential pictures impressed themselves on me. However, one upperclassman, Andrew

S. Low, Jr., cadet first sergeant, made an unusual impression. Low's gaunt build gave him the nickname of "Birdie," and his room was located right across the hall from my roommate and me. As Low would walk up and down the hall in his underwear—plebes were not allowed to leave their rooms unless fully dressed—he would sing, day after day, "The Last Time I Saw Paris." (I sometimes wondered if he knew another song.) But Low had an innate sense of humor that showed a vital touch of humanity through even the rigid plebe system. When we new cadets were first issued our gray dress coats (tunics with high collars and a black stripe down the front) and were learning how to put on the white crossbelts, the confusion was something to behold. Fastening the crossbelts to the cartridge box, tossing the cartridge box over the head, and putting the arms through the belts properly is no trick once mastered. But neither is riding a bicycle—once one learns.

A few minutes before first call for our first parade, Low came across the hall, fully dressed, and witnessed the uproar going on between my roommate and me, the two of us futilely trying to put these unthinkable belts on. Low stopped, asked permission to touch us, and proceeded to adjust the belts for both.

As he headed out the door, I said, "Thank you, sir," knowing full well that all hell would break loose as the result. He stopped in his tracks, turned on his heel, and proceeded to berate me up and down, pulling my chin in as far as it would go. "You never thank an upperclassman, mister," he said. "And you don't apologize either. If you kick an upperclassman by mistake, you don't apologize; you'd have kicked him harder if you could have." After a couple more seconds of painful bracing—chin in, shoulders back, stomach in—he stormed out the door. I smiled to myself contentedly. I knew that expressing appreciation was forbidden but was determined to do so, even though it caused a bit of minor physical suffering. Frankly, my own conception of propriety transcended in my mind this hallowed but somewhat silly "system." The routine was repeated at least twice afterward.

Low's short sermon on the proper hostility of plebes toward upperclassmen was meant to apply only to the West Point system, and his words were spoken at least halfway in jest. Yet my admiration and respect for him were such that I probably took them too seriously. Throughout my cadet years—and for some time after—I could not shake a visceral feeling that being friendly to one's military superiors constituted a form of boot-licking. A psychologist might say that these casual remarks were exactly what I wanted to hear, that they lent a rationale to some already-developed, innate resentment of authority. Whether all this affected my career or not, I don't know. I do know that I remember everything Andy Low said.

The phenomenon of the Army brat plebe was interesting in a way. For some odd reason, even though all new cadets dressed exactly alike and were treated exactly alike, an upperclassman could spot one of us almost without fail. The only explanation would seem to be that Army brats, knowing pretty much what to expect when they entered the Academy, were less shocked than the boy who had left his podunk (home town) with bands playing. Once an upperclassman halted me from a distance. Sauntering up to my side, he asked me simply, "What branch, mister?"

The fact that I was an Army brat and in good physical condition does not mean that I sailed through the first weeks with ease. On the contrary, being previously unaccustomed to shining shoes or paying much attention to my clothing, I made so many mistakes that I soon developed a reputation as one of the "woodenest" plebes in 1st Company. One day, for example, perhaps our third day in beast barracks, I returned from some formation and began looking around for my black tie to go to lunch. It was missing. (My roommate had taken it.) In desperation I made a snap judgment: any necktie at all would be better than none. I fished in my suitcase, pulled out the green tie I had worn for reporting in, and put it on. Once out in Central Area I was descended upon by four members of the Beast Detail, including even the impressive and austere company commander, Cadet Captain Richard M. Horridge. I was bombarded from all sides: "Who do you think you are, mister, Joe College?"

The only acceptable answer was "No excuse, sir." After a short questioning, however, the first classmen realized that, rather than trying to be wise or subvert the system, I was simply stupid. With that they sent me running back to my room to drop off the offending article of clothing and charge back to ranks. I received special attention at lunch that day for being without a necktie, but nothing more was made of the incident.

Another day, while drilling out on the Plain, I was the lead man in a squad going in single file. The command, "Left turn, MARCH!" was given—but not loud enough for me to be certain. Therefore I continued in a straight line. The squad leader, apparently sensing the humor of the situation, allowed me to continue until I developed a definite feeling of loneliness. Finally I dared peek back and found that I was marching all by myself. With a mad dash I turned around and caught up with the rest. Again a few moments of special attention and we continued the drill.

One physical deficiency of mine that caused the upperclassmen more distress than it did me was some sort of loose jointedness which made me "bounce" when marching. My feet could be going along in perfect cadence, left heel properly digging into the ground with every heavy beat, but at the same time my head looked out of step. While everyone else's was going up and down, mine seemed to be going backward and forward. Instructors at drill would observe this phenomenon in amazement and actually were fairly charitable, realizing that I was trying my best, although a couple of them tagged me with the sobriquet "Tanglefoot Eisenwilly." Perhaps in the long run the whole situation worked to my advantage: the reason, I suspected, that I was appointed Battalion Sergeant Major during first-class year—a good job—was simply to "get me out of the company's ranks."

For the first two or three months in West Point my demerits rose until there were only two plebes in the company—one other and myself—who stood out above all the rest. At the end of four weeks I was rated as "deficient in conduct." This caused me considerable concern, as I was not prepared to be deficient in anything, even conduct. True, my father had been a disciplinary case, but of a completely different order. Whereas his misdemeanors had been intentional, skipping breakfast and the like, mine were not. The fact is I was trying too hard and simply had not learned how to budget my time in performing all the necessary trivia. When an upperclassman once complimented me on my shiny "tarbucket" (full-dress hat with pom-pom), I determined that at next inspection that tarbucket would be the best in the Corps. However, this effort was achieved at the price of smudges on belts, inadequately shined shoes, and goodness knows what else. I think I learned a lesson from all this: when time is tight, don't try to be too perfect in any one department. At any rate, I had to learn the hard way. I suppose there was no type of minor gig, such as "dried bubbles on soap bar," that I failed to be nailed for. But I was never caught for anything twice. By late December I had been reported for every minor offense in the books, and now my demerits miraculously dropped down among the lowest in the class. They remained so for the rest of my time on the Hudson.

The West Point that I entered in July of 1941 differed little from that of the days when my Dad had been a cadet thirty years earlier. The yearly routine was nearly identical. As soon as the new cadets had joined the rest of the Corps, for example, we all joined our regular companies at summer camp. Camp Clinton was a flat, dusty area on the tip of the Plain, under the Kosciusko Monument, within full view of the cadet barracks and the imposing chapel on the hill. Life in summer camp was actually more difficult than in beast barracks. For in this new environment the plebes were in a minority and subject to the supervision, not always constructive, of the yearlings (sophomores), who had just completed their own plebe years and were undergoing the heady experience of their new-found freedom and of their petty power. The second-classmen (juniors) were away on the three-month furlough that traditionally came between yearling and second-class years. The days were filled with military drill and tactics. But in addition all cadets, especially plebes, were required to maintain their sidewall tents in the same immaculate condition as when living in barracks.

Toward the end of the summer, when the Corps went on maneuvers, a member of Dad's class of 1915, had he been transplanted into our class of 1945, would have felt at home. Even the outmoded field uniforms were identical: felt campaign hats, full rolled packs, heavy gray shirts, gray riding breeches, and leggings. We were still carrying the model 1903 Springfield rifle. Maneuvers were commanded by the tactical officers, who rode horseback in green blouses and pink riding breeches. The actual maneuvers were conducted, even after the country had gone into partial mobilization, in the leisurely manner of yesteryear. Every day's activity ended with the noon meal. Plebes, while not allowed to fraternize with upperclassmen, could relax. Each cadet was issued $2.00 for the week—with which to go into the small towns nearby to enjoy himself. As always, the cat-and-mouse game went on between tactical officers and the more adventuresome cadets, in which the latter would try surreptitiously to sneak a beer without being detected. (The penalty for being caught was six months confinement to one's room.) At the end of this short respite, the entire Corps moved back to barracks.

Here A Company was fortunate, as we occupied the new South Barracks, built far more recently than those of Central Area. Every floor boasted a toilet! From here on, life settled down; and although a plebe still led a highly restricted life, with a multitude of harassments, he could, if sufficiently circumspect, stay largely out of sight and concentrate on his academics—which of course the upper classes were doing themselves.

I was glad when we began academics. With my preparation at Beanie Millard's, I found the first few months at West Point largely repeated what Beanie had pounded into our heads. As a result, at the end of the first month, I stood first among the A Company plebes academically but still deficient in conduct, a peculiar combination.

Academic success, however, was short-lived. Once my background from Millard's ran out, West Point began to discover my basic limitations.[2] Nevertheless, academics remained the least of my problems in West Point.

In October one day a first-classman, Willis D. Crittenberger sauntered into my room. When I snapped to attention, he said, "Mister, I think you'd like to know that your father just got a star." Without another word he left. This was the first news I had re-

---

[2] In my adult years I have always had a yen to take a course in calculus, just to discover what it basically is all about.

ceived of Dad's promotion to brigadier general. I sat down and wrote him a long letter.

On the night of December 6, 1941, the movie playing at West Point was *Sergeant York,* starring Gary Cooper. Nearly everyone on the post attended and walked back to barracks with the tune "The Old Time Religion" buzzing in their heads. The next morning we in the cadet choir marched up to chapel, singing the old hymn. After lunch that day, I indulged my favorite habit—sleeping all Sunday afternoon. No cadet ever gets quite caught up on sleep. At about three o'clock a classmate of mine from down the hall shook me and said, "Wake up, John, the Japs are bombing Pearl Harbor!" "Baloney," I groaned and rolled over and went back to sleep. At about five, another classmate came in and shook me saying, "Wake up, John, you've just gotten seven demerits for missing choir practice." I jumped up with a start, dressed, and scurried to the bulletin board. Having been consistently negligent about reading the bulletin board, I had not only failed to show up for choir practice but had also failed to initial the gig when it had been posted. (The ante thus resulted in ten rather than seven demerits.) That evening we all knew the news was true. A hush of bewilderment lay over the entire Corps. Louis Jones, one of my closest friends, roomed directly across the hall. His family— Louis was another Army brat—was in Hawaii. It would be days before he would learn that all were safe. I was with him in spirit in his anxiety.

Plebe Christmas was the first time the plebes were allowed to act completely as full-fledged cadets. All three upper classes were gone on Christmas leave, and the plebes had the run of the Corps. Certain men who had distinguished themselves in military subjects were appointed acting cadet officers. The plebe class took over positions such as officer of the guard and carried all normal cadet responsibilities. We were allowed to relax at meals and to entertain our families without the inconvenience of the classroom for about ten days. Mother came up for a while but Dad, having been called from Fort Sam Houston to War Plans in Washington, was unable to come. Once the upperclassmen returned from

Christmas leave, of course, the entire plebe class reverted immediately to its former status.

Through the winter of 1941–42 the situation at West Point was reflecting that of the rest of the country, now at war with Japan and the Axis. All of us had the war very much on our minds, and somehow or other the intricacies of the West Point disciplinary system, unyielding though they were, seemed to hold less significance. My roommates and I tried to follow the progress of the war by the newspapers, but to do so was well-nigh impossible, as it was to all citizens not privy to the facts. The academic year went on uninterrupted, although rumors of all sorts were flying around regarding early graduation.

In the springtime, somewhere around April, the plebes enjoyed another short respite with the upperclasses gone. This time Dad was able to get a day off and come up and see me.

During the visit Dad told me a little bit about his work with General George C. Marshall. He had been informed by Marshall a few days earlier that he would be retained as chief of War Plans for the duration of the war and remain a brigadier general. Dad seemed to expect me to be unhappy at this turn of events but I was not; to me as a plebe the grade of brigadier general seemed tantamount to a god. But Dad, disappointed himself, took it philosophically and at the end of the pleasant visit went back to his duties.

By this time we were definitely on the down-hill slope of plebe year, and as the buds began coming out on the trees we experienced the traditional "spring buck-up" after the quiet doldrums of the winter. The plebes were given more attention; and the closer the end of the year came, the more severe became the upperclass attitude. This resurrection of the beast barracks/summer camp atmosphere caused little anguish. Though June Week was traditionally considered a "hell week" for the plebes about to be "recognized," we knew the end was in sight.

When June Week arrived, the intensity of plebe discipline increased. "Clothing formations," in which plebes were required to change uniforms and report to the basement of barracks in unreasonable time, were common. Nevertheless, it could have been worse, as the bulk of the upperclassmen were engaged in social activities, leaving only a few behind to administer this last disciplinary honing.

Finally the day arrived: Graduation Parade. As the Corps marched out on the Plain, the snarling yearling voices reached such a din that one could hardly hear the military commands. Chins, shoulders, and stomachs were pulled back as never before. At the end of the parade, however, the Corps marched into Central Area, was brought to a halt, and a command was given for everyone to break ranks and shake hands. Even as I write, I feel a tingle at the memory of "recognition." Plebe year was over. We had passed the year-long ordeal and were now yearlings. Though the experience is common to every member of the Long Gray Line, I can remember no recognition of accomplishment that has ever given me the thrill of that moment.

The summer of 1942 brought on drastic changes. To quote Stephen Vincent Benét, the "snug safe world cracked up like broken candy." The Army authorities had now decided that West Point should, for the sake of public relations if nothing else, emulate the feverish activity of the rest of the country and prove that West Point "had gone to war." That summer, which normally would have been a sleepy, languid, existence for the new yearlings in summer camp, turned out to be anything but that. We moved to Camp Clinton across the Plain as had previous classes, but we were issued khaki uniforms and maneuvered and trained intensively in the field at the same time. Standards of spit-and-polish were maintained in camp as in previous years; but the Tactical Department seemed dedicated to running us ragged at Camp Popolopen (since renamed Camp Buckner). For part of the summer our class visited Pine Camp, New York, where, in addition to our own maneuvers, we could witness the newly formed 4th Armored Division in training. Dad's West Point and mine now grew dramatically dissimilar.

Our class spent the entire maneuver time at Pine Camp (now Camp Drum) in pup tents. Every morning at our customary 5:50 hour for rising, we were awakened by the loud horn blown by a large black sergeant known only to us as "Benny." Benny, now a West Point tradition, would swagger up and down the company streets, shouting and tooting unrecognizable tunes. "A-a-a-all right!" he would bawl, "a-all right!" Then he would toot some more and repeat a verse or two, the only printable one of which I can remember went: "I know you'se tired and sleepy too! I don't wantcha but the Major do." Benny was the only compensation for rolling out of the blankets into the cold to start the long rigorous day of training.

But all of us knew we had little cause for complaint. Other men of our age had already been captured on Bataan and Corregidor. This knowledge, in fact, was detrimental to our morale. Whereas a year before we cadets had considered ourselves the nation's military elite, we now felt we were being kept as schoolboys, while real soldiers were being trained to fight overseas.

One aspect that came to light in the course of our training, however, gave us all a lift. Even West Point was now becoming supplied with the latest in military equipment. The old Springfield rifle had been replaced by the new M-1; and the presence of the 37-mm and 55-mm antitank guns for training was proof that American war production was getting under way sufficiently for some equipment to be spared for the secondary purpose of training cadets.

The summer of 1942 caused another revolution in my own life. My father was now for the first time becoming recognized outside the Army. General Marshall had relented on keeping Dad in War Plans for the duration of the war, and in June Dad received his second star (together with considerable publicity in *Time*).[3] One day in camp I received a letter:

June 13, 1942

Dear Johnnie: Confidentially, I am soon to leave the United States for an indefinite stay. Naturally I am anxious to have a few hours with you just to say goodbye and to have a good talk. Today I telephoned to . . . the Adjutant at West Point, and he informed me that any day I could come to West Point next week, you could be excused from normal duties in order to have a few hours with

---

[3] Dad's reputation in the Army was already secure. *Time*, in the article on the promotion, wrote, "The Army said 'Amen.'"

me. He assured me that this would occasion no embarrassment to you, to the authorities there, or to anyone else.

I cannot say for sure what day I can be at West Point, it is possible that I may come late some afternoon, spend the evening, and return the next morning. In any event, I will let you know by telegram about what time to expect me and will telephone the headquarters at West Point, so that a car will be at the airfield to meet me.

Mamie intends to return to the Wardman Park Hotel where she will take a small apartment. She will have room for you when you come down next fall with your pal. Should there be no room in her particular apartment, she can always get an extra one for you. She is looking forward to your visit.

Best of luck. I hope to be seeing you very soon, probably about Wednesday or Thursday. Affectionately,   DAD

P.S. The bosses are certainly giving me a tough job this time. I will tell you about it when I see you.

I immediately applied for a weekend leave to see him off. This would constitute a precedent, but the authorities at the Academy were generous enough to grant my request, and Dad canceled plans to come to West Point. I went to stay with Mother and Dad for a couple of days in their quarters at Fort Myer. On arrival my first question was, "Well, what is your job going to be overseas?"

"Oh, I'm to be the commanding general."

This came as somewhat of a surprise, as the jump from a colonel who was chief of staff of the Third Army at Fort Sam Houston the previous October to commanding general of an entire theater of war in the course of six months seemed astronomical. It was.

During the visit we had the chance for intimate conversations. I told Dad all about West Point and was surprised to find that we had not so much in common on the subject as I had thought. The structure of the place had changed little—this was still June 1942—but our views of it differed. In the twenty-seven years since his graduation, Dad had perhaps developed an overly rosy picture of the place. He thought of it mostly in terms of athletics, pranks, and fun. For my part, since the thrill of recognition, I was finding it less challenging and more drudgery. From plebe year on—perhaps from Pearl Harbor on—West Point was becoming a place that Dad would have never recognized.

Dad was looking forward cheerfully to his new challenge. The only dark spot came one afternoon when we were sitting on the front porch of his quarters at Fort Myer. Word came in that June afternoon of 1942 that Tobruk, heretofore considered an impregnable British position, had fallen during the latest Nazi offensive in North Africa. Nobody had expected this. It made the Old Man pensive for quite a while.

The stay was short, and I returned to West Point. Dad went overseas, and Mother then began busying herself to put the bulk of their furniture in storage and move into the Wardman (now Sheraton) Park Hotel in Washington.

As things were moving rapidly, I had no time to pause and reflect on what would be the effect of Dad's new-found prominence. But I found from that point on that I was treated a little differently, even by my classmates. I was suddenly thrust into a sort of reflected prominence, even though only a yearling. It was a heady feeling in a way and caused little inconvenience—so long as I remained within the cloistered walls of Hell-on-the-Hudson.

When classes resumed that September of 1942, rumors that had been flying around the past spring were becoming true. In order to produce more West Point officers for the war the normal four-year curriculum was now cut to three. This reduction in the length of the course would allow each incoming class to be larger, thereby producing more West Pointers annually. In order to effect this, the former class of 1943 was graduated six months early and became the class of January 1943; the former class of 1944 became the class of 1943; and our class of 1945 was now the class of 1944. Academically, we probably suffered the worst of any, since we had gone through a complete first year under the old system. Now the Academic Board was forced to cram three years course into two. Since the authorities were determined to complete our minimum requirements for bachelor of science degrees, almost all subjects except those relating to engineering were cut out. Social sciences were abbreviated drastically and English was eliminated. The engineering subjects were retained, although also abbreviated. We were given a course in chemistry, for example, without a day's work in laboratory.

Though some would disagree, I had the feeling that morale among the cadets remained rather low for most of the two remaining years until our graduation in June of 1944. The reasons are hardly mysterious. First of all, with the increased tempo, almost all leaves were canceled; our longest was twelve days at Christmas in 1942. In addition, the quality of the staff and faculty deteriorated visibly. Generally speaking—this cannot be taken as applying across the board—the more highly talented officers of the Regular Army were being assigned overseas. Retired officers were being called back for duty at West Point, and many of the tactical officers were drawn for some mysterious reason from the class of 1941, which had graduated only a month before we had entered. No relaxation in the rigidity of our regimen resulted from our stepped-up activities. The wartime aspects of West Point were simply piled on top of them. And yet in all of this we were unable to complain, at least in public. Under normal circumstances we would have felt free to howl; but since men were fighting and dying overseas, we restrained our protests.

Nevertheless, the summer of 1943 was interesting. First came the Beast Detail. Those of us selected were given rigorous preparation ahead of time. For besides the ordinary jobs of hammering the class of 1946 from raw material into organized cadets, all members were to serve as instructors.

Training the new cadets, upon their entry, proved to be a stimulating experience. We soon discovered that the detail went through all the physical grind as our trainees (except for the bracing and compulsory double-timing) and then sat up at night after the plebes were in bed, planning the next day's lessons. But psychologically, the detail held all the advantages; we were on home ground—as the authorities—and whereas the plebe was kept in a constant mental state of wondering "What next?" we were in the saddle. Also we were generally in far better physical condition than our trainees.

The detail was made all the more rewarding because of the fact that the Corps of Cadets in those days practically administered itself. Each company had a tactical officer, to be sure, but that tactical officer remained largely aloof, making periodic inspections and giving military instruction. The administration, duty rosters, routine discipline, enforcement of the all-important Honor System —all were performed nearly independently by the cadets.[4]

Later in the summer the members of the first class were sent out to replacement training centers for about three weeks to serve as acting second lieutenants. This experience gave us some idea of what our duties would be a year hence when we graduated. It was my first experience in dealing directly with our drafted citizenry.

By and large I thought the spirit of the drafted enlisted men was good. I was somewhat appalled, however, at the illiteracy rate. One day while trying to help an earnest man from the mountains to adjust the sights of his rifle, I finally discovered that he knew absolutely nothing about the multiplication tables. The poor fellow's wrinkled brow made a strong impression. "These things are tough, sir," he said, "if you ain't been to school."

The other surprise was the generally poor physical condition of our citizenry. A good many of these replacements, destined for the anti-aircraft artillery, were in the older brackets of the draft. I was amazed at the inability of men in their middle thirties to hold up on a march. It was not a matter of malingering or laziness; they simply couldn't make it. When I stopped off in Washington on the way back to West Point, I was mumbling disgustedly about these "old codgers"—thirty-five years old—much to the amusement of Mother and her friends. (Possibly I was feeling a bit self-important.) With advancing age, it is easy now to realize the difference in stamina between a twenty-year-old and a thirty-five-year-old who has not been consistently active throughout his life.

We had a few days, maybe four or five, at home during Christmas 1943. I was with Mother in the Wardman Park when the news came over the radio of Dad's appointment as Supreme Com-

[4] Since the war years, the trend has been toward closer control by the authorities, with the tactical officers looking over the cadet officers' shoulders to a greater extent. This cautious approach seems deplorable to "old grads" but is probably necessary in the light of the same tendency throughout the Army and government as a whole.

mander for the forthcoming Allied invasion of Europe. All of a sudden that night of December 24, the halls leading to Mother's apartment were packed with reporters. She refused to see any of them. Finally, Christmas morning, someone discovered a lone young woman who had sat up all night in the hall. Mother relented and gave Lee Carson an exclusive interview. In gratitude Miss Carson took me around for a day to meet some of her friends in Washington, including Steve Early, the President's press secretary; Vice President Henry Wallace, who advised us he was studying Russian avidly; and one or two others.

Shortly after the turn of the year, in early 1944, I was sent for by the officer of the day. Dad, I learned for the first time, had secretly returned to Washington directly from North Africa. Colonel Frank McCarthy, secretary of the Army General Staff, who often acted as an aide to General Marshall, was in the OD's office, having come to West Point to pull me out for the remainder of the day. To my astonishment—and to that of the OD—Frank told us that Dad and Mother were on a railroad car pulling into a siding near the East Shore Station down on the river at that very moment. Within moments I was whisked into a staff car for the short ride down to the tracks. During the afternoon a handful of friends from the post also came down for a visit; and as a special treat that evening I was allowed to invite three cadets down for dinner.

After the rest had left, I stayed behind only a few minutes and wished Dad luck. He seemed the same, despite his four stars, but he was obviously rather preoccupied, impatient to get on with his new job of planning the invasion. (His no-nonsense life of the past eighteen months had sharpened his manner somewhat; Mother at one time chastised him for his abruptness. He growled amicably, "Hell, I'm going back to my theater where I can do what I want.")

The reason for the secrecy on the trip was not a question of Dad's physical security. Rather it was an effort to keep the Nazis always in a state of alert. German intelligence mistakenly presumed that Dad had already arrived in London from North Africa, and General Marshall wanted them to keep expecting an invasion any day, which of course would have been an extremely difficult thing for a brand new commander. The secret was magnificently kept, however, and the Washington visit was announced only after Dad had arrived in London.

From that January to June 1944 we of the West Point class of 1944 conformed to the "system," rendering lip service only. We had chosen our branches, bought our uniforms and field equipment. Acutely conscious that we were enjoying the last moments of irresponsibility before taking on the tasks of doing our part in a major war, we relaxed and amused ourselves by making life difficult for the tactical officers who had been making life difficult for us before. I cranked my roommate, Don Carter, to the ceiling of the mess hall one day on a telescopic device, designed for changing the lights. We slept out on the roof in our newly purchased sleeping bags.

In the closing days of first-class year, however, I was still at one point the victim, in my own mind, of the inexorable West Point. For three whole years I had remained on the tennis squad, one of the benefits of which was that such activity excused me from horseback riding instruction. Two weeks before graduation, the tennis season ended and I, along with others, was directed to report to the riding ring. During the year the regular class had advanced to the jumping stage; but those of us who were joining at this late date were not excused. Only about three or four sessions remained, to the best of my memory. Having had no previous jumping instruction, I could never make a complete jump. At worst, I was thrown; at best, I wound up with my arms around the horse's neck, staring into his face from below.

The members of the Tactical Department, many of whom, as I have mentioned, were not much older than we, must have been exasperated with a large part of our class. Perhaps in a way we were enjoying the same abandon that the Old Man had enjoyed years before. This was hardly a commendable attitude; it can perhaps be forgiven because of the unalterable fact that these were our last days as schoolboys before we would face the grim responsibilities that we all knew lay ahead.

Finally came June Week—families, dates, dances, Graduation Parade, and at last Graduation itself.

3

New Grad Among Old Pros

Few single days in American history are more familiar to the average person than June 6, 1944—D-Day—when the Western Allies launched their invasion of Hitler's Europe by landing on the soil of Normandy. Thousands of American and British fighting men would recall it as Civil War veterans did Gettysburg. Other thousands would never live to remember it.

I was not part of the main drama of the day, for by coincidence June 6 was the date that the class of 1944 graduated from West Point. Nevertheless, in a more mundane fashion, it was unforgettable for me also.

I woke up that morning worn out. June Week—the five days preceding graduation at West Point—is hectic. Graduation Parade, the afternoon before, had been an emotional experience. Furthermore, anxious that nothing should delay my clearing the post on completion of the graduation ceremonies, I had turned in my mattress the day before and had tossed fitfully through the previous night on an iron cot with two large blotters as bedding.

As 1st Battalion cadet sergeant major, I took my place to march to breakfast for the last time. The battalion commander turned and regarded me quizzically. "You heard, of course, that the Allies landed in Europe this morning." That was the first I had heard. There was little time to ruminate over the news, however, and no details were available other than President Roosevelt's dramatic announcement to the nation. Therefore, all of us went about our business, turning in our cadet chevrons, packing our footlockers, and preparing to depart.

Although a *Life* photographer had been trailing my date and me for days, when the time came for the Corps to march down to the field house for graduation, I underwent my first experience with big-time publicity. Mother and I found ourselves facing a bank of something like forty photographers, bulbs flashing unmercifully. I felt a swelling of resentment, caused not so much by the photographers' peremptory demands or even by the irritation of the flashbulbs; I hated being singled out conspicuously from those whose comradeship I valued—my classmates. Even after breaking ranks at the field house the chaos continued. The photographers insisted on a picture of Mother handing me a letter that Dad had innocently written. He had intended it to be delivered on graduation day, not realizing the furor that circumstances would create.

The graduation ceremony itself blurs in my memory except for the fact that the speaker that day was General Brehon Somervell, the only man present who had possessed previous knowledge of the timing of the Normandy landings. After the ceremony, however, came another personal shock: I was placed, despite my pleas and protests, in the superintendent's large black car with Mother and the superintendent. The three of us rode like royalty up the hill to barracks, my classmates observing and laughing sympathetically at my discomfiture.

That afternoon I hauled my baggage down to Mother's room in the Thayer Hotel to repack. A couple of weeks earlier I had received secret orders directing me to report to the New York Port of Embarkation the night of June 6 for departure overseas aboard the *Queen Mary*. General Marshall himself had kindly conceived the idea that during this trying period it might be beneficial to Dad were I to spend my regular month's leave with him in Europe. I had been forbidden to tell even my closest friend and that morning had packed my uniforms as if I were proceeding to vacation in the United States like the rest of my classmates. In the Thayer Hotel I unpacked my "suntan" khakis, put them away in footlockers, and replaced them with wool uniforms, as OD (olive drab) was the only uniform being worn in Europe. The process had to be camouflaged; reporters came in a final time to take pictures of Mother and me listening to the radio.

That evening I was picked up by a staff car and, in the custody of a Transportation Corps captain, delivered to the ship. The two of us marched down the dimly lit pier to the gangplank, where the 7th Armored Division had already loaded up, and I was ushered through the corridors to a stateroom. Nine or ten men, huddled in blankets, were asleep. My own was next to the door and I slid into it gratefully. Eighteen hours later I woke up, to be greeted from the various bunks by friendly faces, some of whom were relieved that I was actually alive.

The trip across the Atlantic was pleasant, despite the crowded conditions. An Army division in those days comprised about 15,000 men, a large number even for the *Queen Mary*. My bunk-mates, all lieutenants, were companionable. Someone in his wisdom had decided that I should remain incognito, even among troops on the high seas; nevertheless my identity soon became known. At one point I was sent for by the commanding general of the 7th Armored, but otherwise I simply attended the two daily meals with my new friends in the sumptuous dining hall and took it easy. As the *Queen Mary* could outrun any U-boat or torpedo, she proceeded without convoy. Thus the voyage required only seven days, and we landed somewhere in Scotland on June 13.

As the ship dropped anchor at dawn, Dad's aide, Colonel Ernest ("Tex") Lee, was waiting. Immediately we departed on a luxurious private train for London and Supreme Headquarters, Allied Expeditionary Force (SHAEF), at Bushey Park.

All the way across the water I had been thirsting for information on how the landings had gone, but information had been nil. Tex Lee tried to bring me up to date as best he could on the train trip. Things were doing all right, he said; the lodgement seemed secure; but progress had been slower than originally planned. The British Second Army on the left had not yet taken Caen, originally visualized as an objective for the first day. In the American First Army sector on the right progress was also slow. Nevertheless the bridge-head was sufficiently deep that all beaches and artificial ports were clear of artillery fire and supplies were coming across rapidly.

On arrival at Dad's headquarters I was immediately ushered into his office. It was now early afternoon on D-plus-7 (June 13— seven days after D-Day). Dad had been to Normandy the day before, escorting General Marshall, Admiral Ernest J. King, and General Henry ("Hap") Arnold, but the visitors had left.

Naturally, I was eager to look into the tactical situation as best I could. Things were about as Tex had described them. The landing areas had been joined into a continuous front, and the areas of primary concern were Caen on the east and Carentan on the west. We had been able to get sixteen divisions—British and American —into action.

Two visitors of importance came in that afternoon. The first was Major General Everett Hughes, "Uncle Everett" from Washington days. Hughes was disturbed; he had just returned from Omaha Beach and had come back with the definite impression that the engineer beach party was worn out, ready to drop from fatigue. Supplies were not flowing across to Hughes's satisfaction. Dad leaned back in his chair, picked up the telephone, and put in a call to Lieutenant General John C. H. Lee, commanding the Services of Supply. The call was blunt and to the point. If Lee wanted to keep his job, Dad said, he had better get over there personally and see to it that things were stepped up. The telephone call of about half a minute duration over, Dad went on to other things.

Later in the afternoon Major General Kenneth Strong, the British officer in charge of intelligence for the Allied forces, came in with the latest news. Major General J. Lawton ("Lightning Joe") Collins' American VII Corps, on the extreme right, had now pushed far enough south so that he was now executing his planned swing to the right (west) to cut off the Cotentin Peninsula, later to head north to seize the all-important port of Cherbourg. I sat wide-eyed as Strong gave a run-down on the performance of the nine various German divisions that had arrived in the area. "This division," he pointed out, "has been fighting very badly. There might be a weak spot there." Then, pointing, he said, "But this division here has fought very well." He continued on, portraying a picture of the resistance the Americans were meeting all along the right of First Army. Dad decided that afternoon that in a couple of days, June 15, he would make a visit to Normandy to talk the situation over with General Bernard Law Montgomery, temporarily in tactical control of the ground forces in Normandy.

It might be well to explain the command set-up as of this time. The entire Allied Expeditionary Force and the ultimate responsibility for its performance belonged to General Eisenhower. Nevertheless, the front, being less than a hundred miles long, was at this point a single army group operation. Just as a platoon-size raid would not be commanded on the spot by a major general, so an army group would not be directed in detail by the Supreme Commander. Dad's function at this time was confined to general supervision and coordination between land, sea, and air arms, awaiting the time when the force ashore would be large enough to warrant his taking personal command of all ground operations. Hence Montgomery, his headquarters north of Caen, was the man to whom Dad looked for the direction of the day-to-day ground battle.

This arrangement, though proper, seemed to make Dad a little fretful, like a football player sitting on the bench, anxious to get in the game. He covered his restlessness well, and only one close to him would be able to detect a trace of preoccupation in his manner. But the forced personal inactivity probably accounted for the unaccustomed curtness with which he had barked at General Lee that afternoon and for the eagerness he had showed in wringing out every detail from General Strong on the performance of individual German divisions on the VII Corps front. The decision made to visit "Monty" in a couple of days, Dad seemed to relax a bit.

That evening Dad and I drove over to Telegraph Cottage, a comfortable and unpretentious little house that had been his home for some months past. It was located in Kingston, a suburb to the south of London and in reasonable proximity to both Bushey Park (SHAEF) and Widewing (headquarters of the Allied air forces). It was a small cottage, done in Tudor style, but in an uncrowded area with broad meadows across the road. It was surrounded by enough of a garden to permit him to wander around with a feeling of space. Between the house and the front gate a small mound disclosed an underground bomb shelter. Dad rarely used this shelter and it had been installed only on the insistence of Prime Minister Winston Churchill.

As we were sitting outside enjoying the June weather that first evening, we heard the noise of bombs exploding and guns firing to the south. Dad shrugged; he was aware that the cause was a new type of Nazi weapon, the V-1 (buzz bomb), a pilotless airplane of high speed and heavy bomb load. Apparently the first had appeared the day before. The next day Dad learned that he, as Supreme Commander, was given the responsibility for trying to eliminate this threat.

The V-1s were effective weapons but did not seem to me to carry any decisive potential. I saw several places in the next few days where they had hit, and the damage, while serious, did not seem so devastating as to constitute a major factor in the war at this stage. But Londoners who had lived cheerfully through the "blitz" of 1940 told me that these V-1s created a greater psychological effect than had Air Marshal Hermann Goering's bombers. This seemed difficult to believe, but could be explained by the fact that the people of London had been through the bombing experience before and thought the ordeal was over. They were now facing the buzz bombs with nerves long frazzled from former experience.

There was another element to the buzz bomb—its impersonality. During the blitz, so I was told, people could man the anti-aircraft guns against the German planes and feel they were shooting back at someone. The buzz bomb, even though shot down, would still in all likelihood create the same amount of damage as it would if not hit. And furthermore, it possessed an element of suspense. One could hear the pilotless aircraft coming in and then, ten seconds after the engine cut off, it would dive to the ground and explode. People held their breaths during the waiting period, wondering where this hellish machine would come to earth.

Under these circumstances, it was obvious that the buzz bombs would have to be intercepted over the English Channel, or at least as far out as possible over the southeast corner of England in order to minimize damage on London. The Allied air forces, therefore, were forced to divert some of their fighter squadrons to combating this new weapon. They achieved a degree of success, as it turned out, and the number of V-1s making their way to the city itself was drastically reduced. Nevertheless, neither the V-1s, nor their successor, the V-2 rocket bomb, were completely eradicated until the last days of the war.

Early in the morning of June 15, according to plan, Dad and I rose early at Telegraph Cottage to begin our trip to Normandy for his visit to the British sector. Lieutenant Kay Summersby, an attractive Irish WAC who was Dad's secretary and chauffeur, was on hand to take us in his dull-finished, olive drab Cadillac to the airfield. Air Chief Marshal Sir Arthur Tedder, Deputy Supreme Commander, was on hand. There was ample space aboard the B-17 Flying Fortress and we were told that we could sit anywhere we desired. I chose the bombardier's spot in the nose. Perched up front with nothing but glass between me and the runway, I found the take-off a thrill. The plane was escorted on this trip by thirteen P-47 Thunderbolts. Accustomed as I was to thinking of London as practically on the south coast of England, I was a little surprised how much of the journey was actually made over English soil.

During the first part of the trip over water we could spot occasional vessels, but as we approached Normandy they increased dramatically. And, as the plane neared the beaches, it maneuvered to avoid the numerous barrage balloons protecting the surface ships below. Although the day was dry in Normandy and a hazy sun shone, the ceiling was low, and by the time the B-17 reached the shoreline, it had been forced down to an altitude of three hundred feet, below the height of the balloons. The numerous remaining German obstacles along the beach seemed deceptively peaceful and harmless from the air.

The plane landed on an improvised airstrip in a meadow. Around it were a few shell holes, but Marshal Tedder, who had joined me in the nose of the plane, said he had landed on much worse strips. It was only a couple of miles from the front lines. As we were clambering out of the plane, the co-pilot muttered that he wished those destroyers would quit shooting flak, as it made him nervous. Apparently we had flown in a little close for the Navy's comfort, and someone had put up a couple of 20-mm shells to warn us away.

At the airstrip Air Vice Marshal Sir Arthur Coningham, commander of the British air force supporting Montgomery, was at the field along with a Royal Air Force officer, an aide to General Montgomery.

Monty's headquarters were located near the airstrip. As the aide drove us through the gates of the compound, Dad chuckled at a sign by the road which said, KEEP LEFT! Everywhere else on the

Continent, vehicles drove on the right. The visit was short, as Montgomery was absent; he was off seeing Lieutenant General Omar Bradley at First Army headquarters. A meeting between Dad and Monty was set for 4 P.M. With little delay we departed for the headquarters of Lieutenant General Miles ("Bimbo") Dempsey, commanding the Second British Army.

Dad took Montgomery's absence completely as a matter of course. When he made these visits he in all likelihood stipulated that nobody should alter his schedule. Most commanders antici- pating the arrival of their chief, however, would probably ignore such latitude. It is doubtful that Montgomery was being calcu- latedly impolite, but he lived in a world of his own and liked to go his own way. Therefore, it is safe to surmise that when given such an option he took advantage of it without conscious thought.

The same experience, of the missing commander, was to be re- peated at the other British headquarters during the day; but in those instances the local commanders could hardly be blamed, as Dad adjusted his travels through the sector on the spur of the moment. On the other hand, Monty had to know that the Supreme Commander was coming. Dad's lack of irritation can be explained only by assuming that he was serious in refusing to interfere with his principal subordinate's activities.

As we bounced along the road toward Dempsey's headquarters, I was astonished at the normalcy of the countryside this close to the front. The Norman peasants were working in their fields and had long since ceased looking up when a military vehicle passed. Livestock, particularly cattle, were abundant. Little sign of de- struction was in evidence; I saw no dead animals—not surprising considering that this was D-plus-9—and only one destroyed vehicle. Apparently by the time the British had reached a line this far in- land, the Germans had been retreating so rapidly that no serious fighting had occurred in this area.

At Second Army headquarters we once again found the com- manding general gone. Nevertheless, the staff was present, and Dad conferred with them on the progress in the British sector. One matter that came up seemed minor at the moment. An attack had just been launched but had failed because of lack of coordina- tion between ground forces and air support. Air Marshal Tedder quickly called the airmen into a conference to straighten out the misunderstanding and apparently the problem was solved. In retrospect, however, it is obvious that the problem was indeed not solved, as the terrible experience of the short bombing during the St. Lô breakthrough was later to prove. While at the headquarters, the staff made arrangements for Dad to pick up General Dempsey later.

As we still had about an hour before lunch time, Dad decided to take a look at Bayeux, a famous Norman village and reportedly the home of William the Conqueror. On the way he could visit the 15th Scottish Division. Dad had inspected this unit before and troops moving to the front recognized him. The infantry were marching along in single file on the left side of the road while the vehicles were going along on the right. Our jeep made its way between them. When the soldiers would see Dad, some of them would grin; sentries would salute; some would lean out of trucks and yell, "Ili, Ike!" Dad enjoyed this activity more than any other part of his job. He would wave and yell back to them with a broad smile. Furthermore, it was obvious that his visiting troops about to go into action was a fine thing for their morale. We noticed, however, that the soldiers riding in the trucks showed considerably more enthusiasm than those plodding along the road. After a brief stop at division headquarters, Dad decided to go on.

Only three of us made this trip. Montgomery's aide drove; Dad sat in the right front seat; and I perched in the rear. The conversation as we passed through the pleasant Norman countryside was casual until the aide told of a visit that General Charles de Gaulle had made to Bayeux. De Gaulle, the aide mentioned with a touch of humor, had entered the town the day before and had staged a parade, his first time to set foot on French soil. I could see the Old Man's blood pressure rise. This was the first word he had received that De Gaulle had come ashore. Nobody except the invasion troops, not even self-styled provisional heads of government, were allowed to enter the combat zone without Dad's permission. (Dad had, with the help of King George VI, prevented Churchill's witnessing the D-Day invasion from a British naval vessel—for his own safety.) As if this "oversight" on De Gaulle's part were not enough, the aide went jovially on: De Gaulle had gathered quite a crowd in Bayeux and had made an "I have returned" speech to the French. "The great virtue of the French," De Gaulle reportedly said, "was that they had never submitted to the Germans. Now *with the aid of the Allies* they are reconquering their lost territory." This was too much. Being an outsider, unaware of the struggles Dad had gone through in dealing with this impossible Gaul—reportedly Roosevelt and Churchill had now ceased all communications with him—I could feel a certain humor in the situation; Dad could not. He sat in silence, the back of his neck red, for a couple of miles.

Bayeux was remarkably intact, although an occasional building was damaged or destroyed. The destruction was in no way comparable to what we had witnessed years before in countless French towns as the aftermath of World War I. The people were tanned and healthy, and most of the homes looked prosperous, many displaying flowers in their windows. All of this conflicted with the tales we had heard of how the Germans had abused the Norman population. We pondered the situation and finally surmised that the apparent Nazi leniency stemmed from the fact that Normandy was the breadbasket for Paris. It was in their own interest to let it flourish.

After lunch the early part of the afternoon was spent at Major General Gerard Bucknall's British XXX Corps headquarters, the party having picked up General Dempsey along the way. At about twenty minutes to four we headed back for Montgomery's headquarters. As I sat in the back of the jeep, my uniform had become covered with dust; and when we dismounted the vehicle, Dad turned and told me to shake the dust from my coat. I complied, but when I had it about halfway buttoned up, Monty came bouncing out of his tent. It was an awkward moment, even in a combat zone. However, I was in good company; Montgomery himself was clad in a civilian turtleneck sweater and what I believe were corduroy trousers. His only semblance of uniform was the black tanker's beret he habitually wore. Of course, informality is permissible—sometimes admired—in generals, but seldom in second lieutenants.

It was noticeable, whenever Dad met with Montgomery during this period—and even for years after—how concerned he was to treat Montgomery with every courtesy, even deference. True, Monty's performance often disappointed the Supreme Commander, and the incident five months later, when Dad was on the verge of asking for his relief during the Battle of the Bulge, is well known. However, in all positions except Supreme Commander, Montgomery held a status coequal to that of Dad. He was not only commander of the 21 Army Group; he was also the senior British commander for the invasion. Dad wore the corresponding hat for the Americans. Naturally, as Supreme Commander, Dad was the ultimate boss. But he was obviously determined that any friction that might occur between the two would never be the result of any personal slight on his own part. Their differences would be based solely on military judgment in a common cause. Montgomery, on his part, never showed a noticeable sign of reciprocating.

The trivial incident of the dusty coat, which I find amusing, was somewhat illustrative of the relationship between father and son at this time. We had a deep mutual affection but there existed a certain military wall between us. I was not only his son; I was a young lieutenant who needed on occasion to be straightened out. Without a doubt, with my having been brought up in a more relaxed Army than the one Dad had joined thirty years earlier, I think sometimes he considered me a sign that West Point had gone to hell.

On practically the first evening I had arrived in London, for example, as Dad and I were walking together at SHAEF, I asked him in all earnestness: "If we should meet an officer who ranks above me but below you, how do we handle this? Should I salute first and when they return my salute, do you return theirs?" The question was legitimate to my mind and has never been answered completely to my satisfaction; however, Dad's annoyed reaction was short: "John, there isn't an officer in this theater who doesn't rank above you and below me."

In a way perhaps, had he thought about it, Dad should have been somewhat flattered by my slightly maverick attitude toward spit-and-polish, because my disenchantment with spending hours at shining shoes and polishing brass stemmed partly from an unconscious desire to imitate his own indifference toward such things.

He himself, before he had orderlies to take care of such things for him, had always managed to avoid them whenever possible. He used to shake his head at the loving care with which his friend George Patton would shine brass. When chief of staff of IX Corps at Fort Lewis in early 1941, for example, the then Colonel Dwight Eisenhower, slaving hard at organization and training, habitually wore a wool shirt rather than the more formal blouse and pinks that the commanding general preferred. The general had once mentioned the deplorable condition of Dad's belt buckle. Dad forthwith had given a sergeant a dollar and told him to buy eight brand new belts. It was then the duty of the sergeant, whenever a belt buckle became tarnished, to produce a replacement from his drawer.

I was raised on stories such as this but was expected to perform otherwise.

The correction procedure, furthermore, worked to some extent in both directions. As a cadet, I was disturbed by certain pictures of the Old Man wearing his service cap in North Africa at a rakish angle. I admonished him in a letter that he was disillusioning the Corps of Cadets, and he wrote back promising to do better.[1]

None of this banter, of course, ever reached anything like major proportions; but the two of us never forgot our respective positions despite the relationship. Had I ever, for example even in later years, pre-empted the right rear seat of a car or walked on the Boss's right, I know he would have been annoyed, even though he might have said nothing.

I was excluded when Dad and Monty conferred. The session did not last very long, however, as Dad probably had learned all he needed to know from Dempsey. Soon we were back at the airstrip,

[1] *October 18, 1943:* "I think I really deserved the hiding you gave me on my dress cap. The only point is, it is not a dress cap, it is a utilitarian thing that I use to shield my eyes from the sun and at the same time to allow me to ride comfortably in an automobile or in an airplane. When one wears the stiff wire ring inside the dress cap it has to be taken off if you try to get some rest while in any type of vehicle.

"This is a rotten alibi and if any of my junior officers gave me the same one I would take his head off. However, you are some thousands of miles away and by the time you get this maybe I will put the wire back in the cap and try to conform to regular ideas of neatness in headdress. . . ."

headed for London. Once more I chose the bombardier compartment and again was joined by Air Chief Marshal Tedder, who enthusiastically pointed out various things I would otherwise have missed: some RAF Spitfires flying nearby, naval vessels sweeping channels through the minefields, and in England the Vickers aircraft plant. By the time we reached the London airport, at 6:30 P.M., Dad's staff had become quite concerned. The message telling of our delay had not been delivered.

As we drove back to Telegraph Cottage we were reminded of the lighthearted joshing we had received in Normandy over the fact that London was now under heavier fire than were the headquarters across the Channel. Indeed, if there was any single impression that remained with me from this first glimpse of a combat zone, it was the calm and peaceful atmosphere that prevailed only a few miles behind the lines, where men were dying every minute.

Daily life between Telegraph Cottage, Bushey Park, Widewing, and London was busy and exhilarating. One evening the buzz bombs were hitting close—one in the field across the road. Dad; his British military assistant, Brigadier Sir James Gault; Kay Summersby; and I felt it wise to sleep on the cots in the bomb shelter. As long as such accommodations were not always necessary, I found it somewhat of a lark. On occasion we would play bridge, with Dad futilely trying to bring my game up to standard.

London at this time was to me a romantic and heroic place. In all the city one could feel the excitement of the hour. Before the invasion the atmosphere had doubtless been even more so, but enough drama remained that I felt I was associating with a race of heroes. One evening as I was traveling somewhere in the outskirts of London, I passed a spot where a buzz bomb had struck only a few moments before. With uncommendable curiosity I walked over to survey the damage and was immediately accosted by a tall, taciturn bobby. "Wouldja mind? Rahther busy," he said in a pleasant voice. I failed to understand at first until he repeated his request. He was a member of the team engaged methodically in rescuing the dead and injured—and my presence was not welcome. I suddenly got the message; I excused myself, turned, and went my way.

On June 19 a violent storm struck the English Channel. Allied shipping to Normandy was brought to a standstill for about three days. When Dad heard the news during the late afternoon at Telegraph Cottage, he paused for a few minutes, silent, and asked for a stiff Scotch-and-water. He called Admiral Sir Bertram Ramsay, the Allied naval commander, to ascertain the details. However, there was nothing he personally could do about the situation, and we spent the evening in a rather somber bridge game.

The next day Dad and I hoped to go to Normandy to view the damage on Omaha Beach. Conditions forbade, however, and instead we went to Ramsay's headquarters, where they talked over the situation. It was grim, to be sure, but it carried one fortunate aspect: had the Supreme Commander decided against launching the invasion on June 6, the next date for favorable moon and tides would have been this very June 19, encountering the worst Channel storm in fifty years. More than once during the war, events gave rise to a feeling that the hand of the Almighty was involved in Allied successes.

The day after the visit to Admiral Ramsay's headquarters I accompanied General Hughes on a trip to Portsmouth. Uncle Everett, devoted and emotional as ever, was making this trip to talk to the Southern Base commander and incidentally to show me what was going on. We stopped off at Sandhurst, the British West Point, along the way. When we reached Portsmouth, the scene was dismal. The skies were still gray, although the worst of the storm was beginning to recede. The evidence of its effect was apparent by the stack-up of ships in the harbor, unable as yet to make the crossing. Everett Hughes looked at me, his voice choked and eyes moist. "See that!" he blurted out. "That's what's licking your Dad right now." Fortunately, the storm continued to abate, but the reports from Normandy indicated the complete destruction of the artificial port that had been built at Omaha. Every day Dad hoped to get over there, but one after the other he was frustrated.

During the period of waiting Dad decided to pay a visit to the Prime Minister. We drove to the door of Whitehall, where Churchill was exercising his function as Minister of Defense. The room was simple, with a fairly large-sized table and a huge map on the wall. The three of us sat in straight-backed chairs at one end. England's Prime Minister, slumped limply, was in a bad mood. He stared toward the floor at his side, almost motionless, speaking to Dad but really thinking out loud. "This is the worst weather I have ever seen in my life," he growled, emphasizing every word, as he turned in his chair. Then, raising his voice, "*They* have no *right* to give us weather like this!"

In this respect, it seems that Churchill and General George Patton had an attitude in common. Dedicated to their respective missions, each seemed to feel that the Almighty had an obligation —a personal obligation—to render all necessary assistance to their accomplishments. The Old Man, on the other hand, seemed to view the situation more philosophically. Competitive to the extreme—and imbued with a hatred of Nazism and all it entailed— he appeared to approach his mission of defeating Hitler with the same attitude with which he attacked his opponents in bridge or poker—in both of which he was expert. He appeared to view any situation with the cold, calculating attitude of a professional, confident as he was throughout his life that the Almighty would provide him with a decent set of cards. He never wavered in his faith that he would win, but he appeared not to share the metaphysical feeling that God owed him anything specific, such as good weather on a given day. In short, the Old Man was far more hard-headed than either of his flamboyant friends Churchill or Patton.

Dad's relationship with Churchill was genuinely warm. Personally they were close as two high officials could be under these trying circumstances. Officially Churchill was indirectly one of Dad's two bosses. The Combined Chiefs of Staff (British and American) were Dad's direct official superiors, and Dad on more than one occasion had found it necessary to refuse orders or urgings from either Roosevelt or Churchill at various times pending direct instructions from the CCS.

But sometimes—more often than not—the CCS would refer the matter to the Supreme Commander for decision. Then Churchill, on the scene and vitally interested in the conduct of military operations, would shed the dignity of Head of Government—and perhaps swallow some pride—to come to Dad to exercise his monumental persuasive powers in person. But in so doing, he would base his

arguments on *military* considerations only, even though his real
motivations may have been political. His military arguments, as
in the case of his desire to cancel the invasion of Southern France
(ANVIL-DRAGOON), were often inadequate to change the Old
Man's mind. Discussions were sometimes lengthy and impassioned,
but never did they dent the mutual personal affection between the
two men. Their friendship was all the more remarkable because
the ultimate war objectives of the British and Americans were
in many ways divergent.

But on this stormy day of June 1944, there were no great issues
to discuss between them. Dad had little on his mind other than to
keep contact with his friend, to share his distress, and incidentally
to give me the opportunity to meet this remarkable world figure.
In the space of a few minutes we took our leave and sloshed out
through the rain to the waiting car.

Dad, Tex Lee, and I spent the evening of June 23 in Dad's
"forward" headquarters at the British Naval School near Portsmouth. His trailer was parked on the grounds a few hundred yards
from the school building itself. This was the spot from which the
June 6 invasion had been ordered nearly three weeks earlier. No
security was in evidence, but we gave the matter no thought; Dad
traveled everywhere in the United Kingdom—and later on the Continent—without escort. We had a quiet dinner, and Dad, slouching
on the overstuffed bench that faced his situation map, was thinking
aloud. Pointing casually to the wall, he mused, "As soon as Monty
can take Caen on the left [east] and Brad can take Cherbourg,
then I'll really feel we're here to stay." Despite the setback of the
weather, things were going remarkably well in Joe Collins' drive to
Cherbourg; but around Caen, where Rommel had stacked both
the I and II Panzer Corps, the British and Canadians were finding
the going bloody and tough. We turned in early; the next day
would be long.

Before dawn, June 24, we finally began the trip to Omaha Beach.
The storm had subsided enough to allow disembarkation from destroyer to small boat on the far side of the Channel. By 7:15 the
party was at the Portsmouth dock.

Major General Hughes, Superintendent of West Point Francis

Wilby, Robert Crawford of SHAEF, and others were on hand. We boarded the barge immediately and started out for the destroyer. As the junior member of the party, I was to get off the barge last. Upon reaching the deck of the destroyer, the procedure was to face the ensign (flag at the stern) and salute, then salute the officer of the deck. Unlike the officers of exalted rank, I was carrying my overcoat and helmet, however, and halfway up the ladder the helmet strap became unfastened; the steel pot clanged into the barge below. I scrambled down, retrieved it, and started back up. Tex, in a panic, pulled me aboard, meantime grabbing the helmet and overcoat. I saluted the ensign properly; but by the time I turned to the officer of the deck, he was gone. Sometimes I felt I was a source of comic relief.

After we left the harbor of Portsmouth the destroyer passed a long line of LSTs (landing ship, tank) returning from France. It was a welcome sight, our first visible evidence that traffic was moving. I went to Dad's cabin and slept for a while, waking up at about 10:30. In order to land near Omaha Beach, we first had to switch to a PT (patrol torpedo) boat. The water was very rough and transfer was difficult. However, leaving the damned helmet on board and wearing the coat, I made it this time without difficulty. Close in to shore the party switched to a Duck (DUKW, an amphibious truck) and drove up on the sand.

The beach was a mess. Some ships had been previously sunk on purpose as breakwaters; but the storm the last few days had sunk many more, a large number of which lay on their sides, washed up against the dunes.

From my point of observation, I could see no evidence of the destroyed docks and piers; they had disappeared. All that met the eye was a bay jammed with transports, LSTs, and smaller craft anchored around in seeming confusion. General Bradley, commanding the First U. S. Army, was on hand to meet the party as we climbed ashore. Brigadier General William M. Hoge, commander of the beach party, was also there. After a short while we mounted jeeps with Dad, General Bradley, and me riding together. Bradley sounded quietly optimistic; I could see why Dad considered him a tower of strength. He was at the time short on artillery ammunition and every time a C-47 (DC-3) cargo plane flew overhead, he would happily remark, "There come two more tons of ammunition." He estimated that he would have Cherbourg in two days and said we would have had it sooner except for the discovery of a new type of pressure mine in the sea which prevented the Navy from getting in close enough to fire on the city.

The buildings in this region were almost all damaged, presenting a much worse picture than the one on the British beaches a few days before. One reason may have been that we were closer to the beaches on this trip; furthermore, Omaha was the beach where Dad's old friend Major General (Gee) Gerow's V Corps had run into the only really tough resistance, from a German division which happened to be in the area on D-Day.

As we rode along, I looked for one undamaged house. Not until we reached General Bradley's headquarters, some ten or fifteen minutes later, did I see one. We turned into a small courtyard, surrounded by typical French stone houses of this region, a quaint picture. In the back of this courtyard a road led up a hill and at the top, in an apple orchard, was Bradley's headquarters. He slept and worked in a trailer, with auxiliary tents lined around a field, camouflaged under the trees, all well within sight of the beach. At one end of the field lay the remnants of a German artillery battery, evidently silenced by naval gunfire.

We went in to lunch a few minutes after arriving, where Lieutenant General H. D. G. Crerar, commanding the First Canadian Army, was waiting. Gee Gerow arrived almost as soon as we had sat down. Though I could not be demonstrative, I was overjoyed to see him; it had been years. Shortly Tex Lee and I left the table to sit in the grass and talk with the aides. A chicken was running around loose, but the aides clamped it under a box when they saw the generals come out of the mess tent. I neglected to ask where they had acquired the doomed bird.

After lunch Gerow, Dad, and I sat outside Bradley's trailer for a while. Gee proudly produced some Camembert cheese as a present. He looked fine and was apparently in high spirits. He promised to get Kay Summersby the silk stockings she had asked me to get her as soon as V Corps took St. Lô.

Again, as at Monty's headquarters, the atmosphere was calm and peaceful, although far more informal and congenial. For here were officers who had been lifelong friends, who had complete confidence in each other; no need existed for caution or pretense in their exchanges. As we lounged in canvas camp chairs enjoying the sunlight in the pleasant apple orchard, it was difficult to sense that a struggle was going on a few miles away. There was, indeed, no cause for frenzy or excitement. Things were going well, but real action would have to wait until the *bocage* (hedgerow) country had been cleared. And that process would still require weeks, with American infantry advancing yard by yard—but advancing nevertheless. Operation COBRA (St. Lô breakout) had not yet been thought of except, perhaps, in the most general of terms.

Critics of the military system might be offended to witness the high command casually talking of trivial things. And yet, what else was to be expected? Both Bradley and Gerow had personally been under intense enemy fire on Omaha Beach less than three weeks earlier. Risks, gambles, and physical danger at times lay ahead for all of them, including Dad. But this interlude was one in which all could enjoy, for a moment, a certain relative peace of mind.

After this brief rest we departed so that Dad could inspect the newly arrived U. S. 83d Infantry Division. On the way we passed through the town of Isigny. It was damaged worse than any I had seen. The houses along the main street were all destroyed, and a whole block had been demolished by either artillery fire or aerial bombardment. In some places French sailors, apparently fishermen, were standing around. These Normans were well built, tanned and robust. I wondered how they ever managed to stay on the loose in Occupied France. One thing seemed remarkable, however. In these towns, so badly battered, the people exhibited a far friendlier attitude to the Allies than in those relatively untouched. One Frenchman, recognizing Dad, became excited and ran into his store to get his partner. They both came out to the street and stared. Children waved, as always, and many grown-ups gave the "V" sign. An occasional American flag flew from a window.

General Bradley offered an explanation for the difference between the civilian attitude in this sector as compared to that over on the British side: the people, during the nine-day period since our last visit, had now become convinced that the Allies were there to stay. He added, however, that down in Carentan, when the Germans began a counterattack, the civilians had immediately hauled in all tricolors and American flags and had cooled off their manifestations of friendliness.

We turned off and went along the road due south. General Bradley pointed out the spot he had selected for his future command post. It was in another apple orchard, similar to his present one. He hoped, however, not to be around when the apples became ripe. This future command post was still only seven thousand yards behind the front lines.

The roads we traversed were dusty and crowded. Vehicles moved slowly, bumper to bumper. Fresh out of West Point, with all its courses in conventional procedures, I was offended at this jamming up of traffic. It wasn't according to the book. Leaning over Dad's shoulder, I remarked, "You'd never get away with this if you didn't have air supremacy." I received an impatient snort:

"If I didn't have air supremacy, I wouldn't be here."

We reached the 83d Division in bivouac. The soldiers as always, appeared glad to see Dad. Americans are generally much noisier in their greetings than the British, and some burst into cheers. Others would jump up grinning; still others would burst out in astonished, good-humored curse words.

When the party stopped at one of the regiments, the men were none too energetically digging in. Dad dismounted, talked to a few, and we went on. At one point the party followed along a hedge line, where men were preparing to spend the night. Dad went up to each soldier individually, asking various questions. Sometimes he would ask what a man would do should an enemy scout car appear over the hill. He often asked a man his rifle qualification. Of squad leaders, he often asked how many experts they had in their squads. He fired his questions rapidly and in almost every case would end up with some crack or joke. Such was his way of testing reactions to see how alert and confident the troops and their leaders were.

The 83d Division later went on to write a brilliant record. But on this day the men appeared uncertain of themselves. I had not seen other divisions and therefore had nothing to compare this one to, but the discipline seemed lax. However, the outfit had been aboard a transport waiting to be shipped ashore for some time, and many were still feeling the effects of violent seasickness. They had not yet met the enemy. Dad and I agreed that our impressions might have been unfair—which turned out to be the case.

At 3:30 General Bradley remarked that we had only a half hour to make the boat. We boarded the Duck, switched to the PT boat, and were soon on the destroyer. On the way back we passed another long line of LSTs, this time bound for France.

Parting for the United States at the end of my three weeks' stay amid the drama of the post-D-Day period was particularly poignant. I was leaving just at the time when further great events were about to occur; the break-out was certain to be near. Dad, never one to throw around posies, grumbled one day, "Hell, if you weren't a regular officer with a career ahead of you, I'd just keep you here." Such wishful thinking ran counter to the facts. I was indeed a career officer, and my job was to go through Infantry School at Fort Benning and then join a division to fight. And I could never have borne the idea of spending the war as an aide— even to the Supreme Allied Commander. Dad knew this as well as I.

But I couldn't help feeling a little choked when, on July 1, 1944, Dad saw a group of us off in his B-17 for the thirty-six-hour island-hopping flight home.

4

From the Hudson to the Elbe

The basic course at the Infantry School, Fort Benning, Georgia, was in many ways a vacation. Our West Point class was kept together as a unit and found it a welcome respite from monasticism on the Hudson. The hours were long by normal, peacetime standards, starting at 8:00 in the morning through to 6:00 in the evening, six full days a week. But the sun set late, allowing time in the evenings for tennis, flying, or wandering over to the officers' club for a beer. Newly emancipated, our class probably set some sort of record in the last category.

At Benning we were learning the non-academic nuts and bolts of the infantry trade at platoon and company level. We qualified in the important infantry weapons and benefited from the experiences of officers who had been overseas and had brought back the latest of techniques in tactics, mine warfare, and enemy habits. Military training at West Point had included a good deal of theory and had covered the general functions of all branches; here we were learning a single technique—how to be infantry unit commanders in a specific war.

The days were full, sometimes fatiguing, but our free time was our own. The period was made all the more enjoyable by the appearance of Bo Horkan on the scene at about the same time our class reported. Bo, in the wartime Army as a fellow infantry lieutenant, was an instructor in rifle marksmanship; he was readily adopted as an unofficial member of our class. On weekends, with a couple of fellow students, we would head for Atlanta, Bo's original home, where attractive young ladies, bereft of dates under these wartime circumstances, waited patiently.

During August 1944 Bo and I followed the news from Europe avidly, gloating over the lightning thrusts of the Allied spearheads as they raced across the map of France. This was certainly no repetition of the trench warfare we had learned about as youngsters some sixteen years earlier!

The class as a whole viewed these developments with somewhat mixed emotions; the more gladiatorial types feared that the war might be over before any of us could get overseas and see action. This concern, hardly humanitarian, represented a peculiarity of the professional military man's attitude. Trained all his life to contribute to the nation's effort in time of war, he seldom has the opportunity to put his long preparation into practice. His reputation in the peacetime Army for long periods may well be based on his performance in the previous war. Therefore, so long as a war actually exists, the regular soldier is anxious to participate, giving little thought to his own personal risks.

The course ended about October 1. After a brief graduation ceremony, the infantry members of the West Point class of 1944 scattered, never to be completely reunited. We were allowed ten days' leave and then, on October 10, I reported back to Sand Hill at Fort Benning to serve in the U. S. 71st Infantry Division.

The orders, I think, were probably cut to read the "14th Infantry Regiment," as I have no recollection of reporting in at division headquarters. But in a matter of minutes, it seemed, I found myself in the orderly room of Company B, 1st Battalion, only a few buildings down from both regimental and battalion headquarters. I was to command the 2d Platoon.

Shortly after reporting to B Company I received an unofficial bit of indoctrination on the psychology of the American soldier in contrast to the cadet. It happened that two men were absent without leave. Close buddies, they were both machine gunners, and while unreliable in their attendance records, they were experts; capable of playing their light machine guns like musical instruments. When the first one, a large, sandy-haired farmer named Cody was brought into the orderly room under guard, I eavesdropped to hear what the company commander would have to say behind the open partition. Being AWOL at West Point would, of course, have been a cause for dismissal; and although nothing of the sort, of course, was possible in this case, I nevertheless expected to hear a dressing down that would make one's eardrums sore. Instead of that, nothing but plaintive tones came from Captain Lloyd Engelland's office. "Cody," he murmured, "you can't do this to me; we've had great training here for the last couple of weeks and we just couldn't spare you and Broom."

Cody's answer also was unexpected: "Gosh, Captain, I didn't mean to mess up your training. I just thought I'd go away for a little while." When Cody came out after only a few moments, he was visibly shaken. Turning to one of his buddies, he said, perplexed, "Gosh, I don't know what's the matter with him. Why's he so mad? All I *did* was go over the hill."

Occasionally ridiculous mix-ups would occur in the training schedule. Someone at Army headquarters apparently discovered one day that our instruction in "trench foot" was being neglected; we were six hours behind. Trench foot, a scourge with symptoms resembling frozen feet, resulted from allowing the feet to stay wet for too long a time, eventually destroying circulation. The preventive was really simple. Each man was to carry a pair of dry socks inside his shirt and whenever possible—once a day if feasible—he was to take off his shoes, dry his feet, rub them for five minutes, and put on the dry socks. Such was the procedure. But when I was informed one morning that I was to conduct a training session of four hours on the subject of "trench foot"—outdoors at that—it can be readily understood why I took matters in my own hands and took the company through training in "fire and maneuver" instead.

One of the heady aspects of a command, even of only forty-four men, is the status of being the "Old Man." I had just passed my twenty-second birthday. Nevertheless, I was known by that familiar title among soldiers thirty-five and over. A few nights before the division shipped overseas, Sergeant Sutton, of the second squad, decided to get married. The young lady had come from out of town with no family. Therefore it was only logical that I, as the Old Man, should be the one to give the bride away. Sergeant Sutton may have been approaching forty at the time.

Around the first of December, 1944, the 71st Division received a new commander. Brigadier General Willard G. Wyman, an old friend from Fort Lewis days, whose daughter I used to date occasionally, had been sent back from Europe because of his wife's illness. He had distinguished himself by his gallantry with the 1st Infantry Division on the beaches of Normandy.

Without delay, General Wyman began to retrain the division. We executed company, battalion, and regimental maneuvers, grueling but beneficial. One evening as B Company staggered into the defensive position assigned us for the night, 2d Platoon was placed on the left flank of the regiment. Our sector ran along a broken ridge line facing into a woods. Joyously we found a number of previously dug foxholes that covered our front. I assigned portions of the line to the three squads and the men flopped in their abodes, anticipating a rest. Just before dusk General Wyman and his entourage appeared on the scene. He took a look at my position and sent for me. Without blinking an eye and without a sign of personal recognition, he ordered a complete restructuring of our platoon defense plan. Squads should be kept intact as units and placed in ravines along the military crest of the hill, leaving space between them, covering the voids with interlocking fire. Every man had to dig a completely new foxhole.

A few days later, "critiquing" the exercise, General Wyman, personally, from the stage of the auditorium, produced a water-color picture of this position. He pointed out the error that the un-named platoon leader had made and showed the correction he had directed. I became a subject of much good-natured ribbing within the company but was pleased when General Wyman, the instruction completed, presented me with the painting, done by an unknown artist.

To me this incident has always represented leadership at its best. General Wyman had gotten his point across; had corrected a grievous error; and had done so leaving the junior officer almost elated rather than humiliated.[1]

At Christmas Mother came down to Fort Benning. Activity in the division was slow, and General Wyman, away seeing his wife, Ethel, turned over his own quarters, the so-called "Patton House," to Mother. In off-time she played host to me and a number of my

[1] General Wyman was one of our finest military leaders and rose to head the Continental Army Command before his retirement around 1958. He died in Walter Reed Army Hospital (the day after my father), nearly twenty-five years later. His last act, practically, was to ask me to inscribe his copy of my book, *The Bitter Woods.*

friends. We had a festive time, despite the gloom that had fallen over the entire country as the result of the current German counter-offensive in the Ardennes.

By some circumstance General Wyman came back to the division for New Year's, and Mother moved to the officers' club. He came over and had dinner with us. To my disappointment, he knew little more about the situation in Europe than did I. The evening, however, dispelled the gloom. It went on well past midnight, and when I marched B Company out to the range for firing the next morning, I was slightly bedraggled. The reports of rifles seemed unusually sharp in the early hours of New Year's Day, 1945.

The 71st Division shipped out of Fort Benning a few days later. I had been notified at this point that on reaching Europe I would be yanked out. A couple of weeks before, the high command had seen a general officer disintegrate after the capture of his own son, who had been in his division. Regardless of how it would affect my personal career, both Patton (Third Army) and Bradley (12 Army Group) were determined that the future of one second lieutenant was not worth the burden that Dad would bear by having me as a rifle platoon leader. Both offered to take me as their aides. I was given no choice in the matter and I was embarrassed. If given the choice, I certainly would have stayed, at least in the division.

The trip across the water this time was more tedious than with the 7th Armored Division the previous summer. Since the 14th Infantry Regiment was traveling on a Liberty Ship, the accommodations were far more crowded than on the *Queen Mary*. Furthermore, the U-boat threat was still severe and we were forced to go in a zigzag convoy, thus extending the trip to a total of eleven days. A small incident drove home the seriousness of the business we were engaged in. One night the word rang out that a man had fallen overboard. No effort was made to rescue him in the blackness. The commander of troops simply sent for the doctor and the chaplain. The two officers proceeded to the rear of the fantail, where the doctor studied his watch. After a certain number of minutes, he pronounced the man dead of cold—it took a short time to die in the frigid North Atlantic. The chaplain then said the appropriate prayers, the convoy never budging an inch from its predetermined course.

On arrival in Le Havre in the early dawn of February 6, 1945, I was sent for by the regimental commander. Aware of what was up, of course, I said good-by with deep regrets to my comrades of several months.

Carrying my gear, I was ushered up the gangplank on the top deck where, after minimal amenities, I boarded a small vessel, perhaps a tugboat, on which about a dozen other officers were going ashore early. One of them was General Wyman. Once under way, he beckoned to me to come over. He started the conversation casually. "John," he said, "do you think your men are ready for long marches?" (General Wyman knew that the war would soon enter the pursuit phase.)

I shrugged. "We can do anything we have to, sir."

"Can they march twenty-five miles a day?"

"General, we've done it plenty of times before."

"Yes, but can they do it day after day after day?"

I thought for a moment and answered, "I'm sure they can if they have to."

General Wyman then dropped his casual tone. He turned on me and said, "John, I know you're leaving. I've been proud to have you as a platoon leader in this division and would love to keep you. However, there are some things more important to this war than your career, and I just want you to know that there is not a man in this division who resents your going."

I thanked the general politely and then, excusing myself, walked over to the other rail to stand alone for a while.

After leaving the 71st Division the morning of February 6, I was hustled down to Versailles to spend four or five days visiting with Dad. He was now living in a comfortable house near the Trianon Palace Hotel, where he had been moved as a result of the assassination scare during the Battle of the Bulge.

It so happened that on my visit with Dad the military situation, as during the Normandy visit before, was relatively slow moving. The German salient in the Ardennes had been reduced, and the Allies were slugging away through miserable weather along the

German frontiers to achieve positions from which they could break out across the Cologne Plain. Dad was suffering at the time from either his old bursitis or from a bad knee, and a physiotherapist was treating him. One evening, just after he had had an extensive rubdown, he telephoned Montgomery from his bed. The Ninth U. S. Army (Lieutenant General William H. Simpson), the Second British Army (Dempsey) and the First Canadian Army (Crerar) had been scheduled to attack toward the Roer River. Flooding of the river and heavy rains had held up Simpson's attack. The purpose of this phone call was to make sure that General Dempsey, whose attack had gone off on schedule, really understood that the Americans had been held up by truly overriding circumstances. The maintenance of good feeling between the forces of the two nationalities was a continuing consideration that Dad had to work on constantly. It was never automatic.

Despite his temporary infirmity, Dad's spirits were high. His confidence shone in sharp contrast to his somewhat frustrated state in Normandy when he had been in something of a quandary as to what exactly he was going to do. (It was simply a matter of days before the Ninth U. S. Army would cross the Roer River in the vicinity of Düren and Jülich.) Probably at no time in his life did I ever see the Old Man enjoying such peace of mind as during the European campaign, once the forces were established ashore. He was, during this eleven months, exercising the professional skills and knowledge that he had been developing for thirty years. And he was doing so at the highest levels. Moreover he was exercising his remarkable forte for maintaining morale, sustained by top-flight people. Montgomery was sometimes difficult, but his subordinate Army commanders were not. And the zest with which the officers of the American high command attacked their problems buoyed Dad up. "Enthusiasm" was the word I heard most in describing his army commanders.

During my short stay Dad made an inspection trip to the 71st Division. I went along and turned in my unit equipment to the supply sergeant of B Company. (Army records must be kept straight even during wartime.) I also had a reunion with my former fellow platoon leaders: Jones, Grimshaw, and Harrington. Soon Dad and I departed for Namur, Belgium, where General

Bradley had located his 12 Army Group headquarters. Dad spent only one night, dropping me off in the hands of Bradley.

The morning after Dad left, Bradley called me in for a talk. "Well, John," he said, leaning back in his straight chair, staring absently at a situation map, "there are two things you can do. I could send you to a division and tell them to put you in the operations section of a regiment. That would be an acceptable risk because we're not going to have any more regimental headquarters overrun—at least not in this war. There is one outfit, though, that I have a certain interest in. I'm trying to build some units in the American Army to correspond to the 'Phantom Service' we've had to borrow from the British. They've done great work for me and I don't know what I'd do without them. The two American units aren't ready yet, but so far as I know there are no regular officers in either one and I'd sort of like to have someone in the postwar Army that knows something about them. Nevertheless, either way is all right by me."

I pondered the question for a few moments and answered, "General, as long as I've been pulled out of the 71st Division, I'd feel better if I left for a special purpose. You have an interest in this new type of unit and I think I'd just as soon go there." Bradley seemed pleased; he, like Dad, was much more relaxed than the last time I had seen him on the beaches of Normandy.

Thus it was settled. I was to leave shortly and report to one of the SIAM units (signal information and monitoring), still located at Bournemouth, England. General Bradley ended the conversation. With a slight smile, he said, "Now I guess I had better go back and find out how we are doing with those damn dams."[2]

The atmosphere around 12 Army Group headquarters was calm and businesslike, a reflection of the personality of the commander. In my few days' wait I was able to observe General Bradley at close hand. He had been a great athlete in his day, having once held the record for the longest baseball throw in West Point history. His quiet, high-pitched voice seemed remarkably inconsistent

---

[2] The Schmidt dams which, still in the hands of the Germans, controlled the level of the Roer River.

with his obviously still-powerful physique. Personally he was reticent and this characteristic, combined with his rather homely features, had caused him to be described as a "Missouri schoolmaster." His unruffled exterior, however, combined with his no-nonsense attitude, made him a man that one could admire deeply and feel considerable affection for—but at the same time be not overly comfortable in his presence. He was thoroughly conventional personally and he detested publicity. "Any day I can stay out of the newspapers is a day to the good," he once said to his staff as we were gathering for the noon meal. Quiet or not, he was no man to fool with. Completely honest and straightforward, he suffered from a degree of naïveté that made him, under the surface, a sensitive man who tended to view people in black and white. Hence he tended to have his favorites. In common with many other commanders, Bradley regarded his own headquarters as the highest echelon of the "fighting" zone. Accordingly, all of his staff were required to wear helmet liners and boots, even though the actual fighting was going on many miles away.

Professionally, General Bradley was one to inspire complete confidence. His grasp of the tactical situation—it was really strategic on such a wide front—was impressive. He approached his job with the air of a bridge player who could see that he had adequate cards in his hand to make his bid, even though it might take a little time.

I have often marveled at men like Bradley, whose lifetime careers had included many routine assignments. In the early thirties, for example, he had been on General Marshall's faculty at the Infantry School, in charge of the Weapons Department, an assignment hardly related to that of directing a front of hundreds of miles and over thirty divisions.[3] Furthermore, he, like many other members of the American command, had never heard a shot fired in anger before World War II.

Of course, in observing Bradley, or any officer like him, one must realize that this man was exceptional, having been selected for his position over thousands of other officers with much the same background. Further, the ability to step overnight from lieutenant colo-

[3] In the last campaign 12 Army Group extended about 500 miles and included thirty-five infantry and armored divisions.

nel into positions of high command with apparent ease was a tribute to the Army school system. At Fort Leavenworth the Command and General Staff School concentrates a full year on large unit tactics up to field army level. For officers of Bradley's caliber, the War College later provided a year studying global strategy, to include such broad subjects as fundamental sources of national power. Men like him were products of inherent ability and thorough study under many unsung Leavenworth and War College instructors.

At Bournemouth I reported to the company commander, 3323d SIAM Company, and began to learn my new duties.

The British Phantom Service, which General Bradley was trying to model the SIAM companies after, had grown out of necessity in North Africa and across France. Its mission, in military terms, was "vertical liaison," designed to keep the higher commanders informed of important events on the front lines. A Phantom patrol would consist of three or four vehicles and possibly six to eight men, each headed by an officer. Its major piece of equipment was a high-powered radio that could reach from the scene of action to Army headquarters. Each patrol carried cryptographic equipment with an unbreakable code—unbreakable so long as none of its "one-time pads" fell into the hands of the enemy. Thus the patrol was able to eliminate the usual delays encountered by the normal chain of command.

The 3323d SIAM Company was actually just being organized for its new mission. It and its sister, the 3325th SIAM, being transformed into Phantom-type organizations, were like old dogs learning new tricks. The two units, comprising perhaps 250 men each, were basically Signal Corps organizations, and their original officers had little or no experience with the combat arms and the ways in which standard units operated. Therefore, as a supplement, "line" officers had been detailed to obtain the combat information from the front-line staffs and compose the messages destined for G-3 (operations) at Army HQ. Each line officer was attached to a SIAM patrol, which remained under the administrative command of a Signal Corps officer.

On April 1, 1945, the day that First and Ninth U. S. Armies met at Lippstadt, completing the encirclement of the Ruhr, the company departed for the Continent. While the various patrols were processing to join their future headquarters, I took a couple of days leave, went ahead, stopped off for a day to see Dad, and then proceeded toward the front with Tex Lee, crossing the Rhine at Saarbrucken, planning to spend the night at General Patton's Third Army HQ, now in Frankfurt.

Patton was in a convivial mood, exhilarated by the fact that he was engaged in his favorite type of warfare—pursuit. He had just received a personal blow—his unsuccessful attempt to relieve the Allied prisoner of war camp at Hammelburg—but this seemed to dampen his spirits very little. During the night I came down with a violent intestinal upset, due, I believe, to some oysters I had eaten at Dad's. With medication, however, I soon was feeling better, though I stayed an extra night.

Actually, the delay turned out to be a worthwhile experience, as it afforded me my first opportunity to meet the noted Bernard Baruch, the American financier and friend of Churchill's, who was visiting at the time. The conversation was light. Baruch, a genial man, went out of his way to compliment Patton on his exploits and tell him what a great general he was. Patton, while brushing off the kind words, was flushed with pleasure and as time went on became more and more expansive. "I've been told to hold up and let the rest of them catch up with me," he beamed. "But I'm advancing fifteen miles a day anyhow, though I'm not telling them. Don't want to give the Nazi bastards time to sow minefields." Then pointing at me with mock severity, "Don't tell your Daddy!" I was warned thus more than once, though "telling Daddy" would never have occurred to me; I had my own business to do, and maybe Patton's claims weren't true. Patton would not have cared, however, had I collared the nearest newspaper reporter. His exuberance added to the pleasure of the occasion.

The next day, completely recovered, I picked up my jeep and headed for Marburg, headquarters of First Army, to which the 3323d was to be assigned. I continued on the same day to report to V Corps Command Post at Weissenfels, now commanded by Major General Clarence Huebner, to make arrangements for the arrival of the rest of the patrol. While waiting for the patrol to arrive, I did some side traveling to get acquainted with the attached divisions. During one day I visited the 2d Division, the famous outfit that had held the critical northern shoulder against overwhelming odds during the Battle of the Bulge. On the road going up I found myself in a convoy of troops who apparently had been on leave, as they were wearing their Class "A" uniforms—"ETO" or "Eisenhower" jackets. No weapons were noticeable on them, and wine bottles were being tossed about in profusion. At one point in the road, as my driver and I were going around a bend, I looked to the left and there lying on a bank, the bottom part of his face missing, a dead German stared straight at me. It came as something of an unexpected jolt, but I went on and finished the cheese from my K-ration anyway. A couple of hundred yards farther down the road, about fifty German corpses were strewn around. American veterans, inured to the sights of the battlefield, were not only sitting *among* the corpses eating their rations but some were actually sitting *on* them. It was a dusty day, and I found difficulty in telling the live Americans, sprawled out sleeping, from the dead Germans. Apparently a sharp fire fight had occurred shortly before, for at this point someone came driving up and called for a couple of tank destroyers to clear out a spot of resistance in the woods to the south. To me this atmosphere was a new experience; to the soldiers of the 2d Division it was routine. I arrived back at Corps HQ late that evening, grabbed something to eat, groped my way into a dark farmhouse, and rolled down my bedding.

The next morning was April 13, 1945. At breakfast in the mess the news was that President Roosevelt had died at Warm Springs, Georgia. I, like many others, experienced a sinking feeling; for although I had not been brought up to admire President Roosevelt's domestic policies, I felt the loss of a man who on any count had to be considered a great war leader. Furthermore, Vice President Harry S. Truman was a total unknown except for his role as "watchdog" of the Armed Services during his years in the Senate. Almost simultaneous with receiving this news, I was given a message to report to the airstrip to fly back to First Army headquarters at Marburg. My father, I was told, was there and wanted to see me. This turn of events was frustrating, as I had just completed preparations for the arrival of the SIAM patrol and wanted to be on hand to meet them. However, the orders were clear; and for all I knew, Dad wanted me for something important.

As I settled down in the L-5 liaison aircraft and fastened my parachute and seatbelt, thoughts whirled through my mind. President Truman, it seemed to me, might be making command changes. I remembered Dad's disappointment at being pulled out of the Mediterranean Theater a year and a half earlier, even though the command of OVERLORD was certainly a step to prominence. I wondered if Truman was calling Dad back to be Chief of Staff of the Army, only to let someone else finish the job of conquering Germany.

On arrival at Marburg I found neither Dad nor Lieutenant General Courtney H. Hodges, Army commander, on hand; they were out inspecting. I was told to wait around until they returned. When they strode in, Dad looked at me in astonishment, "Well, what the hell are *you* doing here?"

"I was told to come here," I retorted. "Someone gave me orders and sent me back by L-5."

Dad looked chagrined. "Good God," he moaned. "All I said was that my son must be somewhere in the vicinity. I had no intention of pulling you back from your job." This exchange at least settled one thing: no dramatic event had occasioned my being sent for. Some overly zealous staff officer had merely interpreted Dad's casual remark to mean that he wanted to see me. Such mishaps, I later learned, are fairly frequent occurrences anywhere near the seats of power.

That evening Dad, General Bradley, General Hodges, a group of aides, and I sat around talking. Dad had just sent his message of condolence to President Roosevelt's widow. But the thing most on his mind was the horror camp near Gotha that he had gone through only the day before. The scene of atrocities had left him visibly shaken and he had not yet adjusted the entire episode in his mind. With him on the visit was the reputedly rough-and-tough George Patton, who had become physically ill. Dad had cabled home to ask for a contingent of reporters and legislators to come immediately to witness. "Well, the only speck of optimism I can see," Dad said that evening, "is that I really don't think the bulk of the Germans knew what was going on. When I saw that camp yesterday, I ordered the mayor of Gotha to turn out the towns-people and make them clean up the mess. Last night he and his wife went home and hanged themselves. Maybe there's some hope after all." From there on the conversation turned to other things, including redeployment of troops to the Pacific and the status of the postwar world. At the crack of dawn the next morning I was again in the L-5 headed back for V Corps at Weissenfels.

Within a couple of days after the arrival of the patrol, the command post moved again, this time to its final location on the Leipzig front at a place called Naumburg.

By now my duties allowed a little further travel. A friend and I took off with a jeep and driver during the morning of April 25. We drove north from Naumburg around the east of Leipzig, to a small town on the Mulde River, Bad Düben. The road signs, indicating only one hundred kilometers to Berlin were tantalizing. On the way we passed through the sector of the 104th (Timber-wolf) Division and saw Major General Terry Allen standing beside the road with a big grin on his face. As I had never met the general, we simply kept going. However, it was something of a pleasure to see this famous desperado who, after leaving the 1st Division under a cloud, had trained the Timberwolves into such dashing fighting unit.[4]

When we reached the Mulde River, we were at the front, the limit of Allied advance. By prior arrangement with the Russians, the Allies had halted along the line of the Elbe and Mulde in order to establish a clearly defined demarcation line. The Russians had not yet reached the other side of the river, and thousands of German soldiers were making their way across the remnants of a destroyed bridge, smiling and joking at their good fortune of being able to surrender to the Americans. An occasional German was wounded, but by and large they were quite presentable, having

---

[4] With regret Dad had relieved Terry Allen and Assistant Division Commander Theodore Roosevelt, Jr., from the 1st Infantry Division in Sicily. They were not combat failures, but it had become obvious that the discipline in the division was slipping badly. Both had gone on to justify their retention as combat leaders: Teddy Roosevelt won the Congressional Medal of Honor in Normandy and Allen, given a second chance, trained and commanded the 104th, one of the outstanding divisions to arrive late in the war.

retained their headgear, mess equipment, and overcoats. It was strange, as we approached the river, to see the enemy marching down the road in groups of a hundred, unguarded.

On the opposite bank of the river, an MP was standing. We decided to cross. Here this lone American soldier would count the Germans as they came up. When a hundred had arrived, he would send them across the bridge, delaying the rest for the next batch.

As there was no sign of action, we continued down the road into no man's land. A handful of Americans, with newly confiscated German horses, were having a riotous time galloping up and down. Souvenirs were plentiful—P-38 and Luger pistols, as well as sabers, were strewn all over the roads. We picked up a few. After we had gone about a half mile, however, I began to get nervous and decided that since woods were closing in on both sides of the road, it was best to stop. After all, nobody had guaranteed that every member of the German Army was as intent on surrendering as the ones crossing the bridge.

As we were about to turn back, a burly German marched up, clicked his heels, gave a Hitler salute, and said in English, "I surrender." I was a little shaken, as this meant we were the first Americans he had encountered. However, I was also angered by the Hitler salute. I touched the visor of my helmet and snarled in three confused languages, *"Sie saluten comme ça,* you get it?" I then turned on my heel and strode back to the bridge listening to the footsteps of the man following a few feet behind. The war was certainly over, at least along this front of the Mulde River.

Another trip, sickening but illuminating, took me to the notorious concentration camp of Buchenwald near Weimar. I took only a driver that day and the two of us, wending our way through the winding streets of that former capital of post-World War I Germany, became confused. It was startling how obsequious civilians were when asked directions to Buchenwald. I still have no idea how much those civilians knew about this camp.

Buchenwald had been liberated only two or three days by the time I arrived, and many of the former prisoners remained. American troops were providing them clothing, medical care, and food, but a good many of them, though alive, would still die of malnutrition within a couple of days. I had hardly set foot in the camp before I was approached by a bald-headed little man who offered to serve as my guide. Fortunately, he was a Belgian, a political prisoner, and my French was adequate to communicate. He was still wearing the baggy striped prison clothes supplied by the Nazis and had a certain wild look in his eye, as if fearing that I might miss some aspect of the atrocities that had occurred. He took me through the barracks where the prisoners had slept on stacked wooden bunks. He then took me to the crematorium, where light from the window revealed a half-burned body, not yet removed from the oven. In the room adjacent he showed me hooks on the walls, where prisoners had been hanged at a height just sufficient for tips of their toes to brush the floor. This devilish device would, of course, prolong the agony of death and was probably reserved for special cases, as it would be inefficient for mass extermination.

Outside the crematorium lay a pile of emaciated bodies. It was about fifty feet long and three feet high. Their naked legs—nothing but bones—bore large tattoos identifying whether the victims were Polish, Russian, Belgian, or some other nationality. A few yards away a crowd of former prisoners were standing in a circle, gently kicking three healthy looking corpses with rope burns around their necks. These had been SS (Schutzstaffel) guards seized by the inmates and lynched before the Americans could interfere. As we approached, my guide shouted out in German, "*Amerikanisch' Offizier!*" With deferential politeness, the former prisoners stepped back, opening a gap several feet wide. The situation made me feel a little bit embarrassed; I had a camera but did not want to seem a tourist taking pictures of other men's suffering. My guide felt otherwise; he wanted these scenes recorded, and he kept urging me to take more. It took only a few moments to snap a few pictures and with a word of thanks I turned to leave. The inmates hesitated a moment and when certain that I was finished gave me a nod and a slight smile. They then closed back in again to resume their kicking of the corpses.

The entire episode had a profound and shocking effect. Since the American troops had arrived the camp had been sufficiently cleaned up to eliminate the stench. But the magnitude of the crime perpetrated at Buchenwald was too much to fully comprehend.

Actually it produced a rather numbing effect. Just as one can never fully appreciate the distances between galaxies of the universe, so it was impossible actually to believe that what one was seeing was real.

It took months after witnessing this scene before I could think of the Germans, viscerally, as human beings.

When I had talked to General Bradley the previous February, he had asked me to let him know when I thought I had learned about everything I could from the SIAM unit. Accordingly, some time toward the end of April I dropped him a note asking to be transferred to an infantry unit. In a remarkably short time I received orders to report to Headquarters, 1st Infantry Division.

On May 7 news of the German surrender came over the radio. That night I tried to telephone Dad. Though the call had to go through many switchboards, I succeeded in reaching his house in Reims and talked to Jimmy Gault. Dad was asleep, worn out from the events of the past few days, but I was able to leave my message of congratulations with Jimmy.

World War II in Europe was over.

5

Army of Occupation

V-E Day, May 8, 1945, was greeted by the Allied troops in a remarkably indifferent fashion. In contrast to the wild celebrations at the end of World War I, when soldiers of opposing sides ran into no man's land to exchange helmets and throw their arms around each other, the day was hardly marked. Possibly the reason for our apparent lethargy was the fact that the European campaign had more or less dwindled to an end. In most sectors of the front the units had advanced to their designated final positions, dug in, and simply waited. News of the armistice had leaked in the press a couple of days before. Furthermore, a bitterness existed between American and German troops which, along with orders from SHAEF, precluded fraternization. Most important, perhaps, we all realized that World War II was not over. Japan, while on her knees, had not yet surrendered; the reaction of most of us was that we were merely enjoying a respite before being deployed to the Far East.

In my case, transfer was not an unpleasant prospect. Keenly conscious that the 3323d SIAM Company had arrived on the Continent too late to contribute to victory, I felt that I personally had done nothing to justify my training or further my career. Accordingly, before leaving V Corps headquarters for 1st Division, I had made arrangements with General Huebner to go with him, as I knew that his corps was scheduled for Pacific redeployment.

I reported into Headquarters, 1st Infantry Division, located in Cheb, Czechoslovakia, during mid-morning, May 8. I encountered a rather slow-moving, let-down group of people. The only moment of gaiety during the day occurred in the late afternoon when an American pilot, obviously with more courage than good sense, commandeered a German Messerschmitt-262 jet and entertained the ground troops by doing crazy maneuvers in the sky overhead.

Nevertheless, though I expected my stay with the 1st Division to be temporary only, pending the readiness of V Corps, I still found it an exciting place to serve. It was one of the truly distinguished divisions of the war and, in common with other units that had suffered heavy casualties, it accepted new members easily. There was, to be sure, a certain hard core of old pros that had come over in 1942. These officers, normally fairly senior, were regarded as the "elders" of the group, and every now and then someone who had performed unusual exploits would be pointed out. While all these people took a certain casual interest in me as a curiosity, my presence was a triviality in their lives.

The 1st Division at the end of the war had developed a rather peculiar atmosphere. Completely free of any false modesty, they felt they had won the war single-handed. The saying went that the Army consisted of the 1st Division and several million replacements. One could understand this attitude considering the division's exploits in North Africa, Normandy, the St. Lô breakthrough, and the Bulge. Its more fanatic protagonists, however, were highly jealous of the record of the 3d Infantry Division, thirty-six of whose members had earned the Congressional Medal of Honor—in contrast to twelve for the 1st. "The 3d Division!" one man screamed one day. "I never even *heard* of it!" In their ardor, the men of the "Forgotten 1st" overlooked the fact that the 3d Division had suffered the casualties to correspond with its high number of decorations.

Shortly after the end of the war in Europe, a list came out specifying those divisions scheduled for redeployment in the Pacific. The 1st Division was not among them; it was to perform occupation duty in Europe. Nevertheless, people simply refused to believe such an idea. "They just can't fight that war in the Pacific without the 1st Division!" they said emphatically. They believed it.

All in all, the 1st Division consisted of a family, a very pleasant family, and easy to join. General Maxwell Taylor used to enjoy telling of inspecting a group of soldiers from the 101st Airborne Division. As he went down the line he asked each man whether he liked to jump by parachute. Invariably the answer was positive. At one point, however, he ran across a trooper who said, "No, General, I hate to jump." Taylor, surprised, asked why he was in an airborne division. The man replied, "Well, I like to associate with people who like to jump." This is largely the way I felt about my relationship with these old members of the "Big Red One."

My first contact with a Russian occurred two days after the war in Europe officially ended. A new friend, Major John C. Kelly, and I decided to take a run up to Karlsbad, where Russian and American lines met. We had along with us another passenger and a jeep driver named Robarge. We left Cheb in the afternoon, drove out past the POW area, and proceeded the few miles up to Karlsbad. The road, as always, was jammed with refugees and liberated Allied prisoners. On reaching the outskirts of Karlsbad, however, we were halted by an American MP.

"Have you any special business here, sir?" he asked Kelly.

"No, no, just looking around."

"You can't go in then, sir. Colonel's orders."

John Kelly took his cigar out of his mouth and smiled: "I guess I can find some special business in there."

"OK, sir," the soldier answered, "but don't just drive up to that corner and come back." We promised and drove on in, crossing a bridge and touring the town, stretching our necks to see anything unusual, even though we had no idea where we were going. We soon noticed with vague discomfort that people were staring at us as if we were a group of novelties, but we paid little attention. After all, the war was over.

In towns like this the possibility always existed that some fanatic Nazi soldier would still be holding out for a final, heroic death. We were therefore looking out for snipers; troubles with Russians never crossed our minds.

As we rounded a corner, however, we encountered a drunken Russian, beating up a German civilian. He was brandishing a German P-38 pistol but paused when he noticed us and shouted, "Americanski!" We continued, for obviously he was in no trouble and we were in no mood to protect Germans against Russians.

When we turned another corner about fifty feet away, however, we nearly ran over a middle-aged corpse lying in a pool of blood.

One thought crossed our minds: snipers. I told Robarge to back up in a hurry. Obviously the Russian soldier had been trying to warn us! I hadn't noticed in that first instant, that the corpse in the road was a German. At any rate, we backed up to the Russian, who forgot his civilian and staggered over to us.

He was a youngster, not over eighteen, I would guess. He had blond hair and what were probably open, frank features when he was sober. Now, as soon as he had made certain we were Americans, his features became contorted with ecstasy. "Americanski! Americanski! Americanski!" he repeated over and over again, smiling joyously. As this was the first time we had come in personal contact with a Russian, we were feeling the good will ourselves, and as he lurched around the jeep shaking hands, we answered, "Tovarich!" Sitting in the back seat, inaccessible, I was the last one he got to and had a chance to study him for a fleeting second. His trousers were baggy, close at the ankles, looking like something out of *Arabian Nights*. They had originally been colored with a camouflage print but the filth almost obscured the pattern. He wore a sleeveless black jacket, unbuttoned, and the typical Russian field cap. His skin was covered with large sores—a far from pretty sight.

The boy was not satisfied with shaking hands. Still brandishing his pistol, he stood and shouted, "Me Russkie!" Then he said something in Russian which ended with the word, *"Deutsch,"* holding up four fingers of his left hand and making motions with the pistol. Every now and then he would stop and look at each of us to make sure we understood. I nodded. We were now fairly certain regarding the fate of four Germans, one of whom was probably that character around the corner.

The boy paused for an instant; then, once more intrigued with the idea of meeting Americans, proceeded earnestly to try to kiss every member of the party. Luckily I was out of range, sitting on the floor in the rear. (All later claimed they had managed to avoid being kissed, despite my urging to comply for fear of hurting his feelings.) He went the rounds, excepting me, still moaning "Americanski," stopping only to accept the cigar that Major Kelly was lavishly offering him.

We turned the jeep around and started to leave. After about ten feet, however, Kelly told Robarge to slam on the brakes and back up. Taking out a match, the major gave our friend a light.

Taking off in a hurry, we rumbled right past a young German who was trying to stop us for some reason. Kelly said he would normally have been glad to hear his troubles but was afraid our Russkie friend would show up and take a shot at him—and miss. Not very brave, admittedly, but I agreed with him. We were now, we knew, really in Russian territory.

Activity at "Danger Forward" immediately after the war was relatively slack.[1] The principal problem at the time was the processing of the thousands of German prisoners still coming through the lines, hoping to surrender to the Western Allies. World War II had ended with a large number of German troops as yet uncaptured in western Czechoslovakia, and in other places where the Allies and the Russians had not quite made contact, the German troops kept pouring in. As of a given date—I forget the day—Germans were no longer allowed to surrender to the Western Allies. It was difficult to stop them, despite our strict orders. One night General Huebner at V Corps laid it on the line to Major General Clift Andrus, commanding the division: "After such and such an hour, just shoot them down as they try to come across."

My days with 1st Division were limited, possibly about a month, for Dad wanted me to join him for a couple of events. First came a trip to the United States, part of a home-front morale exercise, in which he was to be accompanied by some fifty servicemen, many of whom had distinguished themselves in the campaign. About June 15 I joined Dad at SHAEF, now located at Reims. Shortly thereafter we departed aboard President Truman's C-54 (DC-4), the plane that Roosevelt had named the *Sacred Cow*. We landed in Bermuda long enough to be fitted out in tropical worsted uniforms, necessary in the American summer. The barnstorming tour was exciting, including dinners, talks in Washington, New York, and Abilene, and a little time off.

[1] Code names were easier to use than designation of units. For example, division headquarters was nicknamed Danger; 16th Infantry, Dagwood; 18th Infantry, Decoy; 26th Infantry, Dextrous; division artillery, Determined.

I was unacquainted, at this point, with Dad's facility for public speaking. I had missed the Guildhall speech in London—probably his most famous—on June 12. Therefore I was flabbergasted when, as we took off for the one-hour trip from Washington to New York, he settled back in his seat and said, "Well, now I've got to figure out what I am going to say when I get there." On arrival he was going to address two million people on the streets and over the radio. I was relieved a couple of hours later when he delivered it successfully, speaking completely without notes.

The stop-over in New York was probably my first exposure to a phenomenon of public life, that is, exhaustion from being killed with kindness. In the elevator after the parade that evening a local official, swept off his feet by the size and enthusiasm of the reception, was beaming and bubbling. I know my weary reaction disappointed him, and I have always been sorry. But all I could think of right then was just the chance to get a little rest.

While in Washington I accompanied Dad and his contingent at a large dinner at the White House. President Truman was all congeniality. I sat at a four-man table which included General Alexander Vandegrift, U.S.M.C., and Undersecretary of War John J. McCloy. This was heady stuff indeed; and my double life, which involves alternating between ordinary citizen and public fixture, was launched.

The entire visit at home lasted about three weeks. Mother and Dad went to White Sulphur Springs, West Virginia, where the Greenbrier Hotel had been taken over by the Army as a hospital. While they rested in the green hills, I attempted to catch up on some of my social life in Washington, D.C.

We returned to Frankfurt am Main, the new headquarters of SHAEF, about the first of July. As there remained four or five weeks before a projected trip to Moscow, it seemed most feasible for me to simply stay in Frankfurt and work in the secretariat of the General Staff (SGS). The SGS in a high-level headquarters performs varied functions, from transporting important visitors to compiling statistics (at that time) on the war. During this waiting period I accompanied Dad to Berlin for his very brief visit to the Potsdam Conference where the "Big Three"—Britain, the Soviet Union, and the United States—mapped out plans for finishing the war with Japan. My only exposure to this exercise was to attend one breakfast given by the President, where I suppose about thirty people were gathered. President Truman, in person, was always the soul of hospitality and cordiality. By this time I was becoming more used to encounters with high-ranking people. Dad's matter-of-fact attitude toward all of them helped to prevent me from being awe-struck.

From my point of view, however, the most significant part of the Potsdam Conference occurred after we had returned to Bad Homburg, Dad's residence outside Frankfurt. Just before going to bed that evening the two of us sat and visited for a few minutes in his bedroom. He was sitting on the edge of his single bed, up against the wall, his .32 calibre pistol lying on the side table. The room was dim, with only the reading light on. He had something on his mind, and finally he came out with it: "John," he said, "Secretary Stimson told me something today. He says that they've now developed a new bomb, based on splitting the atom, that'll be so powerful that it exceeds the imagination of man. They're thinking very seriously about using this against the Japanese. This is, of course, highly secret."

The news was too much for me to comprehend, and I could make no comment. I doubt that I could say anything very helpful, because Dad's reaction was obviously one of depression. He talked quietly and softly, shaking his head slowly as he spoke. Except for that one brief conversation, I gave the matter little more thought. It was the business of somebody else at a high level.

One day during the weeks I was working in SGS, Dad suggested that since I was soon to go to the Far East, I might as well at least see Bavaria. I could go, he said, to Bad Tölz and stay a couple of days with George Patton. This being arranged, I took an L-5 and arrived early one afternoon.

General Patton's aide, Lieutenant Frank Graves, was on hand at the airstrip and the two of us took a command car to the villa, on Tegernsee, a few miles off. When we arrived and dismounted, Frank politely grabbed my suitcase. Immediately the door of the house opened and an irate General Patton came thundering out. His target was Frank. He stood his aide at attention and lacerated

him for what seemed a long time—it was probably only a few moments—for his misconduct in carrying a suitcase. In the course of
the tirade he glanced out of the corner of his eye and said, "Hello,
John," then continued. Without further ado the general turned on
his heel and re-entered, leaving us alone with the driver and the
suitcase.

Frank, apparently accustomed to this type of thing, seemed
unperturbed. After I had been settled in my room we wandered
around the villa, formerly owned by a prominent member of the
Nazi hierarchy. It was complete with every luxury item, including
a gymnasium in the basement. While Frank and I were inspecting
the bowling alleys about an hour after our arrival, we heard a
clap of noise a few feet away. We had intruded on General Patton,
who was busily punching a bag. When the general spotted the two
of us, he walked over quietly and, never looking in my direction,
spoke in a soft tone: "Frank, when you're in combat, you do everything the enlisted man does; but as soon as the shooting stops, you
allow the driver to carry the suitcase." With that the general, apparently with a load off his mind, went back to his exercising.

The next couple of days we visited Third Army headquarters,
the ruins of Hitler's retreat at Berchtesgaden, with its walls covered by the scratched initials of visiting Americans, and even the
"Eagle's Nest," untouched, atop the Alpine peaks. We found some
time for aquaplaning on the beautiful Tegernsee. But the high
points of the visit were the evening conversations with General
Patton.

Patton, as always, was an entertaining man, with a wry sense
of humor. In real life he bore little resemblance to the Franken-
stein monster in uniform that many people picture. He loved
the bizarre and took great delight in keeping any audience in a
state of shock. This he would attempt by his colorful language
and by such stories, in which he took great delight, as his bull ter-
rier Willie's fight with another dog. (A few days before, according
to Patton, Willie had bitten off another dog's ear. After the fight,
Willie had developed indigestion and had thrown up the morsel
in the lap of Patton's resplendent uniform.) His guest the last
evening was General Robert W. Grow, commander of the U. S.
6th Armored Division, a unit that Patton was fond of. The con-

versation covered various subjects but mostly pertaining to war—
this past one and the next.

Patton's legendary emotional nature, which had almost cost him
his career for slapping a soldier a couple of years earlier, manifested itself in even casual conversation. That evening the telephone
rang; it was from the States. Frank Graves whispered fear-
fully that the message might be news that Patton's son-in-law,
John K. Waters, had died of wounds. Happily such turned out not
to be the case, but in describing Waters' wounds, Patton broke
down in tears, meanwhile describing them in earthy terms. Later
on the subject changed to the new VT fuse, a lethal artillery shell
which explodes in the air on approaching the target. Patton, thinking out loud, was musing about the effect this development would
have on future infantry warfare. About the only answer, he concluded, was that all infantry would henceforth have to be protected with armored personnel carriers until they reached the line
of contact.[2]

At one point in the conversation the question came up as to
what uniform Patton should wear at General Bradley's forthcoming
departure ceremonies in Berlin. He wondered, again out loud,
whether he should wear his cavalry uniform with ivory-handled
pistols or dress in a more conventional manner. His chief of staff,
Major General Hobart Gay, had no qualms: "General, those things
are your trademark; you've got to wear the uniform you're known
for." Patton stared off into space for a few seconds, the corners
of his mouth turned down. Without turning, he said quietly, "All
right." The subject was dropped.

As the evening was coming to a close, Patton showed an unusual
human touch. He told me about how much he owed my father
and, tapping the four stars on his shoulder, said emotionally that
he owed all his success to Dad. From what I know of other occasions, Patton was not always consistent on this question.[3]

[2] This has indeed come to pass, and even the so-called "infantry divisions" in
Europe are mechanized, with armored personnel carriers for their infantry.

[3] "During my investigation of the 1943 soldier slapping incident, George came
to see me and in his typically generous and emotional fashion offered to resign
his commission so as to relieve me of any embarrassment. When I finally announced to him my determination to drop the whole matter and to retain him as

The next morning another visitor and I breakfasted alone. By the time Patton had joined us, it was time for me to leave and I stood up and excused myself. The general, exhibiting a little-publicized side, his courtly manners, stood up and conversed politely for a few minutes with our friend, tugging on his jacket, urging him to sit down.

The visit was a rare opportunity to become better acquainted with this unusual man, who unhappily had only a few weeks left to command his beloved Third Army.

Finally came the day for our trip to Moscow. Dad was the guest of the Soviet Government. The long-standing invitation from the Russians was scheduled purposely to include the Physical Culture Parade at Red Square on Sunday, August 12. Early Saturday morning, August 11, the party, consisting of Dad, Brigadier General T. J. Davis, Sergeant Leonard Dry (Dad's driver), and me, took off in a C-54 from Frankfurt for Berlin. When we landed about 9:30 Berlin time, Lieutenant General Lucius Clay and Marshal of the Soviet Union Georgi Zhukov boarded the plane. Zhukov brought with him his aide, an interpreter, a navigator, and a radioman. We encountered some delay, probably because of the intricacies involved in flying over Soviet-held territory, but got off at about 11:00.

Zhukov, Dad's Soviet counterpart in Berlin, was to act as host, and he was to be with us almost constantly on the trip. He was short and stocky, with the good-humored face of a successful man. His lower jaw stuck out prominently. With light blue eyes and a receding hairline, he looked more German than Russian. His erect posture and popped-up chest added to the impression that he was, with all his congeniality, a man of supreme self-confidence. He and Dad, with the interpreter—Zhukov spoke no English and Dad

---

the prospective commander of the Third Army, he was stirred to the point of tears. At such moments General Patton revealed a side of his make-up that was difficult for anyone except his intimate friends to understand. His remorse was very great, not only for the trouble he had caused me but, he said, for the fact that he had vehemently criticized me to his associates when he thought I might relieve him. His emotional range was very great and he lived at either one end or the other of it. I laughingly told him, 'You owe us some victories; pay off and the world will deem me a wise man.' "–Dwight D. Eisenhower, *Crusade in Europe*, p. 225.

no Russian—sat toward the front of the plane at the card table for most of the trip.

I watched them conversing for a while. Communication was difficult through the interpreter, but as time passed, I noticed that formalities were disappearing rapidly. Zhukov asked if he could unhook his high collar and soon had made himself comfortable. He was friendly by nature and liked to laugh, and in his friendliness seemed genuine. He gave no appearance of calculation or discomfiture. I personally believed, however, that he was a little in awe of Dad. The reason, probably, was that he was impressed by the absolute powers that Dad enjoyed in his occupation zone when the two had worked together in Berlin, and by Dad's studied carelessness in displaying them. Zhukov and Dad got along well together, but from the conversation Zhukov seemed hard put to understand Dad's reluctance to join hands with him and beat up a few of the smaller countries of Europe. France and Britain as powers he brushed off.

The interpreter accompanying Zhukov was a tall, fine-looking major, cultured and urbane. He translated easily, with no apparent strain. A likable individual, he was perfect for his job.

The aide was a husky, well-built major, who spoke no English, overly eager to be accommodating and especially to stay out of the way. He sat in the rear and dove into American magazines as though he had never seen a picture book before.

At 12:30 the steward served lunch. Asked whether he preferred pork chops or steak, Zhukov brightened up and said, "Bifteck." He insisted on having some wine to drink before the noon meal and was obviously by this time enjoying himself. General Davis, General Clay, and I joined the other three. We invited the aide to come up and eat with us; but even with Zhukov's permission he was apparently afraid to do so. He insisted that he was not hungry, but I noticed that the steward later talked him into having something to eat back where he was sitting. By some mistake in the orders, I wound up with three pork chops and had to finish them all off. This was easy, as I was in good spirits and had a drink of Scotch to stimulate the appetite. All this was pointed out to Zhukov and I stopped, afraid of establishing a reputation with the Russians that I later would have to live up to.

We landed in Moscow at 4 P.M. Moscow time. Ambassador W. Averell Harriman, his daughter Kathy, some Russian generals, and various people from the Embassy were there to meet us. The Russian guard of honor performed well, stiffly and without lilt, but precise. This was the first time I had seen a contingent of Russians in formation and their goosestepping made me feel vaguely uncomfortable. Dad and Marshal Zhukov reviewed them briefly, and the American party took off for the Embassy Residence.

The Residence was not far from the airfield—about a fifteen-minute drive along the widest street I had ever seen. I was later informed that this street had been created by the eradication of a row of city blocks. People were dressed very poorly; the houses were dingy, crowded and miserable-looking. When we arrived at the Residence, Zhukov took his leave. We were shown to our rooms and soon collected upstairs for a drink. Besides the Harrimans, Mr. and Mrs. Ed Pauley and Major General John Deane, chief of the U. S. Military Mission, were on hand. While we were at the Embassy caviar and vodka started out every meal. We were assured by the ambassador, however, that this was a special occasion.

We were all tired, but after dinner Dad had to go to some meeting. While they were to be gone, Kathy Harriman insisted that General Davis, General Clay, Mrs. Pauley, she, and I go to the ballet. I personally would have preferred to go to sleep. Nevertheless, we went and I enjoyed it. The performance was *Scheherazade*.

Before leaving for the ballet I tried to get a message back to Tex Lee, Dad's aide, in Frankfurt. On calling the U. S. Signal Center in Moscow I was informed that they could not take even a routine message such as "arrived safely" over the telephone. They asked who I was and I told them. The man on the line thought I was a prankster, and in view of a full day I was in no mood for joking. Later I called the Mission and found out that a message had been sent by someone else earlier in the afternoon.

On Sunday, August 12, after shooting a little pool with Sergeant Dry, I went to Dad's room and then our whole contingent left for the parade in Red Square. We arrived at noon and Dad received an ovation from the populace. Whether the people knew who he was or simply recognized him as an American general, I do not know. We were placed in the section of the reviewing stand usually occupied by foreign dignitaries, well crowded and with no place to sit down. A little after noon Stalin and attendants arrived and proceeded to the top of Lenin's tomb. Soon a message came that if Dad cared to, he could come up and bring a couple of others. Therefore, Dad, Ambassador Harriman, and General Deane joined Stalin and his group. My reaction was that it was about time, but later I learned that Dad was the first foreigner ever to be allowed this courtesy.

Red Square was really a large courtyard, which I estimated as about 250 yards wide and 1,000 yards long. The stands, including Lenin's tomb, were in the middle of the long side. A large church was located down to the right, an impressive ornate red building on the left, and across from the stands was what had once been a huge department store, but so decorated as to look like a palace itself. I learned that the Russians intended to tear down this department store because it allowed insufficient space for parades. Twelve pictures of Stalin were visible from the stands.

This Physical Culture Parade, I was told, occurred annually and detailed planning was begun a full year in advance. The number of people participating in this one ranged anywhere from one American estimate of 40,000 to the Russian claim of 150,000. My personal guess was that about 100,000 marched, unless some went around the block and came back on again. All this performance was for the benefit of a couple hundred spectators.

At the beginning a band of a thousand pieces faced the spectators, and what might have been about 3,000 people were drawn up in ranks across the square. When the parade began, these people passed in review, carrying their pictures with them. When they were clear, people came in from side streets, and for an hour and a half, members of the different youth organizations throughout Russia strutted by. Some were Mongols, some were Georgians, some were German-looking Baltic people; but they were all alike in the enthusiastic smiles on their faces and in their splendid builds. Their cocky arm swing, with the elbow going shoulder high and the wrist swinging back and forth in front of the body added to the buoyancy of the atmosphere. The participants must have drilled for months, because every movement was complete precision.

Following this part of the review came demonstrations from every organization—acrobatics and stunts, cheers and dances, all perfectly timed to the band music, which never stopped for almost five hours. It is noteworthy that the cheers did not recount their region's contribution to the Russian war effort, but rather thanked Stalin for having freed them. This continued until 4:45 when all in the reviewing stands, well worn out from standing through the whole thing, sagged into cars and went home.

Despite the fatigue, I left the parade exhilarated. I had never seen anything like it before and probably never will again. Kathy Harriman later told me that all the preparations had been made at night. Some of the performers were professional, others had been brought to Moscow from their provinces a long time ago in order to practice. I was told also that this was probably the only time in their lives that these performers would wear those fancy uniforms and costumes. But in spite of all the cynical explanations on the part of Embassy members, I was still impressed. I could not help thinking of one thing, however: The spectacle reminded me of pictures I had seen of prewar Nazi Germany.

That evening we went out to a stadium to see a soccer game. Though we intended to stay for only one half, Zhukov requested us to remain for the whole game. When the American party arrived and joined the marshals, Zhukov grinned, gave a grunt, and came over and asked me how I liked the girls at the parade that afternoon. Of course, I told him they were great—which was true. He intended, he laughed, to marry me off to one of them, a terrifying prospect since any one of those powerful women could have broken me in two with no effort.

During the intermission we went out to a small room for refreshments. Three or four kinds of wine, vodka, caviar, cakes, and delicacies of all kinds were offered. This was my first initiation into Russian toasting. It takes up the whole meal. There was time, however, to do a bit of sampling of the various wines and cakes, and I was really sorry when we were called back to the stands. After the game was over, Dad and Marshal Zhukov stood up together and

1. "I was born standing at attention." J.S.D.E. fitted out with souvenirs picked up from the battlefields of France, age six.

2. "Dad was engaged in ghost-writing an official guide book [in 1928], *The American Battlefields in France*. This task required a great deal of travel to all the World War I sites. Quite often Bo would accompany us. . . ." The two of us scrambled around some of the many ruins that dotted the French countryside.

3. "Dad worked like a slave in the old State-War-Navy Building (now the Executive Office Building of the White House) and longed for line duty. Nevertheless, his time in Washington . . . set him apart from many run-of-the-mill Army officers. . . ." D.D.E. entering the office of General Douglas MacArthur, Army Chief of Staff, about 1930.

4, 5. "During these years I was being raised among a group of remarkable Army officers . . . whose humanity has rarely been appreciated by the general public. . . ." Two members of "Club Eisenhower" and my "blood brothers"—Major (later General) Leonard T. Gerow (*left*) and Major (later Major General) Everett S. Hughes (*right*).

6. (*Top left*) "Every summer between 1929 and 1935 I was sent to Denver to stay with my maternal grandparents, Mr. and Mrs. John S. Doud." Pupah and Nana at Fort Lewis in 1940. 7. (*Top right*) ". . . Grandmother Eisenhower, the patron saint of Dad's side of the family, was one of the best-humored people I ever met. . . . During these sojourns Grandma would talk about her life as a little girl and delight me with stories of her high-spirited sons. . . ." Ida Stover Eisenhower in Abilene, 1940. 8. (*Center*) *Left to right:* Abe and Ira Eisenhower, Mrs. C. O. (Eisenhower) Musser, and my granddad David Jacob Eisenhower, around 1930. 9. (*Right*) "Granddad had been a tough bird, a disciplinarian as only a Pennsylvania Dutchman can be. He was also well educated and industrious. He had lost his money through the depression . . . and in his later years . . . was in a glum state of mind." Granddad at Abilene, 1938.

10. "Athletically, I decided to specialize . . . I determined that my sport was tennis, a game I had learned . . . in Washington. Therefore I concentrated on that sport. . . ."

11. "In Mindanao a Philippine Army officer . . . presented me with a white cockatoo . . . [that instantly] created a temporary family crisis."

12. "In 1939 Dad's thoughts were now turning toward rejoining the Army in the United States, in hopes of an eventual field command. Besides his desire to get back with active troops, there . . . was a falling out with General MacArthur which, while it never came to a breaking point, resulted in a cooling off of their formerly warm relationship." Dinner for High Commissioner Paul McNutt in 1938. Mrs. MacArthur is on Dad's left.

13. Cadet Chapel, built in 1911, as it appeared from across the Plain of West Point in 1941.

14. "When I got word in camp that Dad was going overseas, I immediately applied for weekend leave to see him off." Dad, Mother, and Mrs. Howard Smith (from Philippine days) sit pensively on the porch at Fort Myer the day before his departure for London in June 1942.

15. (*Left*) "Clamp in those wings; do you think you're going to fly?" In July 1941 the three members of the Beast Detail, here greeting a new cadet, had been in the newcomer's spot. It was nice to have the shoe on the other foot, but we showed little outward sympathy. 16. (*Right*) ". . . when the time came for the corps to march down to the field house . . . Mother and I found ourselves facing a bank of something like forty photographers, bulbs flashing unmercifully." Graduation morning, June 6, 1944.

17. ". . . In all positions except Supreme Commander, Montgomery held a status coequal to that of Dad. He was not only commander of 21 Army group; he was also the senior British commander. . . . Naturally, as Supreme Commander, Dad was the ultimate boss." Montgomery and Eisenhower together in Normandy, summer 1944.

18. "Before dawn, June 24, we finally began the trip to Omaha Beach." The Supreme Commander confers with a couple of his subordinates aboard the destroyer bound for Normandy, June 1944.

19. "[Omaha] Beach was a mess. Some ships had been previously sunk on purpose as breakwaters; but the storm the last few days had sunk many more. . . . All that met the eye was a bay jammed with transports, LSTs, and smaller craft anchored around in seeming confusion." Omaha Beach before the storm of June 19, 1944.

received a fine cheer from the crowd. Unable to speak any Russian, Dad put his arm around Zhukov and this made a great hit.

The next morning I slept until 11:15; only to be informed that the party had already left to see the subways of Moscow. Dad was apparently somewhat put out that I had slept so late, and I anticipated being told for years to come that I did nothing but sleep through the whole Moscow trip.

That afternoon we went to the U. S. Military Mission, where Dad met the American staff. We then went out to the Stormovik fighter plane factory, next to the field at which we had landed. We were oriented on the factory by the manager and then went around to see the people at work. Pictures of Stalin and Lenin, as usual, were all over. The factory force consisted of 60 per cent women and many very young boys. Sergeant Dry, who had been trained in the Chrysler plant in Detroit, explained various things to me as we went along and seemed unimpressed by what he considered antiquated methods. The factory at that time put out at maximum requirements twenty planes a day. They were pursuit ships with a good war record, not very fast, but carrying a heavy load of armament. A test pilot gave a daring demonstration of its performance. After that, we went in for the usual refreshments and toasting and left about 5:00.

That evening at 8:00 Dad, Ambassador Harriman, General Clay, General Davis, General Deane, Mr. Pauley, and I arrived at the Kremlin for a banquet. We were guided up a long set of stairs, through halls covered with beautiful paintings, and arrived in a richly decorated dining room, where there must have been about fifty people, many of them marshals of the Soviet Union. These marshals were generally short and stocky, many of them with shaven heads, most of them more Germanic-looking than I had previously imagined. They were young by our standards for high-ranking generals, and their faces reflected little of the burdens they must have been carrying during the war. Stalin and Molotov soon came in with their retinue. I did not meet Stalin till after dinner, as I had been jostled off in a corner when he first came in and went the rounds. He was a very short man in a white coat with elaborate marshal's trappings. He appeared at this time as a benign gentleman, much older than his pictures indicated.

He was soft-spoken, quiet, and distant. Molotov looked just like his pictures and acted according to reputation—perfectly blank and non-committal.

The impression of the entire scene in the dining room was one of whiteness. All the Soviet officers wore white tunics; and this, combined with the glistening tablecloth and gigantic crystal chandeliers, gave an aura of brilliance that I have never seen elsewhere in untold numbers of formal dinners. According to Russian custom, the dinner was punctuated by a seemingly endless series of toasts. All the big leaders of both nations were included. A Major General Kutuzov sat on my right. He talked French, making conversation possible, but this fact added little to the occasion, as he was about the most joyless character I had ever met. Across the table sat an artillery marshal and a tank marshal. A young man from the Foreign Office, who spoke fairly good English, sat at the end. He kept instructing me what to do, mostly in the line of doing more drinking. He was a likable young fellow, though obviously far from relaxed.

The meal finished, the guests rose and began to move slowly toward the door. Dad beckoned me to come over to be introduced to Stalin. The marshal, staring distantly into space, mumbled some complimentary remark to the effect that I looked like a brave soldier. Then, the amenities taken care of, he and Dad led the way. In the next room we sat at small tables for coffee, the Foreign Office man and me together. We were joined by a kindly looking, elderly gentleman, who reminded me in his demeanor very much of my Grandfather Doud. I did not glean that he was a man of much importance, as his simple gray suit, denoting a civilian employee, was overshadowed by the splendor of the marshals, but I enjoyed his company so much that I looked forward to seeing him again.

The young Foreign Office man then began to tell me my own personal history, surprising but not too disturbing because he probably read American magazines. I was jolted, however, when he told me in detail about my troubles two nights before in trying to get the message back to Frankfurt. I wondered how in the world he had found out about that, as I had almost forgotten it myself. Soon we went into another room to view spectacular movies on the Red Army's capture of Berlin. Marshal Zhukov appeared frequently and was always greeted with cheers by the audience. Immediately after the films Generalissimo Stalin said good night to each of us and left. We went home much earlier than we had hoped.

On Tuesday, August 14, I made sure to be awakened early enough to make the trip to the collective farms. Dad, Zhukov, and our party arrived at a farm at about noon and went into the small administrative building where the general manager, a hospitable, gray-haired little fellow in a dark suit, explained the setup. This collective unit consisted of seven independent "farms," which had joined together. The term "farm" turned out to be a misnomer. The horse barn was considered one farm, the pig sty was considered another, and so on. These were all directed by the manager with the aid of the agricultural expert, a woman of about forty who, it was said, was the brains of the operation. It was interesting to note that for all the pomp and braid surrounding Russian marshals such as Zhukov, people of the soil talked with them freely and as equals. They laughed and joked together. Though the people were, according to our standards, living in poverty, they seemed fairly happy with their lot. One place we visited was a nursery. The Russians really believed in the slogan, "If it moves, salute it." For two days we had been saluting everyone in and out of uniform, but when we saluted the farm woman taking care of the children, I thought this was the end. There were, however, seven people on the farm with the rank of brigadier, and this woman may have been one of them. We visited the horse barn and the pig sty; later we spent some time eating cucumbers and gooseberries out in the fields. The horses were emaciated. According to our hosts, they all had been at the front.

We then proceeded to another place, designated a "government farm," a single unit run directly by the Soviet Government. Whereas the collective farm was supposedly a union of private enterprises (though supervised by the state-appointed manager and the seven brigadiers), the government farm resembled a military organization. The latter was far more prosperous. It had some fine-looking cattle and horses, in contrast to the moth-eaten nags we had seen earlier. Apparently, no animosity existed between the privileged and the underprivileged farms. The manager of the collective farm, in fact, followed us over to the other place, insisting that his people would kill him if we failed to stay for lunch. Marshal Zhukov warned Dad, however, that if we did, we would have to toast everybody in the Soviet Union, including the seven brigadiers. Dad was able gracefully to excuse himself.

That afternoon we took a trip to the Kremlin museum, another first. Members of the U. S. Military Mission came along with us, entering its walls for the first time in the two and a half years they had been in Moscow. The Kremlin is really a collection of buildings within a large wall. Though we had been there the night before, we saw much more this afternoon. In the courtyards, as we wandered around, we came across an ancient cannon, the diameter of whose projectile must have been 2½ feet. The thought, hardly original, hit me that this must have been regarded in its time as the ultimate weapon, the one that would make wars too horrible to fight. We proceeded through various richly decorated rooms. The museum downstairs contained armor dating back to the Dark Ages and jewels remaining from the czars, the value of which undoubtedly ran into the high millions. The Bolshevik hierarchy seemed to have come full circle, as in George Orwell's *Animal Farm*.

That night at 8:00 a buffet supper was held at the American Embassy, with many of the same Russian marshals in attendance. The atmosphere was now all conviviality. The members of the American Military Mission were astonished by the things that happened on our visit, far more so than we, who knew nothing of the usual aloofness between the Russians and foreigners in Moscow. I talked to a Russian major general, who spoke very good English. He was unusually frank and direct. When I mentioned the fear the Germans held for the Russians, he said simply, not jokingly and not bitterly, "Perhaps it is because we are more barbarous than you are." Marshal Zhukov was still acting much concerned about whether I had met any Russian girls.

Somewhere in the course of the evening, I dropped out behind a curtained door for a short breather. I found another American, an officer from the Military Mission, who had retreated with the same idea. As we conversed, he casually mentioned that Russia's foremost hangman, the notorious Andrei Vishinski, who had prosecuted the tremendous purges in 1936, was among the guests. Naturally curious, I wanted to see him. The two of us peered through the drawn curtains and my friend discreetly pointed. Vishinski turned out to be the delightful old gentleman I had met and liked so much the night before. "My God," I moaned, "what an outstanding judge of human character I am!"

On re-entering the main room I was pleased to see that Dad and Zhukov were becoming better pals all the time. They seemed finally to have even worked up a satisfactory sign language. Later the guests were shown an American movie, in which each speech in English was followed by a Russian translation. In the course of the showing Dad received a message from Ambassador Harriman to keep everybody at the house, as he had an important announcement. Zhukov left early, but Dad did his best to keep as large a crowd as possible. The conviviality grew. Local American embassy officers were astounded to hear the Russians and Americans singing the "Volga Boatmen" together, not too off key at that. Then the Russians sang to the Americans and the Americans sang to the Russians. Apparently it was all revolutionary. Ambassador Harriman came back and announced that the Japanese had surrendered. This was cause for more celebrating—though by this time nobody needed our excuse, even such a good one.

Dad's efforts to keep people at the party worked too well on one marshal, Semyon Budënny, always recognizable because of his spectacular handle-bar mustache. The good marshal that night became thoroughly drunk. He insisted on hugging Dad and kissing anyone short enough to come in range. He was a very nice old devil with it all. He told me of his son, who had been six years old at the time of the Revolution. Budënny had joined the Bolsheviks, he said, after czarist soldiers had dashed the boy to death against a wall in front of his own eyes. He pointed out that these czarists were supposed to be gentlemen, whereas he was only a simple farmer.

After two or three hours sleep we left the Embassy early on August 15. Despite the inevitable delay caused by the guard of honor, we were off the ground at 7:00. At about 9:30 we landed in Leningrad, where, after similar ceremonies, a Marshal Govorov conducted the party to his headquarters. In Leningrad the atmosphere was more relaxed than in Moscow. At 10:30 we began a sort of mid-morning luncheon ritual, which consisted of the usual toasting and caviar. (I thought I would never be able to stand the sight of caviar again.) We then took a tour of the city, which included a very remarkable exhibit of the Siege of Leningrad. The statues of Peter the Great and Catherine the Great, the Inner Palace, and the Neva River principally stick in my mind. At 1:00 we were back for another lunch, the same people making the same speeches. Here occurred what I had been afraid of: my turn to make a toast. Fortunately, I had given some thought to what I might say if such an eventuality should come about. All the government leaders had been recognized several times; furthermore, it would seem presumptuous for a lieutenant to be toasting Stalin or Zhukov. I had noted that one man had been left out. Therefore, after an introductory remark regarding the honor of associating with all these high-ranking people, I said, giving my words all the dignity I could,

"I have been in Russia several days and have listened to many toasts. I have heard the virtues of every Allied ruler, every prominent marshal, general, admiral, and air commander toasted. I have yet to hear a toast to the most important Russian in World War II. Gentlemen, will you please drink with me to the common soldier of the Great Red Army."

This approach seemed to go over well and I was grateful that nobody had pre-empted it.[4]

After the meal we were kept by some entertainment—opera singers, violinists, and even recitals of Russian poetry. By mid-afternoon we were off again.

Marshal Zhukov was now completely at home in the plane. Before he took his seat he shed his tunic, half sheepishly, half proudly exposing his blue silk undershirt. Dad offered the marshal the bed; but with a grand flourish Zhukov indicated that Dad rather than he should take a rest. It would have been impossible, of course, for only one of the two to retire, as such would constitute admitting

---

[4] I use the wording given in *Crusade in Europe*, p. 466. As I made no note of what I said, I am willing to accept Dad's version, since it was written in 1948, shortly after the event. It conforms completely to my recollection.

fatigue. Dad had foreseen this, however, and had arranged for a bunk to be made up forward; so both happily stretched out. We ran into a little weather on the way back. I was reading, oblivious, when the interpreter gleefully nudged me and pointed out the window. We were just over the tree tops. At that time the Russian navigators flew only by visual flight regulations, always in sight of the ground no matter how low they had to descend. Apparently the American pilot decided about this time that enough was enough, because soon the ship gave a lurch forward and we climbed above the clouds. As the journey was coming to an end, Marshal Zhukov asked for some magazines for his daughter. Dad and I frantically leafed through the racks, trying to look casual in selecting those that had nothing anti-Russian in them. The abundance of *Time* magazines was no help at all.

We arrived at Tempelhof airport in Berlin at 7:50 P.M. The guard of honor, consisting of U.S. paratroops, was a welcome sight. I observed happily what a snappy outfit they were compared to the stiff Russians we had been seeing for three days. We said good-by to Marshal Zhukov, and I made bold to delay him a second for one last picture. Next morning we returned to Frankfurt.

The timing of this eventful trip to Moscow was fortuitous, as it occurred in the middle of the short-lived honeymoon between the United States and the Soviet Union. Probably it could not have been repeated a year later, certainly not in the same atmosphere of cordiality. Dad had been honored as no foreigner had been honored before. Stalin, though humorless, had been cordial and complimentary. Zhukov, the star of the show, had been hospitable and effervescent. During these four days I developed a warm feeling for him that has never completely disappeared, despite the ups and downs of the relations between our two countries. Little did we know, as we said good-by at Tempelhof, that this honeymoon would soon come to an end.

This story has a short sequel. About two months after the Moscow trip Marshal Zhukov was supposed to pay a reciprocal visit to the United States. When Dad first issued the invitation, however, Zhukov, still landlocked in his thinking, was doubtful about flying the Atlantic. (Dad's greatest exploit, in Zhukov's eyes, was to deliver armies across a body of water, even one as small as the English Channel.) Finally, however, when Dad offered to send me along as his aide—and in his own plane—Zhukov brightened up and accepted. Thus, later in the year, I was looking forward to a trip home. The day I was to leave I received word that the trip was off; Zhukov was ill. We never learned the nature of his illness—diplomatic or otherwise—but Marshal Zhukov, to all intents and purposes, disappeared from our eyes for the next decade. Maybe, with the honeymoon at an end—and with Stalin becoming increasingly jealous of Zhukov's popularity—Zhukov had become too much a symbol of U.S.–U.S.S.R. friendship.

By the time we had returned from Moscow, the two atomic bombs had been dropped on Japan and the war in the Far East was over. No more units would be deployed to the Pacific, and my personal plans for going to the Far East had been canceled. With that prospect gone, I, along with almost all military men overseas, longed above all else to go home. The mere fact of setting foot on the shores of the United States appeared to us in Europe as the answer to all of life's problems. I had particular reasons. With almost four years of high school in the Philippines, thence to Beanie Millard's, and from there to West Point, Benning, and overseas, I felt that since the age of fourteen I had actually seen little of my own country. Nevertheless, I was a regular officer, newly arrived in Europe, and the ruling was that my total tour overseas would span a period of thirty months. I realized the justness of this ruling and prepared to dig in for nearly two more years. As I was on the loose, attached to SHAEF, I had to find a place to go. Certainly SHAEF on a permanent basis was no place for me.

Where the idea came from I have no idea, but I was delighted when I was offered the chance to join Fifteenth Army, located at Bad Nauheim, near Frankfurt. This headquarters, commanded by now Lieutenant General Gerow, had no troops assigned to it; it was simply an organization whose sole mission was to study the European campaign and to determine objectively what had been done right and what had been done wrong. I reported to

Gerow somewhere around the first of September. "Uncle Gee" was putting me, he said, in the G-2 (intelligence) section. I was glad to get back to work again, little realizing that this assignment would be only the first of several intelligence jobs I would hold.

Service with the Theater General Board, as the Fifteenth Army was called, was pleasant indeed. Bad Nauheim had been a resort area before the war, and athletic facilities abounded. The officers were of high caliber and the junior mess was convivial. One of the benefits of this assignment was the fact that I was located only about a half hour's drive from Dad's residence at Bad Homburg. Thus I was able to drive down the road and have dinner with him, while he was there, about once a week.

Dad was a lonely man at that time, let down after the excitement of the war. Jimmy Gault lived in the house and occasionally other members of the SHAEF staff would join them for dinner. One of Dad's pleasures was his brood of Scottie puppies—Telek and Khaki had produced twenty-three in the course of the war, and about nine still remained around the house. Dad was always a believer in keeping his dogs outside, but once in the course of each evening he would open the door and let them all in. They would charge through the house, scrambling up the stairs, exploring every bedroom, leaving an occasional puddle, and finally winding up, all nine of them, piled in his lap.

Before the weather became too cold we would sit out on the back porch after dinner, where a long sloping yard led down to a lily-covered pond. The pups, none of them grown, would amuse themselves rolling down the slope, running back up, and rolling down again. One evening after dinner Dad, Jimmy Gault, and I sauntered down and tossed all nine into the water. Eight immediately headed for the dry ground, all except Lop-Ear, whose deformity made him the least valuable of the brood. That evening "Loppie" distinguished himself. Instead of coming ashore, he took off swimming after the two ducks, encouraged by our applause. Then for a second we feared a crisis: Loppie was stuck in the lily pads. "It's up to us!" Jimmy shouted and headed for the water without bothering to remove his immaculate British officer's uniform, complete with Sam Browne belt and the red tabs of a Scots Guardsman. Dad and I were right behind him. Fortunately

Loppie broke loose and swam triumphantly ashore. Jimmy's uniform was saved and from that time we had a new hero of the household. The only ones who were bored during the entire episode were the ducks, who had merely looked around and paddled away.

The late summer and fall of 1945 was probably the period in my entire life when Dad and I were closest. We would play records —Gershwin's nostalgic "American in Paris" was our favorite— and converse quietly on many subjects.

One evening, as he was riding with me back to Bad Nauheim, Dad said sadly, "I had to relieve George Patton from Third Army today." Patton, it turned out, had made one of his famous off-the-cuff remarks to the press. Frustrated by the fact that almost anyone who could operate a railroad, a signal office, or an electric system in Germany had of necessity been a member of the Nazi party, Patton had in exasperation told the press that Nazis and non-Nazis in Germany were like Republicans and Democrats. His indiscretion had caused a furor. "We could," Dad went on, "survive this tempest. Actually I'm not moving George for what he's done—just for what he's going to do next." Fortunately Gee Gerow was about to go home, so switching Patton to another Army-level post was not technically a demotion, though Patton doubtless regarded it so. Patton soon arrived at Bad Nauheim.[5]

Quite naturally, I was personally a little apprehensive when Patton came to his new command, as I was unsure of what his attitude would be. Nevertheless, his generous nature showed through, and as the officers of the headquarters went through the receiving line, he pulled me aside for a brief and congenial chat. In his typical impish manner, however, Patton had to jar his audience in his remarks that evening. He started out by saying, "I have been here and studied your work today." Then, his voice rising to a pitch, he shouted, "I have been SHOCKED"—and then in a lower tone—"by the excellence of your work."

On Patton's arrival at the Theater General Board the atmosphere among the previously calm, studious staff immediately became electric. One of his first announcements was that he wanted to go home by March. And we were by God going to have all our

---

[5] No personal animosity was involved whatsoever. The two generals went to a football game together in Frankfurt a couple of days after the switch-over.

reports finished by that time! Everyone became frantic, and I am certain that substantial revisions in the studies were made. For the final report, "The Strategy of the Campaign," as I read it, showed the fine hand of the new commander. Even though I felt that First Army had contributed more to victory than had the Third, I noticed that Patton's army was mentioned about three times as often as any other in the theater.

In November Dad went home for temporary consultations. While there he became ill, some sort of respiratory ailment. By the time he was well again, General Marshall had asked for relief from his post as Chief of Staff of the Army and Dad had taken over, without returning to Europe even to pack.

Shortly thereafter tragedy struck. General Patton, on a hunting trip near Mannheim, was involved in an automobile accident. His sedan, I was told, had been hit in the side by the careless driver of an Army truck. His neck was broken, and he was taken to a hospital near Heidelberg. We at Fifteenth Army, shocked and saddened, followed the news avidly every day. For a while it appeared that he might recover, and Mrs. Patton gave cause for hope with her plucky remark, "I've seen Georgie in these scrapes before and he'll come through this one too." Nevertheless, the general did not come through, and about a week after the accident he died. With a friend I drove down to Heidelberg to attend the simple funeral services.

Several of us youngsters were particularly touched when Mrs. Patton, as soon as the funeral was over, came up to Bad Nauheim and sent for the Army brats she knew. In the midst of her grief she was thoughtful enough to call us in, one at a time, for a short visit so she could report back to our families that we were well. She said little about the general, concentrating her conversation largely on her son George, who was at this time a first-classman in West Point. I have rarely been witness to such a gesture of fortitude and kindness.

As it turned out the studies of the Theater General Board had been accelerated even faster than General Patton had foreseen. By early January 1946 the Fifteenth Army was being deactivated, and its former members were in the process of seeking new assignments. My immediate boss in the G-2 (intelligence) section told me he had heard of the setup in United States Forces, Austria (USFA), located in Vienna. Vacancies existed, and shortly after the turn of the year another officer and I drove along the Autobahn, through Salzburg, Linz, and the Russian zone to report to our new assignments.

In Vienna I was sent for by General Mark W. Clark, who had fought his way up through the boot of Italy. Headquarters, USFA was in essence a continuation of the American component of his former 15 Army Group. He was assigning me, he said, to the Allied Secretariat, a rather unusual detail, because he felt that under its energetic chief, Lieutenant Colonel Harold Pomeroy, I would really be put to work and learn something. I was billeted with a couple of other officers in an apartment on the edge of Türkenschanzpark, reputed to be the spot where the Ottoman invasion of Europe had been stopped in 1683.

The secretariat was located in a large building on Schwarzenbergplatz, just off the Ringstrasse, on the edge of the Innerstadt, or Center City. Fortunately the officer I was billeted with, Arthur ("Hotshot") Carroll, had access to one of the section's jeeps, and transportation was easy. Benjamin de Brie ("Brie") Taylor was billeted nearby. Until Hotshot Carroll rotated home, the three of us were practically inseparable. The work of the secretariat was intensely interesting, as we were charged with keeping the records of the meetings of the Allied Council, a four-power body comprising British, French, Russians, and Americans, whose job it was to administer the "liberated" country of Austria. Here I was dealing on a day-by-day basis with not only the French and British but also the Russians. Communication with my Russian counterparts was in French. We kept the minutes of the meetings and made up the agendas. I personally was charged with producing the *Journal,* which published the decisions of the four-power committee.

Meetings were held in a large room with the usual large, hollow four-sided table, each delegation occupying a side. Each country would have about nine or ten officers present. Every issue would be addressed first by the executive committee, which consisted of the deputy commanders from the respective countries, in preparation for the meetings of the Allied Council. A good deal of time was consumed in the discussion of any given topic because of the necessity for translation in three languages. Here Brie Taylor had a tremendous advantage by being bilingual in French and English. Furthermore, he was an extremely gifted writer; and while I felt that I could express myself reasonably well, the breadth of Brie's vocabulary and the smoothness with which he wrote brought home how much I had to learn.

Three characters seemed outstanding in this high-level group, two Russians and one American. Marshal Ivan Konev, the Russian commander, gave every appearance of being a completely straight-line soldier—rugged, with shaven head, light blue eyes, and an open face. At best, dealing with the Russians was becoming increasingly difficult; but we felt at the time that if there had been more people like Konev and Zhukov in actual authority, things would have been easier.

But it was apparent that Konev was not the true boss of the Soviet delegation. The real power was held by a Colonel General Zheltov, the deputy, likewise shaven-headed but with a sharp beak and sharper piercing eyes. At the meetings of the executive committee, Zheltov would lean forward, his bull neck bulging, and speak positively with a pointed finger. Sometimes he would throw in a little English, such as "I agree wiz you," to ease the atmosphere. (His three counterparts would then laugh uproariously.) Zheltov had been a commissar rather than a commander in the Red Army, and this fact made him a hard-liner when dealing with political matters.

It was quite obvious that the only man who could handle Zheltov was our own boss, General Mark Wayne Clark. An actor somewhat in the same category as Douglas MacArthur, Clark was truly an education to watch in action. At every meeting of the Allied Council he would manage to arrive just a little behind the rest. Then, with his towering height, he would saunter slowly around the table—excruciatingly slowly—and, looking down on the top of Konev's and Zheltov's clean pates, would ask them laboriously regarding the health of their families. This grand entrance, coupled with his shrewd intelligence, made the most of a bad situation.

Nevertheless, the Russians continued tying up Danube River traffic, failing to do their share in supplying the people of Vienna, and noncooperating on similar problems.

So passed the winter of early 1946 in a dismal, partly destroyed city, where practically the only recreation was hitting the nightclubs. It was a worthwhile experience, however, if for nothing else than getting some exposure to the Russians at the working level. While they were reputedly cooperative compared to those in Berlin, one incident caught our notice. A Captain Kunin, the only Russian who spoke English, one day indulged in a tennis game with Brie Taylor. A couple of days later Kunin disappeared without explanation.

In late April General Clark, always an extremely personal commander, had apparently decided it was time for me to take over command of an infantry company. Unexpectedly one day he sent for me, pinned on captain's bars, and told me that I was to take over a company of the 5th Infantry, a battalion of which should be arriving in a few days. My exhilaration, as I rode back on the bus to the secretariat, was unbounded. My friends Carroll and Taylor were leaving for home, and I had nothing left to hold me in the secretariat. Besides, to become a company commander with less than two years service was an exalted position, the dream of any member of the class of 1944. Some had achieved it, and it was good to join them.

The 1st Battalion, 5th Infantry, rolled—I should say staggered— into Vienna in early May. To my astonishment, who should show up as S-1 (battalion personnel officer) and headquarters company commander but the ubiquitous Bo Horkan. For months Bo had been stationed near Augsburg, Germany, during the free-wheeling early days of the Occupation; now, completely by chance, the two of us were members of the only infantry battalion in Vienna. When word had reached the battalion commander that I was to be assigned to the unit, it was Bo's duty to recommend what company I should command. In his own calculations, he told me later, I would be best off in Company D (heavy weapons). He had figured, however, that his batting average on accepted recommendations was so low that he had advised my assignment to Company B, a rifle company. Happily his calculations were correct, and I wound up with D Company, which sported as its greatest asset something like seventeen or eighteen jeeps for transportation.

Company D, 5th Infantry, was located in the suburbs of Vienna near Grinzing, a neighborhood made famous by Beethoven and the annual wine festivals. Bo had secured space for selected officers in the villa of Alice Vidiano, a Rumanian countess, right next to one of Beethoven's homes. I was invited to join this group and moved in gladly. D Company itself was in a state of chaos. It was overloaded with officers—perhaps eight of them—almost all of whom were scheduled for return to the United States within a couple of weeks. Needless to say, they were worthless at this stage. The enlisted strength of the company was down to something like thirty, but with the deactivation of the 42d Division our ranks swelled to a figure of well over two hundred in the course of something like ten days. Just to assign these men to billets, feed them, and find them bedding involved a good deal of effort.

One problem was discipline. A large number of the officers and men had come overseas after combat and some tended to work off their energies in channels that were hardly constructive. Drunkenness and venereal disease were rampant. Therefore one of my first acts was to forbid women in the billets after 10:00 P.M. For this I was considered a martinet.

As this was my first company, I attacked my duties eagerly. The major organizational task was to find the right administrative personnel in a morass of rather indifferent souls. Above all, we needed a strong first sergeant. One day a handsome red-headed private, lean and muscular, asked permission to see "the Captain." Over the protests of the acting first sergeant I agreed to see him. Pfc. Bloomingdale (fictitious name), age about thirty, had been a soldier before the war and had at one time in the course of his career, he claimed, reached the grade of first sergeant. His record seemed to indicate that he had been a "twenty-eight-day soldier"—twenty-eight days of hard work and a binge on payday— and had been up and down the ladder of the ranks of noncommissioned officers. Bloomingdale was a shrewd one. Knowing my background, he reported in Old Army style, reminiscent of the 1930s, referring to me always in the third person. He advised me that with his background as a first sergeant, he knew everything there was to know about company administration.

One slight obstacle to using Bloomingdale's services was the fact that he was currently about to be tried by court-martial for participation in some barroom brawl in the establishment we called the "Bucket of Blood," about two blocks up the street from company headquarters. Nevertheless, I wanted to give him a try, as I was desperate. Therefore, after getting the trial canceled, I marched him out to the rear of the barracks, pointed to a certain spot, and told him he would be absolved from his crimes after he had completed digging a hole six feet square and six feet deep. With a bright smile flashing under his small red mustache, he took the shovel and began to work. During the next day my executive officer and I took periodic peeks around the corner of the building to witness the dirt flying out of the growing hole. In an incredibly short time Bloomingdale reported completion of his job. I inspected the hole he had dug and I found it according to specifications. Then, in order to emphasize the ridiculous aspect of the exercise, I dropped a match stick in the bottom and told him to fill it up.[6] This again was done with alacrity, and soon Bloomingdale was ensconced in the orderly room.

Before long, Bloomingdale had proved that he really knew company administration. He immediately began to get the company records in order; and although the rest of the NCOs in the orderly room looked upon him with distaste, he worked long and cheerfully, obviously far more knowledgeable than any of the rest. Within a couple of weeks he was acting first sergeant and was being promoted as rapidly as the regulations would allow. Once he had begun to develop some order out of the chaotic orderly room, however, he began to suffer again from boredom. Off he went on another binge, with some act so obvious that I had no power to cover it up, even had I wanted to. So Acting First Sergeant Bloomingdale became once more Private Bloomingdale and was transferred to another company. The last I heard of him, he had been a drill sergeant but had subsequently been hospitalized with a broken leg as the result of jumping from the top window

[6] This particular form of punishment, I might add, was common at that period, as almost none other, short of court-martial, was effective.

of a second-story building in the middle of the night. I have always held a warm feeling for this cheerful scoundrel, although his career in the D Company orderly room probably lasted something less than three weeks.

By this time Bo Horkan was well aware of my problems with getting qualified personnel, and although the situation was universal in the battalion, he kept an eye out for possibilities. One day a full-fledged first sergeant reported into the battalion and Bo immediately called him to my attention and assigned him to me. His name was Griggs. Sergeant Griggs had served in the 94th Division during combat, and, although only twenty-eight years old, was as hard-boiled as a man who had spent his entire life in the Army. Griggs was truly a difficult one to understand. Conscientious and serious-minded, he had taken the war very much to heart. He was bitterly offended at the irresponsibility of the young replacements whose misconduct was causing the United States to lose the good will of the liberated populations. From the next room I could hear him shouting with a quake in his voice about "the men who fought and died to make this here Occupation possible." He was a handsome man, well-built, with a full head of neatly combed sandy hair and a jutting jaw. Whatever we accomplished in D Company during those few months was due largely to Sergeant Griggs.

Shortly after I took command of D Company, three companies of the battalion were assigned to a *Kaserne*[7] in the city. Truly no company commander coveted this location. In Grinzing we had enjoyed a wholesome setup, where men off duty could walk around outside the barracks in an essentially residential area. But the center of the city of Vienna suffered—like the centers of other cities—from noise, heat, streetwalkers, an excess of bars, and no areas for informal athletics.

One problem, particularly difficult to contend with under those circumstances, was that of venereal disease. With the population practically starving, the streets were loaded with prostitutes, who unabashedly haunted the *Kaserne*. Naturally we had no power to prevent their presence. As a result, the VD rate became the

---

[7] German for "barracks."

most concrete sort of report card that a company received. We in D Company enjoyed remarkable success in fighting this disease, thanks largely to the imagination of Sergeant Griggs. In late August Griggs told me he had made friends with the doctors of a prominent local hospital and had made a tentative agreement with them. If we could collect one candy bar from every man in the company and bring the troops over to the hospital auditorium, the doctors would ask volunteer Austrian patients to walk up and down the aisles showing their physical symptoms. (The candy bars were, of course, the reward to the patients for volunteering.) I was delighted, and a few days later we scraped up almost the entire company and marched them over. The resulting program that the doctors put on was no disappointment. On seeing the physical results of the various types of venereal disease, on both male and female, a few of the less-hardened soldiers became physically ill and had to leave the room. The rest were sufficiently impressed for D Company, 5th Infantry, to go a full seventy-one days without a single case. I doubt that the exercise had much effect on the morals of the troops, but it instilled a fear of the consequences that produced results.

Bo Horkan was returned to the States and released from the Army at about the same time that we moved to the *Kaserne*. Needless to say, he was delighted to go. Possessed of a slightly humorous contempt for such conscientious regular officers as myself, Bo could foresee a tightening of regulations not to his liking. While I missed him personally, I could visualize that Bo's free-wheeling attitude at the time would have little place in our objective of "regularizing" the unit.

In early October 1946, my parents made a trip to Europe. Dad was still Chief of Staff of the Army. As I had now stored up a good bit of leave, I was able to take about three weeks to be with them. I joined them aboard the *Queen Mary* when she docked in Britain. Mother, with her lifelong aversion to flying, had refused to make the trip by air. We proceeded at once to London and stayed in the American Embassy Residence next to Hyde Park. (The ambassador was away.)

One evening Prime Minister Clement Attlee held a dinner for

Dad and his old wartime comrades at 10 Downing Street. Since the event occurred only about a year and a half after the end of World War II, all the generals and admirals were still in their prime. Churchill, now Leader of His Majesty's Loyal Opposition, was doubtless the oldest member present. One would naturally expect a gathering such as this to be happy, and so it was. The remarkable aspect, however, was the surface cordiality between Churchill and Attlee. Churchill's removal as Prime Minister during the period of the Potsdam Conference, a little over a year earlier, had been a blow to him, and I have no idea whether he bore personal animosity to Attlee, who had been his Deputy Prime Minister during the War. I recall distinctly, however, that the morning newspapers that day had told of one of the two calling the other "that wicked man." No sign of antagonism was apparent this evening, however. Perhaps the outburst in Parliament had been merely politics.

Clement Attlee was a perfect foil for his more colorful rival. Small, quiet, bald, even mousy, his retiring demeanor belied the toughness that a man in his position would have to possess. Perhaps he felt as out of place among these high-ranking military people as I. At any rate, he seemed to take pleasure in showing me around 10 Downing Street on an individual tour. At one point, he told me with a broad smile that the first time he had seen this building was some years ago; he had been demonstrating against the government on the streets. The fact that this place was now his residence gave him obvious pleasure.

The next day at a formal luncheon I found myself sitting across from Herbert Morrison, Labourite leader of the House of Commons, and next to Lady Nancy Astor. Lady Astor, born in Virginia, was now the epitome of British conservatism. Furthermore, she was outspoken and uninhibited as to the arena in which she would express her views. Despite the fact that this was a social occasion, she spent what seemed like the entire meal berating Morrison with such admonitions as "Britons never, never, never, will be slaves!" Morrison was unperturbed, chuckling and eating happily with his napkin tied around his neck. He contented himself with injecting a "Now, Nancy" periodically when the good lady would pause for breath. The British, despite their reputation for reserve, seem far more self-expressive than Americans when it comes to politics.

From London our party, including a couple of aides and the air crew, proceeded to Maybole, Scotland, where the Scottish Trust had granted Dad the lifetime use of a flat on the top floor of the forbidding Culzean Castle. After a couple of quiet days, involving bird shooting with Jimmy and Peggy Gault, Dad, Mother, and I departed by automobile for Edinburgh and baptismal ceremonies for Air Chief Marshal Tedder's new-born son. Thence on to Balmoral Castle, in the Highlands, the private home of the Royal Family.

The one thing that strikes an outsider on seeing the Royal Family off stage is their informality. On the two times I have visited there, Balmoral has been full of relaxed, attractive house guests. King George VI and Queen Elizabeth (now the Queen Mother) were a warm couple. Queen Elizabeth took me under her wing before dinner and tried to teach me the steps to a Scottish dance—the "Dashing White Sergeant." I doubt that I was much of a pupil. After dinner that evening, King George and I for some reason found ourselves the last to leave the table. He motioned me to come around the table and sit with him. "What," he asked, "do all your ribbons stand for?" This was a somewhat appalling experience, in that the American Army, for morale purposes, had been lavish in issuing theater and service ribbons. Thus, having no decorations for either valor or merit, my highest ranking ribbon was a yellow one denoting that I had been in military service before Pearl Harbor (the "drafted early" ribbon we called it). The King listened politely and finally broke my embarrassment by pointing out that he also had been presented with the American European Theater Ribbon. A British officer with that amount of color on his coat would probably have been in combat through both the North African and European campaigns.

After dinner the Royal Family held a party in the downstairs part of the castle where all the servants, equerries, and guards attended. Queen Elizabeth, in particular, joined right in. Dad's driver, Sergeant Dry, seemed much more adept at the Scottish dances than I.

The next day we went to chapel with the King, Queen, and

their two daughters, Princesses Elizabeth and Margaret. Soon Mother and Dad left for home and I packed my bags for return to Vienna.

On arrival in Vienna I found the situation with the 1st Battalion completely changed. During my absence the 16th Infantry had taken over the 5th as part of the over-all theater policy of reducing U.S. occupation troops to one division. With a new influx of people from the 16th, we were now duplicated in every important position in the battalion. I was to retain command of D Company, 16th Infantry, which had absorbed D Company, 5th Infantry; but Sergeant Griggs, being far junior to his counterpart as first sergeant, was forced temporarily to step down to a deputy position. I was once again flooded with officers. The battalion was now commanded by a full colonel, a former regimental commander, and battalion headquarters boasted in addition three underemployed lieutenant colonels. Thus we found ourselves with a battalion overloaded with officers and noncommissioned officers but short on privates who could man the guard posts.

As a result of all this, the conditions in the 1st Battalion, 16th Infantry became the most hopeless of any unit I ever observed. The D Company guard posts were still flung far and wide, but the shortage of men to occupy them resulted in a soldier's spending three days on post with only one day's respite in between. In addition, instead of walking post two hours on and four hours off, each man walked three hours on and rested three hours. D Company, 16th Infantry, had plenty of excess equipment left over from the war, which eased some problems so far as the books were concerned, but we were painfully short of winter equipment and the men on the guard posts suffered immeasurably in the snows of the Austrian winter. As we had every rank in abundance except privates, we were forced to use noncommissioned officers up to the grade of staff sergeant to walk post. The *Kaserne* itself was unheated, and the men fortunate enough to be spending the night in their own bunks would light their pot-bellied stoves to red heat. There was nothing to do about these conditions; they were simply built into the situation.

The Vienna Area Command could do little to alleviate these

conditions. For some vague political reason, guard posts could not be eliminated; they were largely protecting U.S. property. Furthermore, reduction of officers and noncommissioned officers and increases of privates was impossible because the privates were simply not re-enlisting. The poor quality of the officers was a matter which could hardly be solved locally. The deputy battalion commander once explained to me that since the 26th Infantry was guarding the Nuremberg Trials and the 18th was earmarked for Trieste, the 16th was receiving the lowest quality of replacements, both officers and men. I could not argue with this thesis, but it hardly helped the problem.

Personally, I took the welfare of my troops very much to heart, and in the presence of the battalion commander complained to Colonel Wellington A. Samouce, deputy commander of Vienna Area Command. With a complete straight face, he asked me, "You are a West Pointer aren't you?"

"Yes, sir, I am."

"Well, I expect those men on post to meet the same standards that you maintained while walking guard post as a cadet."

I said nothing. "Sammy" Samouce, while somewhat of a hot-tempered eccentric, was far from stupid. In giving such instructions, he knew as well as I how completely ridiculous they were. I saluted and left.

Seven years later, when I was finding things tough in the freezing cold of Korea, I said to myself: "Relax. You could be back commanding D Company in Vienna."

My own personal morale under these circumstances was raised by meeting a willowy young brunette, an Army brat named Barbara Jean Thompson. Her father, Colonel Percy W. Thompson, was assigned to a section of USFA headquarters. Women had not been very much of a factor in our lives in Vienna. Social activities centered around a sort of family group at the 16th Infantry Club, including bachelors, married couples, and a smattering of casual girl friends. I had, for a while, taken out a French girl from the Allied Secretariat, but even before going on leave in October I had become weary of playing the role of interpreter between her and my friends.

Barbara and I met at the instigation of a classmate's wife, Mrs. James W. Dunham, who asked me one night to provide transportation for Barbara to a dinner party. This I was glad to do but was not given to believe that "Beattie" Dunham actually considered this arrangement as anything more than chauffeuring. Barbara and I talked little in the course of the evening and when I dropped her at home, she was convinced, I later learned, that she would never see me again.

I felt differently. Although I had been given to understand that she was somewhat engaged to become engaged, I nevertheless called and asked her to the Hallowe'en party at the club. Barbara fitted in beautifully, even though our rough-and-ready crowd lacked the gentility of the generals' aide set she had been exposed to during her first weeks in Vienna. Soon I found myself taking her out frequently and unconsciously staking a claim. Every evening I would pull up to her house in an open jeep, go in and visit with her family a while, and then take her out. Once she was seated in the jeep I would wrap her in two army blankets brought along for the purpose. The two of us would then drive happily through the often subzero Viennese winter toward the center of the city. We went to the Vienna Opera on occasion and sometimes to the Bristol Hotel for dinner. We went often to the less pretentious Regina Hotel where we both loved the trio—violin, accordion, and balalaika—in the downstairs. But generally we stuck with the 16th Infantry group. Barbara found it difficult to understand why I insisted on sticking with this rowdy gang, shunning the smooth, refined "aides" coterie. But she went along with this inverse snobbery and liked my friends. The officers of the Grinzing BOQ (bachelor officer quarters) were soon enamored of her and, though I failed to realize it at first, I was hooked. To fill her daylight hours Barbara got a job in the fiscal section of USFA. How the two of us held up with a schedule of long working days and night-clubbing to late hours I can attribute only to youth.

Somewhere around Christmas, Barbara became quite mysterious one evening at the club. A former boy friend had left her some money, with which she was supposed to telephone him back in the States at a specified time. I became furious, especially when I found myself unable to prevent the call. Now I realized that while

I enjoyed a favored situation regarding competition in Vienna, such was not necessarily the case elsewhere. Therefore in the first week of January 1947, I made my move and proposed. I was surprisingly shaken when she accepted.

Immediately—perhaps that evening—Barbara told her parents of our plans. Therefore, when, a few evenings later, it came time for me to speak to Colonel Thompson, the episode turned out to be somewhat of an anticlimax. Barbara and her mother excused themselves and went upstairs to eavesdrop over the balcony above the living room. Colonel Thompson and I (we knew each other well by now) discussed the North African campaign and the operation of XXI Corps in Europe. In the course of some fifteen minutes of soldier talk, Colonel Thompson said casually, "We've tried to raise Barbara well; I'm sure she'll make you a good wife." We then went back to military subjects and were astonished at the ladies' annoyance when they came thundering down the stairs.

Within a couple of days Barbara and I put in a transatlantic call to my parents. Introducing her over the telephone so many miles away was slightly awkward and Barbara has since said that she approached the experience with some trepidation. I can remember little of the conversation other than assuring Dad that Barbara had a very strong foot. (Through the years Dad had said he hoped we could breed my tendency toward flat feet out of the family.)

Mother immediately mailed my West Point miniature, the traditional Army engagement ring; Barbara and I were delighted to find it fit perfectly. Mrs. Thompson gave a formal ladies' luncheon in early February and our engagement was now official.

About the time that Barbara and I became engaged I received a call from Mike Cavanaugh, my former boss at Theater General Board, now in the G-2 section of USFA. A vacancy existed in that headquarters, and Mike wanted me to come over and be his assistant. I was given about five minutes to decide. With only somewhat mixed emotions I agreed to come.

My reasons for accepting, I admit, were largely selfish. Close as I felt to those of my men who had been with me for any length of time, I considered the deplorable situation in 1st Battalion, 16th

Infantry, completely beyond my control. None of the factors that made duty so difficult for my troops could be affected by me. Furthermore, the oversupervision was getting on my nerves. I had now completed eight months as a company commander in a static situation and could see little more to be learned. Furthermore, I had enjoyed working under Mike before and felt that a change of worlds, to an intelligence section in the hot-bed of intrigue that was Vienna, would be educational. Therefore some time around mid-January 1947 I signed the company over to my successor and simply reported the next day a couple of blocks away.

Duty in the G-2 Section of USFA was not particularly busy but was exceedingly illuminating. For the first time I became conscious of our deteriorating relations with the Russians. While serving with troops, I had found little cause for complaint regarding our Soviet counterparts. But the tension between the two nations was felt in every office of G-2. The first incident that jarred me was the shooting down of an American aircraft, for no apparent reason, over Yugoslavia. As I sat pondering this new realization, Bill Waters, my office mate, leaned back in his chair, laughed, and exclaimed to another man there, "You know, up to this time John has thought the Russians were our allies!"

During this short tour I was able to read background material on the Communist Revolution and study the attitudes of those in power in the Kremlin. I also developed more practice in writing extensive military intelligence estimates.

Time was available in early April for Barbara and me, properly chaperoned by a fairly young married couple, to make a week-long visit to Paris. With the coming of spring 1947, both the Thompson family and I found ourselves on the same train headed for Bremerhaven and home.

6

Police Action

When we arrived back in New York in late May 1947, Barbara and I managed to make matters difficult for everyone connected with our forthcoming wedding. Innocent of the many details involved in a wedding of this size, we put unreasonable pressure on the Thompsons to schedule the event as soon as possible. Ten days after landing was our first deadline; we later relented and accepted a date of June 10, at Fort Monroe, Virginia, Colonel Thompson's next station. In so doing we were by no means being intentionally inconsiderate. But my forty-five-day leave began the day we set foot on American soil, and every day's delay represented a shortening of our rather ambitious honeymoon schemes. How the Thompsons unpacked their bags at Monroe and arranged the ceremony in such a short period remains a mystery to me, although General Jacob L. Devers, commanding the post, allocated the services of an officer full time to help out.

The wedding, because Dad was Army Chief of Staff, was a far more elaborate affair than Barbara and I would have preferred. High-ranking officers and their wives abounded. The ceremony was held in the Casemate Chapel at Fort Monroe and the reception at the officers' club. As we were preparing to leave and Barbara was changing clothes, one officer sidled up and whispered, "Take your time, John; you'll never keep this many major generals waiting again." His prophecy has held up.

Following our honeymoon out West, where we visited friends and relatives we had not seen in years, I reported to Fort Benning, Georgia. Here I took a couple of short courses, principally to occupy the time until reporting to West Point at Christmas.

We spent the first four months of 1948 in New York at Columbia University, where I took courses in preparation for my new assignment as an instructor in English at West Point, to begin in September 1948. Some of the courses were acceptable for graduate credits; others, such as grammar and composition, seemed rather basic. Nevertheless, considering that the West Point class of 1944 had received a minimum of English during our undergraduate years, these fundamental brush-ups were probably called for.

The years spent instructing in West Point were happy ones for us. Two of our children were born there: Dwight David II in 1948 and Barbara Anne in 1949. The friendships we formed there have been lasting. And each year seemed better than the preceding, as experience and personnel changes increased my status among my fellow instructors. During the third year I attained the heady title of "assistant professor" and was able to complete a master's degree in English literature at Columbia. Toward the end of this third year—1950—I applied for a fourth, but the career management people in Washington turned the application down. Nothing could have been more fortunate, for had I remained an additional year, I would later have gone to Korea after the war was over, once again an also-ran.

From West Point, Barbara and I, with our small family, headed for Fort Knox. Here, along with some sixty other infantry officers (out of a class of two hundred), I attended the Armored Advance School. Except for the birth of our second daughter, Susan Elaine, this year was uneventful and not particularly challenging. I improved my golf, developed a better appreciation of the viewpoint of my armored comrades, and learned techniques of field-grade combat duties, both infantry and armored.

One spring day in 1952 I received a telephone call from Washington. On the other end was Major General Wilton B. Persons, a member of Dad's staff at SHAPE in France. Persons was calling to find out what I would like to do after the school year was finished. Dad had made a casual inquiry as to whether a young officer would be useful there in Paris; the staff took it to mean me.

As General Persons talked, I groaned under my breath. Would this be a repetition of what had happened in World War II? Was I once again going to be pulled out of the normal career mainstream and sent to a higher headquarters? That could have been possible, as someone in SHAPE had overreacted to one of Dad's whimsical questions, and the decision was now up to me. Having the burden on my own back was annoying, to say the least. By no means did I relish the thought of leaving my family and going to Korea, where that war was finishing its second year. On the other hand, I sorely regretted having missed active combat in World War II. For seven years I had been an infantryman without the coveted Combat Infantry Badge. And to take positive action to avoid going to Korea was out of the question. I asked, "Where would I be sent, general, if this whole thing hadn't been brought up at SHAPE?"

"Korea."

"Well, Korea it's got to be then." That much was settled; I was not going to be denied combat duty for a second time.

It might be well here to review the course of the Korean War up to the time I received my orders. In late June of 1950, it will be recalled, the Communist North Koreans had crossed the artificial border along the 38th Parallel without provocation and within hours had practically routed the weaker Republic of Korea (ROK) Army. With the backing of the United Nations, President Truman had reacted with force under the UN flag, employing only at first United States air and naval support, but within a couple of days committing ground troops from Japan. The understrength 24th and later the 25th Infantry and 1st Cavalry Divisions were soon proven to be no match for the North Koreans and the United States went into a state of partial mobilization.

As new American divisions arrived, they were steadily beaten back to a bridgehead in the southeast corner of the peninsula commonly called the "Pusan Perimeter." Here the United Nations Forces, now under U. S. Eighth Army, were able to build up strength and in late summer, with the North Korean supply lines now stretched, were able to break out, the route being made possible by an amphibious landing by X Corps (7th Infantry and 1st Marine Divisions) at Inchon, near Seoul. General MacArthur, commander-in-chief of the UN Forces, having obtained authority from Washington, pursued the North Koreans across the 38th

Parallel. By the end of November certain of his units reached the Yalu River, the border between North Korea and Manchuria.

But the American successes had goaded the Red Chinese into action. At the very moment when success seemed within our grasp the Chinese Communist Forces (CCF) were building up in the central highlands of North Korea. General MacArthur, though informed of the presence of Red Chinese south of the Yalu, continued the attack.

In late November the Chinese struck, driving the American X Corps into the sea.[1] The Americans were able to evacuate the X Corps practically intact, however, and promptly redeployed it by sea to Pusan to rejoin the fight. Eighth Army fell back south of Seoul and for the first time X Corps was placed under its command.

From that time on, the two sides fought a seesaw battle in the general vicinity of the 38th Parallel. Eventually the UN Forces gained the upper hand and by October were pursuing the Chinese and North Koreans northward once more. At this time the Chinese and North Koreans called for a peace conference at Panmunjom; the Eighth Army was ordered to halt in place and hold the line.

Now, as I was preparing to go to Korea, the line had been established for some eight months. Both sides had dug in and the bulk of the fighting was being conducted on a series of UN outposts, seized easily in October 1951. Now, in June 1952, these outposts were being threatened by the enemy with increased intensity.

After graduation at Fort Knox our family headed back for Highland Falls, New York, a small town just outside of West Point where Barbara and the children were to stay while I was overseas. Having rented and settled the house, we drove to Fort Sheridan, Illinois, for a few days' visit with Colonel and Mrs. Thompson.

The Republican National Convention in Chicago that nominated Dad for President had just drawn to a close in July 1952

[1] Dad, at Columbia University, was aware through Army briefings, of the situation. I was puzzled when on Thanksgiving evening he muttered absently, "I've never been so depressed about the Korean situation as I am right now." There was no inkling of impending disaster in the newspapers.

when we arrived, and Dad and Mother were still at the Blackstone Hotel. This gave us a good chance for a brief family visit.

We talked of nothing very important, but in the course of conversation Dad gave me one admonition: never get captured. He shrugged off the fact that in infantry combat the chance of being hit by a mortar or artillery shell was always present; but as the son of a new nominee for President, my capture would not only subject me to special cruelties but would also put the Communists in a position to blackmail him. "If you're captured," he said, "I suppose I would just have to drop out of the presidential race."

I assured Dad that this would never happen and told him not to worry. The exchange was not upsetting, as the possibility had occurred to me long before. Since then I have been asked exactly what I meant by this assurance. The fact is I never thought it through thoroughly, and my statement was something in the nature of a response to a warning to "drive safely." There was not, in my calculation, a great danger of capture under existing circumstances. The front was static and a field-grade officer not required to man an outpost was in little danger of ever being grabbed off, so long as he avoided taking unnecessary risks. Yet had I ever found myself surrounded by Chinese or North Koreans, I had every intention of keeping my promise and using my .45 pistol, taking, I hoped, some of them with me.[2]

In retrospect, however, I wonder whether such an action would have been worthwhile. For the Communists, once I was identified, could claim to the world anything they wanted about me, whether I was dead or alive. Thus the blackmail could have been effected in any case if I were simply missing in action.

Dad was not the only one who mentioned this possibility. On the trip over the Pacific and up to the front there seemed to be no shortage of concerned people who would warn me of the possibility of Chinese patrols sent through the lines with me as the target. I had more than one nightmare on the subject.

I said good-by to Barbara at O'Hare International Airport in mid-July 1952 and flew to Seattle, stopping in Denver for a five-

[2] I never fired my .45 Colt automatic in anger. However, after several months in Korea I took it to a firing range one day and discovered that it didn't shoot.

minute farewell with the folks at the airport. At Seattle Uncle Ed picked me up and I made arrangements at the port of embarkation, Fort Lawton, to stay with him in Tacoma until alerted.

While I was in Tacoma we went to the country club for dinner one evening. As Ed introduced me to one of his friends, he said in a jocular way, "John's going over there to fight *your* war."

His friend's answer was a snort: "It's not *my* war." (One would have thought I had started it.)

His remark did not disturb me. It was typical of the American attitude at the time, ever since the Korean situation had become stalemated. News of actions in Korea in most of the nation's newspapers was confined to one-column articles about three inches long on the back page. People were still being killed, but no major movements were occurring to make headlines.

On July 27, 1952, I dismounted from an Air Force C-46 at a strip near the dusty, malodorous town of Taegu. With my duffel bag over my shoulder and a canvas satchel under my arm, I climbed in a jeep and bounced down the narrow dirt road toward the headquarters commonly called EUSAK, the rear headquarters of Eighth U. S. Army, Korea.

The period between departure from Seattle and my arrival in Korea had been in fact rather agreeable. The thirty-six-hour flight from Vancouver, British Columbia to Japan, via a Canadian Pacific DC-4 had included libations and pleasant company. We had arrived at Haneda Air Base in the middle of the night and the military passengers had trundled by rickety bus through the suburbs of Tokyo to Camp Drake. With a couple of days to recuperate and clean up at that replacement center, I had been given the privilege of acting as a courier to Eighth Army in Korea, thus shortening the process of entering the replacement stream and finally getting "settled" in whatever unit I would be assigned to. That moment could not come fast enough for any of us.

So the canvas bag I held under my arm as the jeep jolted from pot hole to pot hole that day in Taegu was my express ticket to my unknown unit. And a welcome ticket it was too.

My elation was, I must admit, temporarily set back by my conversations with high-ranking officers at EUSAK. I was sent immediately to the office of the G-1 (personnel), who seemed bent on telling me his problems.[3] These I would normally have paid little attention to except that his main concern was the depressing lack of casualties among the American troops. He had laid his plans carefully, and what, he wondered, was he going to do with all the incoming replacements when not enough of our men were being killed?

A rather portly colonel, from the Adjutant General's staff in Washington, D.C., was also on hand. This gentleman, in charge of casualty reporting, was far from downcast. Instead, he seemed intent on impressing me with the importance of his position. "Casualty reporting," he pontificated, "is being recognized as one of our most important staff positions. It touches on almost all facets of our activities—public relations, quartermaster, adjutant general's records, everything." As a potential statistic on the books of both of these officers, I found it hard to be inspired.

But again professionalism raised its head. The G-1 said that, as an advance course graduate, I could select the division I desired for assignment. Among the choices were many distinguished units —the 2d, 3d, 7th, 25th, 40th, and 45th Infantry divisions. But the choice was easy. The 3d Infantry Division, descendant of the unit that had inspired me to select the Infantry back in Fort Lewis, was now within my grasp. The G-1 agreed to send me there.

About noon the next day I slung my duffel bag over my shoulder once again and retraced my way to the Taegu airstrip, glad enough to fly out of that desolate place. The plane went through rain and considerable turbulence. In the course of a couple of hours we landed at the K-29 Air Base, near Yong Dong Po, where I was met, amidst the crowd of rather aimless-looking transients, by a young 3d Division captain serving his last few days before leaving.

The next morning, another gray one, was July 29. I finished my processing at 3d Division rear and with a new group of replacements began the long, tedious train ride on the "40-and-8"

[3] The Army staff system breaks down as follows: (G-1), personnel; (G-2), intelligence; (G-3), operations and training; (G-4), supply and logistics. The letter "S" is substituted for "G" below division.

boxcar[4] up to 3d Division headquarters about fifty miles north of Seoul.

Being an individual replacement is generally regarded as one of the gloomy events of a man's career. In World War II this had been particularly true. Indifferent to the welfare of the transients and often disappointed in their own blighted military careers, the commanders of replacement depots in that conflict came to be regarded by American soldiers as little better than concentration camp guards. With miserable conditions—deep mud, poor food, and surly personnel—these camps achieved a hellish reputation in soldiers' minds. Having learned, however, the Army had established a very efficient replacement stream in Korea. I felt it an experience to witness it from the inside; certainly everything within reason was being done to make the trip comfortable.

But with all the improvements in the system, there was no way of escaping the loneliness of the individual, no matter what insignia he wore on his shoulder, as he climbed into an open boxcar and proceeded at the rate of less than twenty miles an hour under leaden skies to an unknown future.

As I sprawled on the floor propped up against my duffel bag, I was subjected to a small bespectacled medic's moaning about the terrible waste of training it would be if a shell should land on his head in a few days. I had to smile wryly at this but was annoyed by the tauntings of a veteran officer whose idea of humor was to berate the poor man on what bums he and various other medical officers were. If for no other reason than diplomacy, it seemed that a medic could be a bad man to offend when going into combat.

The train squeaked to a halt at Chipyong-ni at about six o'clock that evening. The officers joining the division were greeted, escorted to individual jeeps—things were getting better as we went forward—and driven through a gray, treeless wilderness to a large cluster of tents, at which the familiar slanted blue and white insignia of the 3d Division was prominent. After quick interviews all replacement officers were conducted to a large circuslike tent, the division mess, where our spirits were raised by a drink and a good dinner.

---

[4] So named in World War I; capable of carrying either forty men or eight horses.

Headquarters was a long way from the front, but already the spirit of the division was making itself felt, and I think the other officers sensed the same lift. That evening I learned from the division G-1, Lieutenant Colonel Bill Gleason, that I had been assigned to the 1st Battalion, 15th Infantry Regiment.

The feeling of a professional soldier for a unit with a proud record defies any rational analysis. I knew, for example, that the 1st Battalion, 15th Infantry, of July 1952 bore no resemblance to that of April 1940. Units had been reshuffled time and again. But the battalion I was joining was conscious that a unit bearing its designation had a long tradition of China service, that a Lieutenant Colonel Dwight Eisenhower had commanded it in 1940, that its record of decorations—and casualties—in World War II had been unparalleled. Audie Murphy, the most decorated American soldier in the war, had been one of its sons. None of the present personnel had been with the battalion more than a year, but I could not help feeling at home; the spirit of those that had gone before was still with them.

But one practical matter concerned me. For the sake of my own well-being I was anxious that my unit not be publicly identified. If the Chinese were kept in the dark as to my whereabouts, my concern over their special attentions would be much reduced.

The next morning, July 30, I proceeded to Headquarters, 15th Infantry. Here I was interviewed, along with the fretful doctor of the day before and a young American officer of Greek descent destined to be liaison officer to the Greek Battalion, attached to the 15th. The commanding officer was disturbed by the independent attitude of his Greeks. They fought superbly but were inclined to do things their own way. Therefore, the colonel concentrated on pleading with the young officer to discourage the Greek commander, Lieutenant Colonel Nick Tamvakas, from his habit of pulling the wires out of his telephone whenever given orders contrary to his liking.

We new officers were then informed that the 1st Battalion—my battalion—was now in the assembly area preparing to attack the next morning. This prospect took me aback. I had been well trained and had just graduated from the advance course, but to

take over a position as an active battalion S-3 a few hours before
it jumped off into an attack, without a chance to study the terrain
and enemy situation, seemed a little on the stiff side. Actually, I
had nothing to worry about; I simply did not realize yet that every
operation in this stage of the Korean War was being thoroughly
supervised through several echelons of command.

I arrived at battalion headquarters in a reserve area, comfortably
set up under canvas, about mid-afternoon and was immediately
taken in to meet the battalion commander. Lieutenant Colonel
Mills Hatfield was a West Pointer from the class of 1941, who
lectured me on the history of the 15th "Can Do" Regiment and
on the forthcoming operation. I should take the rest of the afternoon, he said, to get rested up for the night's activities. Colonel
Hatfield was a dynamic, emotional man. Part Indian, he had been
an outstanding athlete. He did, however, carry the burden of every
casualty personally. A veteran of six months in Korea, he showed
that the war had taken a severe toll on him.

Before dismissing me, Hatfield mentioned off-handedly that the
reserve area that afternoon had been receiving shell fragments.
These were coming from our own tanks, trying to blow debris
away from the White Front Bridge, the division's lifeline across
the flooded Imjin River. He sent for the presently assigned battalion operations officer, Major Red Allen,[5] and the two of us
headed back to a squad tent. I was to be Allen's understudy before
taking over. In the tent Allen got me an air mattress. I blew it up
and we stretched out to rest. I had been horizontal for about two
minutes when I heard a loud bang and found myself lying flat
on the canvas cot. A shell fragment from the tanks had gone
through the air mattress and cot, missing me by a quarter of an
inch. The fragment was still red hot. "I damn near just about set
a record for the shortest career in Korea," I said to Red. "Maybe
this is a lesson to stay off my back from now on." With this in-
spiration to keep moving, we donned our helmets and wandered
over to the battalion operations tent.

The attack was to be made on a small position—actually a
company-sized objective—called "Kelly Hill" (or just "Kelly"), one
of the tenuous outposts that our forces at that time were clinging

[5] Fictitious name.

to on mountain complexes that were actually in Chinese-held territory. B Company was to make the main assault on Kelly itself while C Company was to take position on a small hill just to the east and A Company was to execute a feint somewhat to the west on Hill 104. All of these positions were located on one complex, the bulk of which was held by CCF.

As we examined the plan, it became apparent that Allen was fuzzy-minded. He had no idea where the 75-mm recoilless rifles would be located. He was vague about the targets to be covered by the 81-mm mortars. What I soon learned was that Allen had been in on almost none of the planning and was merely waiting for me to arrive. A kind and good man—and a very practical man —he had incurred the wrath of some of the powers and his days were limited. He realized this fact and bore no resentment toward me as his replacement. He was sad, on the other hand, that this situation was causing anguish to his friend and classmate, Mills Hatfield.

At about this time the various officers of battalion headquarters began to gather in the squad tent that served as sleeping quarters. Nobody was in the mood to sleep. We therefore all lay awake talking by the light of a gas lamp until one o'clock, the time to get a cup of coffee and move out for the next morning's attack. Hatfield, Allen, and I had a cup together, whereupon Hatfield excused himself and told us to follow him soon. Allen said it would be all right if we delayed for another cup. Soon we were in a jeep making our way toward the front lines through the chill and the foggy night.

A mile or two from the former assembly area, we approached a crossroads where Colonel Hatfield was waiting. Irate, he asked where we had been. Allen shrugged the challenge off; Hatfield mounted the jeep; and the three of us went forward in the line of vehicles.

About three miles from the front the convoy reached the "light line," a point behind the next to last sharp ridge before reaching no man's land. At this point all vehicles went into black-out to conceal our movements.

After what seemed like hours of slow driving, the convoy reached the last valley. All dismounted and began the slow climb by foot to the respective jump-off points through the 2d Battalion's position along the line. This east flank overlooked the majestic, winding Imjin River which, by unfortunate circumstances, split the 15th Infantry in two almost equal-sized pieces.

In Korea almost all of the fighting was done at night; and since UN Forces were defending, it was to our advantage to illuminate the skies to avoid surprise attack. Powerful searchlights, some of them protected in armored vehicles, sat on the tops of the hills. When their beams were directed at the low clouds, the areas in front of our trenches had a brilliance equaling that of a bright moonlight night. It gave one an eerie feeling to see the men struggling up the narrow dirt road sliced out of the side of a cliff, with the pencils of white light over their heads reflecting on the clouds to their front.

Part way up the hill a soldier stumbled and fell. Red Allen was after him like a cat. The soldier had obviously fallen, not from fatigue or from accident, but from fear. After shaking the man a moment, Allen demanded his name. The soldier responded. Allen shook him again and asked him his job in the squad. The man replied almost inaudibly that he was an assistant BAR man.[6] After a few more words and a few more shakes, Allen convinced him that his BAR man needed him. The man got to his feet and with a glassy stare, staggered forward, mumbling that he had to help his BAR man. Here was a member of B Company who had been handled right. Probably he performed well for the rest of that attack.

But a few moments later Allen spied another man lying on the ground. With the same treatment, he was unable this time to make him give his name. In a rage Allen beat and kicked him. The revulsion on the part of others, themselves fearful enough of what lay ahead, was apparent even in the relative darkness of the night. Finally Allen was hauled away and the man was left lying there.[7] A few moments later Allen turned to me as a teacher to a pupil.

[6] Browning automatic rifle.

[7] Shock treatment such as Allen's has undoubtedly saved many a soldier from future disgrace. It is generally accepted when administered by a corporal or a sergeant, but not a major—nor, as with Patton, a general.

In calm tones he explained, "If a man will give you his name, he'll fight; if he won't, you can't do anything with him."

Once at the battalion OP (observation post) on the top of the ridge line, I had a certain amount of time to get oriented before the beginning of the attack. The OP was higher than Kelly Hill and its commanding view over the area of action made it seem almost like a grandstand. The three companies were moving out in sporadic downpours through two lanes cut through the mine fields; soon they were in position. As the dark became gray, I noticed to my astonishment that the dugouts in the battalion OP were occupied not only by Colonel Roye of the 2d Battalion, Colonel Hatfield, and myself; the regimental commander, the division commander, and even the corps commander were there also. All this brass was out to observe what was essentially a reinforced company attack on an isolated outpost!

The attack itself was almost an anticlimax. The artillery preparation was heavy and the troops could be seen moving across no man's land. When the light improved, B Company assaulted its objective. A Company made its feint against Hill 104 and C Company took its position according to plan. It was now early morning, July 31, less than four days since I had arrived on the peninsula and about ten days since I had been in the country club at Tacoma, Washington.

It was soon apparent that B Company's position on top of Kelly Hill had been established; the Chinese had evacuated. A Company, in its feint on Hill 104, however, had been completely repulsed, had panicked, and had wound up behind the second "safe lane" about five hundred yards to the west of our OP. C Company, of course, had no difficulty in occupying their blocking position to the east of Kelly.

Late in the morning Colonel Hatfield turned and told me to go down and tell "that damn A Company to go back out and occupy a position in the valley at the foot of Kelly." Unhappy with A Company's performance, particularly with the speed of their retreat, he was determined that they should not be allowed to call it a day. I hastened to the "safe lane" where A Company was assembled and there for the first time I met Major John Lissner, the battalion executive officer, my immediate superior. John had already been talking to A Company and had found out that the reason for their pell-mell dash to safety was the fact that about 90 per cent of their rifles had jammed in the driving rain and the mud. Indoctrinated with the teaching of the Infantry School, I doubted this was so. I took a couple of M-1 rifles from the various members of the company but was unable to open the bolts. Not satisfied with Colonel Hatfield's instructions, John Lissner then picked up a field telephone to talk to him personally. He returned and repeated the order Hatfield had given me to transmit. Lieutenant Head, one of the platoon leaders of the company, looked over and chuckled as they went out. I admired the boy and we later became friends. Fortunately, like almost all of the rest of the group, he survived the Korean War handily. Also fortunately, A Company encountered no Chinese for the rest of the day. They had been sent, actually, to a place that Hatfield knew was safe.

Having had no sleep the previous night, I was a little foggy our first day on the line, the thirty-first of July. I spent my time touring the front and peering through binoculars to see how B Company was faring on top of Kelly. Without appreciable entrenchments, our troops were taking occasional casualties from incoming mortar fire. Only that evening did they begin to entrench in the darkness and to organize themselves adequately. As nightfall came on, A and C Companies were ordered to withdraw to preplanned positions on the main line of resistance. Colonel Hatfield, as commander of the 1st Battalion, was now responsible for the area.

About ten o'clock that evening a violent explosion rocked the entire hill. Immediately Hatfield sent Allen down to the road to check the cause. On his failure to return, Hatfield sent me. The reason was soon evident: enemy artillery had hit one of our ammunition supply points, killing about twelve men. The bodies— or parts thereof—were strewn all over the ground. Allen's waiting jeep driver, Corporal Smith, had been blown out of his seat and was in a temporary state of shock. I returned to the command post and told Hatfield what had happened. Later Allen joined us, silent when asked to account for his long absence.

Hatfield, Allen, and I remained the night in the temporary CP (command post) where we had spent the previous day. As this was the second night for all of us, we took turns staying alert. In a dugout about three feet wide and twenty feet long, one of the three would pace up and down, falling asleep periodically in his walking and awakening when he would hit the wall. Red and I gave the colonel a break and pretty much split the evening between us while Hatfield collapsed on the floor. He needed the rest more than we.

The next morning, August 1, I saw the sun for the first time in Korea. Our front line was in strong hands. B Company was in the process of being relieved by a company of the 2d Battalion, attached to us for the duration of our stay in this position. Colonel Hatfield told Red and me to head back down the hill and to grab an hour or two of sleep. This we did with relish. By the afternoon, the 1st Battalion, 15th Infantry, was firmly entrenched to the west of the double bend of the Imjin and work had begun in the never-ending process of improving the position.

That afternoon Allen was ordered to return to division headquarters. Whatever his shortcomings as a battalion S-3—which probably consisted mostly of too much independence of mind—I could not condone the treatment he had received. Doubtless his services had been considered inadequate. However, if that was the case, he should have been removed at once. In the meantime, he went through an excruciating personal ordeal of waiting. I thought he showed remarkable stability and objectivity and I have always hoped that the world has been good to Red since he left the battalion.

With Allen's departure, I was now officially the battalion S-3. I came to know John Lissner and Mills Hatfield better—although Hatfield, a moody fellow, kept largely to himself. He was scheduled to leave very shortly and he was tired. I believe he felt that the lives of a lot of men were being expended uselessly. He regarded me with only a mild curiosity and, while I think he would have liked to have been friends, restricted his conversation to official matters. In one exceptional outburst he told how it had hurt to have to get rid of his classmate Red. Then he clammed up.

On August 3, two days after the Kelly Hill action, I was ordered to report to division headquarters. This day happened to be my thirtieth birthday, but of course the occasion had nothing to do with that; I was to talk to the press. On arriving at headquarters, I learned that one reporter had published my unit assignment. Angered by this, I talked to the newsmen in rather severe terms about the amount of interest they were showing in me while exhibiting indifference regarding the important Kelly Hill action. The newsmen for the most part took it as part of the game, although one man from the New York *Herald Tribune,* Mac Johnson, later wrote me in a rather philosophical vein about my outburst. I did not care much about the views of Mac Johnson at the moment; Major General Robert Dulaney, the division commander, agreed with my viewpoint and I went back to the battalion, reassured by his support.

The days on the Imjin were full of new experiences. One illuminated the psychological effect of the "point" system of rotation home.[8] A lieutenant, the pioneer and ammunition platoon leader, had done a dangerous job well, had been decorated, and was highly respected by all members of the battalion. The day his replacement arrived, he was officially relieved from duty but not yet allowed to depart. He retired to his bunker, lay on his canvas cot, and occupied his entire day tracking bugs with an aerosol bomb. This he did for a solid week, never moving. His friends would come in one by one, sit down on a box beside his bed, chat amiably, drink one can of beer, and depart; the lieutenant would converse cheerfully without moving an unnecessary muscle, exerting only enough effort to keep the spray going. When his appointed day arrived, he left with the accolades of the battalion and his jeep headed down the winding road to the rear.

Once settled into position, we tried to maintain some elements of garrison discipline. Colonel Hatfield, for example, had a little fetish that the battalion CP was being guarded sloppily. He told me to see that the guards challenged properly at night, according to the field manuals. One day, before our usual evening trip up the hill, I drilled the sentry thoroughly, rehearsing the ritual time and

---

[8] Persons with enough "points" were reassigned to the States. A battalion on the line received four a month; it required about thirty to go home.

again. Later the colonel and I went up, completed our business, and returned. As we approached the CP entrance, I was expecting a loud "Halt! Who is there?" When we reached the gate, however, no challenge rang out. The jeep stopped and waited. Finally a voice came softly from the darkness: "That *you*, Colonel?"

Those days on the line left vivid impressions of Colonel Hatfield, trudging out to outpost Kelly to check on the welfare of his men, coming back through a "safe lane" well zeroed-in on by the enemy . . . of making liaison with the Canadians on our left, the "Princess Pats," who believed in living like gentlemen within a thousand yards of the enemy . . . of the interminable digging that went on to prepare the position . . . of the pleasure in the evening of walking up on the hill to take a few shots from a tank at likely targets . . . of meticulous planning for counterattacks in the exposed valley along our left flank . . . of talking casually with Colonel Hatfield in the battalion CP while severe Chinese shelling went on . . . of a marine aviator, his Corsair hit by enemy fire, parachuting into Chinese territory within two thousand yards of our front lines . . . of checking the moonlight every night to evaluate the likelihood of an attack. All of these vignettes made a vivid picture in a few short weeks of my life.

Mills Hatfield was probably not with 1st Battalion for more than two weeks from the time I reported. But it seemed like a year or two. During the period of our association, I came to feel great respect for him. Only on his last night did he relax. That evening John Lissner and I were invited into his little log-cabin bunker, dug snugly into the side of the mountain. We had a few cans of beer, took aim at the rats running about the ceiling—which we regarded as pets—and reminisced about West Point. Hatfield left the next day without ceremony.

The 1st Battalion, 15th Infantry, moved off the line in early September. Left in charge of the battalion relief, I spent the night at a crossroads in a heavy warm rain, checking each company as it arrived and directing it to its trucks. I suspected that my days in combat with the 15th Infantry were probably numbered, so I savored every moment. I felt that I was having a good sample of service, if not a long experience, with a fine unit.

Soon thereafter the entire 15th Infantry Regiment was relieved by the 65th. The 1st Battalion moved down to the Kimpo Peninsula to provide the regimental reserve for the Provisional Marine Regiment of the 1st Marine Division. Here, in a quiet sector, we trained and enjoyed the respite. When the battalion was about to move back to rejoin the 3d Division, the blow fell: I was ordered to report to division headquarters at Chipyong-ni. In the meantime we had learned that the 65th Infantry had lost Kelly Hill to the Chinese, with B Company of that regiment being captured almost intact.

I reported to division headquarters for duty with G-3 in a depressed mood. This was hardly eased by the fact that the division was in an uproar over another effort by our sister regiment, the 65th, to regain Kelly. I was astonished to observe the detail in which higher commanders dealt with what was essentially a reinforced company attack. The commanding general of the division was personally checking on the location of every recoilless weapon in the battalion, and the blown-up contour map of Kelly far surpassed in quality anything that had ever been available to our battalion in July. It was no wonder that Red Allen had been in the dark as to the placement of his own weapons!

The move from S-3 and acting executive officer of the 1st Battalion to that of division operations officer was a come-down. In the battalion, the commander who had taken over from Mills Hatfield had practically let me run the outfit, particularly while we were on the line. Now my duties consisted primarily of sitting on an operations desk and, with the aid of a sergeant and a clerk, keeping the map up to date and recording incoming messages regarding troop movements and patrols. The job was hardly one for which I was qualified. And from a selfish, creature-comfort point of view, gone was my jeep, my own wall tent, and my houseboy. This short period represented the nadir of my stay in Korea.

This personal malaise was dwarfed by the frustrations the 3d Division commander was undergoing. Our 65th Infantry Regiment (Puerto Rican) had become practically ineffective as a fighting unit. This regrettable situation was nobody's fault except for some G-1 at EUSAK, who had declared that all English-speaking Puerto Ricans be assigned to other divisions. The regiment had achieved an outstanding reputation in the early days of the Korean War when bilingual NCOs could act as a bridge of communication between our continental (English-speaking) officers and our Puerto Rican soldiers. All these NCOs were now gone. As a result the 65th suffered disaster after disaster.[9]

Paradoxically, the division's difficulties brought about my emancipation from the operations desk. Major General George W. Smythe, who had replaced General Dulaney as division commander, grasped the problem of the 65th Infantry immediately and told my boss, Lieutenant Colonel Henry A. Barber III, that he wanted a staff study written for submission to higher headquarters. I volunteered with alacrity and Hal, after a moment's pause, decided I was the man to do the job.

When I reported to the general's tent, he knew exactly what he wanted. "John," he said, "that regiment can't fight the way it's set up. I want it thrown out of the division or integrated with Puerto Ricans and Continentals like they are in every other division. Now write a study and make it logical." I set to work with enthusiasm. For a few weeks I was to be the division G-3 "projects officer."

I have always wondered whether General Smythe knew what he was doing to me. I was assigned this job only two weeks before election time 1952, an event that the general never referred to but which was much on my mind when I gave myself the chance. The day the returns came in, swarms of newspaper people—perhaps twenty—arrived at division headquarters to sit and watch me like something under a microscope and to report my every reaction. I immediately took refuge in Hal Barber's van, where I could work and not be observed. I did, however, succumb to the wiles of one bespectacled war correspondent who promised to keep me informed on the progress of the election and generously pledged not to disclose my location to any other correspondents. As I worked away, my study nearly completed, the reporter came periodically to the van to deliver news of the election.

He never had a gloomy dispatch. From the very beginning, Dad's lead was commanding; the UNIVAC machines early predicted a landslide. However, the tension was such that with every

---

[9] On one occasion an entire company abandoned their five continental officers on the top of a hill called "Jackson Heights."

report I received from my friend, I reacted with some joyous response, invariably with some normal soldier profanity. What I did not know was that my friend was recording every single word. I later had some cause for embarrassment when my words appeared, every one of them, in print.

When the final results were known late in the afternoon, I responded to the pressure of the press group and went back to my tent where the correspondents were gathered. In a festive mood, I pulled a case of Bourbon and Scotch from under my canvas cot and poured drinks for the crowd. All the reporters, regardless of their own personal political persuasions, joined into the spirit of the occasion. The sound of artillery—outgoing fortunately—was in our ears. One enjoyable aspect was the reunion with the correspondent Mac Johnson, who had been somewhat resentful of my press conference the previous August. He sat on a foot locker, telling me lugubriously that if there were ever any news going out of the war zone whatsoever, the Army would be happy to suppress it. I found that Mac was a fellow I would like if I had a chance to run across him again.

The climax of the day came when some brilliant correspondents decided they needed a picture of General Smythe congratulating me on my father's election. It is difficult to describe how embarrassing a situation like this could be to a young major, assistant G-3 of a division. Nevertheless, the civilian world took over and General Smythe, always a good sport, eased the situation tremendously.

The next break in routine came when I heard that Dad was about to arrive in Korea on the trip he had promised to make during the presidential campaign. In early December I was ordered to report once more to General James Van Fleet's Eighth Army headquarters in Seoul. I was on hand just in time to meet the incoming group.

For some reason or other, the cold weather during these three days impressed me more than at any other time. Perhaps this was because our schedule kept us standing out in the open more than would have been normal; or perhaps the fact that I had been privileged to have a couple of hot showers and a warm place to sleep for the first time in a long while made the cold, when we were out in it, seem more extreme. Whatever the circumstances, Dad's party traveled from place to place, from the 1st Marine Division to Kimpo Airfield, to a couple of American divisions, to the British Commonwealth division, and at one point to a training demonstration, accompanied by Korean President Syngman Rhee, performed by the Capital ROK Division.

The high point of the visit was, to me, an outdoor lunch with my old outfit, the 1st Battalion, 15th Infantry. Here everybody ate in the snow and Dad, bundled up in a pile jacket and thermo boots, talked to three selected young soldiers of the regiment. One of the three was killed on patrol within the week after Dad's departure.

The last evening I accompanied Dad when he called on President Rhee, but the other evenings were informal. The main value of Dad's trip, as I saw it, was the chance for this group of people to become acquainted on a relaxed basis. Along with him Dad had Secretary of Defense-designate Charles E. Wilson, General Omar Bradley, Admiral Arthur W. Radford, General Mark W. Clark, General James Van Fleet, Attorney General-designate Herbert Brownell, and Dad's press secretary, James C. Hagerty. The prospects for the war were discussed behind closed doors; I was not included. In the air was a note of impending command change. General Van Fleet, I picked up, was about to leave, as Dad mentioned to him once that "Max" would be coming soon.[10] General Bradley's tour in Washington as Chairman of the Joint Chiefs was also about over. I do not recall whether Admiral Radford was then being considered as Bradley's successor; but of course such turned out to be the case.

Plans for reorganization of the Defense Department when the war should be finished were reportedly discussed in some detail aboard the cruiser *Helena* when the party returned across the Pacific. However, while Dad was in Seoul all attention was focused on the Korean problem itself. If he already had the germ of the idea which was eventually to bring war to an end, he gave no indication.

Since conversations that I was a witness to were all informal, the information I was able to pick up came in the form of tidbits.

[10] Maxwell D. Taylor, Van Fleet's successor.

One evening, for example, Dad was talking to General Clark, my old boss in Vienna and now commanding the UN Forces, regarding the attitude of President Rhee. With all his faults, Rhee was a truly great war leader. He had been exiled, imprisoned, and tortured by the Japanese, and his devotion to Korea was impassioned. With Rhee, the George Washington of Korea, at the helm, we never experienced the political difficulties that the United States was later to find so frustrating in Vietnam.

But Rhee, aside from his admittedly dictatorial tendencies, suffered from the fact that he had never recovered from his hatred of the Japanese. Clark, according to his story, was having difficulties in keeping Rhee's attention focused on the Chinese Communists. Given the choice, believe it or not, Rhee would have liked to use a few divisions to invade Japan. In a recent conversation, Clark said, Rhee had murmured, "I don't really think this is the proper time to invade Japan."

"No, it seems to me it would be most inappropriate," Clark had answered smoothly.

This must have been the understatement of the year.

Not all the conversations pertained to the major problems at hand, however. At one of our relaxed moments I found myself in a three-cornered discussion with two five-star generals, Dad and Bradley, on the ideal organization of the infantry division. Our points were perhaps technical and theoretical, but the incident illustrates the propensity of soldiers to talk shop and, like other human beings, to differ in their views based on their individual, subjective experiences.

For me personally, one conversation was disturbing. Within a month or two, General Van Fleet told me, I would be sent to Japan. This early transfer was an option given to all personnel in Korea. Only in my case, because my father was President-elect, I was to be given no choice. (Obviously, I was not welcome in Korea among the generals.) While I was later able to fend off the transfer, through Dad's intervention and to General Clark's displeasure, I was coming to realize more and more that Dad's new situation could become a possible cause of inconvenience. At the end of the three days I saw the party off at the airport, bound for Guam. I then returned to the 3d Division.

Almost immediately on my return I was called upon by General Smythe to organize a "skunk hunt." A "skunk hunt" in the terminology of the day, was a ferreting out of potential Communist agents within a division sector. In a static situation of this type, it was inevitable, despite directives, admonitions, and threats, that U.S. units would pick up civilian Koreans as houseboys and orderlies. Also, perhaps, some hostile Koreans may have been skulking around to live off the fat of the land as best they could—we later found a couple of Chinese hiding in the hills—but all bona fide civilians were excluded from the combat zone.

This was a new type of problem—not in the books. Trying to be as logical and fair as I could, I laid out areas for all of the rear echelon elements to begin screening at a preordained moment.

The operation jumped off the morning of December 19, 1952, with long lines of rear-area troops of all sizes and shapes advancing at about six foot intervals across expansive territories, beating the bushes and scaring out all unauthorized Koreans. I observed the operation in comfort from a Cessna L-19 airplane, insuring that the instructions were being followed. At the end of the day, a certain number of Koreans had been rounded up, almost all of whom, I am sure, were merely illegal houseboys. That afternoon I was appointed acting G-2 of the division.

Shortly after this episode, the division moved back to reserve once more and entered into another phase of training. By virtue of my new position as acting G-2, I now had my own van, a small house mounted on the back of a standard truck. Although it was as cold as a tent, I was beginning to feel that I amounted to something. My father-in-law, Colonel Thompson, a veteran of earlier campaigns in the Korean War, had sent me some canned ham and my mother, in response to a rather modest request, had sent with Dad's plane a gallon of cherries and a crate of lemons for making old fashioneds at the cocktail hour. I immediately contributed these commodities to the general's mess, of which I was now a member. All this made for a pleasanter life.

Hardly had we settled back in our reserve position when a bombshell broke.

On January 8, 1953, I received a telegram instructing me to

20. General Omar N. Bradley. Photo taken in early 1945.

21. "By prior arrangement with the Russians, the Allies had halted along the line of the Elbe and the Mulde. . . . The Russians had not yet reached the other side of the Mulde River, and thousands of German soldiers were making their way across the remnants of a destroyed bridge. . . ." Photo taken by the author on April 25, 1945.

22. "Buchenwald had been liberated only two or three days . . . a good many of [the prisoners], though still alive, would die of malnutrition . . . the crime perpetrated at Buchenwald was too much fully to comprehend."

23. "A little after noon, Stalin [invited] Dad, Ambassador Harriman, and General Dean [to join] Stalin and his group. . . . I later learned that Dad was the first foreigner over to be allowed this courtesy." Stalin, his guests, and entourage atop Lenin's Tomb, August 12, 1945.

24. ". . . for an hour and a half, members of the different youth organizations throughout Russia strutted by. Some were Mongols, some were Georgians, some were . . . Baltic people; but they were all alike in their enthusiastic smiles on their faces and in their splendid builds." Physical culture parade, Red Square, August 12, 1945.

25. "No personal animosity was involved [in Patton's transfer from the Third Army]. The two generals went to a football game together in Frankfurt a couple of days after the switch-over." D.D.E. and General George S. Patton, Jr. Note the Fifteenth Army patch worn by Patton on his left shoulder.

26. ". . . Barbara and I managed to make matters difficult . . . we put unreasonable pressure on the Thompsons to schedule the wedding as soon as possible." Colonel and Mrs. Percy W. Thompson at our wedding on June 10, 1947.

27. "The years spent instructing at West Point were happy ones. Two of our children were born there: Dwight David II in 1948 and Barbara Anne in 1949." David Eisenhower being held by his godfather, Bo Horkan, in 1948.

28. "The feeling of the professional soldier for a unit with a proud record defies any rational analysis. I know, for example, that the 1st battalion, 15th Infantry Regiment, of July 1952 bore no resemblance to that of April 1940. . . . None of the present personnel had been with the battalion more than a year, but I could not help feeling at home; the spirit of those that had gone before was still with them." J.S.D.E. newly assigned as operations officer, 1st Battalion, 15th Infantry, 3d Division, in Korea.

29. "The press once delighted in playing up an animosity between [Truman and Eisenhower] which certainly had some basis but has been grossly exaggerated, at least on Dad's part . . . however, the photograph taken when Dad visited the White House for a briefing portrays anything but an atmosphere of cordiality."

30. Eisenhower family reunion on my return from Korea.

31. Dwight David Eisenhower II, age five, hitting a practice golf ball at Fort Benning, Georgia.

32, 33. "On talking with Zhukov that evening, I quickly sensed that this was not the same cocky little rooster we had known in Germany at the end of the war. During the interim we had heard stories that Zhukov had fallen out of favor with Stalin. . . . that evening Zhukov was there, alive but broken. . . . Dad and I concluded that Zhukov was being included in the ruling group only as a façade." Zhukov (*left*) as he appeared in 1945 and (*right*) as we saw him in Geneva a decade later.

proceed immediately to K-14 airfield for transportation to the United States, obviously to attend my father's inauguration. There was much misunderstanding about this episode. I was hardly one to demur about coming back to such an important event; but I had just been appointed to a position which I prized, one which promised promotion to lieutenant colonel. If I were to be away too long the division might have to find a replacement. I sent a message of protest by quickest possible means back to my father.

I received no answer from the United States. However, I was assured by the division chief of staff that my precious spot would be held for me. Without further ado, I took an L-19 to Kimpo and was soon on my way via Tokyo to the United States.

When I landed at LaGuardia Airport in New York, I was surprised to find Dad out to meet me. After a quick stop with Mother in New York, I made my way to Highland Falls, where my family waited for a joyous reunion.

Barbara and I had three or four days at home before going to New York to make preparations for Inauguration. On January 12 I attended one of the preinauguration cabinet meetings.

These preinauguration cabinet meetings were, to the best of my knowledge, the first ever held by a President-elect. The future members of the Eisenhower Administration sat around in a horseshoe-shaped table at the Commodore Hotel in New York and discussed the policies they would try to begin implementing on inauguration. Dad's basic purpose on this day was to give his general philosophy of the responsibilities of each of his future associates, more specifically to stress his basic philosophy that no cabinet member was to think in terms of his own department alone. Obviously remembering his days as Chief of Staff of the Army, he wanted to insure that everyone took the broadest possible view of his own specific job. He read and accepted comments on his forthcoming inaugural address. The group later discussed certain proposed subcabinet appointments.

The figure that interested me most in the new Cabinet was Martin Durkin, the nominee to be Secretary of Labor. Durkin, head of the American Federation of Labor's Plumbers' Union and a firm supporter of Adlai Stevenson's in the 1952 campaign, had been selected because of his high reputation for integrity. The duties of Secretary of Labor, as Dad saw it, were a little different from those of the rest of the Cabinet: that secretary, he felt, should be a definite partisan supporter—a spokesman if you will—of labor.[11]

The other members, while accepting Durkin, seemed prone to regard him as something of a novelty. In for more than his share of banter, Durkin seemed to take what must have been a bewildering situation with remarkably good grace.

After the meeting Senator Henry Cabot Lodge asked me privately about conditions existing in Korea. His son was about to be assigned there as an artillery forward observer. I was able to assure the senator that Korea was actually good duty and, in the present stabilized situation, not particularly dangerous. Lodge seemed somewhat reassured but still skeptical.

After the train ride to Washington the evening of January 19, the Eisenhower party settled into the Statler Hotel. A large, festive family reunion was already in progress.

The morning of Inauguration Day Dad pulled Barbara and me aside. Standing beside the mantelpiece of the presidential suite, he produced a little prayer he had composed, apparently during the service at the National Presbyterian Church that morning. He read it to us with great earnestness and we were moved by the whole idea. He had tried it out on others, Mother at least. Apparently satisfied that he had a quorum of votes, he delivered the prayer before embarking on his formal inauguration speech.

A theologian might smile at Dad's strict delineation of who was doing the beseeching for the help of the Almighty; but the idea, the spirit, was the important matter. Its impact has been proven by the fact that it has been so often referred to in the twenty years since he composed it.[12]

[11] As it later turned out, Dad seemed to modify this viewpoint somewhat and Durkin seemed to take his responsibilities as the "devil's advocate" too seriously. The two soon parted on cordial terms.

[12] "Almighty God, as we stand here at this moment my future associates in the Executive branch of government join me in beseeching that Thou will make full and complete our dedication to the service of the people in this throng, and their fellow citizens everywhere.

"Give us, we pray, the power to discern clearly right from wrong, and allow all our words and actions to be governed thereby, and by the laws of this land. Es-

In my lifetime I have attended five inaugurations, and the ceremonies, once under way, are fairly stereotyped. The main difference between inauguration ceremonies lies in the circumstance of the occasion. Those in which a President is succeeding himself tend to be much more relaxed and jovial, as the guests await the event, than those in which a new political party has just been voted into power. The latter, of course, was the case in January 1953.

Barbara and I were placed up front with Mother for this one—we had left our children with friends in Highland Falls—and the Trumans were treated with every possible consideration, with Mrs. Truman and Truman's daughter, Margaret, up front also. Former President Herbert Hoover was close at hand. But the atmosphere, while correct, was hardly warm. Though I stood almost next to Mr. Truman, he never spoke. Nor did I, out of respect for his obvious desires. The atmosphere was a bit chilly, in fact, with little of the handshaking and visiting among guests that have seemed to characterize other such ceremonies, even the Kennedy inauguration of 1961.

In the course of the morning one mystery was cleared up, or at least mostly so. Dad and I had been puzzled as to who had actually ordered me home from Korea. Neither General Bradley nor General J. Lawton Collins, then Army Chief of Staff, knew anything about it. As Dad and President Truman were driving up Pennsylvania Avenue to the Capitol, however, Dad asked the President if he could throw light on the subject. "Just tell him that that crochety old man in the White House did it" was the answer. Nothing more was said. Since the order had bypassed normal command channels, I conjectured for years that it had gone from Truman to his military aide, Major General Harry Vaughan, thence to the Adjutant General of the Army. It would be nineteen years later, when I visited Mr. Truman at his home in Independence, Missouri, that my theory would be confirmed.

---

pecially we pray that our concern shall be for all the people regardless of station, race, or calling.

"May cooperation be permitted and be the mutual aim of those who, under the concepts of our Constitution, hold to differing political faiths; so that all may work for the good of our beloved country and Thy glory. Amen."

The episode has been widely misinterpreted by any who have been interested. I was pictured as angry about coming home. On the contrary, once my position in the 3d Division was secure, I was delighted. I always appreciated Mr. Truman's kind gesture, and only the frosty atmosphere of the time prevented my expressing it.

It might be well here to touch on the relationship between Dad and President Truman. The press has delighted in playing up an animosity between the two which certainly had basis in fact but has been grossly exaggerated, at least on Dad's part.

At the end of World War II I do not believe that Dad held any opinion one way or another about Truman, not knowing him well personally. He certainly sympathized with and supported his superior—it was impossible, especially in Truman's earlier years, to dislike him—but Dad always referred to him, even in talking to me, simply as "the President." Truman, on the other hand, showed every evidence of regarding both Dad and General Marshall with adulation. Despite Dad's protests, Truman said at one time that if both he and Marshall concurred in any course of action, he would follow it. And there are adequate witnesses to attest to Truman's offering his own help to raise Dad to the presidency if given the go-ahead.

After Truman's upset election victory over Thomas E. Dewey in 1948, however, his own self-confidence grew markedly; and while he seemed to retain his admiration for Dad, he was less lavish in his statements after that time. He selected Dad as the first Supreme Commander, Allied Powers in Europe (SACEUR) in 1950 as the only man capable of performing an almost impossible task. This appointment, while it may have had some political implications, seems to bear out his continuing high regard.

On the other hand, there is no question that Truman's performance as President fell short of Dad's expectations. He was rather alarmed, for example, with what he considered Truman's hesitation of a couple of days in committing ground troops to Korea in June 1950; and when Dad was visiting Washington in December of that year, having just been nominated by Truman as SACEUR, he expressed to me his disgust with the terrified atmosphere pervading all of Washington, from the President on down. Nevertheless, Dad supported Truman's relieving General MacArthur from the Far East Command, sharing the attitude of many others that Truman could do nothing else. And upon departure for Europe in early 1951 there is no question that Dad sided with Truman against Senator Robert A. Taft and other Republicans who, he thought, were trying to cut the President down to size. Dad has written of his secret meeting with Taft, in which he retained some threat of entering politics as a lever to discourage Taft's going too far.

Actually the two men—Truman and Dad—saw pretty much eye to eye on foreign affairs; and in late 1951, while Dad was in Paris, Truman wrote him to the effect that Dad's political plans would affect his own. If Dad were to run for President, the letter implied, Truman would feel safe to retire at the end of his current term.

Dad's announcement in early 1952 that he was a Republican destroyed the rapport between him and the President. Fiercely partisan, Truman, apparently surprised, now regarded Dad as a member of an opposing political camp. It can be surmised that Truman might have considered running against this upstart Republican until his own crushing defeat in the New Hampshire primary of March 1952. After that, it was apparent that Truman would stand little chance of re-election against any Republican; he might not even be nominated by the Democrats. By this time Dad had become convinced that the country could hardly survive another four years of Democratic administration, meaning principally Truman.

The nature of the 1952 campaign was hardly one to cause endearment between the two. Dad was constantly on the attack; and though his actual opponent was Adlai Stevenson, the major issues were Truman's handling of the Korean War and the "mess in Washington." By the term "mess in Washington" Dad meant more than petty graft; he meant as well the fact that Truman had completely lost control of his Administration, particularly in regard to fiscal policy.

After the end of the campaigning Truman seemed to take the attitude that politics are politics, whereas Dad had become so embroiled in the issues that he was dead serious in every accusation he was making. The clincher came when Truman offered Dad the use of his Presidential airplane, the *Independence,* in order to fulfill a campaign promise to visit Korea, adding *"if you still want to go."* This dig hit Dad as tantamount to calling him a liar, implying that his statement was a mere political gambit rather than a pledge.

From that time on the two were on cool terms, and the photograph taken when Dad visited the White House for a briefing portrays anything but an atmosphere of cordiality. After inauguration, communications became practically nonexistent. Truman seems to have been just as sensitive as he was forthright and apparently was hurt that Dad had no intention of drawing on his knowledge and experience in beginning the new Administration.

Dad, being a secure and confident individual, could never carry a strong dislike for anyone for any length of time. But he also had a considerable capacity for simply writing off anyone whose abilities he did not particularly admire—and unfortunately Truman fell into that category.

Truman grew increasingly sensitive. Once, for example, he claimed that Dad refused to receive him for a courtesy call in Kansas City. Nobody I have talked to among Dad's associates has ever admitted to hearing first-hand of the phone call that Truman claimed to have made. I know that Dad would never have been so discourteous, but, in the confusion of the times, Truman might have tried and failed to get through to him. Whatever the facts, Truman, undergoing the withdrawal symptoms of leaving power, took the incident very much to heart.

Several times during the Eisenhower Administration Dad invited Truman to the White House. I drafted one of the letters. Truman always had cogent reasons not to attend.

At the end of Dad's Administration, Truman's pique appeared to have mellowed considerably, although in 1962, at the age of seventy-seven, he allegedly gave an interview for future publication in which he castigated not only Dad but also Richard Nixon and MacArthur in astonishing terms. In November 1963, however, at the funeral of John F. Kennedy, the two former Presidents, accompanied by Mother and Truman's daughter Margaret, lunched together congenially at Blair House. Truman's ability to swing

from kindness to vitriol and back was to me one of his most un-
fathomable characteristics.

The last time I saw President Truman was at his home in
Independence, Missouri, in March of 1972. He and Mrs. Truman
(who had never been a part of the misunderstandings) were the
soul of hospitality. But I do conjecture that the breakdown of the
friendship between these two strong-willed individuals remained
a source of some pain to the thirty-third President of the United
States.

After the inauguration ceremonies the presidential guests were
led into the Capitol for a buffet luncheon. We were then hustled
out early to precede the Inauguration Parade back to the White
House. Nana, Barbara, and I went into the White House lobby
and looked around before the parade arrived. Nana was concerned
that we were breaking all the laws of the Medes and Persians
by entering before Mother and Dad. I could never understand
exactly why. Probably it stemmed from her innate sense of
propriety that we should avoid entering someone else's house
without their invitation. Perhaps she had a little private supersti-
tion. At any rate, I felt little inhibition and the weather outside
was cold. At the appointed time we went out and took our places
on the reviewing stand on Pennsylvania Avenue. The walls of
the White House did not come tumbling down.

The Inauguration Parade was an extravaganza. Twenty years
out of power, the Republicans were losing no chance to pull out
the stops. The ordeal was unreasonably long considering the
weather, but Dad saluted just as smartly for the last float as for
the first. One of the notable incidents was his allowing himself
to be roped—literally—by a brash fellow named Monty Montana
(from Montana). The Secret Service winced but allowed him.
After dark the ceremonies eventually came to a close and the
presidential party retired to the State Dining Room of the White
House where some welcome food had been spread out. Of great
importance to me was the presence of General Gee Gerow, the
grand marshal of the parade. Gee told me that he had received
favorable reports on my performance in Korea which, of course,
coming from a top soldier, set me up considerably. That evening

the family attended the two inaugural balls. Much too late, we collapsed in bed.

For the next couple of days Barbara and I stayed in the Queen's Room in the White House. We were amused that the large room with the double bed was assigned to me. Barbara was assigned to a rather small sewing room in the back. Being generous by nature, and recently home from Korea, I invited her to join me. We were somewhat surprised at the European influence in the Executive Mansion.

Our vacation back in Highland Falls was much too short but had to come to an end. After a few days relaxing and visiting friends I left, heavy-hearted, for the return to Korea. This parting was more difficult than the one the previous July, perhaps because the excitement of Korea was no longer present as a palliative. I climbed in the Secret Service car with Special Agent John Powers and we drove to New York City. The trip back, via Travis Air Force Base and Japan, was swift. I crossed the Pacific in a rather harum-scarum chartered DC-4, to Hawaii, to Wake, to Tokyo. Before I knew it I was landing at a small air strip behind the new 3d Division position, this time on the eastern shoulder of the Ch'orwon Valley.

The nostalgia that had followed me all the way across the Pacific, however, was dispelled very shortly when I rode into the division CP. Almost immediately I was brought in to report to General Smythe, who appointed me *permanent*—no longer a precarious "acting"—G-2, retroactive to the previous December 19.

It was still daylight when I left the general's office to look around. To my astonishment my precious van was nowhere in sight. Everyone was highly mysterious. Mortified and hurt, I was ushered to a hut which was to be my home for the next several months. At least, however, my friend and former boss, Hal Barber, was to share it with me. Much later I discovered that since Hal and I were so close, this was a precautionary measure. Security people were still concerned that the Chinese might try to kidnap me. Hal Barber, one of the heaviest sleepers that I know, was supposedly my bodyguard. When this fact finally came to my attention, I had to laugh at this rather feeble safety precaution.

Our new location was in somewhat more mountainous country than our previous one further west at Ch'orwon. As the continental divide in Korea is only a few miles from the east coast, the almost alpine terrain in the east tapers off as one travels westward. Our position now was almost in the middle of the peninsula and any major Chinese attack toward Seoul would have to overrun us. Our defensive terrain was good. Our main headaches were the high hills in front of us—717,[13] 632, and "Papa-San" (1062). These gave the enemy unobstructed observation over our front lines; but our light aircraft, flying over CCF territory, more than compensated. Our men on the main line of resistance lived their daily lives, protected themselves from shellings, and became at times overly confident. It was difficult to restrain them, for example, from hanging their laundry out to dry in full sight of the enemy. But the patrols were always costly and the outposts always threatened. Our main one, occupied in company strength, stood almost in the middle of the division sector, known as "Outpost (OP) Harry." Fortified elaborately, OP Harry was to become a battle ground of some of the greatest drama that the division was to know in Korea.

In gathering intelligence about the enemy, aerial reconnaissance was of primary value. But coverage of the front lines by the Air Force was almost always highly disappointing, probably because Eighth Army had higher priority requirements. To make up for this weakness, the 3d Division Light Air, equipped with our workhorse L-19s, fitted out their two photographic planes with cameras of exceptionally long focal length. The division light aircraft could thus fly high, fairly safely, and photograph our own front quite adequately. Soon we almost ceased to bother to ask for Air Force reconnaissance.

Strangely, the word came that the news of this division capability had caused resentment in the Air Force, who felt we were infringing on their job. Such is the nature of bureaucracy.

Another source of enemy information was, of course, interrogation of prisoners of war. The trouble here was that we were taking

[13] The hills are designated by the number of meters above sea level. Thus "717" would be a hill, shown on the map, with an altitude of about 2,400 feet.

no prisoners. Rarely did our small patrols in no man's land encounter the enemy at close range, and sending combat patrols into the enemy's trenches cost too dearly in lives. The critical and painful judgment in war is evaluating what anything—terrain, information, or destruction—is worth in terms of risk to one's own troops. Fortunately General Smythe felt that combat patrols into enemy positions to obtain prisoners were simply not worth it.

One experience, however, gave me some sort of a feeling of what we were up against in dealing with the CCF. An enemy attack was made in early spring against Company K of our 7th Infantry Regiment, located under Papa-San. Perhaps half a dozen enemy lay wounded fifty yards from our trenches. Before our men could reach them, however, a heavy barrage of CCF artillery came in on top of them. The fire was accurate; none survived. The Chinese had no intention of allowing their own people to be captured alive.

Only a few days later I got word that a captured Chinese was lying in an aid station. I hurried to the spot with an interrogation team. On our arrival the doctor confronted me with a problem: "Major," he said, "if you keep this man here too long he'll lose his leg. If you think it's worth it, I'll let it happen. The judgment is yours." This balance between humanitarian and military factors worried me, and I hedged, asking the doctor to let me know when the man's leg would be approaching the danger point. When our interrogators began to work, however, we soon realized the man had little to offer of value. No gun positions, nothing. He was evacuated quickly.

We also sent agents through the lines. The attitude of the American soldiers toward these people was something less than warm, and the agents' most dangerous period was the moment they approached American lines on the way back. But since in Korea the action was normally fought at night, our front lines in the daytime sometimes became a model of lethargy. Once, when an agent was re-entering the American trenches in the middle of the day, he could find nobody to report to. He searched in vain for a while and finally found an officer asleep in his bunker. He tapped the officer to awaken him. The American, startled, got up and shook hands with the Korean and then at first chance grabbed a gun and stuck it in his ribs. The man was duly bound and blind-folded before being sent to the rear.

I must confess that the intelligence officer at division level was able to do little to really affect the dispositions of the division. In essence, we studied the maps, decided on logical avenues of approach, analyzed our aerial photos—which gave us 90 per cent of our intelligence—and recommended troop disposition on the basis of judgment available to any trained Army officer. The rest was somewhat of a game played among the so-called "intelligence community."

As the months dragged on in the spring of 1953, the size of enemy attacks seemed to grow. This was welcome as far as we were concerned, because by coming out in the open the enemy was exposed and vulnerable. While our fire exacted heavy casualties, the CCF could do little harm to our entrenched troops. Thus the intelligence information grew and our confidence grew along with it.

The outposts were something else. At the same time, the enemy began to make a really concerted effort to reduce all the outposts along the Eighth Army line of contact. To the best of my knowledge and recollection, our own OP Harry was the only one that survived. One reason it held was the shape of the terrain. By fortunate circumstances OP Harry lay on a table of land slanting toward our position, thus making it easy for us to support it by tank fire on three sides. Another factor was the determination on the part of our new division commander, Major General Eugene Ridings, that this outpost should not fall. Company after company he sent up there, each suffering severe casualties. Two a night went up that hill, one replacing the other. After a vicious four-day battle, OP Harry still held. It was now a pile of powder; thirty thousand rounds of artillery were reported on one night. Later, after the armistice, when both sides were given a few days to clean up their former positions, a friend told me that he had found 3d Division men buried eight feet underground. I have little time for those who say the American soldier performed poorly in Korea.

The routine was broken sharply in the second half of June

1953. By this time it looked as if a truce might be signed. Unbeknownst to us, considerable diplomatic activity had been going on which had apparently convinced the Chinese that they had better cease their obstructionist tactics in the truce talks, still going on in Panmunjom since late 1951.[14]

But although the United Nations and the Communists were coming close to terms, President Rhee of South Korea, who lived and breathed the concept of an attack to the north, remained adamant against any peace that failed to unite the country. He took matters into his own hands. Part of the embryo agreement being negotiated was the return of prisoners of war.

When it looked as if the truce might be signed, Rhee secretly released 25,000 non-Communist North Koreans on the streets of Seoul. These prisoners were of little consequence to either side, although possibly the Communists wanted them for punishment. But Rhee's act implied that the United States could not be counted on to commit its own ally and placed us in a highly embarrassing position of bad faith. (I have learned since that the concern in the White House was acute.) Despite the fact that we were being given no dispatches on the subject, I could well sense, as could all my friends, the seriousness of the situation.

My first reaction was one of amusement. My roommate and watchdog, Hal Barber, was about to be shipped home the day after this happened. His anguish over having his departure delayed somehow tickled my funny bone. I predicted that we might have to fight a rear-guard action all the way to Seoul, although I suppose that this would really not have been a funny thing at all.

As it turned out, no such thing happened. The Chinese pro-

14 Dwight D. Eisenhower, *Mandate for Change*, p. 181: "The lack of progress in the long-stalemated talks—they were then recessed—and the nearly stalemated war both demanded, in my opinion, definite measures on our part to put an end to these intolerable conditions. One possibility was to let the Communist authorities understand that, in the absence of satisfactory progress, we intended to move decisively without inhibition in our use of weapons, and would no longer be responsible for confining hostilities to the Korean Peninsula. We would not be limited by any world-wide gentlemen's agreement. In India and in the Formosa Straits area, and at the truce negotiations at Panmunjom, we dropped the word, discreetly, of our intention. We felt quite sure it would reach Soviet and Chinese Communist ears. Soon the prospects for armistice negotiations seemed to improve . . ."

pensity for turning the viciousness of their attacks strictly on the
ROK divisions now became apparent. This came to a culmination
on the night of July 13 and 14, 1953.

The 3d Division had been on the line on the eastern corner of
the Iron Triangle for six exhausting months. We were being relieved by the 2d Division, and our 15th and 65th Regiments were
already loading in trucks the night the word came that several
miles to the east, the Chinese had hit with several armies[15] against
the Capital ROK Division, one of the finest in Korea. The Cap
ROK had been deployed in the usual manner, with its main
strength on the ridge lines, more or less neglecting the valley between. The CCF had now changed their tactics, gone up the
valleys, cut off the ridge lines, and advanced seven miles southward with comparative ease.

I heard this astonishing news early in the morning in the operations bunker, where I was still on duty from the night before. Our
first reaction, quickly dispelled, was disbelief. Word came to General Ridings that the 3d Division, despite its six months on the
line, was to be shoveled into the breach at Kumsong. This was only
a logical move, I suppose, since no other division in Korea was
sitting with two regiments actually mounted on trucks. General
Ridings acted coolly and quickly. He called in Colonel R. F.
("Red") Akers of the 15th Infantry and Colonel Chester DeGavre
of the 65th. Marking three Xs on a map, he said simply, "Keep
your trucks, 15th Infantry moves first, occupies a position along
route 117A between this X and this X. 65th Infantry follows and
occupies position between this X and this X. Move out."

Immediately I found myself, as G-2, deluged with requests for
maps. As the Kumsong area was some distance away, I was lucky
to have any at all. On scouring my files I found that I had only
twelve. These were given out sparingly, some of them hasty copies
of undetailed old Japanese editions.

But there was no time to lose in preparing for the next action.
Obviously, the Chinese for some reason had paused along Route
117A.

It seemed logical that we should get an advance party to the
Cap ROK command post as soon as possible. I told the division

[15] A CCF army was about the equivalent of a U. S. Corps, perhaps 70,000 men.

chief of staff that I was heading over; he consented. Once aloft in the helicopter I got out my map. At the bottom of Hill 604 on the division's right flank was a fork from which three roads branched out, running generally eastward. The Cap ROK had been deployed with the northernmost of these as its front the day before. The center was 117A, and the southernmost was the road on which the Cap ROK command post was still located, along with the bulk of the medium artillery. These routes were separated from each other by sharp peaks. It was understandable, then, that I studied the map intently, identified Routes 117 and 117A with the greatest of care, not particularly anxious to sit down in Chinese territory.

I found the right road and had the distinction, for what it was worth, of being the first officer from the 3d Division to reach the Cap ROK sector. However, I was glad to know that our own 64th Tank Battalion, equipped with 90-mm M-46 tanks, was rumbling toward 117A, the new front. I learned later that our tanks had caught the Chinese in that vicinity without antitank protection and that the 64th had inflicted heavy casualties. This type of action, for which tanks were designed, buoyed the spirits of our armored types, who had spent boring months firing from static positions. I am inclined to believe, furthermore, that the appearance of these more modern tanks probably identified the 3d Division to the CCF, whose policy it was to avoid engagement with U.S. forces. If so, this circumstance probably saved our lives the next day.

On arrival at the command post I was given a complete briefing on the situation. It was simple. The infantry elements of five battalions of the Cap ROK division had disappeared. Our heavy and medium artillery was largely intact along the road on which we were located. The 555th U. S. Field Artillery Battalion (105-mm howitzer) had lost thirteen of its eighteen howitzers, and anything could be expected that evening. General Maxwell Taylor was at the command post conferring with Lieutenant General Reuben E. Jenkins.[16]

I must confess to a feeling of considerable despondency at the

[16] Jenkins, much to my admiration, stayed the night in the Cap ROK CP. At Fort Benning, a year later, he told me he hadn't expected to survive.

decision to employ the 3d in this manner. Normally, the "book" method of stopping a penetration—as in the Battle of the Bulge during World War II—is to hold the shoulders, denying the enemy the space to reinforce. However, in retrospect, I am inclined to concede that the generals were right, despite the fact that the division would be almost ineffective as a fighting force that night. After all, this attack was being made across hills without even trails, not along roads as axes; furthermore, to abandon 120 pieces of artillery along the rear road was something that just could not be done in good conscience. This I did not consider at the time.

A couple of hours after my arrival, General Ridings and other members of his staff arrived. He had ordered a small "command group" to be with him—primarily the G-2, G-3, division engineer, G-4, the general, his aide, and the chief of staff.

Late that afternoon, the 15th and 65th Infantry regiments dismounted almost simultaneously from their trucks along the rear road and began the grueling climb up the mountains toward 117A in their allocated areas. Tired to the bone, the troops performed in a manner that was almost too much to ask. As usual, I split the night with Daniel Byrd, who had succeeded Hal Barber as division G-3. Dan directed our two sections the first half of the night and I relieved him at one o'clock.

This was the only night in Korea—or rather half night—that I stretched out with my boots on. Even in an infantry battalion I had been confident. But now, because I expected any minute to be surrounded by hordes of Red Chinese, with only headquarters clerks to put up a defense, I could not sleep. My obligation never to be captured weighed heavily on my mind. Before the sun went down I checked the ridge to the rear for escape routes; no paths were visible. Nevertheless, if the division command post were overrun, I would have no further combat responsibilities and should try to make my way out southward, straight up the hill. I wondered, frankly, what I was doing there. Had I broken my agreement with Dad to be cautious by volunteering to precede the division to Kumsong? Should someone have stopped me? And yet my duty, for the moment, was where I was. I could criticize the judgment of my superiors to myself but to even think seriously about leaving was out of the question. After all, it wouldn't be too pleasant for the general or anyone else to be captured either. We could only await developments.

At 3:30 or 4:00 in the morning we began getting news that the flanks of our six struggling battalions, despite the driving rain, were starting to make mutual contact. With every such event our divisional situation improved. Furthermore, we had no reports of Chinese to the south of 117A. Had they continued in the early evening, our two regiments could not have delayed much less stopped them.

We turned out to be fortunate; the Chinese had bolted. The elements of the 15th and 65th regiments made full contact by mid-morning and dug into a reasonable defensive position along Route 117A. Some Chinese prisoners were taken, from which we identified elements of several CCF armies.

The following night, that of July 15, a phenomenon occurred. Five thousand infantrymen from the Capital ROK division determinedly made their way back through the Chinese and into the American lines. As intelligence officer of the division, I wondered how many Chinese were coming along with them. To the best of my knowledge there were none.

From that time on the division headquarters remained in a state of suspense but relative inaction. The Chinese never resumed their attack. Finally, on the twenty-seventh of July, 1953, exactly one year after the day I first arrived in Korea, the war ended. The Chinese celebrated it by a final, heavy bombardment. The truce had been signed; Syngman Rhee had agreed to abide by it; and the same uneasy peace now existing in Korea began.

Two pictures will always remain in my mind on that last day of combat in Korea. One is the look on the faces of the medics as they evacuated the wounded, victims of this last senseless, all-out artillery bombardment. By that act the Chinese gained nothing but increased bitterness on the part of our combat troops.

That evening, with no positive action to be taken, General Ridings' aide and I sat in my suddenly-restored van. I was helping him study for his Regular Army examination. Although the van was protected from anything but a direct hit, the shells were coming in heavily. At midnight they ceased as one. Poring over a textbook on plane geometry seemed an odd way to observe the end of a war.

7

The Long Arm of
the White House

During the years between 1952 and 1958 I experienced the peculiar sensation of being drawn inexorably from straight military
duties toward that awesome institution, the White House. I fought
it as best I could, fighting to retain the identity of myself and my
family. At first I met with moderate success; but as time went
on, particularly after Dad's first serious illness in 1955, it became
a losing battle. Almost imperceptibly my time and preoccupations
were more and more sucked toward the whirlpool until eventually,
while I never lost my basic loyalty to the Army, I abandoned
thoughts of a lifetime military career.

Before January 1953 I had set foot in the White House only
twice, once when Mrs. Eleanor Roosevelt held a reception for all
the children in Washington schools who were currently taking
piano lessons (!) and the second time in June 1945, at President
Truman's dinner for Dad and his veterans of the European
campaign.

In the spring of 1952, after Dad's name had been entered in
the New Hampshire primary, my consciousness of politics grew.
As a student at the Armored School, Fort Knox, I spent many a
late evening huddled over the radio following the results of the
Minnesota, Nebraska, and other primaries. At that time I regarded politics simply as a form of competition. The Old Man
had never lost at anything, and my interest was simplistic: I
wanted to see him win. I gave little or no thought to the fact that
his winning might have a serious impact on my life. When Dad
came home in June of that year to begin his campaign for the
nomination, politics dominated all his activities, and what time
I had with him was sporadic but exciting. During that period he

was engaged in the nastiest phase of the campaign for the Republican nomination. Dad commanded the popular support; Senator Robert A. Taft, sometimes called "Mr. Republican," was the obvious choice of the political professionals. It was an uphill fight for Dad's forces, and the mud-slinging that went on in the spring and early summer of 1952 far transcended anything that occurred during the election campaign itself.

As it turned out, Dad was nominated in July on the first ballot. I heard the proceedings while sitting in a dentist chair at West Point, getting ready for departure to Korea. While Dad's admonition not to be captured made a real impression on me and complicated my tour of duty in Korea, I regarded this matter as a temporary problem only, which would dissipate upon my return to the United States. Politics had by no means turned my head from the career of a dedicated professional soldier.

On my return from Korea in September 1953, I encountered the first invasion of my family's personal life. Parked outside the door of our house was a shiny, radio-equipped automobile with a couple of authoritative-looking young men, whose duty it was to guard our children. We quickly became acquainted and they were soon accepted as part of our normal lives. Guarding the President's grandchildren was considered by the Secret Service as sort of a hardship tour, as it was obvious that the Army would be moving our family from place to place every year. Therefore, at the beginning, only bachelors were assigned. Later on, because of a shortage of single men, this policy had to be abandoned.

At the very outset we made every effort to keep the Secret Service detail as small and inconspicuous as possible. When we moved to my first postwar duty station, Fort Benning, Georgia, Dad decreed that the number of agents be limited to four. This figure turned out to be totally unrealistic in the light of the fact that there were three children to be protected, each going in a different direction, and one special agent could reasonably be expected to stay on the job for only about eight hours at a time. Furthermore, any organization must take into account such matters as vacations, sickness, and so on. As a result, by the time the Eisenhower Administration came to an end in January of 1961, the "diaper detail" had grown to about a dozen men.

As I look back, our relations with the Secret Service in those days were friendly, easy, and informal. Although there was always the prospect of someone's trying to kidnap one of the children, nobody was overly worried in those more tranquil days. We knew every agent personally and considered each a friend. Naturally, I was concerned regarding the psychological effects on the children of being continually guarded. To avoid frightening them, the agents, under their hard-boiled but extremely cooperative head, Bill Barton, did their part. The agents themselves would participate in ball games with the youngsters and try to act as normally as possible. (Occasionally, a playmate would shout triumphantly, "I saw your gun," pointing to the concealed revolver that each agent carried.) By and large, their basic purpose in being around was ignored. In later years at Gettysburg the agents would relax regulations sufficiently to allow the children to send messages over their car radios. Even our fourth child, Mary Jean, (then age five) was proficient in radio telephone procedure. "Man-man [departing] Sunflower [our house] with Grand 124 [David, Anne, and Mary Jean, in order of age] en route Barracuda [church],"[1] she would rattle off with ease.

For my own part, I made it a point to shun any security coverage of me personally. Having a bodyguard trailing around during the performance of my military duties would be an intolerable embarrassment. Furthermore, there was no need for it, as I remained largely anonymous. In this stand I received no objection from any quarter. Undoubtedly, of course, had the intelligence branch of the Secret Service concluded that I was a potential target, the situation might have been different.

As time went on, the long arm of the White House continued to make itself felt. Though it rarely interfered with my military duties, it forced the whole family to continue developing the technique of leading double lives. At Fort Benning, for example, I was commander of the 1st Battalion, 30th Infantry. In that capacity I caught my full share of harassment from regimental headquarters—more than my share I thought at times. But at Thanksgiving Dad came by Benning in his plane to pick up the family

---

[1] We never learned who had conjured up the code name "Barracuda" for the church but it seemed inappropriate.

and take us to Augusta, Georgia; we were now temporarily in the reflected public limelight, on stage and catered to. The holiday over, we returned to the other life, the "real" life at Benning.

This double existence was not particularly new as far as I was concerned, since it represented merely a stepped-up pace of what I had been experiencing since 1942. I was, however, worried about its effects on the children. Fortunately, they proved adaptable. As parents, however, I think it possible that Barbara and I were, for a while at least, more strict than most, in an effort to combat the artificial adulation they received at Augusta and the White House.

On the other side of the coin, I strove to learn what I could from my new opportunities. In the summer of 1954, for example, I spent a month on temporary duty in the White House between assignments at Fort Benning and Leavenworth. Even in such a short period I made friends such as Maxwell M. Rabb, Secretary to the Cabinet, and Brigadier General Paul T. ("Pete") Carroll.[2] In addition, I learned more about Dad and his methods. One day I was told to edit a draft of a "greeting from the President" in observance of a patriotic occasion. The draft was, I thought, too bland and general. I rewrote it, covering the details of the event being celebrated—a good piece of research, I thought, showing the audience how much the President knew about the subject. When the paper reached Dad's desk, I was on the carpet instantly. "What the hell is this?" he roared. "Do you expect a President to sign a bunch of garbage like that? I'm supposed to set the tone; let the other fellows give the details!" I left a wiser young officer.

The year (1954–55) at the Command and General Staff College, Fort Leavenworth, Kansas, involved a highly concentrated course of study. This course, necessary for the advancement of one's military career, was pleasant because of the companionship but extremely demanding. Thus during this period Washington and the White House were fairly remote from our minds.

[2] Max Rabb doubled also as Dad's adviser on minority matters. We have remained close ever since. Pete Carroll tragically died later that year.

In November we had a short visit with Dad and Mother when they flew out to Kansas to dedicate the Eisenhower Museum at Abilene. They picked us up in Kansas City. As we sat aboard the *Columbine* between Kansas City and Salina, I was curious to learn how Dad had taken the defeat in the Congressional elections only a couple of weeks before. He was anything but cheerful. Not only was he facing the prospect of dealing with a hostile Congress but his own personal plans were becoming affected. He had exerted all the influence he could to secure another Republican Congress but still the party showed little sign of the strength he had been trying to build. As a result, the prospect of his own having to run for re-election in 1956 was beginning to enter his mind.

It is unfair to evaluate a person's feelings from a short visit when that person is obviously thinking out loud. But at this particular moment, Dad seemed to regard the prospect of a second term with distaste. After our brief sojourn in Abilene we remained in Leavenworth for the rest of the school year.

The course completed in June 1955, Barbara, the children, and I stopped off to see Barbara's parents, still at Fort Sheridan, on the way to our new station, Fort Belvoir, Virginia. While we were sitting in the kitchen one day a call came through from Washington. Dad was on the line, inviting me to accompany him to the 1955 Summit Conference at Geneva. Immediately I accepted, but as always with a touch of mixed emotions. I never looked forward to the process of shifting gears into the "other" life. Nevertheless, this was one of those many opportunities that I was afraid I would later regret turning down. Therefore, on return to Washington I deposited the family at my parents' new Gettysburg farm and joined the party destined for Geneva. In this instance, Mother was prepared to grit her teeth and go along also. This was a big move for Mother; she was—and is—a "white-knuckle" flyer.

The story of the Geneva conference has been told thoroughly elsewhere. It is dealt with in detail from Dad's point of view in a volume of his memoirs, *The White House Years*. Therefore, I will not attempt to give a rounded picture of it.

By way of background, however, Dad was never enthusiastic over the concept of summit meetings, particularly those in which the foreign ministers had been unable to clear out the underbrush beforehand. In this attitude he was encouraged by Secretary of State John Foster Dulles, who, I believe, retained some of the lawyer's attitude that the professionals should do the bulk of the work and the client should be saved from getting his hands dirty. Nevertheless, public opinion ran strongly in favor of a summit meeting at that time. The President, after all, is the official elected to represent the people, not the Secretary of State. Furthermore, public imagination during World War II had been excited by pictures of the heads of government—Roosevelt, Churchill, Chiang, and Stalin—meeting at exotic places like Casablanca, Cairo, Tehran, and Yalta.[3] Despite the often unhappy results that came out of these meetings, the public had developed a certain unthinking notion that heads of government could solve problems that foreign ministers could not.

Up until this time Dad had continued to refuse to attend any summit conference until the Soviets, by a positive act, would demonstrate a desire to end the Cold War and negotiate in an honest fashion. That event occurred early in 1955, when the Soviets suddenly agreed to the neutralization of Austria and the withdrawal of their occupying troops. This significant step forward gave promise that Stalin's death two years before might presage a new era. Indeed, after the short rule of Malenkov and the assassination of Beria, the Soviet Union was ostensibly being run by a committee of four: Nicolai Bulganin, Nikita Khrushchev, Georgi Zhukov, and Vyacheslav Molotov. Under these circumstances, Dad agreed to attend the conference.

Therefore a feeling of some cautious optimism pervaded the air when Dad and his party, including a formidable number of staff from the White House, State, and Defense, departed from Washington in the *Columbine* on an evening in mid-July 1955. With a brief early-morning stopover in Iceland, we arrived in Geneva late the next afternoon. Mother made the trip well. In Geneva the immediate entourage (family, aides, and personal staff) was located in a comfortable, spacious villa outside of town. The rest, including the press, were located elsewhere.

Immediately on arrival, a flood of advisers began coming and

3 Stalin was not present at Casablanca or Cairo; Chiang was only at Cairo.

going. Secretary Dulles, Robert Bowie, Douglas MacArthur II, and Livingston Merchant were the most frequent; but the parade also included Admiral Radford, General Alfred M. Gruenther, Harold Stassen, and presidential assistant Nelson Rockefeller. Konrad Adenauer, Chancellor of the newly independent Federal Republic of Germany, was on hand for consultation, but of course was not present at any of the meetings at the Palace of the Nations.

As I was not a regular member of the staff, my functions were minimal. I spent some time with Colonel Andrew J. Goodpaster (staff secretary) at the Palace, observed the bulk of the plenary sessions in the large, disagreeable conference room, took Mother sight-seeing one day, and kept a diary. Dad and I also found a little time to hit golf balls in the extensive gardens of the villa.

Although four powers were present at the meeting (France, Great Britain, the Soviet Union, and the United States), all eyes were focused on the Soviet delegation. Their party included the four who were supposed to be sharing the power, plus Andrei Gromyko. Dad, in particular, was trying to ascertain which of the four actually held the reins. He rather suspected that the real boss was the man named Khrushchev, the party chief, but he needed confirmation. In this he used me as best he could. Remembering that Marshal Zhukov had paid me a good deal of personal attention on the Moscow trip ten years earlier, Dad arranged for me to be in the marshal's company as much as possible. He just might, Dad hoped, drop something to me that he would otherwise withhold.

We received our greatest exposure to the Soviet group at a stag dinner held at the villa one evening early in the conference. Bulganin, Khrushchev, Zhukov, Molotov, and Gromyko arrived together, practically walking in step. All were smiles and cordiality, awkwardly so, I thought. During the cocktail period in the garden before dinner, Dad, Zhukov, and I found ourselves talking alone. Zhukov said that his daughter was being married that day but that he had passed up the ceremony because of this opportunity to see his "old friend." Almost reflexively Dad turned to an aide and sent for three gifts, including a portable radio, for Zhukov to take back as wedding presents. Zhukov was visibly embarrassed. He then said softly that "there are things that are not as they seem" and asked if he could see Dad some time alone before the respective parties left Geneva. They agreed to meet at the villa before the conference the last day.

On talking with Zhukov that evening, I quickly sensed that this was not the same cocky little rooster we had known in Germany at the end of the war. During the interim we had heard stories that Zhukov had fallen out of favor with Stalin because of his unacceptable popularity with the Russian masses; we had heard at one point that he had been killed. With the Soviet history of ungentleness regarding those out of favor, we had believed the rumors in varying degrees. But that evening Zhukov was there, alive but broken. He spoke slowly and softly, even a bit shakily. Dad and I concluded that Zhukov was being included in the ruling group only as a façade.

At the dinner Gromyko was given the unpleasant task of acting as interpreter between Zhukov and me. Gromyko was having the most difficult time of all adjusting to this new twist of courting the Americans, and interpreting between a marshal and a major seemed to do nothing to alleviate his pain. But he remained always much on the alert. At one point Zhukov told me, through Gromyko, that he had never, as some newspapers had hinted, been advising the Chinese and North Koreans in Korea. Without thinking, I responded, "Of course not."

Gromyko jumped and turned to me. "Why do you say that?"

Realizing that I had hit something sensitive, I shrugged and said, "Well, I simply never associated the marshal with the Far East." Gromyko seemed to relax.

During a large part of the dinner, attention was given to the conversation at the important part of the table, the base of the "U." Here Dad, with Khrushchev, Bulganin, and Molotov, was speaking frankly and loudly. "It is essential," Dad exclaimed so all would notice, "that we find some way of controlling the threat of the thermonuclear bomb. You know we both have enough weapons to wipe out the entire northern hemisphere from fall-out alone. No spot would escape the fall-out from an exchange of nuclear stockpiles." Molotov in particular, his stone face expressionless, nodded his understanding.

For a couple of days the Big Four conference droned on and

on, the talks made more tedious by the need for translations, as three languages were being employed. Premier Edgar Faure of France was, depressingly enough, noted for his eloquence, and he employed this talent to the fullest, thus lengthening the proceedings. Sir Anthony Eden, British Prime Minister, had less to say, but his stature as Winston Churchill's right-hand man made him a person to listen to. Bulganin, speaking for the Soviets, did provide a bit of ironic amusement. He accused NATO (the North Atlantic Treaty Organization) of being an aggressive alliance. To the expressions of shock around the table, he said with a completely straight face, "NATO *must* be an aggressive alliance, because when we [the Soviets] applied to join, we were denied."

At the end of each day's meeting the assemblage would repair to a spacious back room for a drink. Dad, intent on learning all he could, spent his entire time with the Russians at these gatherings. I realized that the French and British leaders understood, but I still felt a little uneasy about their being left out and tried to be helpful. Once, seeing Eden and Dulles standing alone without a drink, I approached them and asked if I could get them anything.

Eden sprang to life, straightened up, and smiled brightly: "Oh, no thank you!"

Dulles, on the other hand, barely looked up. Glowering, he said laconically, "Had one."

While all this was going on, the secret conferences continued behind the scenes. I was not privy to the subjects being discussed, but the impressive stream of visitors created an electric atmosphere; something was up. On the day before the end of the conference, as I was standing in Colonel Goodpaster's office, Nelson Rockefeller came up and said, "You have *got* to be in the conference this afternoon. Your Dad is going to throw a bombshell."

The room that day had no more visitors than usual, perhaps a dozen in the spacious pews behind the American side of the conference table. Rockefeller and Carl McCardle of the State Department were seated in the front row of seats and Goodpaster and I were sitting right behind them. At a certain point in the proceedings Rockefeller turned around and said, "Now listen. Here it comes." It was Dad's turn to speak.

Dad made his presentation with minimal use of notes. He went on about the dangers of nuclear war and the necessity to guard against surprise attack. He thereupon made possibly the boldest proposal of his career: that the United States and Soviet Union should exchange blueprints of all their respective armed forces and permit each other's airplanes to photograph every inch of their respective territories! Nelson Rockefeller turned around, slapped me on the knee, and gave a triumphant grin. Immediately, as Dad finished speaking, a loud clap of thunder came from the skies and the lights went off. With a chuckle Dad said, "Well, I expected to make a hit but not that much of one."[4] Premier Faure responded at some length and Prime Minister Eden also said a few words. Both had been kept in the dark regarding this proposal because of the last-minute speed with which it was formulated. As the speakers rotated clockwise around the table, Bulganin spoke last. He said smoothly, "That is a very interesting idea; we will certainly study it."

This initiative has since been known as the "Open Skies Proposal."

After the meeting, as we were walking out for the usual cocktail, I happened to be behind Dad and Khrushchev. Khrushchev was talking straight: "That is a very bad idea," he said, "it is nothing more than a spy system." Dad has since written that this was the first time he realized Khrushchev was the real boss.

The rest of the conference seemed an anticlimax. The four powers agreed in principle to Dad's proposal but specified that the foreign ministers would have to meet in October to work out

[4] The authorship of the Open Skies Proposal serves to illustrate one of those phenomena of government, the question of whose idea it was in the first place. As one who was not on the inside of this matter, I can report only the results of my later research on the subject. Dad always insisted that the idea came to him directly off the top of his head at Geneva and, in his own consciousness, this was so. On the other hand, there were at least two principal White House staff officers who had been thinking along these lines. One of these was Harold Stassen, special assistant to the President for disarmament. The other was Nelson Rockefeller, special assistant to the President for psychological warfare. I have since learned from Rockefeller that the idea had been discussed some weeks earlier, at least, in a meeting of the Joint Chiefs of Staff at Quantico, Virginia. However, I am inclined to think that very little of the idea had consciously filtered to Dad before he actually set foot in Geneva. Both Stassen and Rockefeller have been relatively reticent regarding their part in the affair. But both in private have spoken as if the thought had occurred to each independently.

the practicalities. As it turned out, that later meeting was a failure from the start. Khrushchev's will had prevailed in the Soviet Union.

The one aspect of the whole episode that I have always considered remarkable was the alacrity with which the uniformed American military leaders were willing to accept an idea so radical as this. Certainly the proposal made sense. Since ours is an open society, much of the information which would have been obtained by the Russians from mutual photographic reconnaissance was already available to them; we had no such access in the Soviet Union. Nevertheless, the proposal was radical in terms of conventional military thinking, and I considered it a monument to both Radford and Gruenther that they realistically agreed to it so quickly.

On the other hand, given their determination to maintain their closed society, it is not surprising that the Russians chose to turn it down.

On our return to the United States from Geneva I immediately picked up the family and proceeded to get settled at Fort Belvoir. On being shown our quarters, Barbara and I were a little embarrassed; we were located in a colonels' row. Quarters No. 10, Woodlawn Avenue, were similar to those my parents had occupied at Fort Lewis in 1940–41. They were beautiful and comfortable. But I was concerned about the effect of this obvious special treatment on my relationships with my colleagues. The post commander, however, was so delighted with the place that I held back protest. It turned out that the Secret Service had requested we be assigned to a separate house rather than a duplex and that it be of brick construction. With these criteria, nothing else was available. Fortunately, my direct boss, Lieutenant Colonel William Porter King, lived in a similar set of quarters directly across the loop. Nobody protested, at least not to my knowledge.

The work that first year at Belvoir was unusually rewarding. I had the distinction of being the only Leavenworth graduate in the "associate arms" section—that is, all non-engineers—and therefore spent most of my time rewriting the tactical problems on which the Engineers based their teaching. This fact gave me considerable status which had nothing to do with my family name.

One petty matter, however, was indicative of the direction my family's lives were moving. One day somebody from White House communications appeared to install a direct telephone line from Quarters No. 10 to the White House switchboard. I was horrified. "We're too damned accessible to the White House here as it is," I howled. "Never!" The targets of my fears, actually, were not Mother and Dad. But I suffered from an obsession that people like social secretaries, staff officers, and sometimes cabinet members, while respecting the President's and First Lady's privacy, would never extend the same courtesy to us. They would be hounding Barbara, in particular, whenever the spirit moved them. The communications man beat a retreat, but the lack of a special phone actually provided little insulation; it simply meant that the White House operators would have to go through a couple of extra motions to reach us. But at least we had only one telephone—which would not be interrupted by the White House—instead of two.

On the afternoon of Saturday, September 24, 1955, as I was preparing to leave the Fort Belvoir golf course, Special Agent Richard McCully, a member of the children's detail, came in the club house. "You'd better get home," he said. "Your father's had a heart attack. We don't know how bad."

As I drove home, the events of the past years, particularly the last three, went through my mind. An era seemed to have passed —and a short one at that. Heart attacks were not taken so much in stride in those days. At once, I called the White House switchboard and soon was talking to Major General Howard M. ("Doc") Snyder, Dad's physician, at Fitzsimons Army Hospital in Denver. It seemed that Dad, vacationing in Denver, had suffered the heart attack—a coronary thrombosis—the night before at the Douds' house on 750 Lafayette Street. He had been taken to the hospital and tests had now confirmed the diagnosis. Dad had insisted that I should not bother to come out to Denver, and Doc Snyder, on his part, felt that my coming was not really necessary. He could keep me informed. Mother sounded strong.

As I was pondering this turn of events, the telephone rang; it was the Air Force aide, Lieutenant Colonel William Draper. Bill was determined to go to Denver with the *Columbine,* to stand by, and he strongly urged me to go with him. I was easily convinced. I obtained authority and the next morning met Bill and several others at Washington National Airport.

At Lowry Air Force Base I was met by Press Secretary Jim Hagerty. On the way to the hospital he gave me a run-down. "If you would divide heart attacks into five different degrees," he said, spreading the fingers of one hand, "the President's would be considered in the third category, moderate, not severe but not slight either." At the hospital I checked in with Mother, who always seems to rise to the occasion, and right away was taken into Dad's bedroom, where he lay propped up in bed under an oxygen tent. He motioned me to a seat.

Obviously under sedation, Dad spoke quietly. "You know," he said with an air of wistful detachment, "these are things that always happen to other people; you never think of their happening to you." He then pointed to a table and asked for his billfold. He had made a successful bet with his friend George E. Allen over something a couple of days previously and, as was his habit, he wanted his gains passed on to Barbara. (Mother later told me that the billfold had been all he could think of the night before when he was being carted to the hospital.) All in all, Dad was peaceful and resigned; throughout his life he was a good patient, as he considered his welfare to be the responsibility of the doctors, not of himself.

I stayed at Fitzsimons a few days, sleeping on the same ward as both Dad and Mother. The doctors told me all they could: the first forty-eight to seventy-two hours were critical. As to the percentages: well, statistics showed that 80 per cent of all first heart-attack patients survived. I sat in on the little conferences between Jim Hagerty and the doctors, in which they discussed what should be put out to the press. By Dad's direction, nothing was held back. His memories were too vivid of those days in 1920 during which President Woodrow Wilson, on the second floor of the White House, was completely out of contact with the world, his only communication being through his wife. In Dad's case, the bulletins were so frank as to give him a blush of embarrassment when he later read them: timing of bowel movements and the like. But the press appreciated being told the truth; and the medical details, while perhaps a little annoying to laymen, were necessary for doctors over the country to interpret what was really going on.

During much of the waiting time I visited with Mother. She was receiving floods of mail from all over the country and was determined that she would answer every letter by hand. "If these people take the trouble to write me," she declared, "I'll write them back." At the time I thought she was out of her mind, but somehow over the weeks she was successful. Doubtless it proved excellent therapy for her own spirits to have something, no matter how overwhelming, to do.

On my own part, I was able to make only one small contribution. The difficulty with thrombosis patients, I was told, is that after the pain of the first hours, they feel perfectly well. The problem, then, is to keep them quiet without their becoming fretful. No drugs can help heal the heart tissues; some doctors are even doubtful regarding the real usefulness of the oxygen (although they dare not omit it); only time can heal. With this in mind, I went down to the music studio in the basement of the hospital and selected a collection of soothing records to be played in Dad's room—Brahms, Debussy, Tchaikowsky. Dad had them played over and over and, by the time he later left the hospital, had his visitors amazed at his recognition of certain classical music.

I made one later weekend trip to Denver, this time carrying a wire recording of greetings from the children. Vice President Richard Nixon turned up while I was there, and we returned to Washington together in the *Columbine*. While visiting with Mother, the Vice President made one wry observation. "Mrs. Eisenhower," he smiled, "I don't mean to sound disrespectful, but you know the President's watchword in this Administration has been 'moderation.' So if he had to have a heart attack, it seems appropriate that he would have a 'moderate' one."

By this time Dad had progressed enough to talk business in a general way. He had conferred, for example, with Secretary Dulles about preparations for the ill-fated foreign ministers' meeting in October, the follow-up to Geneva three months earlier. He had actually signed a couple of critical documents within a couple of days of his commitment to the hospital. But the doctors had advised against reading the newspapers, as much of the petty material printed therein could be worse for him emotionally than truly substantive issues. During my second visit, however, he was allowed for the first time to see a newspaper. The large headlines confirmed the break-up of the romance between Princess Margaret of Britain and RAF Group Captain Peter Townsend. Dad tossed the paper aside: "If that's all they have on their minds, then things are OK." The next day Dad was wheeled out in the sunshine to be photographed by the press wearing a pair of red pajamas they had given him. Over the left breast pocket were inscribed the words, MUCH BETTER, THANKS.

From that time on, Dad's progress became more visible. First he took a few steps and then he graduated into limited stairclimbing. By early November he was ready to return to Washington. However, when informed that he would have to proceed to and from the airplane in a wheelchair, he demurred. If it meant only a few days difference, he said, he would stay in the hospital until he could appear on his feet. Thus the trip back was postponed; he and Mother returned to Washington on November 11, Veterans' Day. He spoke from the steps of the airplane in the autumn sunlight: "The doctors, they say, have given me a reprieve, if not a pardon." Despite the fact that he looked well, few, if any, dared hope what a spectacular reprieve he had really been afforded.

Time passed. A little over a month after the folks returned from Denver, our fourth child, Mary Jean, was born at Walter Reed Army Hospital. Meanwhile, Dad was undergoing a difficult time of decision. The doctors, including the renowned Paul Dudley White, had proclaimed him fit to run for another term as President. Doc Snyder, in fact, even when Dad was hospitalized at Fitzsimons, had volunteered that his life expectancy might be improved should he run a second time rather than withdraw to a life of inactivity. And strangely, Mother was one of the first to seriously contemplate the possibility of his continuing in office. I would have thought that she would be the first to want him to retire and conserve his strength. But she, knowing Dad as she did, agreed with Doc Snyder that inactivity would be fatal. And she had another reason, an almost mystical feeling that Dad still had more to contribute. "I just can't believe that Ike's work is finished," she sighed as the three of us talked at Fitzsimons.

To me, at that early date, the prospect of a second term was startling. There existed some doubt in the minds of many, moreover, as to whether the American public would vote for a man who had suffered a coronary. But that intangible was Dad's problem: the doctors had put the onus squarely on him.

I will never know exactly how Dad felt emotionally about a second term: probably he was ambivalent. His outward actions and utterances gave every evidence of indecision up to a remarkably late date. When riding to the church on Christmas Day 1955, for example, he mused, apparently thinking out loud, "I *told* the boys four years ago that they ought to get someone who'd want to run again for a second term."

Apparently Dad was testing himself, testing whether his new regimen—which really called only for an hour's rest before lunch and avoiding losing his temper—would allow him to do his job to the fullest. At the same time, he seemed to be inviting the views of the family. Milton came down to Belvoir one day and we discussed the matter. Milton felt personally that Dad should not run again; the record of the first four years would be enough to establish him as a great President, and another term might not be worth the risk from many considerations.

I decided to put my thoughts down on paper, as I find this device useful in avoiding a mental merry-go-round. I pecked out a long letter in the form of a staff study, giving facts bearing on the problem, reasons for running, and reasons for retiring. At the end of this rather prolix document I recommended his bowing out. Dad—and especially George Allen—expressed admiration of the piece of work, but Dad made no commitment.[5]

A meeting Dad held at the White House on the evening of Friday, January 13, 1956, seemed to have the greatest single influence on him. He had gathered a group of men, all of them in the Administration except Milton, to present their views. After

[5] Appendix A.

dinner Dad went around the circle and each adviser spoke his piece in turn. Milton, his views known to Dad, refrained from speaking but acted as secretary. To a man they recommended running for a second term. The gist of the reasoning was fairly simple: polls showed that Vice President Nixon was not yet ready to defeat a candidate like Adlai Stevenson. His youth, above all, was against him. Further, the argument went, Dad had gathered about him the finest group of subordinates that had ever served an Administration; the country deserved a continuation of their services.

I do not like to think of myself as a cynic. But I cannot avoid the visceral feeling that the self-serving element affected the advice Dad received. On the other hand, I wonder what else he would expect from the "fine group of subordinates" themselves.

Of course, even such unanimity, had Dad felt otherwise, would never have swayed him. His colleagues were telling him what, by that time, he wanted to hear. In early February he announced his availability for a second term on nationwide television. Historians will differ on the wisdom of that decision, influenced to a large degree by their sympathies with the principles of the Eisenhower Administration; but in the election the next year the people of the United States showed that they approved. Even the New York *Times* came out for him.

After the announcement in February things quieted down for a while, as Dad's renomination was a certainty. Interest was rejuvenated, however, by a much-publicized movement, led by Harold Stassen, to "dump" the Vice President. As Stassen was currently still the assistant to the President for disarmament, he was required to take leave without pay while indulging in his political maneuvers. I was not a witness to any of this but personally regarded it as a most unfortunate episode. Stassen soon backed down.

But more complications lay ahead. On June 6, 1956, I received a telephone call that Dad had been struck by some serious abdominal ailment and that I should hasten to the White House without delay. Bill Barton, chief of the children's Secret Service detail, drove me up. En route we received word over the radio that there was no longer cause for hurry. Bill and I had no idea whether Dad had recovered or had died.

When we arrived at the Southwest Gate, Mother was waiting. I then learned that Dad was suffering from a serious intestinal blockage and had been removed to Walter Reed a few minutes earlier by ambulance.

When we finally got to see him, Dad was suffering severely and was really in no mood for visitors. The blockage had been in the ileum, a small tube which connects the small and large intestines. The doctors seemed a little surprised to discover this malady, considering ileitis as a young man's disease; but the diagnosis accounted for the attacks that Dad had suffered periodically for years, sending him to bed with a swollen belly and considerable pain. A group of ten eminent surgeons, both military and civilian, were on hand to consult. In view of the seriousness of an operation on a patient with a cardiac history, they were holding off as long as they could.

Major General Leonard D. Heaton was the surgeon in charge of the case, but the most prestigious doctor present was the late Isidor S. Ravdin, from the University of Pennsylvania. Time and time again Ravdin urged his colleagues that it was time to move.

Finally, at about midnight of June 6, the conferees were nearly unanimous that the time had come to operate. Only one doctor held out. The rest, however, balked at going ahead without a unanimous opinion.

Some time after midnight Dr. Walter Tkach, who had been keeping me informed, came up and said, "If we don't move soon, we are going to lose our patient." I could do nothing. Finally the dissenting doctor agreed, but Mother, who clung to the belief that the operation was unnecessary, refused to sign the permission papers; I did so in her place.

Dr. Heaton then came in to Dad's bedside and said, "I think we had better go inside and look around." At first Dad failed to understand. When the message got through, he gave a quick nod and said calmly, "Go ahead."

Mother, Milton, and I sat in a waiting room. At about 4 A.M., the operation was finished and pronounced a success; Dad's heart had held up well. I left the hospital the next day because, in his discomfort, the last thing in the world Dad wanted was companionship.

The operation for ileitis, despite the fact that it turned out well, had wide repercussions. First of all, it intensified the health issue for the 1956 political campaign. This situation was exacerbated by the fact that for a long time Dad was unable to absorb food, and the weight loss was noticeable. And, with a temporary loss of stomach muscles, he walked slowly and hunched over. (I never saw him look worse until his last days.) As he progressed, certain columnists such as Drew Pearson and Doris Fleeson were hotly contesting the prognostication of the doctors that Dad's recovery would be complete.

One matter of significance occurred during this period when Dad was incapacitated: the cancellation of our promise to aid Egypt in financing construction of the projected Aswan High Dam. In good health Dad might well have exercised a restraining influence on Secretary of State Dulles in making this move—but that is only a conjecture. It did, to the best of my knowledge, represent the only instance in which Dulles made a policy move without consulting Dad first.[6]

A matter of lesser importance involved the meeting of the Presidents of American republics in Panama, originally scheduled for that June. Without the President of the United States, such a meeting would be practically meaningless. This problem was handled by a simple postponement. Later in the summer Dad was able to attend and, while he had to minimize his personal activity, the conference was successful. The other Presidents appreciated the fact that Dad had made the trip to Panama still wearing a surgical drain.

The role that our family played in the 1956 presidential campaign was minimal. The episodes I have mentioned actually took me away from my regular duties very little. The habit of employing the whole family as a political phalanx was not yet in vogue. However, we attended some events quietly and in the background.

[6] They later exchanged at least two memos on the wisdom of the way the cancellation was handled. Twice Dad wrote Dulles asking if we might not have done better; both times Dulles replied emphatically that everything had been handled perfectly. See Dwight D. Eisenhower, *Waging Peace*, pp. 33, 34.

Barbara and I were present at the San Francisco Republican National Convention in August where the Eisenhower-Nixon ticket was boisterously rubber-stamped. Here I argued unsuccessfully against Chairman Joseph W. Martin's gimmick of making my son David the "honorary chairman" of the convention. "How many votes is that worth?" I asked Thomas E. Stephens, a political adviser. "None" was the answer. I still lost; I could keep David from the convention but could not affect what the chairman would do from the rostrum.

By this time Dad was looking like himself again, robust and alert. The timing had been fortuitous if not miraculous. At the St. Francis Hotel I acted as a sort of aide in Dad's apartment, the link between the President and the outside world for a good part of the day. One afternoon, as he was taking a rest before going out, I had to tell Dad that a Navy patrol plane, over international waters, had been shot down by the Communist Chinese. There was, of course, nothing that he could do, for the moment at least; but the incident drove home once again the fact that the President never leaves his job, even though engaged in political party activities.

As the campaign progressed, it heated up. Back in 1952 Dad had said that had he known Stevenson would be the Democratic nominee he himself would have stayed in uniform. Now, in 1956, he no longer felt that way. Stevenson, once again the Democratic candidate, was becoming more and more desperate, bringing into the political arena questions I considered outside of politics. The most publicized of these was the matter of nuclear testing. Stevenson was able to conjure up sufficient experts—experts always disagree—to prove that governmental policy in the nuclear field was condemning millions of innocents to death. Premier Bulganin of the Soviet Union understandably supported his contention (probably no help to Stevenson politically). Though the United States later observed a moratorium on nuclear testing, I felt, as did many, that the matter was too technical to be treated as an emotional political issue, and I held Stevenson at fault. My previous high regard for the governor was restored only years later when he was ambassador to the United Nations. But I think that making nuclear test policy a political issue in the presidential campaign cost him votes in 1956.

With the health issue, the test ban issue, and others, the press delighted in giving the impression that the election would be close. Being not too astute politically, I was taken in by all this. One day in early October I marched into Dad's Oval Office considerably agitated. "You've got to get moving," I said. "You're going to fall behind."

Dad sat back and roared with laughter. "This fellow's licked and what's more he knows it! Let's go to the ball game." Off to New York we went; Secretary Dulles, up to his ears in troubles over Suez, was also drafted to go. I am sure that Dad enjoyed this first game of the 1956 World Series more than I; I am also sure that I enjoyed it far more than the preoccupied Foster Dulles. The fact that the Brooklyn Dodgers beat the New York Yankees that day seemed not to impress him.[7]

In late October and early November everything popped at once. On October 22 the Hungarians, giving vent to years of pent-up frustration, broke out in a hopeless rebellion against their Soviet masters. One week later the Israelis, after repeated American pleas to desist, jumped off in the Sinai Desert and began to decimate Nasser's Egyptian forces. Thus Dad had three problems on his hands: Hungary, Suez, and the election. The election, typically, took last priority. One personal incident casts some light on Dad's attitude.

On the evening of October 30 the two of us were talking in the bedroom on the second floor of the White House. The subject uppermost in our minds was the Israeli military success in Sinai and Prime Minister David Ben-Gurion's defiance of our pleas to cease use of force. "Well," Dad mused. "It looks as if we're in for trouble. If the Israelis keep going—and if the UN says so—I may have to use force to stop them; conceivably that could entail the use of all kinds of weapons. Then I'd lose the election. There would go New York, New Jersey, Pennsylvania, and Connecticut at least."

[7] The Yanks went on to win the series, 4–3.

"Wowie!" I moaned, "Couldn't you hold off taking action until the election is over?"

"That might be too late. We'll just have to see."

Fortunately, from a domestic political viewpoint, the British and French solved the dilemma. On October 31 Prime Minister Eden issued his famous ultimatum to President Gamal Abdel Nasser of Egypt. The waters were now so muddied that the Israeli operation sank to secondary importance. The United States introduced a resolution in the United Nations—as mildly worded as possible—condemning the action and calling for cessation of the use of force. The British bombed Cairo. Several days after the issuance of the ultimatum and the bombings, the British launched a feeble land attack at the mouth of the Suez Canal with insufficient forces and ceased operations when censured almost unanimously by the UN. Nasser scuttled enough ships in the Canal to block it to all traffic. It took months to clear up the political mess and force an Israeli withdrawal back to its borders.

The presidential campaign still on, Adlai Stevenson logically used the whole affair as an example of the "bankruptcy" of the Administration's foreign policy. It was to no avail, for in times of crisis, the American people traditionally rally behind their President. On Election Day Dad polled about 35.6 million votes as against a little over 26 million for his opponent. He picked up 457 electoral votes. Stevenson won 73—all from the South, up to that time solidly Democratic in presidential as well as local politics. But the Republicans failed to regain either house of Congress.

During the summer of 1957 I took on my first job of real responsibility in the White House. Brigadier General Goodpaster (promoted in January), at Dad's insistence, was planning a leave of about three weeks' duration in New England, his first since joining the White House staff three years earlier. A caretaker was needed; therefore Dad arranged for me to be put on temporary duty between assignments to hold the fort. Andy Goodpaster, because of his energy and intelligence, had by now taken over an impressive array of unrelated duties that seemed to fit nowhere else. Besides the normal functions of daily briefings to Dad (now the "Boss") and ensuring that national security actions were coordinated, *not* predigested, when they came for presidential decision, he supervised the production of the daily "staff notes" and, as staff secretary, had assumed responsibility for supervising office allocation (even parking spaces) and for monitoring the budget of the White House. His position was beyond description, and few people could simply step in and take over permanently. However, on a temporary basis it was not too difficult to perform the daily essentials.

I moved into the office adjoining Andy's to become acquainted with my duties about a week before his departure. Generally, I would be involved with national security affairs—State, Defense, Atomic Energy Commission, CIA—and Lawrence A. ("Art") Minnich, the regular assistant staff secretary, would continue to perform his normal functions pertaining to domestic affairs.

One day in mid-August Colonel (later General) Bruce Palmer, the officer specified for liaison between the Army and the White House, asked to come see me. During the visit he gave me a fact sheet concerning a proposed Army missile—the Pershing—with a range of something like five hundred miles. The missile was running into difficulty at the Department of Defense level and both he and I knew—although neither of us said so—that by dealing directly on this matter (from Army Staff to the White House) we were violating the chain of command in bypassing the Department of Defense.

Nevertheless, I studied the paper and took it in to the Boss. To my relief, he showed considerable interest in this successor to the Redstone missile and told me to set up an appointment within the next couple of days with the Army Chief of Staff, General Maxwell Taylor. As it turned out, General Taylor was out of the country; but General Lyman Lemnitzer, the Vice Chief of Staff, well conversant on the subject, was available. The Boss directed —and I agreed wholeheartedly since it got me off the hook—that Defense Secretary Charles E. Wilson be present also.

When the day arrived, Wilson had managed to assemble a formidable group of advisers to accompany him. These included Deputy Defense Secretary Donald A. Quarles and Admiral Arthur Radford (retired the week previously). General Lemnitzer called me up the evening before: "I'm certainly going to be outnumbered in that meeting tomorrow; do you suppose we could get Secretary [of the Army Wilbur M.] Brucker in?" Without difficulty I made the arrangement with Tom Stephens, the appointments secretary.

The meeting that morning was as intense and as disagreeable as any I ever attended. Charlie Wilson and his group were, of course, quietly furious about having the matter brought up at all. More important, they were wedded to the concept that the Army should be restricted to missiles of two hundred-mile range. Admiral Radford, arbitrary by nature but usually a wily infighter, overplayed his hand this time. He *told* the Commander-in-Chief how things were: "If a weapon fires more than two hundred miles," he said, "it has to be transferred to the Air Force, according to our rules." I could see the Boss react.

"No service," the Boss declared, "will be restricted from developing a weapon for the mere reason that it fires too far." He admitted that he had no intention of putting the Army in the long-range strategic arms business; but he could visualize close ground support of our troops in Germany by weapons located in areas farther to the rear, such as the Brest Peninsula. The Pershing missile could fit into this category. The Army had won.

As the group filed out of the office, I observed their reactions closely, with some trepidation and some amusement. Charlie Wilson was in the depths; he walked past me without looking up or speaking. Admiral Radford, with a wide but mirthless smile, took with him the briefing chart I had previously made for the Boss, apparently implying that something sinister would come of it. Quarles, always the gentleman, gave me a glance out of the corner of his eye and chuckled. Secretary Brucker and General Lemnitzer were exultant.

Despite the decision rendered at this meeting, I had the distinct feeling that everything possible would be done in the Pentagon to obstruct the Boss's concept. It would be easy, in a bureaucracy of that size, conveniently to forget that the meeting had ever been held. Andy Goodpaster and I habitually kept records of every conversation held in the Oval Office, but this is the only one that I ever took to the Boss for approval. He read it over, initialed the upper right-hand corner, and underlined the word "mere" in the critical sentence. I then excerpted portions from the record and, with a cover sheet indicating the Boss's approval, sent it to the Pentagon for the guidance of those involved.

This episode certainly represented the most flagrant violation of the "rules" that I have ever consciously committed. Furthermore, backing and filling continued for some months before the decision on the Pershing was actually implemented by the new Secretary of Defense, Neil McElroy. Nevertheless, I have always felt a certain degree of proprietorship whenever the Pershing missile, now long deployed in Europe, is mentioned.

When Andy Goodpaster returned from New England, I switched over to a new tour of duty in Joint War Plans Branch, Plans Division, ODCSOPS,[8] Army General Staff. While this Pentagon assignment was not really a part of the White House experience, I think it can be considered indirectly so. The matters we dealt in, war planning, were of vital concern to the President as Commander-in-Chief. Furthermore, our family now lived in Alexandria, in easy range for attendance at White House functions. For example, when Queen Elizabeth II and Prince Philip of Britain visited in the fall of 1957, Barbara, the children, and I were present a good bit of the time and the two of us attended the dinners.

Work in the Pentagon was unlike anything else I have ever encountered. One's first reaction on arriving, unless one is eaten up with ambition (and thinks this is the place he will get ahead), is bewilderment and a certain degree of frustration. The office I was assigned to was considered quite a plum. When the Army Chief of Staff desired a position paper on strategy or force levels, the requirement came to "Joint War" for strategy or "Army War" for force structure. It was amazing how quickly a requirement could come down the ladder to the bottom, me, and how long it would take—and how many great minds would have to examine the result—as it went back up. But one of the rewarding aspects was the chance to deal with my Naval and Air Force counterparts. We bargained with each other at our level much as the Joint Chiefs of Staff horse-traded at theirs.

Physically, the Pentagon is gloomy, especially in the middle —that is, the B, C, and D rings. On the outside, the E Ring,

[8] Office of the Deputy Chief of Staff for Operations.

and on the inside, the A Ring, one might see the out of doors more frequently. On the E Ring, where the generals are located, one can even enjoy the view of the Potomac River or Arlington; not so where the bulk of the offices are buried away.

The hours in the Pentagon were by theory not too long, 8:15 to 4:45. However, to show the proper attitude, one should stay much later; 6:45 to 7:00 was about proper for a truly dedicated officer. In some spots this schedule was necessary; in other places it could have been avoided. (A good deal of the daytime was absorbed in waiting for the generals to have a spare moment.)

One occasion in the winter of 1957 Washington experienced a severe blizzard. An announcement came over the radio that all but "very key people" should stay home. *Everyone* in Joint War put on his snowshoes and made it in.

At that time (1957-58) each of the military services was preoccupied with trying to obtain the largest share of the budgetary pie. They were also in competition for the prestige of what service would have hegemony in each of the "unified commands." The Army seemed at the bottom of the heap. And yet the old pros developed an amused detachment about the internecine competition. My immediate boss and a long-time veteran of the "Joint arena" one day told of a terrible uproar the Army had been engaged in with the Department of Defense over some proposed Navy weapons system. The deeper he got into the story, the more animated and enthusiastic he became. His eyes were bright with intensity. Finally I asked, "Colonel, how did it come out?"

He suddenly stopped and stared at me. "Oh, we lost!" he said cheerfully.

The fact of the matter was that the Army was smarting under the impact of the so-called "new look" in military defenses. This term meant in essence that the Army was being cut back from its high force levels of the Korean War; and at the same time the Air Force, with its new missiles, was absorbing a bigger percentage of the budget. The Army's natural reaction, unofficial of course, was to try to discredit the Administration—to prove that the Boss was making grave errors in his reshaping of the military establishment. And I was in the office that was supposed to originate these positions! Once I demanded that my name be taken off a paper I had drafted, for by the time it had reached the deputy planner, Colonel Philip Mock, the contents had been so sharpened that I asked to be excused of any responsibility. Mock looked at me for a moment and nodded, "John, I respect that. I'll take your name off." Phil was not always so gentle, but I had great admiration for him. I was delighted when he finally attained the three stars of a lieutenant general. As commanding general, Fifth Army, he was the one, twelve years later, who was to present Mother with the flag from the coffin at the Boss's funeral.

One personality at Department of Defense stood out above the rest, Deputy Secretary Donald A. Quarles. By the time I arrived Charlie Wilson was packing his bags and the new Secretary, Neil McElroy, had not yet taken the reins. Quarles was making most of the decisions. Don Quarles had spent a good deal of time in the Pentagon, having previously served as Secretary of the Air Force. As such, he doubtless retained much of his Air Force orientation. He thus became the "paper tiger," the target of the Army's wrath and frustration. I shared those emotions to a large extent, although from the time of the "Pershing" conference I had always recognized him as a gentleman. Only later did I come to realize that in all his pro-Air Force positions Don Quarles was faithfully representing the Administration. His untimely death in 1959 was a real loss.

On the afternoon of November 25, 1957, about three months after reporting for duty in the Pentagon, I received a call in my office from Andy Goodpaster asking me to come over to the White House to help him out "on something." I went blithely, just as glad to have a short respite from Joint War, and arrived in less than an hour after the telephone call.

At the White House I soon learned that the Boss had suffered what was almost certainly a stroke. Two neurologists were present from Walter Reed but they could tell me very little, pending developments. I immediately went up to Mother's room, and there General Snyder explained what had happened. Dad had experienced dizzy spells at his desk early that afternoon, and on trying to communicate with his secretary, Ann Whitman, had found that his powers of speech were gone. She had sounded the alarm for

Andy, who had gently but firmly steered him to his bed in the White House. The stroke might be minor, Snyder went on, but the exact nature had not been determined. He believed that standing in the cold that morning during ceremonies for visiting King Mohammed V of Morocco might have caused a spasm in one of the small capillaries of the brain. Plans had already been made for Vice President Nixon to stand in that evening at the formal dinner.

As we were waiting, a figure appeared at the door. Who should it be but the Boss himself, clad in his brown-checked bathrobe! To our horror, he plunked himself down comfortably in one of the easy chairs as if nothing had happened. Mother gasped, "What are you doing up, Ike?"

He countered fairly audibly with a question of his own: "Why shouldn't I be up? I have a dinner to go to."

It took a couple of minutes for the three of us to convince him that he was in bed for the evening, and it appeared that this was the first time he realized the extent of his condition. Finally he got up and ambled back to his room, mumbling to himself about the Heads of Governments Meeting of the NATO Conference in Paris two weeks off. Softly but quite clearly, he said, "If I can't make that meeting, I'll have to quit. Anyhow, I couldn't leave this job to a better man than Dick." Back in bed, resigned, he went to sleep.

That evening Mother carried on, playing her role at the dinner for Mohammed V. The King, apprised of the circumstances, was of course quite understanding. Dad remained in bed, with Doc Snyder sitting with him half the night and I the other.

When the Boss woke up the next morning, he began to look around the dimly lighted bedroom. He pointed to his favorite water color, a Turner depicting Culzean Castle from the shoreline. It portrayed some outlaws of old, smuggling illicit goods into Scotland. Dad began to burble, trying to name it.

The more he tried, the more frustrated he became. He thrashed on the double bed, beating the bedclothes with his fists. By this time Mother and Doc Snyder had joined us and each was shouting any word that came to mind. Finally Mother hit upon the official title of the picture, "The Smugglers." When she blurted it out, Dad shook his finger at her in a gesture demanding a repeat. But even having heard the word, he still couldn't say it. Later in the morning he was successful.

The Boss's recovery, however, was remarkable. Within a couple of days he was up and around and able to communicate haltingly. By Thursday, three days after his stroke, he was able to attend Thanksgiving services. By the end of the week he was determined that he was going to make it to Paris.

After the original crisis that Thanksgiving, I returned at once to my duties in Joint War. I was ordered, however, to go to Paris with the Boss on December 13 in an aide capacity. Here I might add parenthetically that it is difficult to step into a busy staff like that of the White House or Joint War for a few days and do much of anything useful other than odd jobs, a little editing, and expressing of opinions—the last of which is normally the least welcome of one's contributions. As long as the Boss was holding up well, this trip was somewhat of a vacation.

The Heads of Government Meeting in the Palais de Chaillot was, however, significant for several reasons. First, this was the year that the nations of NATO, with exceptions, agreed to the stationing of nuclear weapons on their soil. While Americans tacitly accept that nuclear weapons are stored in unknown spots around our country, the idea is not quite so easy for Europeans. For one thing, the weapons we store are our own and controlled by us. Not so in their cases. The willingness of many of the NATO nations, therefore, to so participate in the over-all NATO defense was a noteworthy act.

Another aspect of the trip which was surprising to all of us was the exceedingly warm welcome the Boss received whenever he stepped outside the door. The streets were lined with people. This was an unusual phenomenon for the Parisians, accustomed as they are to visiting heads of state, but it was particularly significant in late 1957, only a year after we had participated in their humiliation over the Suez. Quite likely the fact that the Boss was determined to come to Paris after a serious illness, even at the risk of his life, caught the French imagination.

But the critical unknown was the question of the Boss's own performance. It exceeded the expectations of all of us. True, he was forced to read his formal talks, but this was hardly noticed. The occasion that gave me the most concern was the visit he paid to SHAPE, his own headquarters of five years before. He thought he was going informally, quietly; but when we drove through the gates we discovered that General Lauris Norstad, Supreme Allied Commander in Europe (SACEUR), had turned out the entire headquarters, formed up in the courtyard, for a ceremony. On seeing this, the Boss took off his hat in the cold and said a few words, in this vein:

> . . . After forty years of wearing a uniform, it would be strange if I felt still quite as natural with my civilian hat as I did with my military cap. But I want to indulge, for just a moment, this feeling of homesickness, the fun of going and seeing some of the people of SHAPE, not because they are the same ones, because there's only a few left here of five years or so, but they are the same ones carrying the same mission, doing the same job that all of us here started in 1951. . . .
>
> So, to all of you greetings, good wishes, good luck, and I hope that your homes are warm and nice, and the kids are in good health and everything is going fine with all of you—with all of SHAPE—from whatever nation you are.
>
> Good luck. Thank you. Good-by.[9]

Despite my own disapproval of the entire exercise—it was too much to take on, I thought—I have to admit that I was touched. More important, the Boss had proved that his recovery was to all intents and purposes complete.

A sequel to the trip was less cheerful. Since the Boss was still not at his best, he decided that the report to the nation over television should be a joint program between him and Secretary Dulles. The President gave a few introductory remarks and then introduced the Secretary. With all his qualities, Secretary Dulles was something less than a spellbinding speaker. As he droned on, the Boss inadvertently chewed on his glasses, gnawed on pencils, and examined the ceiling. After the program, Mr. Truman was quoted as saying, "I think I was as bored as the President was." This format was never employed again. Fortunately the situation never again called for it.

[9] From *Public Papers of the Presidents, Eisenhower, 1957,* p. 843.

That fall of 1957 and early part of 1958 constituted probably the lowest point in the Boss's Administration. A certain slump always sets in during the year after a President is re-elected. In a way he is already a lame duck, though he may still have three years left in his term. And when elected under the dramatic circumstances such as those which surrounded the election of 1956, the letdown the next year was understandably severe.

But even recognizing these circumstances, this period was exceptionally difficult. Not only did the American economy begin to slip into the 1957–58 recession but the nation was jolted by the launching of the Soviets earth-orbital satellite Sputnik I on October 4, 1957. This event sent off a wave of unreasoning hysteria, which the Boss did his best to combat. The first United States satellite, Explorer I, was put into orbit by the Army nearly four months later.

It is notable, though perhaps only coincidental, that the Boss's stroke occurred during this very difficult period, between the launching of Sputnik I and Explorer I and during a period where an economic recession was shaping up. His dispatch of troops in September 1957 to enforce school integration in Little Rock, Arkansas, had caused a furor in the South. The remarkable thing was not that the Boss experienced difficulties during this time but that he was able to recover and regain the control of the situation.

Explorer was never intended to be the "official" United States satellite program. After we had accepted the commitment, at the Rome Conference of 1954, to orbit a satellite during the International Geophysical Year (1957 through mid-1958) a project, Vanguard, had been established to make use of a booster to be designed from scratch by the Navy. By early 1956 Andy Goodpaster had learned that the Army, using a modified version of the Redstone missile, had boosters available and sitting on the shelves that could do the job early in 1957, months before Sputnik. But directions to the Department of Defense to keep the White House informed of this alternate prospect evaporated into limbo, and the Boss was preoccupied with other things.

The rationale for ignoring the Army's capability and for starting from scratch with the Navy's Vanguard was that Vanguard would theoretically contain nothing secret; everything about it could be made public, available to all nations. Dad swallowed this line of reasoning, egged on, I am sure, by Charlie Wilson and Admiral Radford, neither of whom bore any noticeable affection for the Army.

The end result was that the Russians put up a satellite—two in fact—before the first American success, a humiliating national experience.[10] Only when the new Defense Secretary, Neil Mc-Elroy, was told by Major General John B. Medaris and Dr. Wernher von Braun of the Redstone (Jupiter-C) capability was the ultimately successful Explorer taken out of mothballs and readied for firing on January 31, 1958.

The success of Explorer I had many unpredictable implications. The size of the satellite it placed in orbit was small compared to the 184-pound Sputnik I or the 1,100 pound Sputnik II. Nevertheless, with its instrumentation, it provided more scientific knowledge than the Soviet products. The Army's achievement in this venture, strangely, while lauded by everyone—the Boss was elated the night it went—did not endear the Army high command long to the rest of the White House. I sensed a feeling that the Army represented an upstart second only to the Soviets in the White House.

In mid-February 1959, the Vanguard program finally succeeded. The Boss in his elation sent a letter of congratulations to the superbly capable Admiral Arleigh Burke, Chief of Naval Operations.[11] Along with it went a bottle of Burke's favorite Scotch, Chivas Regal.

A few days later the Boss had folded in his inside coat pocket a letter which he was showing with glee to anyone he could corner. It happened to be an acknowledgment from Admiral Burke.

Admiral Burke's letter, dated February 18, 1959, began in proper formal military style:

My dear Mr. President
My deepest appreciation for the bottle of Chivas Regal. Your

[10] The first Vanguard exploded on the ground after the successful launching of Explorer I.

[11] Burke was the only member of the Joint Chiefs asked to stay on for six years, in contrast to the normal four.

thoughtfulness and kindness in sending it to me will remain in my memory for a long time to come. It is my exceedingly good fortune to be able to accept it on behalf of the many capable and loyal Navy People who have contributed to the Vanguard program . . .

The second paragraph continued in the same vein but expressed approbation of the Chivas Regal and indicated that the admiral was enjoying the libation while writing this letter. The third paragraph, containing a couple of misspelled words, exclaimed how much clearer were the problems of the Navy with the aid of the "suberb Scoch." The letter continued to degenerate until it reached the last paragraph:

Shanks again ferthe bug juice. Besh damed burobon Iever had. Shuris good shtuff. Jus like mipappy uset tom ake. Shurdo tank yu fur shis jug an tha dayoff. Itch bout tyme I adda day off to do sum cleer serius thimpking. Shur haz hellpt. Everthig ish cleer as cannbe now. Mush quitnow an fine anodder bodel odish delic iuocius boos.

> Very respectfully,
> ARLEIGH BURKE

The Boss had immediately answered as follows:

Your letter of the eighteenth gave me a needed chuckle. The reflected mileage from one, repeat one, bottle was tremendous!

Through all this period, during the satellite problems, I was still assigned to Joint War Plans, Army General Staff. During that time also, in July 1958, came the landings in Lebanon. The whole situation gave me some measure of difficulty in the form of divided loyalties. The Army, I thought, was receiving less than its justified share of credit for launching Explorer: in the same spirit I resented the fact that the marines were accorded so much publicity in the Lebanon operation that very few people outside the Pentagon realized that the bulk of the eventual force were soldiers.

This was a selfish service viewpoint, I admit, but I think I was partly sharing the paranoia that was afflicting the General Staff at that time. Probably my feelings were exaggerated by a belief that things did not have to be so bad for the Army, that if the Boss were exposed a little more to the Army viewpoint, he could do something to rectify the morale problem. If my attitude was narrow-minded, I have little defense. But when I was sent for to report to the White House for permanent duty under Andy Goodpaster on October 20, 1958, I went with a sense of relief. My period of divided loyalty was at an end. But at the same time I was being drawn once more into the Boss's orbit.

8
Worker in the Vineyard

When former Governor Sherman Adams of New Hampshire resigned as assistant to the President in the fall of 1958, the White
House staff was reorganized and my ties with the White House
became more involved. I reported for duty on the White House
staff within a couple of days after Andy Goodpaster's call.

Adams was a fine, dedicated, honest public servant. He was
highly loyal to the Boss but at the same time gave the impression
that he enjoyed his powers a little too much for the tastes of a
large number of people of both political parties. The indiscretion
he committed, that of accepting rather trivial favors from a man
he admired—and then innocently asking a federal agency to give
this man's problem priority attention—was a matter of carelessness, not venality. It was a peccadillo compared to the galloping
corruption in many other administrations. But having offended
so many people, Adams found that when his error was made public he had few allies outside the White House. Finally he realized,
though he fought the idea, that he was a political liability for the
President, indeed the whole Republican party. He resigned volun-
tarily but lingered around the White House for a few weeks before
returning to New Hampshire.

The Sherman Adams case, along with that of Air Force Secretary Harold E. Talbott some years earlier, has always struck me
as particularly tragic. The fickle public can easily forget the contributions of a man, no matter how significant they may have
been, and remember him principally for his downfall. Anyone
engaged in public service would be well advised to study the circumstances behind these unconscious indiscretions that can brand
a man, however unjustly.

Governor Adams was replaced by Major General Wilton B.

Persons, a retired Army officer. General Persons had spent a significant part of his military career in working with the Congress. He had served with the Boss at SHAPE and had subsequently become the principal legislative liaison officer in the White House under Governor Adams. Theoretically, Persons was given broader powers than Adams had held. Their methods of operating, however, were diametrically different. Where Adams gave the impression of autocratic hostility, Persons made full use of his soft Alabama accent and twinkling eye. He had a soldier's vocabulary—which offended nobody—and a disarming sense of humor. ("If they don't do like we say, we'll just take our ukuleles and go home.")

Under Persons the organized staff—as apart from the Boss's personal staff, consisting of Tom Stephens, Jim Hagerty, Ann Whitman, and the military aides—was organized in three principal sections: domestic issues (Robert Merriam), legislative liaison (Bryce Harlow), and staff secretary and national security (Andy Goodpaster). This breakdown is the greatest of oversimplifications; it leaves out the legal counsel (David Kendall) and the National Security Council (NSC) staff (Gordon Gray). It would be utterly impossible to draw up a schematic organization chart for the White House; everyone more or less designed his own job. Since there was always more than enough to do, nobody stepped on anyone else's toes.

I mention this organization simply to identify where I fitted in. Art Minnich and I were Andy Goodpaster's two principal subordinates in his capacity of staff secretary. Art handled domestic affairs generally and I assisted Andy in his national security responsibilities. Thus, in pure theory, I reported through Andy, through General Persons, thence to the Boss. Since my desk was located only a few yards from the Boss's, the theory really had little application in practice. Actually, Persons preferred things this way. He declined esoteric security clearances for types of classified material that Andy and I held—for the U-2 program for example—and everything worked harmoniously.

This organization included one flaw that, with other people involved, could have caused friction. Andy Goodpaster, with title of staff secretary, handled all matters pertaining to immediate national security problems; Gordon Gray, on the other hand, located across the street, bore the title of Special Assistant to the President for National Security Affairs. In this capacity Gordon handled long-range planning such as the NSC policy papers. But the man handling long-range policy needs to know what is going on currently and vice versa. The dividing line is difficult to draw. In this case, the potential pitfall was minimal because the positions were held by two selfless individuals, totally dedicated to helping the Boss. Competition or self-promotion never entered the question. The two simply kept each other overinformed.

When I arrived for duty at the White House, the first item of business was to define exactly what my job would be under Andy. On my own part, I preferred to be assigned to a specific area of responsibility in which I could operate fairly independently under his supervision. Andy was not so inclined. Either for my own education or in order for him to keep his hand in on all issues, he decided that I should assist him across the board in all his activities.

One area he gave me specifically, however: the daily intelligence briefing for the Boss. Andy would pick me up in a White House car at our house in Alexandria at about 7:30 each morning and on the way in to work we would talk over what was going on at the time. By our arrival at about 7:45, I would have on my desk several daily intelligence brochures, from State, CIA, and Defense. The volume of material was far too vast for the Boss to go through personally. Therefore I would select the items of greatest importance, make notes, and be prepared to give him a run-down whenever he was free. In other matters, I simply worked as Andy's understudy.

One of the big obstacles regarding the daily intelligence briefings was to find an open space in the Boss's schedule. In the early morning, before appointments began, he was always busy signing letters he had dictated the day before. When I would barge into his office, I was not always welcome. More than once, his way of saying good morning would be to slap his palm on the desk and growl, "What the hell do you want?" I took this impatience completely as a matter of course and, after I had plunked myself down in a chair facing the desk, he would relax and listen. Needless to say, I confined myself to the essentials and tried to find convenient times of day to brief him.

Sometimes, in slower periods, I would save up my material for a day or so. Soon I learned to check with Tom Stephens to find when the Boss might be going somewhere in the car. I would then ride along with him and, in a relatively relaxed mood, he would be receptive. If a report of vital importance had come in, such as word of Khrushchev's threatening to blockade Berlin, I would of course battle my way into the office, sometimes holding up a scheduled appointment for a couple of minutes.

One of our major activities was that of monitoring the Boss's meetings with his cabinet members and others. When Andy had taken over as staff secretary in 1954, he had developed a policy of accompanying every visitor that went into the Oval Office. Andy would look over the scheduled appointments and decide which meeting he would monitor and which he wanted me to handle. We did not take shorthand, but, being fairly well acquainted with the material beforehand, we were able to get the essence of each conference with little difficulty. John Foster Dulles was the only exception to this rule. Dulles often saw the Boss alone and unfortunately kept scanty memos himself. As a result, some important conversations between the two are lost to history.

One technique I developed during this period turned out to be useful, not only during my White House assignment but after. I studied the Boss's writing style and analyzed it. He had always been good in English; for a while as a cadet he had stood at the top of his class in that subject. But his style was completely unpretentious. His vocabulary was remarkable—sometimes he would come up with a word that would make the press head for their dictionaries—but he eschewed purple phrases and quotable statements. Perhaps he could never have mastered the MacArthur blank verse, even had he admired it. He thought of his writing as simple, direct English, and he had been able to a great extent to resist the wordiness of "federal prose" over the years.

I never forgot the lesson I had learned back in 1954, while on temporary duty, when I had been sternly corrected for pretentiousness and pedantry in my drafting. It is difficult to write for another person even under the best of circumstances, but it was a source of pride to me to be able to redraft wordy material into something the Boss would sign.

The relationship between a father who happened to be President and a son working on his staff was one problem that I never found serious. Between the two of us the situation was eased by our common military background. In person I always called him "Dad," and we spoke our minds to each other frankly. However, when speaking of him in the third person, I would use the common term "the Boss" and sometimes even slipped unconsciously into "the President." This was no affectation; with other people using formal terminology, it was only natural.

The situation was easier, I believe, than it would have been if my father had been president of a corporation. At least in the White House, nobody was concerned that I would inherit the job. Therefore, I felt that I was treated as just another staff officer by my colleagues unless a tricky or unpleasant issue came up which someone would ask me to discuss with Dad at some "informal, opportune time." After a period, I became conscious one day that I was getting more than my share of the bad news to take in—such items as the latest developments regarding the shooting down of the U-2 over the Soviet Union or of the RB-47 over the Baltic in 1960. When I discovered that was the case, I found it amusing but quickly decided it was inevitable. The only problem in the long run was with the Boss himself. He was a man who in his later years (in contrast to those days of slave labor during the thirties) chose to leave his worries at the office. From the White House days to the end, I think he unconsciously associated me with work—and bad news at that!

Toward the end of 1959, when the Boss began his program of extensive traveling abroad, I found myself as a member of the advance teams that visited the various capitals to make preliminary preparations. Experience proved the necessity of sending representatives close to the President ahead of time. An ambassador on the spot was in a poor position to judge in detail the desires and needs of his visitor. The "standard" team, headed by Tom Stephens, consisted also of Jim Hagerty, myself, and others. By the time we included officers who would have continuing responsibility for a given capital, members of the Secret Service, and communications personnel, the team filled the Special Air Missions Boeing 707 to the last seat.[1]

This type of duty was tiring but stimulating. Normally, the party would spend only about a day and a half at each stop, and much had to be accomplished during that short time. Our first chore, not always easy, was to establish ourselves with the local embassy as speaking authoritatively for the President. Here was always a potential clash, for some ambassadors—usually self-important political appointees—tended to take their positions as the "President's representative" too literally and disliked being told by a group of White House staff officers what the President could do and what he could not. Normally, by the time we had arrived, a tentative schedule would have been submitted to Washington by the local embassy, and we would probably have copies of these plans. But the Boss had requirements that the local embassy could not foresee regarding security, rest periods, food, and even location of telephones and buzzers where he would sleep.

The most common controversies that Tom, Jim, and I encountered involved the Boss's schedule. He was required by the doctors, for example, to rest for an hour before the noon meal. The local ambassador would take note of this but, anxious to squeeze the utmost from a presidential visit, would schedule luncheon for one hour after the termination of the preceding ceremony. This plan obviously was not good enough; that hour included travel time (sometimes a half hour) to his place of rest, undressing, and dressing. If an ambassador would stand his ground and refuse to budge, Jim would look at me and I would go into the family act. "Mr. Ambassador," I had to say more than once, "the doctors are adamant on this full hour's rest. The President is going to countries other than this one, and we've *got* to save his strength. If you can't find some way to comply with this requirement, I just have no choice but to recommend to Dad that he cancel coming here." It always worked.

[1] There were three Special Air Missions Boeing 707s equipped for the President's comfort. Whenever the President was aboard, regardless of which one of the three planes was employed, it was designated *Air Force One*. This procedure has since been changed as the requirement for more sophisticated equipment accompanying the President has arisen. Now one specific plane is so designated.

A lesser point that had to be sold, this time to the local government, was the question of press and TV buses following close behind the President's car. From the local government's viewpoint there was question that these buses would somewhat mar the appearance of the motorcade. Here Jim Hagerty would carry the ball. "Mr. Minister," Jim would say solemnly, "I appreciate your position. But you must realize that only a few thousand people right here will be seeing the motorcade. These press buses will beam the spectacle to the whole world, and millions around the globe will witness the warmth of the reception your people give the President." This appeal to the national pride of the local minister invariably carried the discussion. I can remember no instance where the press buses were finally denied.

This team operated through Europe, the Middle East, and North Africa in November 1959; we did the same in Latin America the following January. And no sooner had we returned home, worn out, than we would then turn around and join the Boss on the "official" visit. Thus we made every circuit twice.

In June 1959 Barbara moved the family to Gettysburg and I lived in a room on the third floor of the White House on weekdays. Time for reporting to the office in the mornings was the same, but I was only about three minutes from my desk. In the evenings I would plan to stay in the office until 7:00 P.M., as before. However, on most "normal" days I received word about 6:30 that the Boss, having finished his work and practiced a little golf on his putting green, would like me to join him on the second floor of the White House for a cocktail. Dad would lounge in his overstuffed easy chair, with the telephone available at his side. Sometimes we would be alone but usually, as the Boss was a gregarious individual, there would be a visitor or two on hand to pass the time until 7:30 dinner.

By all odds the most frequent of these visitors were George E. Allen, a close friend from World War II days (likewise a friend of both Roosevelt and Truman), and General Alfred M. Gruenther. Allen and Gruenther were ideal companions, as both, being men of the world and geniuses in their own fields, had no axes to grind. From each, Dad knew he could receive intelligent and disinterested opinions. Business of the day, however, was rarely discussed unless the Old Man, with something particularly perplexing on his mind, brought it up. Conversation generally ranged over a wide spectrum of subjects, from baseball to horse racing (George Allen's favorite hobby) to the stock market to politics.

George, on his part, was a superb conversationalist and entertainer. He possessed a well-recognized sense of humor, one of the pleasant features of which was that the butt of the jokes was almost invariably himself. He was much overweight, and one of the Boss's favorite diversions was to give George instructions on taking care of his health and to lay wagers with him as to how many pounds George could lose in a certain time. But George lacked motivation and almost invariably lost. An admirable trait of George's was his loyalty. An old friend of Truman's, he never once uttered a word derogatory to the former President, even though he knew that Dad and Truman were not on the closest terms. "I'm a Truman man," I once heard him say. Unfortunately, Truman did not realize this fact and said so in public.

General Gruenther, on the other hand, had an equally acute sense of humor but of a different kind. He was a wag and a kidder. His mind was always working at top speed and conversation with him, no matter what the subject, was rarely low key. In this last respect he and the Boss were much alike.

The three of them—Allen, Gruenther, and the Boss—played bridge together a great deal, both at the White House and in his cottage at Augusta National Golf Club. But Dad and Gruenther, with their expertise at the game and uncharitable reactions to any blunder, were both considered impossible to play with as partners; therefore they always had to play together. George loved to play against them. A born gambler, he figured that his luck could more than offset their skill. This was invariably the pattern when the three would play with William Robinson, Clifford Roberts, W. Alton ("Pete") Jones, Barry Leithead, and other friends of Dad's from both New York and Washington. Without a doubt the Boss's capacity at this stage of life to leave his work at the office contributed immeasurably to the fact that he left in good health, with no sign of slowing down.

The morning of Monday, November 10, 1958, appeared to be just another day. World affairs—the big issues—seemed to be quieting. The Red Chinese threat to Quemoy and Matsu, Taiwan's offshore islands, had tapered off to the point where the Reds were issuing more pompous statements and less artillery fire. This situation promised to sputter out, which it did. The domestic crises over the federal troops in Little Rock had done likewise. Furthermore, we in the White House had recovered, at least partially, from the sting of the defeat in the congressional elections. From a personal viewpoint, Andy Goodpaster and I had just returned from a stimulating visit to Europe in the company of such atomic pioneers as Dr. Edward Teller and Dr. Norris Bradbury. Everything appeared to be leveling off to business as usual—as much as business as usual ever applies in the White House.

That Monday morning, however, we learned that Khrushchev had reopened the issue of the status of West Berlin, a running sore since the days of World War II.

Khrushchev's initial declaration did not take the form of a definitive ultimatum. He declared his intention to turn over administrative control of East Berlin to the Pankow (East German) regime and called on the Western powers to begin negotiations with them looking to a withdrawal of Allied forces from the city. The portent was ominous, however, and the move created a furor within the Western governments and in the press. The Boss, seeing nothing to react to immediately, held his tongue.

The complicating factor in the whole situation was the fact that each of the Western powers—United States, France, and Britain—viewed the situation in somewhat different lights. The British seemed most willing, as a matter of accommodation, to go along with Khrushchev; the French, now under Premier Charles de Gaulle, were inclined to a stiffer attitude, although De Gaulle refused at first to commit himself. The Boss, reflecting not only his own convictions but sensing those of the American people as a whole, rejected outright any action which might imply a recognition of East Germany. Any such recognition would only render the reunification of Germany all the more remote. Further, Chancellor Adenauer, architect of the new West Germany, was adamant on the subject.

The situation threatened to become acute a few days after the Khrushchev declaration, when the East Germans held up a U.S. convoy destined for Berlin on the *Autobahn* at Helmstedt. The vehicles were delayed only a little over eight hours; but in the interim, both General Norstad[2] and the Joint Chiefs of Staff were cranking up for immediate military action. The Boss restrained them, and when the convoy was released, this immediate threat subsided. Subsequent convoys were delayed for shorter periods. Quite possibly the Soviets and the East Germans were not operating in perfect harmony.

On November 27 Andy Goodpaster sent me to Augusta with a summary of the positions of the governments as we knew them at the moment. Messages had been pouring in, and it was my job, under Andy's supervision, to distill the various viewpoints from the reports. This effort was complicated by the fact that the reports we had were not necessarily all authoritative. Some encompassed the views of the so-called "working-level" officials rather than the final considered, balanced views of those in authority. Thus I went to Augusta armed with a collection of information that would confuse and frustrate any President.

I reported to the Boss in his little office above the pro shop, overlooking the Augusta National Golf Course. The peaceful scenery outside belied the peril of the world situation in which the Boss, slouched on his chair in golf clothes, was in the final analysis the key figure. One by one, I went over the reports, the Boss becoming more and more restless as every divergent opinion among the allies manifested itself.

Some of the news, to be sure, was good. The allies were working through their embassies in Bonn on a joint reply. At the very least, none favored outright withdrawal from Berlin; the points of disagreement actually centered around tactics: timing, procedures, and the extent with which we could deal with the East Germans as Soviet agents. The "Soviet agent" idea, a brainchild of the State Department, had been rejected by the Boss from the outset. Of all the subtleties, the most disturbing was a British "working-level" paper suggesting that we deal with the East German government and eventually recognize it. Even M. Couve de Murville, French Foreign Minister, was reported to favor "low-level" dealings.

Within moments the Boss had Secretary of State Dulles on the telephone. "What the hell are the British up to?" he roared. As he

2 Supreme Commander, Allied Powers in Europe (SACEUR).

listened, Dad seemed to calm down a little. Things had changed drastically even from the time I had left Washington. The British "working-level" paper, happily, had been disavowed by Prime Minister Harold Macmillan; that was a relief. But the Secretary had bigger news: Khrushchev had lifted the immediate threat. But he gave the Western powers exactly six months, to May 27, 1959, at the end of which, he declared, Allied rights in Berlin would cease.

This ended the immediate crisis and created a new one. All talks during those ensuing six months would be conducted with the Soviet threat hanging over the heads of the negotiators. It was up to us, Dad mused, as he sat chewing on the bow of his glasses, gazing over the first tee, to ensure that this threat would not split the West asunder.

The first time that the Boss formally addressed the Berlin situation among a large group of his advisers was the morning of December 11, 1958. Immediately following the meeting of the National Security Council, he called the Vice President, Under Secretary of State Christian A. Herter, General Maxwell Taylor, Deputy Secretary of Defense Don Quarles, Secretary of the Treasury Robert B. Anderson, CIA Director Allen Dulles, and members of the White House staff into the Oval Office. (Secretary Dulles was in the hospital for a check up.) This meeting involved a preliminary discussion of an extremely abstruse set of ramifications, complicated by the old bugaboo of diverse views among the European Allies.

In view of the magnitude of the stakes involved, one might expect a meeting of this sort to be either frenzied, gloomy, or at least tense. On the contrary, the atmosphere on the surface was routine. As each officer filed from the Cabinet Room through Ann Whitman's office, he took his place in a more or less accepted location. Under Secretary Herter this day was sitting in Secretary Dulles' normal chair, behind the desk to the left of where the Boss swiveled back and forth, either scribbling, talking, or looking at the ceiling.[3]

[3] For some reason, the Secretary of State always sat in that spot, possibly because most of the papers being handed to the Boss came from State but also, one

The Vice President sat squarely opposite the President across the desk. Quarles and Taylor sat together at the end and others ringed themselves around. Members of the White House staff snuggled up close behind this first ring of officials. I was frantically taking notes.

The conversation seemed not unlike those which I had witnessed among the high command in World War II. Certainly a larger number of people were present and, since this was a subject which had not been highly coordinated among departments, each official spoke his mind in turn without being called. The tone was quiet, thoughtful, and businesslike, with no histrionics and nobody trying to upstage another. As with all such meetings, as time went on and everyone's views became more and more clear, the Boss tended to move to the center of the stage. By the end of the session he was doing most of the talking, giving what conclusions he could, based on the scanty facts available, for all to take back to their own offices and continue to do their homework on.

Everyone present was well aware that the Western Allies lacked conventional power in Europe to fight the Soviets on the ground. (The forces of the Warsaw Pact countries, opposing NATO,— most importantly the Poles and East Germans—were largely discounted, as the Soviet forces alone were superior in numbers to ours.) The group was seeking a general approach to make it clear that the West would not tolerate a Soviet abrogation of previous agreements, meanwhile avoiding resort to the final drastic action of general nuclear war. Should Soviet actions provoke us to this cataclysmic recourse, we could have, at that time, damaged their homeland all out of proportion to the capacity to retaliate. And yet the consequences to Europe and America, even in 1958 when we held overwhelming nuclear superiority, would have been dire indeed.

The matter of achieving a solid position with our Western Allies was complicated by the fact that confusion seemed to exist in all governments. Two international conferences in Western Europe would be involved with the same subject, the ambassadorial meeting of the four Western powers in Bonn and the NATO ministerial

suspected, because this was the most advantageous angle from which to look over the Old Man's left shoulder.

meeting, for which Foster Dulles was preparing, to begin in a couple of days.

Of the two the Boss decided that the most effective forum would have to be the NATO ministerial meeting. This emphasis was logical, since agreements among the foreign ministers would carry more weight than those among ambassadors. On the other hand, the very format of the NATO ministerial meetings, comprising so many countries, was awkward.

The degree of the use of force in the event of blockade—its gradual application—constituted the crux of the discussions. Here the conferees held various ideas, but nobody seemed to be very positive. If a convoy were to be stopped at Helmstedt, for example, should the United States send a reinforced battalion to fight its way down the *Autobahn* or should the force be as strong as an armored combat command? Possibly the size of the unit was not an overriding question. Even an armored combat command could be easily swallowed up by Soviet forces before reaching its destination. The Boss then put his finger on the essence, the more realistic contingency. The Communists could obstruct ground access to Berlin without resorting to the direct use of arms. They could merely demolish bridges and blow craters in the *Autobahn* and railroad lines. Without firing a shot, the Soviets could say, "So sorry, the ground access routes are in a state of disrepair." Only in the case of obstructed air access would combat action be necessary. An aircraft dispatched from Frankfurt to Tempelhof could be halted only by shooting it down.

Other complications had to be faced. One was a recent statement by Willy Brandt, then mayor of Berlin, indicating that he might be wavering. His position, however, was still unclear. A second was the virulent hostility with which his countryman Konrad Adenauer viewed any dealings whatsoever with the East Germans. But the densest complication of all still remained the attitude of the British. The Boss summarized: "If our policy is going to be to force the Soviets to bear the onus of being the first to resort to arms," he said, "then we had better get this to the British as soon as possible and give them time to study it."

Toward the end of this preliminary conference Vice President Nixon, thinking out loud as were the rest, got to the core of the situation in a way that turned out to be prophetic. "It seems to me," he said, "that we've got to consider what Khrushchev is really after. I can't believe that he's angling for war. I really think he's after a summit conference and this is his way of forcing it." In the electric atmosphere of the moment this remark went almost totally unnoticed.

Thus this first meeting ended with little decided except to declare that we would stand firm and deal only with the Soviets. "That message to Khrushchev from the Paris meeting," the Boss said, "should make it plain that the U.S. does not want war, and we realize the Soviets don't want war either. But if they deny us our rights, then we'll have to reassess our position. They've got to know that we're willing to put our whole stack in the pot. The other day a lady [Queen Frederika of Greece] advised me that we should ease world tensions by making a generous offer to the Soviets, so generous that they and the world will recognize it as such. But it must be something short of surrender.

"That," the Boss said, shaking his head, "will be the trick of the week."

The day after this meeting Secretaries Dulles and Herter came in. Dulles was leaving for the NATO ministerial meeting in Paris the next day. When he showed the Boss the opening statement he planned to make, the last sentence of the last paragraph immediately caught the President's eye. It began, "Because NATO meets these tests . . ." The sentence, he felt, presented too rosy a statement of the performance of NATO at that point. Getting on the soapbox a bit, the Boss continued: He had worked hard for NATO himself; but he had become discouraged at the continuing European pressure on the Americans to keep forces of six equivalent divisions while they themselves were withdrawing. Despite the economic resurgence of Europe—indeed, they were beginning to become formidable competitors—their vehement protests against any prospect of United States force reductions was making him weary. He brushed off information regarding West German progress in building their army and went on to complain that the British were selling generators in Mexico City at half the U.S.

price. At the same time, we were spending about 10 per cent of our gross national product on world defense. The wording was changed to read: "These are the ends which NATO serves . . ."

"The NATO allies should be reminded," the Boss went on, "that the U.S. maintains the nuclear deterrent to general war, the umbrella under which they live; we assist peripheral nations around the world: we maintain two divisions in Korea; and we supply the capability to deal with such problems as Quemoy and Matsu. It seems," he growled, "that the Europeans ought to be able to provide at least the ground forces for their own defense." Dad then reviewed his trip around Europe in early 1951—Andy Goodpaster had been with him—and reminded us all that NATO had been established on the assumption that five years would be the maximum for large American deployments in Europe. He had no intention of running out on our commitments, he hastened to add, and realized that West Germany was currently restricted to twelve divisions. Why, he wondered couldn't the West Germans produce twenty instead?

"Twenty German divisions," Dulles answered, "would probably scare the French."

The Boss snorted, unimpressed, "U.S. resources," he summarized, "should no longer be regarded as inexhaustible."

Foster Dulles then brought up the recent behavior of General Charles de Gaulle, who had taken over as Premier of France the previous May. On the basis of past personal experience, the Boss warned Dulles to be prepared for De Gaulle to take the most extraordinary actions. He told the story—a favorite of his—about his confrontation with De Gaulle over his plan to evacuate Strasbourg while the Battle of the Bulge had been raging. De Gaulle, in Churchill's presence, had threatened to withdraw French forces from SHAEF command and Dad had told him to go ahead, since the Americans and British could win the war anyway. But he also told De Gaulle not to expect another round of ammunition nor any other kind of support.

Halting his tirade, the Boss conceded that he recommended no such course of action for the State Department at this time; he was simply illustrating the kind of thing De Gaulle was capable of.

Three days later we received good news. The NATO foreign ministers, meeting in Paris, declared that the West would never negotiate with the Communists while under threat. The NATO nations other than the four most principally involved (United States, Britain, France, West Germany) associated themselves with this position. The governments of the four were in the process of drafting identical answers to Khrushchev's statement.

In the middle of January 1959 came the first sign that the posture of firmness with restraint was showing some promise. Khrushchev seemed to begin a gradual, almost imperceptible retreat. Soviet Deputy Premier Anastas Mikoyan came to Washington, ostensibly to visit the Soviet Ambassador, Mikhail Menshikov, a rather unlikely story. Not unexpectedly he asked to see the Boss. I met him in Tom Stephens' office before he went in, and we conversed casually for a few moments. He was particularly interested in the painting of Dad, done by another Thomas E. Stephens, that hung in the office.[4] Mikoyan himself was a personable, outgoing personality, who resembled the man behind the counter in a meat market rather than a Communist Politburo member. Though he confined himself to repeating the Soviet line, still his very coming seemed significant. Presumably, he had been sent to begin muddying the waters.

By the end of January 1959 the Boss was ready for a full-scale meeting to review our contingency planning, always looking forward to the fateful day of May 27—when Khrushchev's "six months" would expire. Time had passed for the members of the Administration to study the situation in detail; furthermore, Secretary Dulles, back from Paris, was armed with the thoughts of our NATO allies. His subsequent discussions with members of the Defense Department had brought into focus the differences in their viewpoints.

[4] It is easy to confuse two men, both named Thomas E. Stephens. One was the artist, who must have done a couple dozen portraits of the Boss; the other was Dad's appointments secretary, an astute political aide who had been on board off and on since the beginning of the 1952 campaign. Though the former was British, the two had once lived within a block of each other in New York City.

In reality, this meeting was a continuation of that held on December 11, 1958, with essentially the same cast of characters. The issues remained the same, to wit, a decision regarding our own policy to meet the Soviet threat and the all-important corollary of what our allies could be persuaded to do.

The technicalities regarding the possible escalation of the Allied responses to Soviet recognition of East Germany were difficult indeed. Such recognition would mean the Soviets' turning over control of the *Autobahn* to the East Germans, which would be intolerable. Already, at every checkpoint on the land routes to Berlin an East German (GDR) official was present. Whereas we would continue to refuse to allow this GDR official to approve or disapprove our right of entry, to stamp passes, or search trucks, it would, nevertheless, be unreasonable not to show a pass at least to identify a given convoy as military.

The main split between Dulles and the Defense Department was over the immediacy of limited military action. The Joint Chiefs of Staff (JCS) believed that, once a convoy was stopped as of May 27, an instant move should be taken. A small armored probe, involving scout cars rather than tanks, should pass the barrier and proceed until it was stopped. Further, the Joint Chiefs had recommended preparation for possible large-scale use of force if things came to a head on that day in May. It should include units capable of meeting major resistance, carrying bridging equipment to cope with the passive resistance actions that the Boss had pointed up earlier. Dulles, on the other hand, felt strongly that sudden actions of this type would be misconstrued around the world. Indeed, he said, in many countries such acts would be viewed as aggression on our part.

The two viewpoints were clearly defined. General Nathan Twining, chairman of the JCS, with a healthy military suspicion of diplomats, was afraid the United States might make some move, go halfway, and quit. We should, he believed, be ready to risk general war on the spot.

In this difference the Boss leaned on the side of Foster Dulles but for somewhat different reasons. One division, he said, reiterating his former thinking, could never be sufficient to do the job; and without our Allies behind us, we would have no line of communications to depend on. Even Adenauer, the President said, would probably not go along with a "Berlin or bust." In a situation as ticklish as this, we must give peace forces a chance to do their work.

After the arguments went back and forth, the Boss declared that if a convoy should be stopped on May 27, it would pull back. We would then institute an airlift to Berlin, evacuate dependants from the city, withdraw our ambassador to Moscow, and break relations with the Soviets. We would then take the matter to the UN and begin preparations for possible general war.

In the meantime, however, between the end of January and May 27, the Boss agreed to reinforce our troops in Europe, not by deploying additional units but by sending sufficient replacements to fill those vacancies which normally exist in peacetime configurations. This move should *not* be made public, for a publicly announced reinforcement would only commit Khrushchev further and cut off any line of retreat he would like to take. It should be made obvious enough, however, that clandestine Soviet intelligence would pick it up. Let the Soviet spies work for us—and in the cause of peace.

In the course of the meeting, it was readily assumed that the West would be forced soon to enter into negotiations with the Soviets. A second-level meeting, it was decided, would not truly violate our determination to avoid negotiating under threat. A summit conference of heads of government was out of the question; but a meeting of the foreign ministers might avert the crisis before it could come to a head.

This conference, like that of December 11, was conducted quietly, with everyone freely expressing his own views. On the surface it appeared no more tense than a normal meeting of a corporate board of directors. But there was no escaping the drama. The Boss, as he wrote later, recognized that "we were risking the very fate of civilization on the premise that the Soviets would back down from the deadline when confronted by force.[5] And yet he felt he had no alternative—because our backing down would mean eventual disaster.

[5] *Waging Peace*, p. 342.

This January 28 meeting terminated what might be considered the first phase of the Berlin crisis. The United States Government had, for its own part, decided on the course of action it would take when the time of grace expired.

Soon thereafter Secretary of State Dulles began what was to be his last trip to Europe. The White House had received news that British Prime Minister Macmillan was planning a trip to the Soviet Union toward the end of the month, and little time remained to achieve what meeting of the minds might be possible with the British.

It was a good thing Dulles went. Macmillan, still worried over our determination not to permit East Germans to act as Soviet agents, seemed to believe that the current status of Berlin could not long continue, at least not after Adenauer was out of power. De Gaulle, by contrast, began for the first time to indicate his true feelings. He was willing to adopt a hard line more rapidly than either the Boss or Dulles had visualized. The memories of Allied failure to take action when Hitler occupied the Rhineland in 1936 were still with him. Adenauer, on his part, was becoming more openly suspicious of the British, probably rightly so. The outcome of Dulles' visit produced one item on which all could agree—the reaffirmation that a foreign ministers' conference with the Soviets should soon be held.

Immediately upon his return Secretary Dulles turned over his duties as Secretary of State temporarily to Under Secretary of State Christian Herter. He then entered Walter Reed Hospital for observation of the abdominal pains he had been suffering.

Khrushchev then took another step to confuse the situation. At the meeting of the 21st Party Congress he inserted a remark that he would welcome a visit by the Boss to Moscow. This prospect created excitement in the papers, but the Boss countered in a press conference that it was hardly to be construed as a formal invitation. The gesture, however, opened the way for the Western powers to propose a meeting of the foreign ministers.

Prime Minister Macmillan began his trip to Moscow in late February. While there he kept the Boss informed of every move. He was treated well at first. After a warm welcome, however, Khrushchev suddenly delivered an insulting speech and broke an engagement on the excuse of a toothache. On reading Macmillan's cable reporting this new turn of events, the Boss remarked that he personally would have gotten in the plane and headed home. Nevertheless, Macmillan stuck it out; and after a four-day trip around the Soviet Union returned to Moscow where the atmosphere was once again more cordial. By swallowing his pride, Macmillan probably eased Khrushchev's problem in his gradual backing down on the Berlin crisis.

A few days later Khrushchev took his next step, calling for a summit meeting on the Berlin crisis. However, he conceded that the West would never agree to such a conference without a foreign ministers' meeting first. Therefore he gave way and agreed to the lower-level conference as a prelude to a summit, a major concession. The Vice President's earlier prediction seemed to be coming true.

On the morning of March 5 the Boss held another meeting in his office. By now, the American position was fairly well settled and some of the limited actions had been accomplished. The slight build-up in Army forces, the movement of the Second Fleet to the North Atlantic, and the positioning of an additional tactical air unit in Turkey were approved. However, the Boss refused to deploy an additional division to Europe and put in abeyance a proposal to stop all flow of dependants to Berlin. The attitude of Mayor Willy Brandt was still a matter of some concern. Brandt still seemed amenable to making all Berlin—East and West—an international city with the understanding, presumably, that he would be mayor.

As in all meetings, the matter of degree of force necessary to hold open ground access routes to Berlin came up. Here, to my amusement, the Boss's military background raised its head in earnest. He pointed out a little pontifically that holding open an access route involves more than just occupying the road from shoulder to shoulder. This would be more a matter, he went on, of a three- to four-corps operation, holding considerable territory on either side of the road.[6] This was a consideration that everyone else present, in their state of confusion, had simply brushed under the rug. All realized he was right; everyone also knew that the entire U.S. ground forces in Europe comprised *two* corps—and weak ones at that. No further mention was made of trying to hold open the access route by force.

The major consideration now, however, was domestic public opinion. A large segment of the population, it appeared, was becoming restless, impatient for some outward sign of American reaction to the Khrushchev ultimatum. More specifically, many felt that we were failing to make adequate military preparations for a showdown and were somewhat baffled by the fact that the Boss, in the light of the Khrushchev threat, insisted on continuing his previously announced reductions of U.S. armed forces. To explain the Administration position, Vice President Nixon and General Persons urged that the Boss invite the leaders of both political parties in the two houses of Congress (specifically Senators Lyndon Johnson and Everett Dirksen and Representatives Sam Rayburn and Charles Halleck) for a briefing the next morning, March 6. Herter, on the other hand, was skeptical. He advised quietly that not too many details of our diplomatic tactics be given to members of Congress. Too much exposure would, he said, make any retreat by Khrushchev more difficult. And, Herter added, "When a microphone is placed in front of a politician, he has a tendency to talk."

At this point Dad exploded: "Tendency, hell—a compulsion!" Nevertheless, the meeting with congressional leaders was scheduled.

By the time the legislative leaders arrived the next morning, the plan had already altered. The Boss, doubtless at the suggestion of General Persons and Bryce Harlow, had decided that the morning group was too limited; four people could not adequately cover a

---

[6] A corps is actually not a fixed unit. The largest unit of prescribed size and strength is the division. A corps comprises two or more divisions with supporting engineers, artillery, and others. I never asked Dad what size corps he had in mind in making this statement, as the question of ground warfare, being so preposterous, was academic. Based on his World War II experience, Dad doubtless had in mind at least four divisions per corps, one of them armored. Many corps in that war grew so large as to dwarf this figure.

wide enough spectrum of opinion. Rather than expand the morning meeting in the Oval Office, however, it was decided to hold a second one late that afternoon in the ground-floor library, to include Senators Alexander Wiley, Richard Russell, J. William Fulbright, and Leverett Saltonstall; and Representatives Leslie Arends, A. S. J. Carnahan, Carl Vinson and Robert Chiperfield.[7] Since the members from the Executive Branch—Nixon, Herter, McElroy, and Allen Dulles—were the same, and since there was no overlap of congressional leaders, the two meetings can to all intents and purposes be regarded as one.

In both sessions CIA director Allen Dulles, after some introductory remarks by the Boss, gave the assembled group a general intelligence briefing covering such subjects as the strengths of Soviet ground and air forces, the sizes of Allied garrisons in Berlin, access routes, political attitudes in Germany, key personalities, and the trade situation between East and West Germany, particularly Berlin. The Boss then gave a general run-down of our basic objectives. In both cases, he asked Secretary of Defense McElroy to give a summary of the interim military measures and contingency planning. Acting Secretary of State Herter described some of the diplomatic intricacies. Both meetings were then thrown open to a give-and-take discussion.

This day was an educational one for me. Aside from my regular duty of keeping the record, I was able to observe these members of the Legislative Branch in action. True, I had met all of them time and time again at White House social events. Senator Johnson, for one, had been particularly solicitous on a recent plane trip from Washington to Austin, Texas. Furthermore, for a certain period of time Andy Goodpaster and I had attended the weekly Republican legislative leaders' meetings. However, this was the first time I had seen members of both parties in action under a situation of real pressure.

The most startling aspect of the discussions was the difference in basic approach between members of Congress and those of the

[7] The evening meeting thus broadened the congressional participation to include the senior Republicans and Democrats on the Armed Services Committees of both houses, the Senate Foreign Relations Committee, and the House Foreign Affairs Committee.

Administration. Somewhat to my disappointment, I detected that some of the legislators had real difficulty in viewing the Berlin situation as a whole. No matter how exalted the position a senator or congressman might hold, I learned at first hand, his viewpoint is ultimately influenced by the attitude of his own constituents.[8]

I was a bit astonished also to observe how little some of the legislators actually knew about the Berlin situation. In the morning session, for example, Senator Dirksen was uncertain at first that the distance between Frankfurt and Berlin was substantial—that Berlin lay well behind the line of contact between NATO and Communist forces. Such an observation is probably unfair to Senator Dirksen; his responsibilities as Minority Leader were confined mostly to domestic issues. As the morning wore on, moreover, his grasp developed remarkably. Finally he put together his recommendations for a public statement: (a) we have explored the situation and will maintain our rights and responsibilities to the people of Berlin; (b) we have agreed to stand firm but are willing to negotiate; and (c) our military capabilities are adequate for our particular position in the world.

These constituted to my mind about as good a summary of a U.S. public position as had been drafted by anybody.

Sam Rayburn, for some reason, seemed the most worried. Perhaps Rayburn was influenced by the fact that his district of Texas (which includes Denison, the Boss's birth place) was a rural area where isolationist sentiment may have been strong. Repeatedly he exclaimed: "Let's do all the talking we can. I would rather talk than fight."

Rayburn's fellow Texan Lyndon Johnson had a completely different outlook. Johnson, in this instance, seemed to be thinking politically and looking at the state of Texas as a whole. He felt, in contrast to Rayburn, that we should make a point of showing sufficient firmness. Johnson made plain his desire to return from this meeting to the floor of the Senate and recommend specific

[8] George Allen had written about this fact of life eleven years before in his book, *Presidents Who Have Known Me*. In his chapter "Juice" (influence), he had observed that legislators can very rarely be bought by money or material inducements. However, with an eye to re-election, they are particularly vulnerable to anything that means votes at home.

actions to strengthen the President's hand. Continually he pleaded, "Isn't there *some*thing we can do to help out?" The answer had to be negative. The Boss intended to go ahead with his 30,000-man reduction of the Army. And a resolution regarding the "sense of the Senate" would cause infinitely more harm than good in our subtle dealings with Khrushchev.

Johnson was obviously disappointed that he would be unable to make a personal gesture on the floor, and I had the uncomfortable feeling that he failed to grasp the breadth of the problem. Nevertheless, he accepted the outcome with grace and good humor.

The afternoon session was conducted in a somewhat more sophisticated vein than that of the morning. For the men being briefed in the ground-floor library were men who possessed more background in defense and foreign affairs and who, in some cases, had vested personal interests other than pleasing their own constituencies. It appeared to me—although such generalizations are risky—that those whose positions were most secure at home were more apt to think in national terms than were those not so fortunate.

Outstanding in the two meetings was Senator Russell of Georgia. True, he had to ask whether Berlin was part of NATO—a good question—but, after being assured that our military forces were adequate, he was satisfied with the Administration's approach. Like the rest of us, he regretted the fact that the West lacked the ability to accomplish our objectives by conventional strength on the ground. He did, however, quickly recognize the Boss's insistence that to maintain ground forces of adequate size to match the Soviets, we would have to become a "garrison state" and that we therefore relied on our nuclear deterrent. When the matter of the role of Congress came up, Russell was emphatic: "You do what you have to, Mr. President, and come to us afterward." The Boss grinned and assured Russell that if it came to an emergency, he need not worry.

I was amused by the directness of some of the questions. At one point Russell asked, "What about the Germans? Can our Germans lick their Germans?" This particular point was answered by the Vice President, who referred to Allen Dulles' briefing. East

German forces were unreliable, Nixon said. The Soviets would not depend on them.

Russell's fellow Georgian Representative Vinson, seemed to understand the situation adequately, but it was obvious that he believed there was no harm in using it for his own purposes. As chairman of the House Armed Services Committee, "Uncle Carl" harbored a paternalistic attitude toward the military services. Though he favored the Navy, considering it almost his personal property, he was still strongly opposed to the impending force cuts in the Army. These, he asserted, could never be explained in terms of the present crisis.

Senator Fulbright also opposed the planned troop cuts. He understood the Boss's position himself, he said, but was not sure that his constituents would. He also picked up the problem the Boss had addressed weeks before, that of limited non military harassment along the *Autobahn*. Russell came up with a solution: Bailey bridges.[9] What, then, if someone fired at the engineers putting them up? At this point the Boss had to admit that we really did not know in detail what would be done in every contingency; we would have to see what developed.

At one point the discussion wandered away from Berlin to the question of the Mutual Security Program, more commonly referred to as "foreign aid." Russell was an avowed opponent and Fulbright also was far from enthusiastic. This afforded the Boss a chance to insert some strong words in its favor. Fulbright, intentionally or not, referred to the program by the term the Boss disliked, then stopped himself and chuckled, "Oh, pardon *me*, Mutual Security!" No progress was made toward a meeting of the minds on this issue and all knew that none would be made. It was soon dropped.

Further, no decisions were made in the two meetings of March 6; none was expected. The purpose was to inform the congressional leaders and indulge in a certain amount of give and take. Though it was impossible to gauge the extent to which this frank communication filtered out to affect public opinion, my guess is that it was substantial, certainly worth the time and effort.

[9] Prefabricated military bridges capable of quick construction and heavy loads, much in use during World War II. Named for their designer, Sir Donald Bailey.

Bryce Harlow and I walked out together. I was slightly dazed; these men were certainly a different breed of cat. "Well, you've got to realize, John," Bryce said in his soothing way, "these are tough birds. They've all risen to where they are over the dead bodies of a lot of opponents."

By this time Khrushchev had broadened the Berlin issue to involve the future of all Germany and of European security in general. Foreign Minister Adam Rapacki of Poland had come up with a scheme for Europe that seemed to have captured the imagination of Harold Macmillan in London. It was dubbed the "Rapacki Plan" and called for a thin-out of both NATO and Warsaw Pact forces on the European continent. The idea, which is still being discussed today under the new name "mutual balanced force reductions," had some appeal. It would have been, however, impossible to negotiate at that time. Warsaw Pact forces would always remain a threat to Western Europe, even if Soviet forces should withdraw partly into the Soviet Union. To the Boss, the fear was always that Harold Macmillan, in his desperation to find some way to negotiate his way out of the current crisis, might be willing to agree to a totally unrealistic, unenforceable agreement.

In this atmosphere the United States Government was now busily engaged in preparing for a visit by Prime Minister Macmillan on March 20. The Boss asked Acting Secretary Herter to check with the British ambassador, Sir Harold Caccia, to find out from London what Macmillan would want to talk about. It was obvious, with the amount of time allotted for conversations, that the two could never spend the entire period talking only of Berlin or even European security. There were other issues to discuss, of course. One of these was the prospect for an agreement to cease nuclear testing in the earth's atmosphere. Nuclear underground testing of small weapons, the Boss believed, could continue in the absence of an all-encompassing agreement; but in the interest of the whole Northern Hemisphere, no more shots between the ground and space should be conducted.[10]

[10] It was not until 1963 that such a limited nuclear test-ban treaty was agreed upon by the powers involved, with the exception of France and Red China. Never-

On the day of Macmillan's arrival, March 20, we all of course watched with curiosity as the Prime Minister, stony faced, accompanied by a couple of aides, marched into the Oval Office. Things went swiftly and soon the small group left for Camp David, with a stop-off on the way to visit the ailing Secretary of State John Foster Dulles. They then proceeded to Camp David.

This conference, the first of a series of Camp David meetings with foreign heads of government, was held in an ideal atmosphere. The two principals and their advisers—perhaps a dozen in all—sat comfortably in a large circle in the living room at Aspen Cottage. Experts came and went, fleshing out the crowd. With the principals thus relaxed, some of the uneasiness with which both sides had approached the meeting began to dissipate; the talk became warmer and more frank.

In this first session Macmillan gave a detailed description of his Moscow visit—nothing, actually, that we did not already know from his messages. At one point, however, his eyes moist, Macmillan waxed emotional. The British, as he saw it, were not prepared to face obliteration for the sake of two million Berlin Germans, their former enemies, especially over issues such as the color of passes for motor convoys and the nationality of those who stamped them. Eight nuclear bombs, Macmillan said, would wipe out thirty million Englishmen and destroy the entire British economy. The Boss reminded him that in case of general war, the United States would be the prime Soviet target. More Americans would die than British.

I had met the Prime Minister personally only once before, in 1945, when he had visited Dad in Bad Homburg, after World War II. He had made little impression on me at the time except as a tall, austere, reserved man with a mustache that made him look somewhat like a walrus. He showed none of the flair of Churchill and lacked even the outgoing friendliness of Eden. I found him a rather uninteresting personality, though I realized that, as he had been Dad's British political adviser in North Africa, the Boss was fond of him.

---

theless, the United States had previously decided on a one-year unilateral restriction on testing, much to the discomfort of the Atomic Energy Commission (AEC) and the military.

Following the first afternoon session Dad decided to relieve the tension. He took Macmillan by helicopter to the nearby Gettysburg farm. Part of Dad's evolving scenario for visitors was a trip to my family's home, the Pitzer Schoolhouse,[11] on the edge of the farm. The two came for a while and left; I remember no details. But in the light of the barrage of visitors that Dad brought to our house in the ensuing months, Barbara and I have always been sorry that we kept no guest book.

At Camp David the next morning, Macmillan was expressing apologies for his show of emotion the day before. The Boss seemed perplexed; he said he hadn't noticed. I never queried the Old Man on things like these. I was an Army officer doing my duty, not consciously a future recorder of events. But I found it difficult to visualize that a person as sensitive as the Boss would have failed to observe Macmillan's state of emotion. Possibly he was concentrating so hard on the issues at hand that he was oblivious for the moment. Or possibly he chose to overlook what might have been an embarrassing episode for his friend. I only know that he shrugged it off.

The most touchy question that had to be decided at this Camp David meeting was agreement on conditions for a summit conference. It was already concluded that a foreign ministers' conference was in the offing, but the point of contention was the relationship between the foreign ministers' meeting and a possible later summit. To complicate matters, a statement by the Boss in a press conference three days before Macmillan's arrival had been misconstrued. His words had been:

> It is my hope that thereby all of us can reach agreement with the Soviets on an early meeting at the level of foreign ministers.
>
> Assuming developments that [would] justify a summer meeting at the summit, the United States would be ready to participate in that further effort.[12]

This statement, fuzzy, had been interpreted by the press—and by Macmillan—as meaning that regardless of the outcome of a foreign ministers' meeting, he would meet subsequently with Khru-

[11] Originally, a one-room schoolhouse—converted and enlarged by the previous owners—that we had bought for our home in 1957.

[12] *Waging Peace,* p. 350.

shchev at a summit. This, Dad vehemently declared, was a misinterpretation. The foreign ministers' meeting, he insisted, would have to promise a real prospect of mutual understanding, sufficient to make a summit worth while, before he would accede.

This issue became the crux of this Camp David meeting. The professional diplomats spent hours trying to work out mutually acceptable wording for public consumption. Finally, on the morning of the third day, they came up with a compromise:

> The purpose of the Foreign Ministers' Meeting should be to reach positive agreements over as wide a field as possible, and in any case to narrow the differences between the respective points of view and to prepare constructive proposals for consideration by a conference of Heads of Government later in the summer. *On this understanding and as soon as developments in the Foreign Ministers' Meeting justify holding a Summit Conference,* the United States Government would be ready to participate in such a conference . . .[13]

All was well; the meeting had been a success.

By spring 1959 it had become obvious to all, including Secretary Dulles himself, that he would live only a short time. For months after he had been stricken with his second attack of cancer, everyone, including the Secretary, pretended that he would recover. But now, on April 16, knowing the facts, he resigned as Secretary of State. The Boss was at a loss to find a way to express not only his appreciation for Dulles' invaluable service but also his own heartfelt sentiments. Certainly there existed the Medal of Freedom, our highest established civilian decoration, but that medal had been presented to several other public servants. In Dulles' case the Boss wanted to do something special. With adequate warning time, a special presidential medal could have been struck—and in looking back it is obvious that it should have been. However, to do so would have meant beginning work on the medal during the period in which we were all outwardly assuming that the Secretary would recover. There was nothing for the Boss to do now but to present the Medal of Freedom with a cover letter, saying

[13] Italics supplied.

in his own words how inadequate this award was in the Boss's mind.

This letter completed, Dad called me in and asked me to deliver the medal and the letter to Ward 8 at Walter Reed—to Foster Dulles himself if at all possible. Dad was unable to go. I went with some feeling of trepidation, very conscious of the significance of the occasion and unaware of the atmosphere prevailing.

I was greeted on arrival by Mrs. Dulles, Dulles' sister Eleanor, and his secretary, Phyllis Berneau. They greeted me cheerfully, and while we sat in the adjacent living room, Mrs. Dulles went to the bedside and quickly returned, saying that the Secretary was asleep. The ladies appeared touched and delighted with the award. They asked me to express their appreciation to the President. After a short chat, I departed, realizing that I had been in the presence of three very brave ladies.

During the spring of 1959 Sir Winston Churchill came to visit the United States. The object of his visit was purely unofficial and sentimental, as he had been out of office as Prime Minister for four years. On arrival in Washington on May 4, Churchill came to the White House and stayed in the Queen's Room, on the second floor where he and Dad had met the first time, over seventeen years before.

Over the course of the years I had previously been exposed to Churchill on at least three occasions. The first was in June 1944, during the storm over the Channel. At No. 10 Downing Street in 1946 and at the English-Speaking Union in London in 1951 there had been time for only a handshake. But this evening we were to gather for a small dinner in the Family Dining Room on the ground floor, children included. As Mother, Dad, Barbara, and I waited in the West Hall for Sir Winston, it was something of a shock to witness the difficulty with which he made his way down the long hallway from the Queen's Room. He had recently suffered a stroke, and one side of his body was nearly paralyzed. He was, however, able to walk unaided. As we conversed in the West Hall and later at dinner, it was sad to observe the degeneration of his faculties. Within a couple of feet of him, Dad turned and said to Barbara, "I only wish you had known him in his prime," apparently certain that he would not be overheard. At dinner, seated next to him, I found it extremely difficult to make myself understood but was complimented by his obvious efforts to listen. For health reasons he had given up his beloved brandy and cigars.

All in the White House had a feeling that here was a chance to see one of the great world figures for the last time. Everyone knew, of course, of the deep affection the Boss held for Churchill and all felt personally involved. It was quite obvious that the former Prime Minister was taking grave risks with his health by making this trip. Dad gave two stag dinners in his honor, and on the day Churchill left the White House to move to the British Embassy, the entire staff was out on the north lawn of the White House, simply hoping to get a glimpse as he rode out alone, in the back seat of his limousine, holding his hat in his hand motionless, as a gesture of greeting. This demonstration of esteem on the part of a relatively blasé White House staff was the largest and most sincere I witnessed during my period as a member.

In the course of Churchill's informal visit, our daughter Susan, eight years old and quite a horsewoman for her age, became so taken with the former Prime Minister that she painted a water-color of a horse to give him. I first learned of it the day Churchill was to depart for his embassy. Sue marched up as I was going out the door for work and said, "Give this to him." When I inquired about the identity of "him," it turned out to be Mr. Churchill himself. The way to handle such a matter, of course, was to contact Anthony Montague-Brown, Churchill's aide, give him the picture, and later inform Sue that the mission had been accomplished. This I did. We were astonished a couple of days later when Sue received a letter of thanks from the former Prime Minister on embassy stationery, encouraging her to continue with her painting and hoping that she would enjoy it as much as he did. It was signed by Churchill himself, in shaky but legible hand-writing.

When Under Secretary of State Christian A. Herter was sworn in as Secretary on April 20, 1959, we in the White House could immediately sense a change in style. Tall, gaunt, bent over, soft-spoken, a bow tie his trademark, Chris Herter almost epitomized one's picture of the Boston Brahmin in the best sense. As soon as he took office, Andy Goodpaster and I tried an experiment; we began monitoring all meetings between Herter and the Boss, even private ones. We never received an inkling whether Herter objected or not. Even if he did, he was too much of a gentleman to indicate it. On our part, we were happy; because from then on our records of historic decisions would be more complete.

Four days after becoming Secretary, Herter flew to Geneva for the beginning of the long-awaited foreign ministers' meeting. This exercise proved to be a farce from the beginning. It was obvious that Soviet Foreign Minister Gromyko was worse than powerless: he was belligerent. And the British, with their eyes always on a summit meeting, seemed to regard the conference merely as a *pro forma* gesture to placate the Americans. About this time the Boss learned that Macmillan had already agreed to a summit while in Moscow the previous February; his exasperation, though brief, was formidable. In plain terms the Boss felt he had been let down. The warmth of the relationship between the two had been damaged.

The meeting of the foreign ministers did, however, have one salutary aspect. At least the East and West were talking. While Khrushchev had made several informal statements previously to the effect that the May 27 deadline was not really to be considered an ultimatum, still one of the Western objectives was to insure that the passing of that date would not be crammed down Khrushchev's throat. Therefore, while the foreign ministers did little more than glare at each other—and while the Boss exchanged exasperated messages with Macmillan—the time went by. Contingency plans, of course, were always present in the event that Khrushchev would take action; but the possibility of their use was now beginning to look more remote.

On May 24, 1959, John Foster Dulles died at Walter Reed Army Hospital. The four foreign ministers at Geneva thereupon took a recess and flew to Washington for the funeral. The ceremonies were held on May 27. Purposely, no notice was taken of the fact that this was the expiration date of the ultimatum.

The thaw in the atmosphere continued, at least on the surface. For some months the United States and the Soviet Union had been planning an exchange of exhibitions in Moscow and New York. The Russian exhibition in New York was to open in late June; the American exhibition in Moscow, some time between July 4 and 20. Soviet Deputy Premier Frol Kozlov was coming to the United States to open the Soviet show, and the Boss asked Vice President Nixon to do the honors for us in the Soviet Union. The mutual exhibitions were arranged and organized, although periodic Soviet obstructionism in Moscow sometimes baffled Harold McClellan, in charge of setting up our pavilion. Perhaps the Soviets still felt some ambivalence about the whole idea.

One element of the American display, the art exhibition, caused a temporary but annoying furor. The Boss had delegated the selection of American paintings to a group of fine arts "experts." Although only 10 per cent of the works were supposed to be abstract, some of those selected raised the blood pressure of many Americans. (Khrushchev later took pleasure in chiding us by remarking on his difficulties in telling whether many were right side up.) One painting in particular, entitled "Welcome Home," portrayed an impressionistic version of a group of unattractive, overstuffed capitalists entertaining a grotesque major general with his mouth full.

For his own part, in his enthusiasm for the exhibition, Dad had contributed one of his own paintings to hang in McClellan's office. The piece, a copy of a splendid photograph of my son David (probably about four years old), was one of Dad's best. It was already in Moscow when the art flurry kicked up in the press. The Boss forbade its display and ordered it returned.

Deputy Premier Kozlov arrived in the United States in late June, and a large group of us went to New York to view the Soviet exhibition in the Coliseum. The display was impressive though ponderous. Understandably, emphasis was placed on Soviet space achievement; replicas of Sputnik I and Sputnik II were prominently located for all to inspect.

Kozlov himself was a mysterious figure to most of us. Though theoretically number-two man to Khrushchev, he was, nevertheless, little known to Americans. A large, stocky man, probably in his mid-fifties, with a full head of gray hair and a spectacular set of white teeth, he was friendly and ebullient—as only a Russian can be when things are going well. When we reached the art exhibit,

Kozlov could tell that we liked what we saw. With a wave of his arm, Kozlov told the Boss to take his pick; he could have any one he wanted. Two in particular caught Dad's eye. One depicted a Russian soldier and his family. The other entitled, "Spring Is Approaching," was a panorama of a snow scene with a sparkling blue stream in the foreground. Dad selected the latter. (He later confided to me that he actually preferred the picture of the Russian family but had chosen the snow scene because it had a simpler frame. Dad did not want it construed that he had selected the painting with the fanciest frame in the building.)

A couple of days later Kozlov came to the White House before leaving for a trip to the West. The visit confirmed what all of us had surmised: that beneath this broadly smiling exterior rested the mind of a Communist as tough as any. Nevertheless, his very presence in the United States was significant, and Kozlov seemed to appreciate the courteous treatment he received.

While Kozlov was traveling around the country, the Boss learned that Khrushchev, at a press conference, had expressed a desire to visit the United States. This hint, while appealing, was not immediately picked up. Dad was still determined that any meetings with the Soviet leader should be contingent upon signs of visible progress in the still-floundering foreign ministers' meeting. He reacted by sending an informal verbal message to Kozlov as the Deputy Premier was departing on July 12 for Moscow. Under Secretary of State Robert Murphy was directed to indicate that *should the foreign ministers' meeting provide results which would justify a summit meeting,* the Boss would then be glad to see Khrushchev before such a summit occurred.

A few days later, in a meeting with the two Under Secretaries of State, Douglas Dillon and Bob Murphy, the President was in for a shock. Murphy had misunderstood his instructions and had issued the invitation without conditions. He had omitted the proviso that the foreign ministers' meeting should *previously* show progress. Murphy frankly admitted the error.

The Boss was now boxed in. His entire position—that he would not see Khrushchev without signs of progress at Geneva—was destroyed. The Khrushchev visit was to become a fact regardless. Naturally, nothing much more could be expected from the foreign ministers since the Soviets no longer had incentive to make concessions.

This episode, which occurred shortly after the death of John Foster Dulles, is interesting primarily as it points up the way that Dad and Dulles had formerly operated. In military terms, one could compare the Eisenhower/Dulles relationship with that of Generals Robert E. Lee and Thomas ("Stonewall") Jackson. Lee laid the basic plan and knew that Jackson, given flexibility, would understand and carry out his wishes. The Boss admonished his embarrassed lieutenants, both capable men and loyal, by pointedly describing the meticulous way in which Dulles had always insured that he understood the nuances of his own desires. But the matter was now academic, and the speed with which the Boss adjusted to a new situation might possibly indicate that he was not displeased, viscerally.

With the invitation to Khrushchev now accepted—and a return invitation to visit U.S.S.R. issued—the Boss decided immediately to do his best to rectify the situation with his three Western Allies; he would make a trip to each capital before the Premier's arrival on September 15 and consult with Macmillan, De Gaulle, and Adenauer. In the ticklish business of maintaining trust among allies, it is harmful to give one's partners the impression that they are merely onlookers, while two superpowers decide the fate of the world between themselves. In the present situation, consultation with our three friends beforehand could fend off this feeling, at least partially.

I was put in charge of managing this particular journey, probably because during the preparation period I would be located at Gettysburg, where Dad had set up a temporary office for the summer. Tom Stephens, Captain Evan P. ("Pete") Aurand, and Colonel Robert L. Schulz would act as advance men—Tom for Bonn, Pete for London, and Bob for Paris. This would be the first elaborate presidential overseas visit. Dad had, to be sure, gone to Panama, the Bahamas, Paris, and even Geneva while in office, but these other trips had been one-stop affairs. This one, being so involved, had to be planned and directed centrally.

The first problem was timing. Dad had come up with the idea of seeing De Gaulle first, arriving on August 27, the fifteenth anniversary of his significant official call on the Provisional President just after the Liberation of Paris in World War II.[14] De Gaulle quickly exhibited a lack of interest in commemorating this date, however; he would be in Algeria at the time. Therefore, after much adjustment of schedules, Dad decided to proceed directly to Bonn on August 26, thence to Britain for a few days, and to Paris last.

As we were planning this trip to Europe, public interest continued to center on the forthcoming visit of Khrushchev to the United States. Thus the Boss had two major items on his mind: (1) what to say to our European allies and (2) how to handle the Soviet leader almost immediately thereafter.

On August 5, 1959, Dad and I flew down from Gettysburg to the White House so that Vice President Nixon could give a complete report on his own visit to the Soviet Union, just completed. Except for several of us on the White House staff, only Under Secretary of State Dillon and the Boss's youngest brother, Milton Eisenhower, who had accompanied the Vice President to Moscow, were on hand. As I feverishly scribbled notes, I was impressed by the manner in which Nixon was able to brush aside the travelogue aspects of the trip and concentrate on much-needed advice regarding Khrushchev and how to handle him.

Actually the Vice President was dealing with two subjects: first, a series of "do's" and "don'ts" regarding the Boss's projected trip to the Soviet Union and, second, how to approach Khrushchev personally. These remarks regarding Khrushchev, based on concentrated experience, were particularly illuminating. "Above all," the Vice President said, "don't let the Russians wear you down. They'll do everything possible to do so. For example, I don't recommend going all the way out to Siberia; that's too exhausting. On the other hand, you should get out of Moscow and visit places like Kiev and Leningrad, where you'll find the reception a good

[14] This call in 1944, which indicated U.S. recognition of De Gaulle as Provisional President of France, had meant a great deal. De Gaulle had mentioned it warmly often.

deal warmer. Frankly, I would delay the Russia trip as long as possible; the longer you wait, the longer Khrushchev has to remain on his good behavior." The Boss agreed, saying that he was now contemplating waiting until December.[15]

Turning to the personality of Khrushchev himself, Nixon tended to cast cold water on hopes that the Premier would be impressed by the standard of living this country was able to afford its citizens. "Khrushchev is a man with a closed mind," the Vice President said, "and the only thing he'll understand is the power of America and the unity of her citizens. The only long-range answer to the Russian problem, as I see it, is a gradual opening of the doors through mutual contacts. There's a great opportunity here. I was surprised at how hungry the Russian people are for news of the outside world.

"When Khrushchev visits here," Nixon went on, "I'm sure he'll refuse to see any American missile sites. He refused to show us any, saying that the time was not yet ripe; and I am sure that he will avoid the precedent of seeing any of ours, since you are going to Russia later."

The Vice President knew what he was talking about. He warned that Khrushchev could not be handled like any ordinary important visitor. He would have a large entourage along with him and one man, a high-ranking American official, should be put in charge of coordinating the entire visit. As many stag meetings as possible should be scheduled, as Khrushchev preferred it that way. "Further," he warned, "be prepared for Khrushchev's penchant for light-hearted needling, even in toasts. Again," he repeated, "be aware of his efforts to wear you down. Khrushchev is not a sick man; he simply wore himself out when he visited Poland. He drives himself unmercifully, and when he's not working on you, he'll have Mikoyan or Kozlov standing in for him."

When the meeting came to an end the President asked his lieutenant to give essentially the same report to the Cabinet. The Vice President agreed. Subsequent events proved the accuracy of his analyses.

---

[15] With Khrushchev's agreement, the trip was delayed even further, scheduled for some time in the summer of 1960.

All of this was out of my line of direct concern at the moment, of course, as my primary preoccupation was the Boss's trip to Western Europe, only two weeks away. In this capacity I was snowed under by the intricacies of planning. The series of scheduled events continued to grow. New requests came in every day for alterations of schedule. Transportation means had to be decided on, not only between capitals—that was easy—but between the airports and the cities. Would the Boss go by car or by helicopter? Travel by car would give the maximum exposure to the people, who obviously would like to see him; on the other hand, travel by ground transportation is slow and unpredictable when crowds are involved. And care had to be taken to preserve the Boss's energy for the real purpose of the visits—substantive talks.

An item which may seem trivial was the problem of the gifts which a head of state normally presents to his counterparts in host countries. These were not state visits, of course, but it soon became apparent that the Boss would see the heads of state in each country—President Theodor Heuss in West Germany, the Royal Family in Britain, and, of course, President de Gaulle in France. This selection was made more difficult because of the paucity of funds available for such purposes in the State Department. As a guide, Wiley Buchanan, chief of protocol, estimated that we could spend about $300 per gift—in other words, for a mere memento. For the Royal Family we decided on a fine, sophisticated radio. (First we had to check to ascertain that there was no MADE IN JAPAN engraved on the bottom.) A gift for General de Gaulle required a more extensive search. Finally, with the help of Lieutenant Colonel Vernon ("Dick") Walters, we procured a small but beautiful piece of Steuben glass entitled, "The Cathedral." It exceeded the estimated expense a little but was such a natural for De Gaulle that we all looked forward to the moment when the Boss would present it to him.

Finally, all preparations completed, we returned to Washington. The Boss and his party left before dawn on Wednesday, August 26.

We landed at Bonn 6:30 P.M. local time. Adenauer, of course, was on hand and after a brief ceremony the party climbed in our allotted vehicles for the trip into town. From the outset we were astonished by the wild enthusiasm of the crowds. The people on the streets numbered several times the populations of the towns we went through. It was odd, I thought, that the Germans should exhibit such an unusual outpouring of affection for their former conqueror. True, the Boss had been instrumental in pushing through the Western European Union (WEU) which had restored the Federal Republic to a respectable place in the Western community and allowed Germany to become a member of NATO. But such a fact is the kind of thing that goes into diplomatic memoirs and the fine print of newspapers; by no means could his role in restoring Germany to her place among nations have been known to the entire population. The only logical answer was that West Germany, whose existence was being threatened by the Soviets, regarded the Boss as the leader—the symbol—of the nations that would protect them.

By the time we reached the Embassy Residence it was already dark, and the crowds had closed in, making it difficult enough for the Secret Service to whisk the Boss himself into the front door. The rest of us had to fend for ourselves, and it seemed a minor miracle when we finally made it. We went to bed early. It had, after all, been a twenty-seven-hour day and had provided satisfying proof of the Boss's stamina.

The next morning we realized we had a problem in getting back to the airport that evening. The hour-and-a-half delay coming in had been fatiguing but had caused no difficulties. The return trip, however, had to be made on time, as we were destined that evening for London, where delay would cause much inconvenience. Therefore somebody—either Tom Stephens or a Secret Serviceman—came to me with a strong recommendation that the Boss take the helicopter—the crowd situation would be simply too unpredictable. I knew that this would not be an appealing subject to broach but I was relatively accustomed to carrying the bad news. At first Dad demurred, but finally, encouraged by Ambassador David Bruce, he agreed that we should ask the German government. At least the change in plans could then be made public to prevent crowds gathering on the streets only to be disappointed.

After a morning call on President Heuss the Boss spent the

rest of the day with Adenauer at the Palace of Schaumburg. At the first session the two heads of government reviewed the Berlin situation. When the Boss asked, however, about the possibilities of increasing contacts between the East and West Germans, Adenauer was disappointingly pessimistic. The East Germans, he said, were the ones who made trade and cultural and social intercourse all but impossible. And naturally, the Pankow regime enforced its will on its people with brutal, iron-fisted methods.

The interesting aspect of these talks, however, was Adenauer's admiration for and close relationship with General de Gaulle. De Gaulle's staunchest ally at this point in history, strangely, was now France's traditional enemy of yesteryear. There was more, of course, than sentiment that prompted Adenauer to support De Gaulle. Algeria, in the process of shaking off the domination of the French, was promoting discussion of the French-Algerian problem in the United Nations. The French—specifically De Gaulle—refused to even discuss the matter in that body, thereby placing himself in a bad light. If forced to the wall, the United States, with its anticolonial background, would have to vote with the Algerians, particularly if the French refused to defend themselves. Adenauer's concern, however, was that the Algerians would never have been able to fight without the aid of the Communists. By deduction, therefore, he concluded that a free Algeria would necessarily be Communist-dominated. By the domino theory, Morocco and Tunisia would soon follow. Adenauer did, however, promise Dad to communicate with De Gaulle in hopes of convincing the French that they should at least discuss the matter in the UN.

At the end of the lavish lunch that day, Adenauer made a flattering but inexplicable gesture. As everyone was leisurely exiting the room, he shouted out in a commanding voice, "Herr Major!" Since I was still at my seat and knew there were no other majors in the room, I turned in his direction. Der Alte solemnly raised his remaining glass of white wine. Baffled, I returned the salute. Perhaps Adenauer was expressing a recognition of the young Americans who had participated in freeing his beloved Germany from the Nazi regime fourteen years earlier. Perhaps he was merely looking for an excuse to finish off his glass of Rhine wine, which he dearly loved. I had no way of knowing.

The afternoon session was remarkable in that the two principals became so engrossed in their private conversation that neither one sent for an adviser. While a lot of high-priced—and sometimes fairly self-important—help sat expectantly in the next room, the two heads of government talked on beyond their time. With difficulty someone extricated the two and all left for the helicopters a couple of blocks away.

We reached the airport in comfortable time and the departure ceremonies were brief. One thoughtful touch was the rendition of the "Official West Point March" by the German Army band. This meant a lot to at least three persons aboard the aircraft: Dad, Andy, and me. Bill Draper turned the nose of the 707 westward for the short flight to London. The day was far from over.

When we arrived at London International Airport, Heathrow, dusk was almost upon us. Harold Macmillan and the Boss went through a brief ceremony, the minimum, of course, as this was not a state visit. In the course of the proceedings, I was surprised to see the Royal Air Force honor guard lower the colors in salute, actually draping the Union Jack to touch the ground. Such is the difference in custom. As a youngster I had believed—one of those fanciful boyhood legends—that a soldier allowing the American flag to touch the ground would be taken out and immediately shot. Not so the British. To them the monarch is their national symbol, not the flag. Perhaps, I thought, it is really more sensible to have a person as a symbol rather than a piece of cloth. On second thought, however, if George III had been merely a piece of cloth, Britain might not have lost her American colonies.

The throngs in London were, as the night before in Bonn, enthusiastic but the procession was not held up. I gave the reception little notice, as I remembered the tumultuous mobs Dad used to draw in London just after the war. The Boss, however, felt differently. He afterwards confided his amazement and said that Macmillan had likewise been overwhelmed. One reason they half-expected the reception to be cool was the fact that this was Dad's first trip to London after the Suez episode of 1956.

The next morning at 7:15 the Prime Minister was at the door. Dad, Doc Snyder, Sergeant John Moaney, and I were to make an overnight visit with the Royal Family at Balmoral Castle in Scotland. Prince Philip was on hand when the plane landed at Dyce Airport, near Aberdeen, and soon the small cavalcade was making its way to Balmoral, a good distance away in the Grampian Mountains. At about noon we arrived at the gates of the castle, where a company-sized guard of honor was drawn up. The Queen arrived and joined Dad in trooping the line. We then drove into the grounds, insulated from public view.

Balmoral Castle is a comfortable place but not lavish. Dad occupied the same room on the first floor as on our previous visit thirteen years earlier. The rest of us were at hand right down the hall. There were, of course, plenty of footmen to take care of everyone's needs, but otherwise the atmosphere was informal.

One of the appealing customs the Royal Family observed was that of changing the seating arrangements at each meal. At noon that day I was placed next to Prince Philip, that evening next to Princess Margaret (where I was unable to convince her of the virtues of benedictine and brandy as an after dinner cordial). As was customary, the household held other guests, personal friends of the Queen and Prince.

That afternoon Dad and I were invited for a trip around the castle grounds. The Queen drove the station wagon deftly and Dad sat in the front seat. Princess Margaret and I sat in the back. Occasionally we were held up by a small barrier in the form of a sapling log, its end resting on two posts, extending across the road. It would then be up to the Princess and me to pile out of the back seat, remove the obstacle, and replace it after the station wagon had passed through. Several of these were encountered along the hilly dirt roads, but nobody ever explained their significance.

For his part, Dad was enjoying the sojourn thoroughly. The absence of visible security people gave him a sense of escape. However, as we were nearing our destination we encountered one of the presidential Secret Service Detail standing by the side of the road looking rather smug. The Old Man's disappointment was obvious.

Eventually we joined the rest of the guests in a small clearing, where a modest stone cottage stood by a lake. Before long we were inside with the Queen preparing tea and scones over a charcoal broiler. Afterward we all cleared the table, but the Queen herself did the bulk of the dishwashing, with Dad pressing hard to help as much as he could. No servants were around; this was the Royal Family's method of getting away from it all.

The next morning everyone breakfasted in his own room. At 9 A.M. the Queen and Prince came down to say good-by. Before leaving I produced the Boss's gift, the AM/FM radio. To my dismay it failed to make a sound. Prince Philip, quite accommodating, said not to worry, as the reception was very bad around there. Exasperated, I blurted out, "But this thing doesn't even produce static!"[16]

At the Dyce Airport Prince Philip took his leave and we were off once more on the Queen's Flight, destined for Chequers.

On arrival at Chequers, the official country residence of the British Prime Minister, Macmillan and the Boss got down to business right after lunch. Strangely enough, with the panorama of mutual problems, the first subject was that of U.S.-leased bases in Trinidad, possibly chosen as an ice-breaker.[17]

The house at Chequers was the gift to the British government some years back on the part of a wealthy American. Parts of the house were over four hundred years old and had once been the property of the Cromwell family. The house is ideally set up for conferences. The main hall is large enough for a sizable group to gather in a horseshoe around the gigantic fireplace. On the second floor a number of guest rooms can house the members of the delegations. One could walk from his bedroom and look over the balcony to observe the proceedings below.

In the course of the afternoon I took my secretary, Polly Yates, down to the nearby abbey where she was to be housed. This ancient building had not been used by the Church since the days of Henry VIII and was now a school. It was meticulously kept and the beautiful lawns and towering boxwoods were a spectacular sight.

[16] A chagrined Pete Aurand had the radio replaced in a matter of days.

[17] In 1940, it will be recalled, President Roosevelt had leased several bases in Britain's Atlantic and Caribbean island colonies from Prime Minister Churchill in exchange for fifty old U.S. destroyers. The duration of the lease was to be ninety-nine years. The difficulty was now the status of the Trinidad base in the light of the imminent independence of the island.

After a short visit with Polly's hosts, I returned to Chequers. A makeshift golf game was in progress. A golf bag was lying on the ground next to the retaining wall surrounding the house; and the Boss, Macmillan, Selwyn Lloyd (the Foreign Secretary) and U. S. Ambassador John Hay Whitney were having a competition —the Americans against the British—to see how many hits each side could make against the bag from a distance of about 150 yards. When the Americans came from behind to tie the match, both sides apparently decided this was the diplomatic time to quit.

Later that afternoon I occupied myself in our office on the second floor, writing acknowledgments for the visit at Balmoral. As it turned out, there were about fifteen people deserving of a note of thanks for their role in arranging the one overnight stay in Scotland. At about time to quit, I was alone; the telephone rang and I identified myself. I soon learned to my consternation that the caller was a reporter. The gentleman's voice brightened when he heard my name, and he asked questions regarding our reaction to the magnificent reception in London two days earlier. I answered as politely as I could, saying that the Boss and his party were all delighted, and got off the phone as quickly as possible.

That evening, Dad, Herter, Macmillan, and Lloyd conferred privately. Meetings with the British were always eased by the fact that the two nationalities speak relatively similar languages.

The next morning, Sunday, I was awakened by a roar: "What the hell have you been doing talking to reporters?" In haste I dashed into the Boss's room. There on the front page of one newspaper was a long article written by my caller of the afternoon before, blessed with much by way of embellishment. I explained how I had been trapped but was unable to account for the embellishments. Soon Andy, who had heard the summons, came to my rescue. He looked the article over quickly, then convinced the Old Man that I had truly been misquoted. Fortunately Andy hit upon a phrase in the story, "We were knocked sideways by it all." This is a typically British expression and foreign to my lexicon. Dad, mollified, merely grumbled and restated—unnecessarily—that it was not the function of the White House staff to give press interviews.

That afternoon the two delegations discussed the all-important question of a proposed nuclear test-ban arrangement with the Soviets. There was some difference of opinion among experts as to the size of weapon that could be fired underground without being detected from another continent. That evening after dinner the Boss, Andy, and I went over the talking points that Dad was to use in his joint television appearance with the Prime Minister the next evening. All had agreed that the program should be unrehearsed. But since we all knew that the viewpoints of the men still differed regarding the conditions for a summit conference, his statement had to be exact. Actually, no assistance was really needed.

The next evening Dad and members of his party, having returned to London, went to No. 10 Downing Street for the television program and dinner. While the Anglo-American group was mingling about with a cocktail before dinner, I spotted former Prime Minister Clement Attlee (now Earl Attlee) sitting alone, possibly feeling an outsider among all these Conservatives. On the grounds that Attlee had been our host at the same residence in 1946 I introduced myself. We sat and reminisced about that gathering, thirteen years earlier.

When the television show began, Macmillan and the Boss opened by referring to their long personal friendship and to the importance of close Anglo-American relations—allowing, of course, that the two nations had had their differences. They emphasized their mutual objectives of peace, which both would pursue in their dealings with each other and with other nations. The matter of the emerging nations and their relationship to the British Commonwealth was touched upon, as well as trade. The important part of the exchange, however, pertained to the prospects for a summit conference with Khrushchev:

MACMILLAN:
. . . Now the first war [World War I], I feel, ought never to have happened. It happened by mistake. I believe if we had the same kind of international meetings as we have now, it wouldn't have happened. . . .

Now we are in a situation, I felt there was a danger we might drift into something by mistake—bluff—counterbluff—lack of understanding on both sides—and drift into something. . . . And that

is why I set about my journeys last February . . . and I think I
am bound to say that they haven't turned out too badly. . . .

I have always wanted a summit meeting and I believe your ini-
tiative will put us in a position to get it under the best conditions.

EISENHOWER (later):

I will not be a party to a meeting that is going to de-
press and discourage people. Therefore, we must have some prom-
ise of fruitful results.[18]

In other words, the Boss at this point in time was still holding
out for progress at the foreign ministers' meeting; Macmillan was
already committed to a summit. Actually, the two men had
different problems. The British population, for some reason, looked
back with a brighter view of the summit conferences of World
War II than did the Americans. Perhaps Yalta had dimmed American enthusiasm. Furthermore, Harold Macmillan was facing elections that October; the Boss was not.

The dinner that evening was remarkable principally because of
the presence not only of the Boss and the Prime Minister but of
three former Prime Ministers as well: Winston Churchill, Anthony
Eden, and Clement Attlee. Each spoke briefly. I wonder how often
such a high-powered event has occurred in history.

The next day, Tuesday, September 1, the only event scheduled
was a private dinner in which Dad's old British war comrades
gathered for a reunion. The following morning five or six helicopters arrived on the spacious lawn of Winfield House, the Embassy residence. By 8:50 A.M. we were airborne, destined for the
stickiest part of the trip: Paris.

As *Air Force One* taxied up to the ramp at Orly Field, Paris,
we all felt a certain uneasiness, although not very much was said.
The reason for the suspense, of course, was the fact that we were
now coming to deal with an almost unknown quantity: De Gaulle.
To the best of my knowledge the Boss had not seen him since just
after World War II—fourteen years earlier. Certainly the two had
not met since De Gaulle's election to the French presidency. In

[18] *Public Papers of the Presidents, Eisenhower, 1959,* pp. 622–26. Italics supplied.

34. "I am sure that Dad enjoyed this first game of
the 1956 World Series more than I; I am also sure
that I enjoyed it far more than the preoccupied Foster
Dulles. The fact that the Brooklyn Dodgers beat the
New York Yankees that day seemed not to impress
him." The game of October 5, 1956, played while the
Suez crisis in the Middle East was heating up.

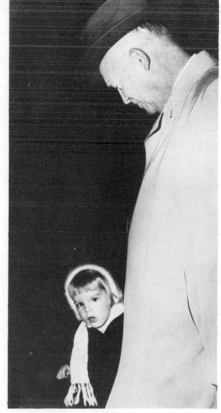

35. The President and his youngest grandchild, Mary
Jean, return from Augusta after Thanksgiving holiday,
November 1958.

36. "When Undersecretary of State [Christian A.] Herter was sworn in as Secretary on April 20, 1959, we in the White House could immediately sense a change in style. Tall, gaunt, bent over, soft-spoken, a bow tie his trademark, Chris Herter . . . epitomized . . . the Boston Brahmin in the best sense."

37. (*Opposite*) "Shortly after noon on September 15, 1959, the Boss . . . was on hand to meet [Khrushchev] at Andrews Air Force Base. . . . The amenities were brief and formal. The Boss read his welcoming talk to emphasize the nature of the visit. The merciless sun reflected off the white concrete adding to the grim impression: the two squinting principals looked even more belligerent . . . than they felt."

38, 39. Two stalwarts of the White House staff: Press Secretary James C. Hagerty (*right*) and General Andrew J. Goodpaster (*left*).

40. ". . . the gracious reception at the Vatican by Pope John XXIII, with his little talk in broken English commenting on our common first names. . . ."

41. ". . . poverty-stricken Afghan peasants peering in the car, with the magnificent Hindu Kush mountains as backdrop. . . ."

42. Jawaharlal Nehru.

43. ". . . a bobbing elephant ride in an elaborate Indian howdah. . . ."

44. "In the spring of 1960 General de Gaulle paid a state visit to the United States." De Gaulle with Mother at a dinner given in his honor.

the meantime, of course, the White House had been deluged with reports on De Gaulle's positions, particularly toward NATO and Algeria. We had no idea whether De Gaulle planned to play down the visit with a cool reception; we rather suspected that he did.

On disembarking, however, we found that our concern, at least as far as the warmth of the reception went, was unfounded. An impressive crowd was present, replete with all the splendor of the picturesque Garde Républicaine. The French Air Force band rendered their own arrangement of "The Star-Spangled Banner," far superior I thought to the official American version. De Gaulle's speech of welcome contained cordial references to the Boss personally and to the United States in general.

On the way into Paris the crowds grew more dense. By the time we were in the city they were substantial, although they failed to duplicate the wild enthusiasm of those in Bonn and London. Along the route the motorcade stopped mysteriously for a moment and then went on. Soon we were being escorted into the magnificent Quai d'Orsay Apartments, the official guest house where President de Gaulle insisted on entertaining his important guests. For a few minutes after arrival, Dad and his handful of aides went from room to room exclaiming over the marble bathrooms and luxurious furniture. Dad's bathroom boasted a gold bathtub; my room, next to his, had an equally elaborate silver one. Soon a small group gathered to compare notes and go over the planned itinerary. It was to be, we noted, a highly ceremonial affair.

That afternoon at 4:00, after a formal but pleasant luncheon at the Élysée Palace, the talks between the two Presidents began in earnest. A group of fourteen people gathered in a rather modest room at the Palace of Foreign Affairs, Quai d'Orsay. The weather outside was pleasant, and the two heads of state sat facing each other across the middle of the oblong table. This session, we realized, was to be the critical moment of the Paris visit. Despite the pageantry and De Gaulle's effusive welcome, the question still remained as to how he would behave when settled down to discuss substantive issues.

As I was seated next to the wall a couple of feet to the left of the Boss's back, I was in a choice spot to observe every movement and change of expression that might flit across De Gaulle's face. To my relief—and somewhat to my surprise—De Gaulle presented his views in a quiet, objective, almost impassive tone, although there was no doubt of the intensity of the feelings that lay beneath this sober exterior. On the Berlin question and the Khrushchev visit De Gaulle had little comment. As we had learned earlier, his views and the Boss's were nearly identical on these matters. Having practically passed these matters over, however, De Gaulle's attitude intensified when he turned to the subject that bothered him the most: the relationship of France to the rest of NATO.

De Gaulle was, he claimed, a strong advocate of the North Atlantic alliance—as he chose to interpret it. He preferred to view the alliance merely as an agreement between independent countries and he was opposed to a unified international military command such as SHAPE. French soldiers fighting under the banner of an international organization would, he felt, lack the dedication and verve they would show if fighting only for France.[19] Both sides presented their thoughts with no expectation of swaying the other. The conversation was frank and the two cheerfully agreed to disagree. As it turned out, De Gaulle took no further action to withdraw France from the military side of NATO during the period of my father's administration.[20]

On the Algerian problem De Gaulle was adamant that the Algerian rebels represented only a small group of self-appointed revolutionaries. The situation was still in a state of flux, but De Gaulle still harbored hopes of retaining not only a French Community in black Africa but also Algeria, which he claimed was a part of Metropolitan France. As to the next meeting of the UN, he refused to reconsider his refusal to discuss Algeria. However, in a couple of days he planned to make a statement promising free elections in Algeria.

[19] This view, of course, was well known to all of us, as De Gaulle had previously withdrawn the French fleet from the forces earmarked to SACEUR in the event of war. It would cooperate he had said, but not be under SACEUR's command. The loss of the French fleet—hardly a potent force—had not been a major blow. Nevertheless, the principle that De Gaulle espoused was unacceptable to the United States as well as to the rest of the NATO countries.

[20] Later De Gaulle backed up his views by withdrawing all French forces from SACEUR and inviting Supreme Headquarters to leave the country, although France remained theoretically in the NATO alliance.

That afternoon at the Hôtel de Ville, General de Gaulle pulled out all the stops. The crowds were tremendous and he spoke in phrases that only a Frenchman could provide. He ended his talk with these ringing words: "Long live General Eisenhower! Long live the President of the United States! Long live America, forever the friend and ally of France!"

The day was long; the ceremonies at the Hôtel de Ville lasted until 6:50 P.M. As we were scheduled for dinner at the Élysée Palace at 8:30, Secretary Herter came to Dad's suite to compare notes. While we were talking Dad mentioned the reason for the pause on the way into town that morning. Frustrated at being hunched over in their convertible, the two Presidents had asked the driver to lower the top. The driver had been agreeable but had at least twice failed to obey. Eventually, at a predetermined point, he had, on his own volition, stopped the vehicle and complied. By this time Dad had surmised the reason: the motorcade had been proceeding through a Communist district and the Sûreté had given directions that the top be left up to prevent someone's dropping a grenade into the back seat. (The orders of the driver's immediate boss superseded those of the President of the Republic.) I remarked idly that any assassin worth his salt would know enough to hold a grenade for two or three seconds after pulling the pin, thereby achieving an airburst. Secretary Herter looked at me aghast: "Well, aren't you a nice fellow!" he gasped. I shrugged. I had been thinking only technically.

At the formal state dinner, representatives from all of the countries of the new French Community (De Gaulle's version of the British Commonwealth) were represented. These were an interesting group and distinctly pro-French. One of the guests, a short, handsome black from the French Congo, a priest, wore a white monk's habit, though I was told he had been defrocked. He was particularly friendly and promised to send the Boss a small elephant as a memento of the occasion. (He later followed through on this promise, somewhat to our dismay, but the gainer was the Washington Zoo.)

The next day the Boss and his party transferred for the day from the Quai d'Orsay to the American Embassy Residence, where Dad was able, in accordance with custom, to return De

Gaulle's hospitality by holding a luncheon. He presented his gift of the Steuben glass "Cathedral." De Gaulle was predictably moved.

That evening we headed for the Palace of Rambouillet, the magnificent summer residence of the French Presidents, some distance out of Paris, to spend the night. The atmosphere remained cordial, even convivial. While the strictly intimate conversations were going on, Doc Snyder and I spent some of the time rowing around the palace lake, enjoying the scenery. When the whole group gathered, the two principals spent a good deal of the time in conversation, as will happen with a couple of old soldiers. At one point, to my dismay, Dad called me across the room to recite Shakespeare's version of Henry V's exhortation to his troops just before the Battle of Agincourt, a passage I had committed to memory in the course of my studies at Columbia University. Feeling like an awkward schoolboy, I stood beside the table and quoted the passage, "We few, we happy few, we band of brothers! For he who sheds his blood with me today shall be my brother . . ." My discomfiture was exacerbated by an uneasy feeling that, though the quote illustrated the Old Man's point—the affection between comrades in arms—the fact that those words were uttered by an English king about to defeat the French might not sit well with De Gaulle's Gallic pride. I watched his face for an indication; he remained impassive.

That evening I was housed in a room directly above Dad's in a tower of the château. The room was, I was told, the one in which King Francis I had died. It was chilly and I was grateful for the bearskin blanket. As we were contemplating the next day's trip (to Culzean Castle, Scotland) before going to bed, Dad mumbled that he wished he had a couple of bridge friends. I suggested that he call them at home and ask them over. Within hours two of his friends, Bill Robinson and Pete Jones, were on a jet headed for Prestwick.

On the morning of September 4, we mounted helicopters on the grounds of the château and bade farewell to President de Gaulle after what had proved a stimulating visit. De Gaulle had wanted to go to the airport but on this point at least he gave in. For had he gone, Dad would later feel obligated to reciprocate in Washington, breaking an iron-clad precedent.

In the course of the trip from Paris to Prestwick Dad scribbled out messages to be sent by radio from the aircraft to his hosts. After a short time we landed at Prestwick and went by car to Culzean Castle. Pete Jones and Bill Robinson appeared almost immediately thereafter, sleepy but ready to begin the bridge game.

In the midst of our planned stay, news came from Washington that the situation in Laos, where the Communist Pathet Lao were invading, was degenerating. With much regret, the Boss canceled the rest of the respite and we headed back to Washington, arriving on Sunday, September 6, 1959. Thus ended what was for me the most exciting trip of the Eisenhower Administration.

9

Twilight

When we arrived home from Europe the upcoming Khrushchev visit was only a week away. Though he said little, it was obvious that the Boss was uncomfortable; he had not forgotten that this visit was coming to pass under circumstances contrary to his own instincts. He was resolved to be courteous and polite but not effusive.

In preparation, the State Department busied itself frantically composing the usual position papers and "think pieces," but these appeared of secondary importance. After all, the Boss, having lived so close to this Berlin and European security issue, needed little by way of background material. The thorny problems lay in the physical arrangements for the visit.

Security was one of them. At that time (1959), protection of a foreign dignitary rested in the hands of the State Department; the Secret Service was not involved. There were, of course, dire predictions concerning the reactions of various Americans. Khrushchev was hardly a popular character, and in the eyes of many of our citizens of Eastern European ancestry, particularly the Poles, he was a symbol of oppression. Added to the hostility of this segment of the population, whose feelings ran deep, was always the possibility of violence on the part of lunatic groups who would conspire to make trouble for any major world figure.

Aside from security, certain protocol problems had to be resolved. For in our efforts to be correct we wanted to make sure that Khrushchev would be handled in a proper manner. As he was not by title a "head of state," his visit would have to be classed as "official" rather than "state." If Khrushchev should come in the capacity merely as head of government, he could not be given the trappings of a state visit—exchanges of dinners and the like. The

State Department hounded the Soviet Embassy on this question: Is Khrushchev head of state or head of government? The Soviet Ambassador Mikhail ("Smiling Mike") Menshikov must have gone through certain agonies over this matter. The Soviet Union actually had a titular president, but Menshikov's future was tied to that of Khrushchev.

The Soviets finally came up with the only logical compromise, that Khrushchev was visiting the United States in the *capacity* of head of state. With this status given due publicity, an embarrassing situation was avoided. The Boss could meet his visitor at the airport and observe the exchange of hospitality as if Khrushchev were President of the U.S.S.R.

The Boss himself participated actively in planning Khrushchev's visit. It was amusing how viewpoints differed regarding the things that Khrushchev should see in the United States. Dad had made the offer to show military installations, but Khrushchev, as predicted, had been at pains to refuse. But people came up with plenty of places for him to see. The governor of South Dakota suggested that Yankton, being a "typical" American town, would be ideal. The mayor of Los Angeles felt that nobody could appreciate the U.S. without visiting his city. Even the Boss, on his part, thought that Khrushchev should stop off and see his own home town of Abilene. In all the planning the Soviets were surprisingly stubborn, specifying what the Premier (Chairman) would like to see and apparently making a point of ignoring our recommendations. Their preferences were acceptable, and Dad could later remind Khrushchev that his own people had made the schedule.

Given the intricacies of the situation, the Boss had early agreed with Vice President Nixon that one man should be placed in charge. He made a wise selection in Henry Cabot Lodge, our ambassador to the United Nations.[1] Lodge, a smooth, self-assured aristocrat, was also a tough-minded individual, whose adroitness in verbal slugging matches with the Communists made him ideal for this

[1] I was amused at the Boss's directive regarding Lodge's title for this job. He was to be designated as the "President's Personal Representative," the subtlety being that Russian ambassadors, being strictly messenger boys, held little prestige in the Soviet Union. Hence Lodge's normal title "ambassador" would be unimpressive to Khrushchev.

challenging chore. But troubles with Ambassador Menshikov were not over. One evening a couple of days before Khrushchev's arrival, a message from the State Department came to the Boss as we were having a cocktail before dinner. Menshikov, it appeared, was being arrogant about the arrival ceremonies. By Soviet custom, he claimed, he, as ambassador, should mount the steps of the aircraft and proceed in, accompanying the Chairman on the way out. Why this was so important to Smiling Mike was unclear, but we quickly surmised that he wanted to pass on some message before Khrushchev met the Americans. Menshikov had the reputation, probably justified, of maintaining his position by sending exaggerated messages to Moscow, telling of the deplorable conditions in this country—while at the same time disarming the people around Washington with his suave, friendly manners. Menshikov, we conjectured, was in a bad spot and wanted to say a word to Khrushchev before the Chairman could look around and see for himself how misleading his messages had been.

Be that as it may, when Menshikov's position was reported to Dad, he dismissed it abruptly, almost casually: "Tell him he'll do it our way or he'll go home." This curt directive solved the problem.

Shortly after noon on September 15 the Boss, with a considerable contingent of officials and staff, was on hand to meet the gigantic Russian TU-114 transport as it ponderously sat down at Andrews Air Force Base and waddled its way up to the ramp. The plane, a turboprop, was reputed to be the largest in the world at that time. The day was warm and brilliant and suspense filled the air. A few children from the Soviet Embassy were on hand with immense bouquets of flowers.

The amenities were brief and formal. The Boss read his welcoming talk to emphasize the official nature of the visit. The merciless sun, reflected off the white concrete, added to the grim impression: the two squinting principals looked even more belligerent, probably, than they felt. On the way back to Blair House moderate-sized crowds stood impassively as Khrushchev went by. No disturbance of any kind was encountered.

Khrushchev, as it turned out, was actually in an ebullient mood. He had achieved his objective of coming to the United States and had met a reception which, while hardly heart-warming, was at least correct and uneventful.

At about 3:20 that afternoon the Vice President, Secretary of State, and Llewellyn Thompson (U.S. ambassador to the Soviet Union) joined the Boss in the Oval Office. Ten minutes later Chairman Khrushchev, followed by Minister of Foreign Affairs Gromyko, Ambassador Menshikov, interpreters, and a couple of others joined the Americans. The group conferred around the Boss's desk much as in any routine staff meeting.

Khrushchev, carrying his usual excessive weight, was suffering from the Washington heat. His first act on entering was to present the Boss with a replica of the object the Russians had just dropped on the moon. Understandably, the Boss was not exactly pleased. The Soviet moon shot, occurring only the day before, seemed hardly a coincidence. Nevertheless, he accepted the gift with composure. "After all," Dad said later, "the fellow might have been sincere."

The Boss opened the conference. He had no desire, he said, to restrict the subjects to be covered, but time was particularly short that day. Therefore, he continued, it might be best to utilize this meeting principally to plan the rest of Khrushchev's trip. From the beginning, this exchange unearthed some of the problems we would face. The Chairman, for example, misled as he was about the United States and our political structure, could not conceive that statements made by our press or by local American officials could originate from any source other than the government. The Boss tried to explain that he himself was often the object of a great deal of criticism from the press and opposing politicians. Khrushchev was stony, unconvinced.

Little time passed before Khrushchev, still smarting from his "kitchen debate" with Nixon in Moscow, turned his wrath on the Vice President. How, he demanded, could he be well received in the light of certain remarks Mr. Nixon had been making? No visitor would be welcome in the Soviet Union, he went on, should he, Khrushchev, so express himself about him. The Vice President retorted by reminding the Chairman of the speeches he had made when he, Nixon, had visited Moscow. Khrushchev thereupon turned to the Boss and said, "You read these speeches; you be the judge." Ludicrous as the situation was, with Khrushchev's asking

Dad to be a referee between him and the Vice President, it still gave hope that some rapport between Eisenhower and Khrushchev might be possible.

The first conference finished, the Boss took Khrushchev aside and talked alone for a few minutes. They then left for a helicopter tour around the city, which was accepted only when Khrushchev was satisfied that the Boss himself would go along. At the end of the trip Khrushchev was delighted. He had, to be sure, criticized much of what he had seen—American mobility, for example, and our life style of individual housing. But he was intrigued by the helicopters. In fact, he asked if he could purchase three of the same model for his own use.

Dinner that night was a routine state-type affair with all its attendant glitter and pomp. Khrushchev and his family, according to the tenets of Communism, refused to wear dress clothes. Instead, all—including the normally resplendent Menshikov—came in business suits. Before dinner a small group gathered on the second floor of the White House, and Barbara and I had the chance to converse with Khrushchev's family. His wife, we learned, though she looked like a peasant woman, was a scientist in her own right, holding a Ph.D. His son Sergei regaled Barbara with the prospects of what fun she would have in Moscow, with inside-outside swimming pools, heated for the winter. Two daughters were there, Rada and Julia. Rada, a plain but attractive blonde, was accompanied by her husband Alexei I. Abzhubei. Rada and Barbara hit it off, and Rada seemed genuinely disappointed not to be allowed loose for a visit and private tour. Barbara, for one, felt particularly sorry for the ladies. Whereas the men in the party seemed at home in their business suits—Khrushchev determinedly so—the women seemed quite conscious of their plain dresses.

The memorable event of the evening was Khrushchev's toast. In making it, he confirmed that he was indeed unable to leave politics aside, even at a social event, and launched into an extemporaneous discussion of the relative strengths of the two countries. A few days before in Moscow he had stated that he would "bury" us—meaning, he explained later, economically. This evening he put the frosting on the cake and said:

What we should now do is to strive together to improve our

relations. We need nothing from the United States, and you require nothing that we have. It is true that you are richer than we are at present. But then tomorrow we will be as rich as you are, and the day after tomorrow we will be even richer.

After dinner Khrushchev was entertained by Fred Waring and his Pennsylvanians. Though I enjoy Waring's singing group very much, I thought at the time that in future evenings it might be complimentary to throw in something Russian. Therefore, when Khrushchev was out West the next week, Pete Aurand and I contacted the Marine Band ensemble, who were going to entertain at Camp David, and asked if they could learn some Russian melodies. We came up with a list, to include "Dark Eyes," "Katushka," and "Stenka Razin," favorites from Vienna days. The idea was that at Camp David the ensemble would alternate between American and Russian tunes. I checked the repertoire with the State Department (God knows why!) and received negative advice on "Stenka Razin." Reason: it was a tune from czarist times. I respected their advice, but later I told a Russian-American and he hooted. "Stenka Razin," the song of the river bandit, had nothing to do with the czar; it was a Russian folk song that Khrushchev would have particularly enjoyed.

The dinner at the Soviet Embassy the day after Khrushchev's arrival was notable for its lavishness. Though catered locally, it included vast quantities of delicacies flown in from Russia. The Russians, as many of our troops learned right after the war, are notably hospitable; Khrushchev, in addition, was determined not to be outdone. During the day the Chairman had faced a large gathering at the National Press Club. I recall watching his performance on television with fascination. His reactions were slowed a bit by the difficulties in translation; but when he finally understood each question, his reactions were always strong, one way or the other. He could smile, glower, or roar. With all his responsibilities in the Soviet Union—and with his inevitably dangerous rise to power—Khrushchev had probably never gone through a grilling by a free press. He stood up well, I thought; while the experience appeared to irritate him, he probably found it a bit of an education.

Khrushchev arrived back in Washington after his Western trip on September 25. The tour had been eventful and Cabot Lodge, having accompanied him throughout, told the Boss of his own personal ordeal. We were most interested in Khrushchev's violent reaction at being denied permission to visit Disneyland in California. (We later learned the facts. Soviet police had felt that adequate security could not be provided at the drop of a hat, and our people had agreed. Nevertheless, Khrushchev blamed his disappointment on the mayor of Los Angeles.) He had experienced a very frank exchange with an independent American farmer in Iowa, one Roswell Garst. After his return he and the Boss, together with advisers, headed the next day for Camp David.[2]

As with the Macmillan visit some months before, I maintained something of an amateur standing during this series of meetings, commuting between Camp David and our nearby Gettysburg home. However, I drove up for breakfast the morning after the party's arrival. Khrushchev and the Boss sat opposite each other in the middle of the medium-sized dinner table. Observing from one end, I watched fascinated as the Chairman went into action. With his shaven head, wearing a white, embroidered, collarless shirt, he presented an unusual appearance. He sat leaning forward, both elbows on the table, speaking slowly, distinctly, even ferociously. The Chairman ate little, so engrossed was he in his own words, punctuated by continual wagging of his right index finger.

One would have thought that Khrushchev was conducting serious negotiations of enormous magnitude. Actually he was telling war stories about his experiences in World War II as a commissar with an army group at Stalingrad in 1942 and at Odessa in 1943. Occasionally he would throw in a little aside such as a remark on how the Red Army discouraged looters: they shot them. But all of this tirade must have had a purpose. While it appeared to be merely reminiscing, he seemed, the longer one listened, to be trying to make a point, to establish in the Boss's mind that Khrushchev himself, although a commissar, had actually habitually taken the side of the field commanders against Stalin, to whom he referred with contempt. Conceivably he was attempting to establish some sort of old-soldier rapport.

[2] The Boss for some reason had been reluctant to use Camp David for the conference. However, Khrushchev was very intent on going there, probably for its intimacy and prestige.

The closest thing to a kind remark that Khrushchev made about Stalin was that the latter had appreciated and admired Dad's actions as Supreme Commander in the last days of the war. In this he was doubtless referring to Dad's decision to halt Western Allied forces on the Elbe and Mulde Rivers and his acceding to Stalin's request not to push into Prague in Czechoslovakia.

At one point Khrushchev, relaxing for the first time, mentioned Marshal Zhukov. "Don't worry about your old friend," he said, "he is living happily in retirement, doubtless writing his memoirs."[3]

I personally was most entranced by his description of the Odessa operation. Here Stalin had ordered a massive attack, which the local commander had considered suicidal, estimating a probable loss of 300,000 men. Khrushchev, according to his story, had sided with the army group commander and had tried to reach Stalin by telephone. Zhukov had ostensibly blocked the call. The attack had gone off as scheduled and the losses had turned out to be approximately what Khrushchev had predicted. A couple of years later, Khrushchev went on, Mikoyan, apparently somewhat in his cups, had chided Stalin about this bad decision. As Mikoyan was happily rambling on, Stalin was rising from his chair. Khrushchev averted disaster by assuring Stalin that the Soviets would have lost 300,000 men in that spot regardless of whether they had attacked or defended.

After breakfast that morning, as the group was milling around, I found myself standing next to Khrushchev and his interpreter. Head leaning forward and glowering into space, he mumbled, perhaps thinking aloud, that he was suffering from some kidney ailment and therefore had brought along his own drinking water. I hardly needed the message, although he may have wanted me to pass it on.[4] But even on such a casual subject, his intensity still burned.

That afternoon, as was now becoming customary, the Boss brought Khrushchev over to the Gettysburg farm by helicopter.

[3] As with everything Khrushchev said, I took this statement with a grain of salt. However, years later in Brussels, the Soviet ambassador presented me with a copy of Zhukov's memoirs, showing pictures of the marshal in his old age.

[4] If the Chairman was apologizing, he need not have. The Boss took his own drinking water all over the world.

This time Dad decided for some reason not to bring his guest down to the Pitzer Schoolhouse; instead, Barbara scrubbed up the four children and I drove the family over to Dad's place.

In these informal circumstances Khrushchev was at his best. He sat at the end of the glassed-in porch and assumed the role of the beneficent grandfather. Pointing to the children, one by one, he asked their names. Then he would give each the Russian version. (Strangely, he was unable to translate "Susan," which means "serenity." Maybe there was no such word in his vocabulary.) He then specifically invited my entire family, including the children, to accompany the party on the Boss's forthcoming trip to the Soviet Union. The children were excited at the prospect (David was eleven at the time); I was horrified. To my mind, our battle to avoid spoiling the children by excessive publicity and attention was difficult enough without this exercise.[5] When I told Dad a couple of days later that the children were not available, he showed his irritation. But he recognized that in this case, since I was their father, my word stood.

Khrushchev distributed trinkets to the children, including little red-star pins. When I caught David wearing one to school a couple of days later, I explained in no uncertain terms exactly what it stood for. "If Khrushchev could take us over," I fumed, "guess what family would be the first to be shot." (Later on in the year Khrushchev followed up his folksy approach by sending Russian toys to the children and sending the family an elaborate set of Russian Christmas ornaments.)

The whole meeting at Camp David has been recorded by the Boss in *Waging Peace*. Nevertheless, the episode which best illustrates the significance of the whole meeting deserves elaboration. On the last morning, a Sunday, the Boss had gotten through to Khrushchev that he, the President, would never attend a summit meeting under a threat such as still officially existed regarding Berlin. The two walked together in the woods, accompanied only by Khrushchev's interpreter, to avoid the Chairman's being overheard by Gromyko and Menshikov. Khrushchev agreed that the threat of unilateral

[5] When Khrushchev, after breaking up the May 1960 summit meeting, withdrew his invitation for us to visit Moscow, my mother never abandoned her conviction that Khrushchev did so because of his hurt feelings over my unreasonable stand.

action by the Soviets on Berlin would be lifted. This was acceptable to Dad, who replied that this action removed any barrier to a summit meeting. There matters stood for the moment.

At lunch that day, after a talk with Gromyko, Khrushchev exhibited the inexplicable hostility he seemed to harbor by turning once more on the Vice President. He spoke to Nixon in harsh terms, exceeding the rules of decent manners. After the meal was over, he told the Boss in private that he could not include his earlier agreement in a joint communiqué. The Boss retorted that this meant the summit and trip to Russia were off. Khrushchev quickly rejoined that he would stand by his word if only he could explain it to the Politburo first. Finally they concluded that the Boss would make this agreement public two days after Khrushchev had departed and that Khrushchev would later confirm it.

Khrushchev left Camp David and the United States in high spirits, apparently relieved and flattered by the reception he had received. He did indeed, in the months following, consistently refer to the "Spirit of Camp David," as if the entire episode had been one of camaraderie, sweetness, and light. This piece of fiction was useful for his purposes but was hardly shared by any of us in the White House.

On Monday, September 28, 1959, the President, in subtle terms, announced at a press conference what had transpired between him and Khrushchev at Camp David:

> Now, the Chairman and I discussed the Berlin question at length. As you know, *no specific negotiations can be carried out in such question as this without our allies,* but you will have read the communiqué which brings up this point and says that negotiations are to be reundertaken, after making proper arrangements, in the aim to get a solution that will protect the legitimate interests of the Soviets, the East Germans, the West Germans, and above all, the Western people.
>
> Over and above this, we agree, in addition to what the communiqué said, that these negotiations should not be prolonged indefinitely but *there could be no fixed time limit on them.*[6]

[6] *Public Papers of the Presidents, Eisenhower, 1959,* p. 395. Italics supplied.

Immediately Khrushchev, in Moscow, confirmed that any time limit on negotiations on Berlin was lifted. The Berlin ultimatum of November 27, 1958, had evaporated. In its place was the agreement for a summit meeting, which Vice President Nixon had predicted Khrushchev wanted many months earlier.

After Khrushchev's departure the atmosphere in the White House relaxed somewhat. It would be an overstatement to say that we fell into a state of euphoria; but we were relieved that Khrushchev, still glowing from the visit, was, by the tone of his speeches and references to the "Spirit of Camp David," obviously trying to ease tensions. During the autumn President Adolfo Lopez Mateos of Mexico came to Washington and, since the Camp David location had now become a matter of prestige, the meetings were held there. Once again, as had become habit, they came down to visit the Pitzer Schoolhouse. In checking the records I find that during the visits of Lopez Mateos there were two other heads of government visiting Washington at the same time. And also during the period of the 1959 Berlin crisis, we were undergoing hearings in the Congress on defense policies and the United States was suffering from a protracted and damaging steel strike. It is impossible for a President to concentrate on any particular problem, even Berlin, exclusive of many others.

By November the Boss had decided to make a series of trips to various countries, particularly along the perimeter around South Asia. He realized that his remaining time in office was short—only a little over a year left—but he was well aware that he still enjoyed a considerable prestige around the world and decided to make maximum use of that standing for the benefit of our relations with others during his last months in office. It would be useful, he thought, to be seen personally in various nations and to assure populations of underdeveloped countries of the peaceful intentions of the United States.

It is sometimes difficult for Americans to realize how suspicious the populations of nonnuclear countries—particularly the developing countries—are of American attitudes and intentions. History shows that we have really exhibited a fairly warlike background.

Our nation won its independence from the British, not by passive resistance but by force of arms. Shortly thereafter the fledgling nation dared to take on the British Empire once more in the War of 1812. In 1848 the United States, in a war almost as unpopular as that in Vietnam, seized about 60 per cent of the territory which was claimed—but not controlled—by Mexico. Only about eighty-five years after the founding of the Republic, the United States went through the throes of one of the most virulent civil wars in history.[7] In 1898 we decimated the remains of a tottering Spanish Empire and then, in a conflict seldom recognized for its scope, took possession of the Philippines at the turn of the century. In two world wars, especially the second, the United States amassed vast armies and armadas, and in August of 1945 became the only country ever to drop an atomic bomb on an enemy.

Add to this history the fact that in the 1950s the nations of the world had developed a feel of being the pawns in a chess game between two superpowers, both loaded to the teeth with nuclear weapons which could spell the doom of friends, foes, and neutrals alike. It was primarily to put at ease the minds of those potential victims of a supreme holocaust that the Boss decided to make his series of state visits.

The selection of countries to be visited was an evolutionary thing. When Vice President Nixon first brought up this idea at a dinner in December of 1958, he actually had in mind a trip to the Far East. Dad, however, held a long-cherished ambition to visit India, and the trip was first designed with that as an objective. But to go to India required also a visit to Pakistan—and since the Pakistanis had their differences with Afghanistan, that country was included also. Iran, Turkey, and Greece soon followed. It was decided to bypass Israel and the Arab countries of the Eastern Mediterranean, not only because of the amount of time available but also of the delicacy of the situation in that region. At the end of the planning stage, eleven countries were included.[8]

The trip itself extended from December 3 to December 19, and a

[7] The Civil War killed or maimed about a million men out of a population of about thirty million.

[8] Italy, Turkey, Pakistan, Afghanistan, India, Iran, Greece, Tunisia, France, Spain, and Morocco.

complete description would fill many pages. For my part, the most enjoyable phase of the trip was being a member of the advance party with Tom Stephens, Jim Hagerty, and others.

One matter of fundamental importance had to be completed before the Boss could leave on the main trip. This was the question of control of American nuclear weapons in the event that the Soviets should attack the United States or our NATO Allies during such periods as the Boss would be out of contact with the Department of Defense. In the event of surprise attack, war plans in those days called for use of our nuclear weapons, but the decision to employ them was always correctly reserved to the President personally. Now, as we were preparing to go to far points of the earth, we realized that a situation could arise wherein it would be impossible to reach the Boss in sufficient time; reaction would have to be immediate. Communications were good, but there were always those moments such as during motorcades among teeming mobs when we had to admit that he would be temporarily out of touch.

Elaborate plans had been long in the process of formulation for the delegation of this presidential power to the Secretary of Defense in case of dire emergency. But wheels of government turn slowly and the wording of this authorization, a sheaf of papers perhaps a half inch thick, had been at least eighteen months in its redrafting and polishing. It just so happened that I had carried this action for the Army General Staff when assigned to War Plans in the Pentagon, and Andy Goodpaster had turned it over to me when it reached the White House in its near-final form. There were still, on the day of our departure, a few details the Boss wanted changed. Therefore I was in and out of his office several times during that day, making last minute changes.

On the surface there might appear a certain irony in the picture of a President and his staff feverishly completing arrangements for general war on the verge of departing on a mission of peace. Nevertheless, in his role as Commander-in-Chief, the Boss could never leave the country exposed to attack, no matter what the purpose of his trip. The Boss approved the final plan within the hour of departing for *Air Force One*.

One aspect of the trip caused a slight amount of confusion. My mother, recognizing her limited physical stamina, felt it impossible to go along. However, Barbara was available and more than willing. On learning of her invitation, Barbara threw herself into preparation for this major foray into our "other" life. Shots, diplomatic passport, purchase of clothes, decisions on what to take—all these were involved. In desperation she called on Pat Nixon, who, as wife of the Vice President, had been through this type of experience many times and who had always managed all her own details personally. Pat gave invaluable advice and even offered to lend Barbara her own personal luggage. Fortunately, it was not necessary to accept this generous offer.

It was accepted, however, that Barbara could not officially be considered the Boss's "hostess." Therefore, we had to leave it up to each embassy to make its own interpretation of her role. As a result, she was treated as Dad's hostess in countries such as Pakistan, India, and Spain, but not in Greece. In most of the Moslem countries no problem existed; the important affairs were stag. I personally felt considerable sympathy for the local ambassadors who had to take this protocol decision upon themselves.

As it turned out, protocol meant nothing; Barbara and I simply had to evaluate the situation in each capital, whether she would act as Dad's hostess or as the wife of a junior staff officer. But in the meantime, she made a substantial contribution to the good-will aspects of the trip, visiting hospitals in Pakistan, villages in India, and a harem in Afghanistan. In this activity she was encouraged and assisted by General Alfred Gruenther, now retired and president of the American Red Cross, who notified his offices in nearly all the capitals we were visiting to set up some program for her, coordinating with the local embassies, of course. On the evening the party entered Athens a small boy, in his eagerness to see the parade, had climbed up on a wall. The wall had crumbled and the boy was in serious condition in the hospital. Barbara and I learned of this while visiting the Acropolis. Without hesitation Barbara hurried to see him. The visit elicited some publicity and the Greek press seemed quite appreciative of the gesture. Fortunately, the boy later recovered.

Among the interesting and prominent personalities we were exposed to on this trip, the one that made the greatest impression on me was Prime Minister Jawaharlal Nehru of India. To me the man was inscrutable. I had met him once before, in 1957, when he had come for lunch at the White House, but that had been a brief and formal interlude. Now, witnessing him at close hand for over three days, I found him all the more complex. Unlike Vice President Radhakrishnan, whose lofty Hindu superiority was unmixed, Nehru was something else. On the surface he appeared interested in his guests. He took a particular liking to Barbara and made it a point to see to it that she tasted all the various kinds of exotic Indian fruits. In her presence he seemed almost outgoing.

And yet one felt that behind Nehru's impeccable manners he was hardly sincere—acting. That probably was the key. For whatever his other qualities, Nehru was a consummate actor—even a poseur. On the evening of our arrival in New Delhi, while President Rajendra Prasad was formally greeting the Boss atop a high platform, Nehru was not part of the ceremony. Nevertheless, he sat on the back steps, his chin resting on the back of his hand, staring bored into space for the benefit of the multitudes. He lost no chance to joke in public about his personal difficulties in dealing with two Presidents at one time; and one evening, while addressing a half million people at a rally in Old Delhi, Nehru, having been informed that the break-up of a soccer game necessitated a delay in our departure, simply extended the exercise by ad-libbing smoothly in Hindi for an extra half hour.

I personally was perplexed by it all—by the statue of British King George V facing the Rashtrapati Bhavan (President's House) in New Delhi, by the portraits of the former British Viceroys on the walls of the dining room, and by the attitude of Nehru himself. I asked Dad how he interpreted it all. "Well," he said thoughtfully, "the thing you've got to realize about Nehru is his basic resentment of the white man. To tear down the statue of George V, as we Americans would probably do—to him that would be too uncivilized. Keeping these things from the past is, in a way, a form of superiority."

I am no student of India or of the Hindu religion, but Dad's off-the-cuff observation answered the riddle as well as anything that I could come up with.

There is a major misconception that a state visit of this nature entails long, serious deliberations establishing new policies, which are formalized in due course by normal diplomatic intercourse. To be sure, in almost every nation visited, the local government would present its requests regarding increases in American aid. The Boss would listen patiently and promise to place the matter under review on his return home. But by and large, anyone who tries to regard these various meetings as "summits" in the true sense is doomed to disappointment.

Actually, these trips move so rapidly that it is impossible for anyone fully to absorb all the interesting things he is exposed to. Nevertheless certain highlights for me remain: the gracious reception at the Vatican by Pope John XXIII, with his little talk in broken English commenting on our common first names . . . the seething mobs of Indians at Connaught Square, New Delhi . . . the breathtaking beauty of the Taj Mahal . . . a bobbing elephant ride in an elaborate Indian howdah . . . poverty-stricken Afghan peasants peering in the car, with the magnificent Hindu Kush mountains as backdrop . . . the peace of the Mediterranean as viewed from aboard the flagship of the Sixth Fleet . . . the clanging and jolting train ride from Marseilles to Paris . . . Charles de Gaulle, blind without his thick glasses, greeting visitors at the Élysée Palace though unable to recognize them until moving inside . . . mounted Arab horsemen lining the Moroccan road, firing salutes in the air with their antiquated muskets . . . the thousands of citizens out to meet the Boss on our return to Washington in the frigid early morning hours.

During February of 1960 the Boss made a similar successful good-will visit to Brazil, Argentina, Chile, and Uruguay.

The meeting of the heads of government of the United States, Britain, France, and the Soviet Union, the long-awaited Summit, was scheduled to begin in Paris on May 16, 1960. Progress in the direction toward some understanding at least seemed good. Before the Boss's Asia–Europe trip of December, for example, Khrushchev sent him a message of good wishes for success. On the hardheaded side, we wondered rather vaguely what might be accomplished at this meeting, and all felt some uneasiness regarding the outcome in world opinion if no accords could be reached. But the outcome would decide.

On May 1, 1960, an officer came over from CIA to tell Andy Goodpaster that a photo reconnaissance plane, of the type that had been overflying the Soviet Union with impunity since 1956, had gone down over Russia. This reconnaissance plane, soon to become famous under the name of the U-2, was designed to fly at an altitude out of range of Soviet surface-to-air missiles. Khrushchev obviously had known of these repeated reconnaissance flights but had refrained from mentioning them, doubtless because by so doing he would admit Soviet inability to deal with them. The flights had been programmed because of the Soviet rejection of the Open Skies Proposal of 1955 at Geneva.

When Andy heard of the loss of the plane, he did, of course, report it without delay to the Boss. He also, of course, told me. Our immediate reaction, however, was not one of concern over its implications but of sympathy for the pilot. We had been assured categorically by the director of CIA, Allen Dulles, that no man would ever be taken alive. This knowledge cast a pall of sadness over us but was soon submerged in other events.

On the evening of May 3 Mother and Dad generously gave a party in the White House for a sizable group of Barbara's and my friends. The next morning I left on a trip to New Mexico to visit atomic installations at Sandia and Los Alamos. On my way back I read in the newspapers that Khrushchev had announced the destruction of the American aircraft and had taken the matter to the Supreme Soviet, disclosing a part of the evidence available to him. In Denver, where I dropped off to see my ailing grandmother, I called Mother and asked how the Boss felt about the news. His relayed message was understandable: "He says, 'Do you think I *ought* to like it?'"

I arrived back in Washington, troubled, and headed for Gettysburg, where I habitually acted as liaison between the Boss and the staff. That afternoon, Saturday, May 7, Andy called me from the White House. "Just how tough are things, General?" I asked.

"About as tough as they can get," he answered. "They've got the pilot alive." Thus collapsed all the statements that National

Aeronautics and Space Administration (NASA) and the State Department had issued.

The U-2 had, in fact, been so secret that its true purpose had not been disclosed between departments and agencies of the government. As it was admirably fitted out to be a weather reconnaissance plane, it flew many such missions under NASA control in various locations. NASA truly believed that weather reconnaissance was its only mission. Thus, when this particular plane went down on May 1, NASA issued a statement that a weather reconnaissance plane had become lost and was overdue. State Department had confirmed this impression. All of this would have held up except for the one "impossible" contingency—that a man be taken alive. Under this circumstance, the conventional intelligence practice of disavowing intelligence sources would never hold up.

At the National Security Council meeting on Monday, May 9, the Boss announced that he would take full responsibility for the missions. "We're going to take a beating on this," he said. "And I'm the one, rightly, who is going to have to take the brunt."[9]

Dad since has been blamed in some quarters for assuming the responsibility. I cannot see how he could have done otherwise. For one thing, it was true; he had approved flights for periods of a week at a time. (The plane went down on the last day of an approved week.) For another, there was no point in sticking with a discredited "cover story" with the pilot, Francis Gary Powers, in Soviet hands. Finally, the Boss instinctively would rather take the responsibility for making an error in judgment than be accused of not knowing what was going on in his Administration.

The timing was bad, admittedly. However, I cannot think of any good timing for such an occurrence. Our luck had simply run out.

The Boss reinforced the Secretary of State's previous statement at his press conference on Wednesday, May 11. He outlined the necessity for these flights and indicated that we would continue. Before leaving for the Paris Summit, however, the Boss suspended them.

9 Until Khrushchev's announcement, the only people in the White House aware of the U-2 program were the Boss, Gordon Gray, Andy Goodpaster, and me. Soon thereafter everyone in Washington was claiming to have been in the know.

After that, Khrushchev never missed a trick in his efforts to wring the last drop of propaganda out of the incident. He made threatening remarks, canceled the visit of the chief of the Soviet Air Force to the United States, and finally mysteriously decided to arrive in Paris a couple of days in advance of the scheduled Summit date, May 16.

The Boss spent the day of May 14 with Bill Robinson in the White House. They went to Burning Tree Golf Club to view a bit of the tournament being held there and then came back for work until about six o'clock. I joined Dad and Bill at about this time and after a 6:15 supper, an outwardly relaxed President took off from the White House lawn at 7 P.M. for Andrews Air Force Base. Twenty minutes later, after an informal send-off by a delegation of perhaps a dozen people, the party was off the ground and the wheels were up.

The weather was gray and slightly chilly at Orly Field near Paris. Again ceremonies were minimal, although for the French the word "minimal" translates to a somewhat different meaning than it holds for Americans. Traffic was light and miraculously the motorcade reached the Embassy Residence in a record twenty minutes.

During that same Sunday morning the Boss, in the upstairs living room of the Residence, conferred at length with the Secretary of State and later, the Secretary of Defense. The discussion ranged across the board but, as always, the subject of the U-2—or to put it more precisely, Khrushchev's next move, with the U-2 as a backdrop—hung over us all.

At one o'clock, the members of the household, namely Ambassador and Mrs. Amory Houghton, the Herters, Andy Goodpaster, Jamie Houghton, Dad, and I, went to lunch in the downstairs living room. At the end of the meal, word came of Khrushchev's action to date. The Chairman had put on a demonstration in his meeting with President de Gaulle during the morning, demanding that the United States (1) apologize for the act of sending spy planes over Russia, (2) renounce any intention of so doing in the future and, (3) punish those responsible. If the United States failed to do this, Khrushchev had said, he would be "unable" to attend the Paris Summit.

This news produced concern, but the Boss declared that this was no time to be bulldozed. In early afternoon he left for the Élysée Palace to meet with the other three Western heads of government. Dad had already decided not to revise his current positions, particularly since Khrushchev, at the end of his discussion with De Gaulle, had agreed to attend the next morning's session in any case.

Supper that evening was held in the Residence dining room downstairs. Dad wanted to get together with Macmillan as soon as possible and it fell to me to make the arrangements. Therefore I had to excuse myself from the table from time to time. It was now too late for a meeting that evening (supper was not served until about nine o'clock); we set up a meeting for the two over eight o'clock breakfast the next morning.

Macmillan arrived for the breakfast conference on time. At about ten minutes to nine, Philip de Zulueta, Macmillan's assistant, and I went out to the office to collect the various papers the United States had issued pertaining to the U-2 incident. By the time that Assistant Secretary of State Charles E. ("Chip") Bohlen and others joined Dad and Macmillan, a full-scale meeting was under way. Soon the draft of the statement the Boss was to issue at the first formal meeting was produced. Although the statement refused Khrushchev's demands, it did state that no further U-2 flights over the U.S.S.R. would be undertaken but not because of Khrushchev's ultimatum. Tactics were discussed regarding how the chairman of the meeting, President de Gaulle, would handle things. When this meeting was completed, part of the party took off amidst some flurry at about ten minutes to eleven.

I sometimes wonder if history will bother with such situations as this morning conference. Here was a group of about fifteen people, all speaking their minds, their ideas supplementing each other's. The President was drawing upon the ideas of all, regardless of station, observing no difference on the basis of the rank of the adviser. The determination of all was unmistakable and the Boss never lost his composure.

Indeed, at times of crisis such as this the Boss would always be at his best, keeping matters in perspective. When he left the Residence for the first meeting of the Summit after this grueling couple of hours, he walked with amazing bounce.

At eleven o'clock word came back to the Residence that the Summit session had begun. I felt a certain relief that the meeting had even opened, for a little over an hour before this had looked almost impossible.

The morning dragged on slowly. Those of us "minding the store" waited anxiously for news. As the time progressed, my own feeling of optimism rose, since at least the session had not broken down in the first five minutes. After what seemed an interminable stretch, we were notified at about 2 P.M. that the President was on his way back to the Residence.

As the car pulled up to the drive, we all peered out the window. Andy Goodpaster was riding in the back seat with the Boss, and Andy's grim look told the story that things had not been a success. Dad appeared completely unperturbed, but when the three of us went to the downstairs sitting room, the story began to unfold. We were immediately joined by Ambassador Houghton, Chip Bohlen, and Livingston Merchant (now Under Secretary of State); soon the build-up was so complete that we once more had the entire U.S. delegation present.

The story of Khrushchev's tirade at this meeting has now become well known. What some people do not know so well is the degree of difficulty the Boss experienced in keeping his temper during the long-drawn-out polemics. Most excited of all was Bohlen, who appeared livid with rage—and who, being a linguist and a former ambassador to Moscow—had been forced to listen to Khrushchev's statement in three languages.

Immediately, the group began to discuss the statement the Boss might make to the world. Jim Hagerty and Andrew H. Berding, Jim's counterpart in State, were there by this time, taking occasional notes as the Boss and Bohlen briefed the rest. The Boss, for his part, decided early that he would issue his statement in a moderate key, but he was anxious that the world know the full story. He designated Bohlen as the primary witness to speak to the press. Bohlen was more than anxious to do so. I was amused that one gesture of Khrushchev's had disturbed him particularly—

when the Soviet Premier, hands raised above his head, had declared his "hands clean" and his "heart pure."

At about three o'clock, luncheon was served and a small group went to eat. Bohlen and Hagerty worked on the statement between bites in the front office. Luncheon itself was animated, since the group were still recovering from the drama of the morning's activities. Under the surface, we all felt the impact of the insults, all harboring strong resentment and bewilderment at Khrushchev's violent conduct.

After lunch the Boss sat down and completed the job of editing the public statement. He then retired to his bedroom at about 4:15 to get a couple of hours' rest. Before turning in, he asked me to draft a letter he might send to heads of the various governments he had visited during the preceding year, explaining to them as best he could what had befallen. Later, after having approved them, Dad dressed for dinner and went downstairs. It was now 6:30.

In the living room Dad sat for a while, alone. Macmillan was on the way to visit De Gaulle and would come by shortly. This meant a late supper and late evening. The Boss spent about forty-five minutes walking through the gardens, and, apparently relaxed, making small talk with the office secretaries.

At about 7:15 Macmillan arrived and the two of them walked in the garden for a while and later sat down alone in the living room. Macmillan then left.

The next day, Tuesday, May 17, I went down to the first floor about 7:30 to look over the reports and shortly thereafter went upstairs to the living room for breakfast with Dad. After a good night's sleep, he appeared much refreshed. Andy, Jim Hagerty, and Secretary Herter were already on hand. The Boss was pleased to have a message from the Joint Chiefs of Staff expressing their support. The latest rumors had it that the Russians were now peddling the idea around town that some of Khrushchev's demands had been met, stressing the cessation of U-2 flights over the Soviet Union. They were indicating, according to these rumors, that perhaps a phone call from the Boss to express regret over these flights would be sufficient to keep the Summit going. Khrushchev would drop his demands that the people connected with the flights be punished if Dad would personally apologize.

Generally speaking, however, the course of action for the morning seemed simple. The three Western powers were to meet at ten o'clock in the Élysée Palace. The Boss was then going to ask that De Gaulle call a full-scale meeting for any convenient time. If the Russians refused to attend, then they in fact would have broken off the Summit.

Reports on Khrushchev's activities continued to conflict. One said that he had told a sidewalk press conference that he would leave the next day (Wednesday) unless the Americans acceded to his demands. Another indicated that he planned to stay around for a couple of days. His airplane crew, according to the Secret Service, had checked out of their hotels. All of this ferment by the Soviets seemed to represent an effort to create a war of nerves.

Since Dad had some time on his hands—and since golf seemed to be impractical—he and Macmillan decided to go for a drive to visit SHAPE Headquarters and the little village of Marnes-la-Coquette where Dad had lived as SACEUR.

Upon arrival at the house Dad had been a little taken aback to note that the press had followed him. However, after taking a few pictures they kept their distance. Dad and Macmillan toured the back yard and the interior, the Boss obviously enjoying the sojourn immensely. After a few minutes, they remounted their vehicle for the half-mile trip to the office of the mayor of Marnes-la-Coquette, who had been Dad's staunch friend for many years. I followed after.

The mayor was not in his office when we arrived, but a messenger soon found him. Encumbered by considerable corpulence, he came running across the square. He was a hearty man, and his delight at this visit knew no bounds. Obviously he had not been notified in advance, for he had a two-days' growth of beard. He briskly ushered the Boss and Macmillan into his small office. In this room, devoid of a rug, were a table and about eight chairs. On the wall were pictures of the Boss, General Gruenther, General de Gaulle, and Louis Pasteur. The mayor made a point of saying that the two most distinguished citizens of Marnes-la-Coquette were President Eisenhower and Maurice Chevalier, without specifying priority. It soon became a problem to find a graceful way of terminating the conversation, in view of the exuberance of the Mayor. Dad somehow eased his way out, however, and by 12:30 the motorcade, with expert motorcyclists on its flanks, headed back for the British Embassy. On the way I received a message by radio that an important message for the President was waiting.

On our arrival a half hour later we learned that a full-scale meeting was to be held that afternoon at three o'clock. Khrushchev apparently had driven some hundred kilometers out in the country to visit a small Russian cemetery. When reached there by the French and notified of this meeting, we were told Khrushchev had canceled his 3:30 press conference and said that if President de Gaulle wanted him to attend, he would do so.

Once back in the American Embassy Residence, the Boss set about drawing up a statement to assure the world that the Summit that afternoon did not signify that the West had accepted Khrushchev's "conditions." Jim Hagerty and Chip Bohlen went to work again and the statement was approved and duly issued.

Lunch was at about 1:45, served in the main dining room of the Residence, relaxed as usual. As we had all suspected before our return, the crisis of the entire exercise had been passed. After the initial meeting with Khrushchev, the tone had been set, and everyone seemed to feel now that we had done the best we could with a bad situation. We all felt the Boss had gone as far as he could to make such a meeting possible without losing dignity.

At about three o'clock the Boss left for the meeting at Élysée Palace. At about ten minutes after five o'clock, however, he was back. Khrushchev had not, in fact, turned up and had instead held a belligerent press conference announcing his immediate departure from Paris.

By now the Boss realized that nothing constructive was going to transpire and had now become interested primarily in Khrushchev's leaving town. Mother called, much concerned for his well-being.

At one o'clock on May 18, the following day, the Boss, Ambassador Houghton, and I drove to the Élysée Palace for lunch with General de Gaulle. After the meal the group went out to sit in the beautiful gardens for coffee and brandy. De Gaulle seemed completely unperturbed by all these turns of events; perhaps he had never put much stock in the Summit anyway. However, we all knew what he had whispered to the Old Man that bleak first morning: "No matter what, I am with you."

By the time the guests began arriving for the cookout dinner at 7:45, Dad was already hard at work charcoal-broiling steaks in the small back yard of the Embassy Residence. Cares were past; he was relaxing. The Old Man, a gourmet, loved to cook, and he went about this hobby with the same concentration he brought to bear on everything else. It had a therapeutic effect on him, and Mother has remarked that whenever something important occurred, Dad's inclination was to head for the kitchen.[10] He conversed lightly with all, especially with Mrs. Lauris Norstad and Laura Houghton, doubtless one of his favorite hostesses. As always, however, when the steaks were about ready, he gave a sharp announcement—command is more accurate—for the guests to drop what they were doing and head for the dining room. The initiated knew that this was not an idle utterance. Everyone had to be in his place so that the steaks, when served, would be perfection. So it was this evening.

After dinner, while the men were sitting in the back living room, we began to discuss a message which the Democratic leaders (Rayburn, Johnson, Stevenson, and Fulbright) had sent for delivery to Khrushchev, urging him not to break up the Summit. Secretary Herter had answered, notifying those involved that the message was overtaken by events as the Summit was now a dead issue. But he had promised to send the message on if the senders insisted. Apparently, Doug Dillon had received a phone call in Washington that afternoon insisting that the message be transmitted. Finally, Herter went to our makeshift office to phone Senator Johnson. Apparently two phone calls had been made; in the first, Lyndon Johnson had expressed irritation over the fact that the message had not already been delivered. In the second he had been more conciliatory. Apparently, the complicating factor had been Johnson's speech on the floor of the Senate, declaring that the Democrats were behind the President, during which he had been

---

[10] On hearing of the news of Pearl Harbor, for example, Dad went straight to the kitchen and began to make vegetable soup.

applauded "on the President's behalf" by all, led by Senator Dirksen.

Accordingly, it was finally agreed that the message should be sent the next morning by the Embassy to Khrushchev with a cover memorandum to the effect that it represented an expression of the "unity of America." This useless exercise occupied enough time so that it was settled only by midnight.

On Thursday, May 19, we left at about 7 A.M., for the Gare des Invalides to board helicopters for the trip to Orly. At Orly, though the staff were hurrying to the plane, I paused to listen to "The Star-Spangled Banner" played once more by the French Air Force Band. This time the rendition was unusually meaningful. De Gaulle had stood by the Boss throughout and had made it clear that he would continue to do so. An abortive Summit was over, and an old friendship renewed.

In spring of 1960, General de Gaulle made a state visit to the United States. Unlike most of his formal rituals, he had real business to accomplish, to solidify a united position for the forthcoming Summit Conference in Paris. The serious talks were, as usual, held at Camp David; and also as usual, the Boss went through the ritual of bringing De Gaulle to the Gettysburg farm and then down to the Pitzer Schoolhouse.

In our home, De Gaulle became a changed man from the austere, aristocratic role he usually assumed. Though in public he pretended to speak no English, he unbent in private and actually spoke it quite well. The family were alarmed for a moment when our four-year-old daughter, Mary Jean, toddled up to him and reached for his thick glasses, which he had to use after a cataract operation and about which he was very vain. With a slight, benign smile, however, De Gaulle looked at Mary and said, "I must wear these to see: poor me!" Mary Jean was soon distracted in other directions.

In the months following the May 1960 Summit, Khrushchev persisted in his policy of harassment and vituperation. He had, at Paris, withdrawn his invitation for the Boss to visit Moscow. (The Boss, on his part, commented wryly that Khrushchev could have done that without coming all the way to Paris.) In June the Communists and left-wing Socialists in Japan were able to muster enough by way of demonstrations to force the Japanese Government to cancel its invitation to the Boss to visit Tokyo; they could not guarantee his security. On July 1, 1960, the Soviets shot down an American RB-47 aircraft over the Baltic Sea.

But through all the unpleasantness, which probably had some adverse effect on Nixon's 1960 election campaign, one fact remained: Khrushchev had completely dropped his November 1958 ultimatum on Berlin, at least for the duration of the Boss's presidency.

In the spring of 1960 I began my last major project in the White House, that of preparing for the Boss's postpresidential years at Gettysburg. This entailed securing an office, finding secretarial help, and—most important—making sure that the presidential papers were in order.

A President in recent times has been well taken care of by the nation when he leaves office. In earlier years when a President departed, he was completely on his own. However, the Presidential Retirement Act, already in effect, would entitle the Boss to a $25,000 a year pension, an office to be provided by the General Services Administration, an allowance of $50,000 a year to provide salaries for office help, and a widow's pension of $10,000 for Mother after his death. The amounts have increased dramatically since 1961, but these were the figures that we had to work with.

Dad's situation in planning for retirement to Gettysburg was unique. In 1952 he had resigned his commission as General of the Army so that he could be a bona fide civilian while running for office. (By special law, all five-star generals, so long as they kept their rank, were supposed to remain theoretically on active duty for life.) When Dad left office in 1961, he had no real financial need for reinstatement of his rank, as the presidential retirement benefits were of course adequate and much exceeded those of a five-star general. Yet for sentimental reasons, and in order to be able to keep a couple of members of his military family (specifically Sergeant John Moaney and Colonel Bob Schulz), Dad hoped that his military status might be restored. The problem here was that the retirement prerogatives of the two positions obviously could not be additive. Such an arrangement would have been unfair to former Presidents Harry Truman and Herbert Hoover; no Congress, Republican or Democratic, would stand for it.

Fortunately, though the Congress was controlled by the Democrats, the Boss was on warm, friendly terms with its leadership, particularly Senate Majority Leader Lyndon Johnson and Speaker of the House Sam Rayburn. Bryce Harlow was able to work out a compromise with the Congress creating a special law that would reinstate the Boss's military rank but give him only the normal ex-presidential benefits. The only privilege that went with this arrangement was authorization to keep three active military personnel on his staff at Gettysburg, with the proviso that their salaries should be deducted from the $50,000 allotted for his office expenses.

The bill was pushed through Congress by Representative Carl Vinson (a former opponent on the 1958 defense reorganization bill), without a murmur of opposition. After the Boss left office, President Kennedy signed it into law, retroactive to Dad's original date of rank, December 1944. (The retroactive feature meant nothing in terms of dollars; it simply placed him where he had previously been in the five-star lineup, behind MacArthur and ahead of Arnold and Bradley.)

Fortunately, in early 1960 Major General Willard S. Paul, a retired officer now president of Gettysburg College, offered a fine building at 300 Carlisle Street, the college president's residence, for Dad's use. General Paul himself was not occupying it at the time, as he preferred to live elsewhere. The house was ideal for the Boss's office.

By this period, incidentally, I had made my mind up definitely to leave the Army. There were many reasons, stemming back to 1957, but I had now mentally crossed the bridge and was prepared to resign effective January 20, 1961. I planned on settling down in Gettysburg, where Barbara and the children had moved during the summer of 1959.

Finding an adequate office staff in Gettysburg was difficult. Not many secretaries in Washington were enthusiastic about moving to a small town. Polly Yates, for one, felt she had to stay where she was; her whole life was centered there. I understood her position but was delighted when Lillian H. ("Rusty") Brown, one of General Persons' secretaries, agreed to go with me. Also, Ann Whitman, the Boss's secretary throughout the eight White House years, was willing, for a while at least.

The physical problems of the future office were soon taken off my shoulders when Bob Schulz decided that he would stay with Dad and work out of Gettysburg. Bob had been with the Boss since 1946 and knew his personal business thoroughly. He could take over responsibility for setting up the office and hiring the rest of the staff. For this he was admirably equipped, and I could forget everything else and concentrate on my main problem, that of the Boss's papers.

The matter of presidential papers, in which I am involved to this day, has always interested me. By historic precedent, from the days of George Washington, the papers of a President have been considered his personal property, and, at the end of his tour, he takes them with him. This is, I believe, a correct arrangement, as it protects a former President from any attempt on the part of his successor to make use of them for political purposes. Furthermore, a former President is entitled to have the records of his Administration available to him for reference and future writings.

But the problem has become immeasurably complicated since the first days of the Republic. The volume of mail, for example, has increased to the point where, even in the 1950s, the White House would receive something like fifteen thousand letters a week. Furthermore, with the growth of the White House staff from a couple of clerks to its impressive current size, the volume of paper generated "in house" is tremendous. For the "papers" of the President include not only his own personal correspondence but also the official communications of his staff. Finally, the matter of security classification has complicated the issue. Many of the papers bear the stamp "Top Secret"; others go even farther, carrying esoteric code names covering information of extremely high, specialized sensitivity. The various categories of papers, therefore, had to be separated and each treated accordingly.

A final consideration, not to be overlooked, is the fact that a

President's papers have, by their historic importance, considerable monetary value. But this fact, we believed, represented a potential liability. For, we reasoned, if a President's family should inherit these valuable papers without being able to sell them because of their security classification, the inheritance taxes could theoretically represent an intolerable financial blow. The Boss, recognizing this potential embarrassment, early put it in his will that what papers remained in his possession at the time of his death should automatically become the property of the United States Government.

Fortunately, a nonprofit group known as the Eisenhower Foundation had long before, on a private basis, secured the funds to construct the Eisenhower Center at Abilene, Kansas, which encompassed both a museum and a handsome presidential library. The library had the capacity to receive all the Boss's papers, with room to spare.

The Boss's will being taken care of, our problem was to arrange for the transfer of the still privately endowed library at Abilene to the ownership of the government. Such an action was necessary in order for the United States National Archives to provide a staff and actually run the building. Accordingly, the prescribed exchange of letters was drawn up between the Boss and former Admiral Franklin G. Floete, then head of General Services Administration, setting forth the exact terms. Drawing up the letter required a team of several people, including private attorneys, to reach a wording that took care of all the technical pitfalls. Eventually, on April 19, 1960, the complete exchange was made public and submitted to the Congress. Timing was important, as law required the letters to rest before Congress for 180 working days before the provisions could go into effect. If we were late, there would be no place to send Dad's papers as of January 20, 1961, where they could be available to him. We made the deadline and the government accepted ownership of the library in time.

For planning purposes, we divided the presidential papers into three basic categories. The first, incredibly voluminous, consisted of the correspondence and memoranda of nearly the entire White House staff, excluding only those of the Boss himself, Gordon Gray (concerning the NSC), and Andy Goodpaster's (mine included). This vast bulk was to be sent immediately to Abilene, where the researchers could begin to sort it out.

The second category consisted of the highly secret, esoteric material (for example, the Gray and Goodpaster files) requiring a more sophisticated degree of protection than could be afforded in Gettysburg. Here the Army came to our aid. These papers were to be stored in Fort Ritchie, about a half hour's drive from Gettysburg. As we anticipated little need for the Boss to refer to these papers, the distance away from his office was not considered prohibitive.

The third set of papers, the "Whitman files," consisted of the Boss's own letters and memoranda written over the previous eight years. This set, the smallest of the three—and the most important—filled twenty-four safes. These were to be delivered to the new office at Gettysburg and would be accessible to Dad himself and to his writing team.

For the papers of the second and third categories at Ritchie and Gettysburg, I was designated informally as custodian. I was to retain my high-level clearances for access to the Boss's presidential papers. (Such a designation was logical, as the only other individual previously holding such clearances was Andy Goodpaster, who was aching to get back to straight Army duty.) While not specifically stated, it was understood that my clearances pertained only to the Boss's papers, not to material of similar classification produced after the end of his Administration.

In October 1960 I was beginning to show signs of exhaustion, which prompted the doctor to recommend that I get away for a couple of weeks. On hearing this, the Boss reacted instantaneously and ordered me to take a two-week vacation in Puerto Rico. After two weeks in the Caribbean, Barbara and I came back refreshed.

While in Puerto Rico we received the news that the New York *Times* had come out in favor of Senator John F. Kennedy over Vice President Nixon in the coming presidential election. As the *Times* had supported the Boss twice, this came as a shock and put some damper on an otherwise delightful rest. This was the first inkling I had of a substantial possibility that Vice President Nixon might lose the election. It is extremely difficult for those in power to visualize their own party can ever be voted out.

The night of the election Barbara, Dad, a friend, and I watched the returns on television. At about midnight, with the returns so discouraging, Dad gave up and went to bed. Barbara and I held out until about 1:30 A.M. The next morning we learned that the election had come out much closer than predicted by the commentators and their computers. Nevertheless, by about 9:00 the result was definite. Kennedy had won.

I went into the Oval Office and Dad and I sat silently, the Boss slumped in his swivel chair staring at nothing through the window to the South Grounds. I rarely saw him so depressed. "All I've been trying to do for eight years," he finally said, "has gone down the drain. I might just as well have been having fun." He had one small decision to make: whether to go to Augusta as planned or to stay over in Washington to meet the Vice President when he returned that evening from California. Almost physically I shoved Dad into his car and rode out with him to the airport. His conscience assuaged, Dad needed little urging.

That evening I joined the crowd gathered to meet the Nixon party. The night was damp at Andrews Air Force Base and the dark was penetrated only by a few floodlights. The crowd in general had not yet felt the impact of what had happened. All were subdued but surprisingly cheerful. The camaraderie among people who, from different parts of the Government, normally had little chance to get to know each other, was remarkable.

When the Vice President came down the steps of the plane, the floodlights were in his eyes and he could see very little. He finally recognized me I had been shoved up front and later recorded in his memoirs that I was there to "represent the President." Possibly he was disappointed; but I have always hoped he realized the circumstances that necessitated the Boss's absence.

After the election the atmosphere around the White House was subdued. Even in the face of the facts it was very difficult viscerally to realize that we would all soon leave. Few of the current staff would have remained in their jobs even had Nixon won the election; he would have brought in his own team. Nevertheless, we could not help a vague feeling of rejection, that the American people had disapproved of our own efforts over the past years. Given the circumstances of an active political campaign, of course, with neither candidate an incumbent, this feeling was irrational; nevertheless, it was inevitable. General Persons said once, slowly and thoughtfully, "I'm just going to keep my mouth shut. If I can't say anything good about the boys coming here, I'm just gonna say nothing."

On December 6, 1960, President-elect Kennedy was scheduled to come to the White House for a briefing. As one of my odd jobs, I was placed in charge of physical details for the visit. Nothing much was needed except to arrange for a military cordon to line the driveway from Pennsylvania Avenue to the door of the West Wing. All military services were represented. According to custom, no honors were to be rendered. General Persons did, however, discuss the matter with Clark Clifford, Mr. Kennedy's representative, to ensure that the President-elect understood.

Senator Kennedy arrived at the appropriate time, sitting alone in the back seat of his limousine. This was a thoughtful, perceptive move on his part. The sensitive people he was coming to see were expecting a flood of assistants to be with him—a sort of Roman triumph. Some of his future staff were already there, to be sure, but they had traveled separately and inconspicuously. Before the President-elect arrived, several staff people had sidled up to me and hinted that they would like to meet him. I asked the Boss if that might be possible; he thought it would be fine. Therefore, before the formal conference began, a sizable group filed into the office to meet Kennedy. The Senator was surprisingly boyish-looking, probably because of his thick shock of hair. However, his warmth and modesty were impressive. He greeted each one of the staff as if it were a distinct privilege. After that, a restricted group met in the Cabinet Room to discuss the problems facing the nation at that particular time.

The night before Kennedy's inauguration, January 19, 1961, involved an odd combination of circumstances. I spent the latter part of the afternoon proceeding from office to office with two janitors, picking up the last of the presidential papers, the few that had been considered necessary for operation up to the final minute. Once these eight safes of material were removed, the outgoing

Administration would be occupying offices with no documents available. As with every change of Administration, the new staff would come into empty quarters and begin their own files. As I was finishing, a few snowflakes began to fall; it took little time to see that it was snowing in earnest. At about 6:30 Secretary of Defense Tom Gates called. "Tell your Dad," he said, "that I'm turning out the whole Army to keep the streets clean." As it turned out, the streets were highly passable the next morning, and the inauguration went without a hitch.

That evening of January 19, however, the conditions were so bad that a good portion of the White House staff was stranded and forced to spend the night in the bomb shelter, the only time that had happened in eight years. I understood that something of a party was under way there, and I would have liked to join it. However, Barbara and I were tired and turned in on the third floor early.

The morning of the inauguration, the atmosphere in the West Wing of the White House was eerie. With no papers to sign or examine, we simply idled away the time. Dad spent a good deal of the morning leaning on his safe talking with Ann Whitman and others. For my part, I had decided to wear Army uniform that day to avoid the top hat the President-elect had requested. I simply went to my desk—there was nowhere else to wait—and propped my feet up until the time to go from the office to the mansion.

The farewells in the office were, not surprisingly, full of emotion.

When I arrived, the servants, most of them in tears, were lined up saying farewell to Mother and Dad. They had, after all, been together eight years. Soon the Kennedys, the Lyndon Johnsons, and a small entourage arrived in time for a short visit and a cup of coffee. Sitting on a settee in the Red Room, I passed a few moments telling Jacqueline Kennedy how she would love the house and how great the servants were. I doubt that she heard much; her mind understandably was on the immediate future.

Soon the group took their places in the procession to head for the Capitol. As the car carrying Barbara and me pulled out, the three military aides gave us a salute. I choked up a bit. Our direct connection with the magnificent White House was over.

The historic view of the Eisenhower years is currently in the process of change. The labels formerly tagged on it by the more extreme commentators are beginning to disappear. It has been termed a "do-nothing" Administration. As a matter of fact, those who take the time to read even parts of the Boss's memoirs must realize that those years were active indeed for the President. The period during which the world was adjusting to the fact of nuclear deterrence was dangerous.

At the advent of the Eisenhower Administration, the United States enjoyed a vast military superiority over the Soviet Union. During that Administration and for some time after—witness the Soviet backdown in Cuba in October of 1962—our strength was such that the Soviets could never afford a move that would provoke the unleashing of our nuclear power on a first strike. Thus the Boss was able to defy Soviet threats in every major crisis, including Suez in 1956, Lebanon in 1958, Quemoy-Matsu in both 1955 and 1958, and finally Berlin between 1958 and 1960. As time went on, we continued to possess this superiority, but the power on both sides was growing to the point where our arithmetic advantage was becoming academic.

Perhaps during the Eisenhower years we were at times, as Dulles termed it, on the "brink" of war. More than once I went home to my family with a hollow feeling in my stomach for fear that the next confrontation might result in a military holocaust. But this never happened, largely because of the Boss's policy of restraint while maintaining our own "big stick."

As a side issue in these brief comments, it might be well to mention the extent of United States involvement with South Vietnam as of the beginning of 1961. It has sometimes been hinted that our involvement in that country began with the Eisenhower Administration. Such insinuations, probably politically motivated, are without basis. True, on New Year's Eve 1960 a serious meeting of high-ranking officials from State, Defense, and the White House was held in the Oval Office regarding Indochina. However, the subject was Laos, not Vietnam. And at the end of his White House memoirs the Boss expressed regret that he had left a messy Laotian situation as a legacy to his successor. He made no mention of South Vietnam.

Certain figures are pertinent. In dollars, military assistance to Vietnam for the last six months of 1960, for example, came to $42.6 million. Thirteen other countries received more during the same period.[11] Of these thirteen, Turkey, Italy, Japan, and Korea received three times the amount sent to South Vietnam. Taiwan received twice as much.

In fiscal year 1961 (July 1, 1960, to June 30, 1961) the United States had 701 military advisers in Vietnam (an increase of only ten, from 692, as of December 31, 1958), in contrast to 1,242 in Taiwan and over 2,500 in Korea, and in Korea we maintained two U.S. divisions. These figures hardly presage the stupendous American military involvement that occurred in succeeding Administrations. All this was not by chance. Dad once described the prospect of a land war in Asia as a "nightmare."

The reason why the Eisenhower years appeared quiet to the public stems, in my opinion, from two sources. First of all, the social upheavals of the 1960s had not yet arrived. It is true that the Boss, having been poor himself as a boy, was not instinctively an avid social reformer. Personal opportunity rather than personal security was his watchword. But he believed deeply in the equal rights of every individual, as witness his sending the 101st Airborne Division in 1957 to enforce integration at Little Rock and the passage in that year of the first civil rights bill in nearly a century after the end of the Civil War.

But the second element, which should not be overlooked, is the fact that the Boss administered with smooth efficiency. His favorite sport provides an analogy. Those who watch professional golf on television are often inclined to run out to the nearest course as soon as the tournament is decided because the professionals have made the game look so easy. The Eisenhower Administration, with matters handled deftly and in low key, made the running of government appear routine. Such professional handling of the world's problems, while it made poor copy for the newspapers, served the nation's interest well and is only now coming to be appreciated. It will be appreciated more when the Boss's intimate papers from Abilene are made public in the near future.

---

11 Belgium, Denmark, France, Italy, The Netherlands, Spain, Greece, Iran, Pakistan, Turkey, Taiwan, Japan, and Korea.

When one considers the national temper of 1952, he must admit that Dwight Eisenhower was elected on the basis of his military background. At that time the Korean War, while stalemated, was costing the United States many lives every day. The Chinese, as well as the Russians, were being pictured through our media as ten feet tall. The public cried out for a man with stability and proven decisiveness to protect the country from this external threat. The Boss demonstrated these qualities in office, although his motivation for running for the presidency was doubtless heavily influenced by his conviction that the Democrats, too long in power, had become both profligate and inefficient.

Probably his strongest point as President and Supreme Commander was his ability to command loyalty among persons of stature. With the size of the government (as with the Allied Expeditionary Force of five million), no one man can handle all the details. Therefore, the quality of government is influenced to a large degree by the quality of men and women the chief can attract to serve and remain. It was only natural that the Boss should have enjoyed a distinct advantage in this respect, as he was an established world figure before he came to the White House. Nevertheless, had he been a different personality, he would never have retained the loyalty of those who initially flocked to his service. I can bear close-hand witness of his thoughtfulness toward all who were serving under him. His schedule of appointments in the course of a day as President was appalling; and while he tended to be a hard taskmaster with his staff, he invariably found the time to go out of his way and add the personal touch.

One salient policy that Dad adhered to in the military he carried over to the presidency: to accept blame for failure while giving credit to others for success. This policy, even as a soldier, appeared on the surface to have drawbacks. He had never been glamorized, for example, to the extent that Douglas MacArthur was glamorized. Nevertheless, those united with him in a common cause felt a deep sense of personal association, were they soldiers of a combat division in Europe or members of his presidential Administration. This aspect of his character was not the type of thing to make headlines, but I feel deeply that it brought results.

Quite possibly my father, as President, should have modified his policy of self-effacement when he went from the military to the presidency. Jim Hagerty, I believe, though a brilliant press secretary, held the Old Man too much in awe. And the Boss himself, understanding the problems that the nation was faced with—and expecting a sophistication among the population that did not exist—was prone to downgrade the "Hollywood" aspects of the presidential position.

After all, people in general tend to look to their government for a certain amount of entertainment. President Truman is remembered largely in the quote, "Give 'em hell, Harry!" Yet every individual must operate according to his particular personal style. Dad achieved best results by doing things his own way. And the people seemed to have a way of seeing behind the headlines. The overwhelming landslides of 1952 and 1956—and the general agreement that the Boss could have been re-elected in 1960 despite his age and illnesses—bear out their wisdom.

10

Vignettes from the Decompression Chamber

Some place along the line Dad picked up an anonymous poem that seemed to fit his philosophy perfectly and he enjoyed quoting it often. The poem itself was addressed to anyone prone to consider himself indispensable.

> . . . Take a bucket, fill it with water,
> Put your hand in—clear up to the wrist.
> Now pull it out; the hole that remains
> Is a measure of how you'll be missed. . . .
>
> The moral in this quaint example:
> To do just the best that you can,
> Be proud of yourself; but remember,
> There is no Indispensable Man![1]

The Boss left office in January of 1961 under conditions far different from those of an outgoing President today. President Kennedy broke precedent by allowing Dad's personal Secret Service bodyguard, Special Agent Richard Flohr, to remain with him for a couple of weeks; but at the end of that time Dick left and the Boss was in every respect a private citizen.

This fact was bound to cause certain psychological adjustments. But the Boss's attitude was simple: he had done his best for eight years, had experienced his triumphs and setbacks, and was perfectly happy to let someone else carry the burden. Naturally, he was disappointed that his own party and his Vice President had been voted out of power, but if he considered this turn of events a reflection on his own Administration, he never showed it. Al-

[1] See Appendix B.

though his former associates resented the efforts of the new Administration to tear him down—a common practice in politics—the Boss was determined never to take action nor to speak words that would hinder the efforts of an Administration that, in his words, was "trying to run the country."

Very shortly after our return to Gettysburg on January 20, 1961, Dad and Mother left for Augusta. When they returned about two weeks later I was shocked and worried at the Old Man's demeanor. His movements were slower, his tone less sharp, and he had time even during the work day to stop and indulge in what would formerly be considered casual conversation. I feared for his health. Fortunately, I could not have been more in error; the Boss had simply relaxed.

Small incidents brought home our new status. It was a peculiar feeling when the Boss slid into the right front seat of our car the first time I drove him alone to the office. And one night, returning from a party in Gettysburg, he insisted on climbing out and opening the gate while I drove through. All this in contrast to the former days of chauffeur-driven limousines and vehicular escorts. To the observer the Boss seemed to undergo little or no conscious psychological adjustment.

The equanimity with which Dad and Mother adjusted to their new life, however, was hardly shared by the rest of us. I have thought often of Eric Hoffer's warning in his magnificent book *The True Believer* that those most frustrated and dissatisfied are not the perennial poor but the "new" poor—those who have been somewhere and have been cast out. Psychologically, I believe that the former members of a White House staff fell into Hoffer's new-poor category; our irritation over the glee with which much of the press treated President Kennedy's "honeymoon" period disturbed us for a while. We were hypersensitive.

New episodes, however, came up to prove that the Boss had really not been forgotten. One day in the summer of 1961, as he and I were driving back from the golf course, he became pensive for a moment. "Maybe you won't believe it," he said, "but this fellow Khrushchev has had the temerity to hint that he would like to reinstate the invitation to go to Moscow. John McCloy has just come back from the disarmament talks and told me that Khrushchev had approached him on the subject. Of course I'd never do it, but why Khrushchev would bring up such a thing sort of beats me." He sat for a while, obviously mulling the whole thing over in his mind. As the events later turned out, the United States and the Soviet Union were soon at loggerheads again over Berlin and nothing more was said about it.[2]

Khrushchev's extraordinary move seems to substantiate a remark Ambassador Whitney had made in Paris in May 1960, that Khrushchev, at the Paris Summit, had been acting like a woman scorned. Though it is impossible to assess all the reasons for Khrushchev's performance at Paris, this subsequent invitation confirms one element at least, that Khrushchev valued Dad's friendship and was in all likelihood personally frustrated when Dad, by refusing to meet his demands, made a continuation of their personal relationship impossible.

While Dad was still in office, we were never conscious of dangerous persons. The Secret Service intercepted all threatening mail.[3] But the Pitzer Schoolhouse was too accessible to overcurious tourists—it was located about a half mile down the road past the main gate to Dad's farm, and anyone trying to get a look at the farm from the road would be disappointed and probably continue to the first turn-around, our driveway. Through the years we had become used to thoughtless people who would stick their cameras over the hedge to take pictures of the children; once a large yellow tourist bus drove into our yard. But in those days the Secret Service detail took care of such matters and the incidents were minor.

With the end of the Eisenhower Administration, the incidence of tourists fell off. But now various disturbed people, not yet realizing that the Boss was no longer the Great White Father, continued to come. In the course of those three and one half years we remained in Gettysburg after Dad's presidency, over half a dozen deranged persons found their way to our unprotected domain. In

[2] This unpublicized invitation was confirmed by Mr. McCloy in a letter dated April 3, 1973; see Appendix C. He was, at the time, U. S. Coordinator of Disarmament Activities.

[3] The only time during which there seemed to be cause for concern was during the furor over the Rosenberg espionage case when I was in Korea in 1953. Dad wrote me at that time that he had doubled the Secret Service detail on the children.

all cases but one, they were initially looking for the Boss and tried to use us as a means of getting to him. At least two were openly dangerous. Only a couple of months after our settling in Gettysburg I found myself loading a souvenir M-14 rifle to cover the Boss's departure from his office in town to his car. I had good reason: a disturbed former sergeant, who had verbally threatened the Boss's life, was on the loose in Gettysburg and no State Police were in sight.

During a relatively short period of my life I was able to indulge the flying hobby. It remains extremely important in my recollections. One reason, I think, stems from my peculiar position in life. Almost everything else I have done during my adult years has been affected to some extent by my name—by my father's position, if you will. This includes my career in the Army, in the White House, and even in writing. But in the air I had no name; to the Federal Aviation Agency (FAA) I was simply Comanche Nine-Nine POP (so named from her license number, 5499 Papa). The quality of my landings, navigation, and judgment were mine alone. Only once did I run into trouble.

It started out as a routine flight. On the morning of August 3, 1964, my forty-second birthday, I got up early to make a trip from Phoenixville[4] to Gettysburg and, as always, called "Weather" in the Harrisburg weather office. It was a gloomy, overcast day with scud lying low in the sky, but Harrisburg assured me that I could expect a 3,000-foot ceiling all around the area. This being satisfactory, I went to Pottstown, checked out my plane, a Piper Comanche, and took off.

I was well aware that weather predictions around the Gettysburg area were poor. The forecasters could report on conditions at the Harrisburg airport but they had virtually no sources of information on localized weather to the south. Nevertheless, I was flying over familiar territory and Pottstown, Lancaster, York, and Gettysburg —all provided with fine airfields—were only a few minutes apart. The entire trip normally took between thirty-five and fifty minutes, depending on wind direction.

The leg between Pottstown and Lancaster was about as pre-

[4] I had moved my family to Phoenixville in September 1964.

dicted. Visibility was not what I would have liked as I went over Lancaster; but there was, after all, a radio station (OMNI) located on that field and I could always turn back to that airport if conditions worsened. West of the Susquehanna River I crossed over the city of York. The ceiling had now dropped to something like 1,200 feet. At this low altitude my radio, for navigation purpose, had become practically useless. At the far edge of the city I discovered that, under these conditions, I was not so familiar with every landmark as I had thought. Taking a guess, I followed an unfamiliar—and wrong—road out of York. Though temporarily lost, I was not concerned.

Forced down to about a thousand feet, I spotted a town that looked familiar. The water tower of East Berlin, Pennsylvania, was well-nigh unmistakable. I had now located myself; I was north of the Lincoln Highway, not too far from the York airport. To get my bearings, I circled the town once to make absolutely sure that this was East Berlin and then headed south by magnetic compass, always aware that just to the east of the field stood hills a little bit higher than my present altitude. Within a few moments the York airport appeared below me, just off to the left.

For a moment it crossed my mind that it might be wise to sit down at York. After all, this airport was only a forty-five-minute drive from Gettysburg. To sit down there would involve only a phone call to my Gettysburg office and my secretary could easily drive out and pick me up. On second thought, however, I decided otherwise. Here I was in my own back yard, with the clearly defined Lincoln Highway leading straight to Gettysburg—and no hills at all between me and my destination. I headed west down the Lincoln Highway.

As I proceeded for the last few minutes of the trip, the ceiling became lower and lower. Rain was beating on the windshield of the plane and I was now forced down to something like 500 feet. The die had been cast, and I continued past Abbottstown and New Oxford. Soon, going even lower, I saw Gettysburg sprawled before me.

For years I had known the town of Gettysburg about as well as anyone could know the topography of any place. As an instructor in West Point, I had studied the terrain in detail as a buff

45. "De Gaulle seemed completely unperturbed by all these turns of events. . . . we all knew what he had whispered to the Old Man that bleak first morning: 'No matter what, I am with you.'" President de Gaulle, Prime Minister Harold Macmillan, and the Boss at the Élysée Palace during the abortive summit meeting of May 1960.

46. "Barbara made a substantial contribution to the good-will aspects of the eleven-nation trip of December 1959, visiting hospitals in Pakistan, villages in India, and a harem in Afganistan."

47. "In June 1959 Barbara moved the family to Gettysburg and I lived in a room on the third floor of the White House on weekdays." Our daughter Susan riding horseback in Gettysburg at age eleven.

48A. ". . . Commanche . . . 5499P . . . was for me ideal. . . . when talking by radio to a flight service station . . . my name was not 'John Eisenhower'; it was 'Nine-Nine Papa.' "

48B. "Ken McCormick and Sam Vaughan [of Doubleday] spent a great deal of time in the early part of 1963 in Gettysburg, especially after the Boss had returned from California in the spring. . . . The impression is still with me of papers flying all over the office, covering our desks like a Pennsylvania snow drift." *Left to right:* Bill Ewald, Ken McCormick, and Sam Vaughan.

49. Farewell call on President Nixon before my departure as Ambassador to Brussels. Mrs. Nixon thoughtfully joined us in the Oval Office. May. 1969.

50. "The champagne that day tasted especially good." Traditional *vin d'honneur,* in which the new Ambassador invites his military escort, General Georges Vivario, and the commander of the Horse Guards for a glass of champagne at the Embassy after presentation of credentials. May 14, 1969.

51. "...the Belgians...can look to their King and Queen and say that their royal couple is the most attractive reigning pair in all of Europe." King Baudouin I and Queen Fabiola of the Belgians.

52. Anne and her husband, Fernando Echavarria, and daughter, Adrianna.

53. Secretary of State and Mrs. William P. Rogers visit Brussels for the NATO Foreign Ministers meeting, December 1970. *Left to right:* J.S.D.E., Mrs. Pierre Harmel, Minister of Foreign Affairs Pierre Harmel, Mrs. William Rogers, Secretary of State Rogers, Barbara Eisenhower.

54. "But ahead, though as yet uncharted, lay a new life." The family gathers for my fiftieth birthday, August 3, 1972. *Seated, left to right:* Susan E. Bradshaw with daughter Caroline, Barbara, Mother, granddaughter Adrianna Echavarria, Anne Eisenhower de Echavarria. *Standing, left to right:* Alexander Bradshaw, Mary Jean Eisenhower, the author, Julie Nixon Eisenhower, David Eisenhower, Fernando Echavarria Uribe.

of the Civil War battle; I had known the names of every road and every spot before ever laying eyes on the place. And yet a new experience was in store: I had never realized what a pinpoint a small town is when one is flying over it at 150 mph at an altitude of only 400 feet. In an instant the town was out of sight. And to make matters worse, Doersom's Airport was blacktop, difficult to pick up even under ideal conditions. The situation was becoming downright unpleasant.

I turned Nine-Nine POP on her right wing and decided to keep circling the town until Doersom's Airport should come into view. I had plenty of gas; but if I lost sight of the town I would be in real trouble, as there was no assurance that the weather behind me at York and Lancaster was any better than here.

Finally, after a couple of circles around Gettysburg, I spied Doersom's. Keeping the airport always in sight, I cautiously maneuvered around and flew over it toward the south. Then, taking no chances of losing sight of it, I made a steep 180° turn to the north, letting down toward the runway. I had no interest at this point in wind direction; I would be landing uphill and the runway was long enough to handle Nine-Nine POP even with a slight wind to my tail.

As I made my last bank, however, I glanced at the turn-bank indicator; it indicated a bank of over 60 degrees. "My God," I thought, "I could have spun her in here at 300 feet!"

The landing was safe. Nine-Nine POP sat down nicely and I taxied up to the gas pump at the north end. Don Sullivan, the proprietor, stepped out of the door of the office and, giving me a quizzical look, pointed to the sky. Annoyed for a moment, I burst out, "Do you think I don't know how it is up there? Let's get a cup of coffee!"

I immediately called Barbara to tell her I was safe. She was perplexed. The weather back in Phoenixville was not too bad; furthermore, a Gettysburg friend, in small-town fashion, had already called her to say she had seen my plane go overhead. Little had the well-meaning friend realized that the most dangerous part of the trip, the last few moments, was still ahead when she made her call of reassurance.

The episode I have described is in a way grossly misleading. The entire trip took only an hour, in contrast to the usual fifty minutes, and the time in which I felt myself in trouble covered only about fifteen minutes of that hour. That fifteen minutes, out of a total of 450 hours of private flying, represents the only situation I ever got into that could by the remotest interpretation be called a "scrape." On the whole that represents a rather small fraction, and probably few drivers of automobiles could say the same. Normally, it is much easier on the nerves to fly than to drive, not only mile-for-mile, but minute-for-minute or hour-for-hour.

Furthermore, flying provided me a certain relaxation from the routine of other work. It was a sedentary sort of relaxation, to be sure, but satisfying. In the air I thought of little other than the business at hand, of flying the aircraft. On November 22, 1963, for example, when I got the news of President Kennedy's assassination, I was stunned like all other Americans. Naturally, there was nothing to do, but I was in no mood for working. My secretary and I sat for a few minutes in stupefaction. Finally, I asked, "Do you want to take a little flight?" She agreed without hesitation. The two of us drove out to Doersom's, rented a small Cessna 150, and simply cruised around the Gettysburg area. The flight lasted only twenty-five minutes. But there was nothing to say, and cruising around for a while was the most graceful and peaceful way of saying nothing.

Only once did I ever take the Boss up in a plane. On August 28, 1963, we planned a trip to Berryville, Virginia, to see the first volumes of his *White House Years* come off the press. The auto trip would be a long, tiresome one; therefore I offered to take Dad in a plane and he readily acceded. As Bill Ewald was going along, I decided that my Tripacer would not be sufficiently roomy and powerful. I took an Aeronca two-seater from Gettysburg Air Park over to York, rented a Cherokee from Oscar Hostetter, and brought it back to Gettysburg to pick up the other two.

As it turned out, I failed to allocate adequate time and arrived at Gettysburg a couple of minutes late. (I had, of course, intended to be at the field when he arrived.) The Boss was always cranky about punctuality, but this day he practically roared his displeasure. I knew that if he could have backed out of the trip gracefully, he would have. Dad held a private pilot's license from thirty years before, having logged about three hundred hours. However, in recent years he was accustomed to four-engine planes—*Air Force One*—and this was his son at the controls.

Bill and I had anticipated this tension to some extent. We had prepared a cocktail-shaker of Scotch-and-water and had placed some glasses aboard. We also brought along a portable radio and some magazines, all for levity. The Boss merely smiled wanly and asked where the hostesses were. He refused Scotch and took his place in the co-pilot seat.

The weather that day was beautiful, not quite CAVU (ceiling and visibility unlimited) but close enough to ensure a pleasant flight. Furthermore, I had been into Winchester before; and although the black runway was a little obscure, I could foresee no problem. I would have recommended that he go earlier by car had I foreseen any.

The first part of the fifty-minute trip was tense, and the Boss sat grim-faced. I knew better than to try making conversation. Furthermore, I was worried, not about the flight but about the prospects of bringing on another heart attack through the tension. When we passed Frederick, however, and approached the Potomac, I gestured toward a large white cross-runway, nearly at the horizon. "That's Martinsburg, West Virginia," I said.

Immediately the Boss relaxed; though he said nothing, I could read his mind: "Apparently this young pup at least knows where he is." He picked up the chart, figured our position, identified towns on the Potomac, and began quizzing me on landing techniques.

"Exactly what is your airspeed when you set her down?"

"I don't know, Dad, I flare out at about fifty-five or sixty but I'm watching the runway when we actually touch."

Although my answers seemed to satisfy him, my every move was scrutinized, even supervised, from that point until we had landed at Winchester and taxied back to the ramp. Doubleday people were out in force. I was grateful that someone snapped a picture as we were parking—a record of a memorable occasion. (I have since lost it.)

After going by car to Berryville, Dad checked over his new book with delight and saw, probably not for the first time, the way the gigantic presses turn out so many volumes in a day. Soon we were on our way home.

This time the Boss suggested little detours to check out Harpers Ferry and, as we approached Gettysburg, asked that we go down to about 1,500 feet so he could check if Mamie was at the farm. On landing, Bill went with the Boss and I returned Oscar's Cherokee. If the Secret Service had then been assigned to the Boss, we would never have had this minor escapade.

As time went on and I developed more flying time, my horizons and my ambition grew. Somewhere along the line I read an article about the first transcontinental mail delivery. The pilot, in a completely open airplane—and well bundled up—carried a sackful of mail from coast to coast, having made some sixty stops, a few of which were crashes. His wife followed along on the ground in an automobile. This article brought home something I should have realized: a cross-continental trip is nothing but a series of short hops. Accordingly, I got out a planning chart and began thinking seriously about such a venture, figuring to bypass the Rocky Mountains by taking the El Paso route. I bought all the necessary sectional charts, possibly fifty in all, and planned the flight in detail. In the meantime I was doing as much cross-country flying as possible, partly to test the effects of pilot fatigue. I went to Lawrence, Massachusetts, to pick up David from school, took friends to Hartford, Connecticut, and took Bill Ewald to Cape Hatteras. With the Hatteras trip I was content that everything was ready.

My purpose in flying to San Francisco was to attend the 1964 Republican Convention. At first Barbara had agreed to go with me, but as it turned out her confidence in my flying ability somewhat paralleled that of the Boss. I was fortunate that Don Swope, a friend from Gettysburg, possessed the nervous system and the faith in the next world to go along as a passenger. We left early on July 6 amidst a certain amount of publicity in Gettysburg. Ideally, we would have liked to have made the trip in three days by way of Springfield, Missouri; El Paso; thence to San Francisco. We were, however, plagued with some bad weather and some minor engine trouble. The trip, therefore, actually consisted of stops at Springfield; Pecos, Texas; El Paso; Phoenix; and San Francisco—twenty-seven hours flying time. The five days involved can be matched in days by driving an automobile—but at considerably more time and strain. I shot home movies but later found that most of them were taken on the ground. As a result, the reel turned out to be a collection of pictures of the various control towers at the airfields where we landed.

I returned to Gettysburg alone a couple of weeks after the Republican Convention, going this time over Reno and Salt Lake City to Big Springs, Wyoming, and on the second day to Park Rapids, Minnesota, to visit Dr. and Mrs. Malcolm Moos. When I arrived back in Gettysburg, feeling rather full of myself, I found a meeting in progress between the Boss and the editors from Doubleday. My welcome was rather low-key, "Well, we've been sort of looking for you." The trip back required only eighteen hours in the air.

After the move to Phoenixville it turned out that flying became less and less feasible. The only satisfactory airport, Chester County, was about forty minutes away. No longer was Doersom's Airport only about five minutes from home. With lack of practice, I began to get uncomfortable flying cross country and finally, with some emotion, parted company with Nine-Nine POP.

I sometimes wonder whether I will ever fly again as a steady hobby. The prospects seem dim for the foreseeable future in that the same conditions exist as at the time when I gave it up. And yet I am unwilling to completely foreclose the possibility, for I know of no satisfaction that quite equals "greasing in" a plane, coming to a halt about a third of the way down the strip, taxiing her up to the gas pump, and going in to join the gang for a cup of coffee.

But even if I don't, I am grateful to flying for the distraction it gave me during the period of the "decompression chamber."

11

The Writing Game

Although in early 1969 I was lucky enough to be the author of a best seller—*The Bitter Woods,* published by Putnam's—when someone asks about taking up writing as a full-time career, I usually say "Don't." Fascinating as the activity is, anyone depending for his entire livelihood on book writing is letting himself in for anguish, anxiety, frustration, and possibly a touch of starvation. Regardless of a person's inherent writing ability, he must consider the hard facts, principally finances.

Suppose an individual has an unusual story to tell—which is rare—and he secures a contract with a publisher, rarer still. Suppose further that he receives an advance that looks extremely good on the surface, say something over $25,000 (extremely rare). The writer must then pay his expenses (travel, office, secretary perhaps) and spread the remainder over two or probably three years. He would do better financially in almost any kind of steady job—or on welfare. In this atmosphere his family and his recreations suffer, for a day away from work is a day lost. The writer is not paid for being present at his desk; he works to create a product that does not write itself.

In view of these facts, most authors must do other things to pay their bills. Thus, while the main subject of this chapter is the writing game, I would be giving a wrong impression if I failed to mention some of the other activities that I engaged in during the years between 1961 and 1969. Books were merely the central, most intriguing part of my work.

I had little background for a writing career. By the end of the Boss's Administration I had published only one article on a specialized military unit in World War II (the SIAM company) for

Military Review at Fort Leavenworth. I was a captain at the time, and my $25 honorarium remains probably the most important fee I ever received for such activity. My standing was high in West Point English but not spectacular. I must have had the writing bug to some extent, however. The 1944 *Howitzer*[1] observed that I wanted to be a writer. Rebellion, probably, against West Point reveilles.

The three years of instructing in English at West Point, however, were significant to me; and when I took my master's degree in English literature at Columbia during my spare time, I learned research methods which I have never seen reason to change. Later, a good deal of my time as a staff officer in the Army was spent in writing. But federal prose is a different language from straight English, and when I began to get involved in writing for publication I found that I had to develop a completely new technique.

During the period when I served as assistant staff secretary at the White House we put out a volume of material in our daily memoranda of conferences that amazes me to this day. It had no literary value, but the mere habit of writing so much obliterated most of the mental hazard that many face in putting pen to paper.

Toward the end of the Boss's Administration I became convinced that he should write his memoirs. Therefore, in preparation for his postpresidential years in Gettysburg, I urged him to take on this activity as his main occupation.

Actually, this was far from a radical recommendation, as writing is almost the only dignified occupation a President can follow after leaving office. Certainly his status in the world would preclude him from being, for example, sales manager of a corporation. Besides, it is, I believe, generally accepted that a President owes it to himself and to history to give his own version of what he did while in office and why. In the case of the Boss, self-justification seemed to have been a minor consideration. He was content in his own being that he had performed a necessary task to the best of his ability and that that phase of his life was over; he was looking to the future rather than to the past.

On the other hand, the 1960 political campaign probably influenced Dad's thinking to some extent. In a way, his ultimate

[1] The West Point yearbook.

decision to write his own account of his White House years bore some similarity to his decision to write *Crusade in Europe* in 1948.[2] When accusations were hurled around in 1960—accusations such as the mythical "missile gap"—his interest grew. In approaching the question of presidential memoirs he realized, of course, that he would not write pure history. No one man could write a complete history of the times—but as with *Crusade in Europe,* he agreed it might be well to get the facts on the record as he had viewed them.

Finally the Old Man agreed that the memoirs should be done and he further accepted my offer—I had decided to resign from the Army as of January 20, 1961—to be his chief assistant. Fortunately, he had retained close contact with Doubleday's Doug Black and the three of us talked over the forthcoming memoirs while the Boss was still President. In the meantime, the Army had offered me two years' leave without pay, which simply meant an option to return to the fold as of early 1963.

We wasted no time in getting the project under way. The Kennedy inauguration in January 1961 took place on a Friday. That evening the entire family returned to our respective homes in Gettysburg. On the next Monday morning, my secretary Rusty Brown and I turned up at 300 Carlisle Street, Dad's future office, and began to get organized. Bob Schulz and Ann Whitman were still in Washington, desperately trying to handle the Boss's current mail, which was still substantial despite the fact that he was now a private citizen.

Rusty and I found ourselves very much alone in our suite on the ground floor of the building. We had plenty of room but nothing to work with except for two desks, some still empty filing cabinets, and a typewriter. We went to the local print shop and procured supplies of yellow pads, bond paper, carbons, pencils, and other office materials. Soon our working documents began to arrive—the *Public Papers of the Presidents,* the speeches of the Secretaries of Defense, the bound copies of the *State Department*

<hr>

[2] Dad had at first shown a minimal interest in writing *Crusade in Europe,* considering it an exploitation of the work and sacrifices of others. However, when book after book on World War II came out, most of them full of inaccuracies, Douglas M. Black, president and chairman of Doubleday and Company, convinced him that it was up to him to set the record straight.

Bulletin, and Dad's personal files from the White House. In addition, we had copies of the Sunday editions of the New York *Times,* the New York *Herald Tribune* and the Washington *Evening Star* covering the entire period of the Administration. Doug Black came down from New York and checked over our situation to ensure we had everything we needed. His interest and generosity during this period were much appreciated. Mother and Dad, for their part, took off for warmer climates, first to Augusta National and then, after a few days at Gettysburg, to California.

Actual work began slowly, and Rusty and I spent a good deal of our time carrying boxes of papers, filling files, and arranging our quarters. By March, however, I had produced a rather detailed outline of the projected two volumes and had sent copies to the Boss and to Doubleday. The outline was a challenge. I had been present in the White House for only a portion of the entire time covered. Nevertheless, with the files and the newspapers and a small booklet—a yearbook—produced by the staff just before Dad left Washington, I was able to cover the subject fairly well.

In making this outline, I followed an earlier-agreed-on organization. Kenneth ("Ken") McCormick, then editor-in-chief of Doubleday, had specified that he would like a presidential campaign to be covered in each volume; the plan called for the first volume to end at the time of the Boss's decision to run the second time, in February of 1956, and the second volume to pick up at that point. I was proud of that outline for, though its details were changed often in subsequent months, its essence remained the same throughout the nearly four years of the project.

At the outset it was clear that one man would be unable to do all the research. The mass of detail would be too great; also I felt that I lacked sufficient background to do justice to the domestic side of things. Doug Black and I thereupon set out to find a full-time colleague. After searching through several names, we came up with a man who turned out to be ideal for the position—Bill Ewald. Dr. William B. Ewald, Jr., had been a staff officer in the White House during the early years and had then become assistant to Secretary of the Interior Fred A. Seaton. He had spent the year of 1959 with his wife traveling around the world under an Eisenhower Exchange Fellowship. Though Bill was now well employed at International Business Machines, it took him only a few days to accept the job, despite the fact that it entailed a considerable cut in salary. His joining us was made possible only by the help of Thomas J. Watson, Jr., then president of IBM, who agreed to release him for a couple of years and hold his job open.

For our day-to-day work, of course, it was necessary to have a Doubleday editor to serve as the company's representative. The project was major from Doubleday's viewpoint; the contract that Doug and the Boss signed on February 1, 1961, was a generous one indeed—almost unrealistic I thought at the time. Nevertheless, no single project can be so important as to command the full time of the editor-in-chief. Doug had his man already selected, Samuel S. Vaughan, a senior editor, thirty-two years of age—shockingly young, I thought, looking down from the dignity of thirty-eight myself. The three of us—Bill, Sam, and I (assisted at times by Ken McCormick) made a good team. We had our differences in our preoccupations, but we conducted business with remarkable harmony.

When the Boss returned to Gettysburg in the spring of 1961 he was able to attack the first chapter, which covered his decision in 1952 to run for the presidency. On this subject no researcher could be of much help. The records covering the period while Dad was Supreme Commander in Europe were sketchy. The appointment books at the time had been kept in scribbled notebooks, and few memoranda had been kept of the various conversations that the Boss had held with Senator Henry Cabot Lodge, General Lucius Clay, his friends Bill Robinson, Cliff Roberts, Barry Leithead, the aviatrix Jacqueline Cochran, and others who had been influential in bringing about his final decision. Accordingly, he wrote this chapter almost entirely from memory, reinforced by what notes I was able to provide. This same situation obtained generally through the succeeding chapters on the presidential campaign of 1952 but now stimulated by press accounts—not all of them favorable—of his relations with various political leaders and the adroit way in which his team handled the nomination in the bitter battle between Eisenhower and Taft forces in Chicago.

When the text reached the White House period, the situation changed. We now ran into a problem somewhat peculiar to the presidency. When Dad was writing *Crusade in Europe,* he had the facts completely straight in his mind and had dictated the original text in the course of about one hundred days. That book dealt with a series of events in World War II—over about two and one half years—which never repeated themselves. In dealing with the presidency, however, it would be very easy to become confused regarding the month—or quite often the year—in which certain events had occurred. The President's routine is a cyclical thing. Every year he delivers a State of the Union Message and submits a Budget Message; Congress meets and adjourns yearly, and its composition changes every two years. Hence the Boss found himself far more dependent on written records than had been the case when writing about World War II.

As a result, Bill Ewald and I gradually fell into the habit of providing rough drafts of almost every chapter. These drafts the Boss would cut down, lacerate, and redo time and time again. In many instances the end product would bear little resemblance to the original draft. The chapter on the Indochina crisis of 1954, which I researched for some three months, serves as a case in point. Mesmerized by the records, I produced a first version of something over a hundred typewritten pages. This the Boss cut to about half size—and it probably still remained too long. With all our labors, it soon was quite obvious that the best parts of the Old Man's memoirs were those that he wrote himself. But considering the magnitude of the project and the other demands on his time, we could find no better way to operate.

Originally, Bill and I thought that I would dig through the personal files located in Gettysburg and he would confine himself largely to the Library of Congress. However, this scheme turned out to be impractical, for although Bill specialized in domestic issues and I specialized in national security and foreign affairs, still a great amount of domestic material resided in the Whitman files that I was working on. Thus, Bill spent more time in Gettysburg than he had originally planned, and as it turned out we became less arbitrary on the division of subject matter. A more efficient researcher than I, Bill was able to handle the domestic chapters and research an occasional national security chapter. The two of us habitually would agree on a draft text before we would submit it for the Boss's extensive processing. Fortunately, neither one of us was afflicted with exaggerated pride of author-ship—if we had been, we could never have survived the Boss's murderous editing.

One problem the researchers and editors encountered in making recommendations to the Boss stemmed from our somewhat dif-ferent outlooks, Ken and Sam on the one hand and Bill and me on the other. I think it irked Sam occasionally when I would refer to the difference in attitude of former members of the government (Washington) and of the publishing house (New York); but I feel that my point had validity. The question of Senator Joseph R. McCarthy of Wisconsin, for example, serves as an illustration.

McCarthy, the vicious demagogue of the late 1940s and early '50s, was undoubtedly one of the greatest thorns in the Boss's side during his early days in politics. In the 1952 campaign the Boss had been trapped into a tacit endorsement of McCarthy. He detested the man and his methods, and his original scheme had been to make his own campaign swing into Wisconsin *before* the nominating convention met at Chicago. Thus, with his policy of avoiding endorsement of one Republican over another before nom-ination, he could have kept his contact and association with Mc-Carthy to a minimum. But the political staff erred—I do not like to think they intentionally sabotaged the Boss—and the visit was set for some time *after* Chicago. From the convention on, Dad felt obligated, as a matter of practical politics, to endorse all Re-publicans. For to openly repudiate McCarthy at this time would have been to insult the Republican voters who had nominated him. Dad was infuriated by this blunder on the part of the staff but went through the necessary political motions, contenting him-self with "reading the riot act" to McCarthy in a private meeting on Dad's train. Later, while in office, he had maneuvered behind the scenes to bring about McCarthy's censuring in the Senate and subsequent political downfall.[3] McCarthy had by 1954 broken openly with the Boss and practically called him a Communist.

Nevertheless, by the time 1961 had arrived, McCarthy was four years dead, and his censuring in 1954, over the opposition of a

[3] See *Mandate for Change* (1963), pp. 316–31. See also Appendix D, hitherto unpublished.

great number of influential conservative Republican senators, had erased him as a political force three years before he died. Therefore Bill and I tended to view McCarthy principally as a very nasty political problem that had been duly taken care of. But in this respect Bill and I underestimated the intensity of feeling which existed among those groups that McCarthy had abused, which included the intellectual and the publishing worlds. The editors saw McCarthy from the viewpoint of outraged idealists, whereas Bill and I looked at the problem more pragmatically.

The story was eventually drafted with a certain amount of compromise, not on the facts—they were there—but on emphasis. And of course the Boss finally refined the text his own way.

Other problems came up, of course, such as our tendency in the drafting process to end the treatment of every problem on an up beat. Bill and I, as former members of the Administration, naturally felt that things had by and large been handled masterfully and very few serious governmental problems had gone unsolved or unimproved. But the editors, also naturally, looking at the entire book, saw it as too much of a series of success stories. They would have liked to have seen the Boss bare his soul and admit to more mistakes—which, it happened, neither the Boss, Bill, nor I felt was justified.

All such matters were, of course, ironed out, thanks, in the final analysis, to Sam's and Ken's objectivity and their realization that this was ultimately to be Dad's book. I cite these differences as the exceptions rather than the rule. For despite the stresses of this type of work, our mutual friendships and respect continued steadily to grow throughout the whole effort.

In late summer of 1962, after Bill and I had worked about a year and a half, I made the error of inducing the Boss to let me submit a very rough draft of the manuscript of the first volume to Doubleday. Up to that time Bill and I had been working pretty much alone with the Boss, while Sam had remained in the background, giving encouragement but not participating to the extent he later did. Actually, we would have been wise, as it turned out, had we in Gettysburg produced one more draft, the best we could do. However, the Boss assented, and I sent the rough manuscript to Sam. The editor concealed his misgivings at first, but asked if

I could come to New York for about three weeks. As I was still technically in the Army, I was able to stay at Fort Jay, Governors Island, and came daily by subway to the publisher's offices at 575 Madison Avenue.

In retrospect, I realize that when I turned over the manuscript I was unconsciously expecting the reaction to be fulsome admiration; I was in for a jolt. Sam and Ken reserved large blocks of their time—almost all—for the period I was there. We three sat in a conference room and tore the entire text apart, reorganizing, cutting, and fleshing out background facts. The impression is still with me of papers flying all over the office, covering our desks like a Pennsylvania snow drift. It was an exhausting experience, but the results were worth it. We now had a text we could work on, although it was far from polished.

Ken McCormick and Sam Vaughan spent a great deal of time in the early part of 1963 in Gettysburg, especially after the Boss had returned from California in the spring. We threw papers around once more in a manner similar to that of the previous fall. Sometimes there was a real question as to who possessed the "official" manuscript. With patience, however, the first volume began to shape up. Even the galley-proof stage required considerable detailed revisions. As a result of this experience, I concluded that writing is at its most painful when the author first receives the editors' comments. We would submit no more half-baked texts of the second volume, I resolved.

During the process of helping on Dad's books I developed a certain set of misconceptions regarding the normal relationship between author and publisher. Actually, Sam was doing a great deal for the Boss that the author himself is normally required to do. This included procurement of photographs and maps, writing of captions for the photos, and such. I was later to realize how much Sam had done when I went into the writing business for myself.

One somewhat surprising aspect of writing a book is the fact that, in my experience at least, the title is almost the last thing decided on. In this choice the publisher has a great deal of say, and the matter seems to be one of negotiation, with each side possessing a veto. We had always tacitly agreed that the two volumes together would be called *The White House Years,* but the choice of a title for the first volume was particularly difficult. Harking back to the revolutionary feeling that swept the country in 1952 (in 1963 the campaign of 1952 did seem revolutionary; today it appears as a continuum), all thought that some word implying "change" from the Truman days was necessary. We settled on *Mandate for Change.* Today we all refer to that volume simply as *Mandate,* which it should have been named in the first place.

On September 27, 1963, came the big day: the first copy of *Mandate* was delivered to my office in Gettysburg. It happened that the folks were in New York that evening, so I flew the book up for them to see. The Tripacer made the trip from Gettysburg to Flushing Airport in two hours, and soon I was rushing downtown by taxi to the Waldorf. I don't know who was more thrilled to see the volume—the author or I. Mother and George and Mary Allen were at the apartment when I came in, and we passed around the single volume, everyone wanting to see it at once. Mother was thrilled to see the dedication: "To Mamie." The Boss had decided to surprise her. That moment—when a book comes out between covers—is the thrill of the writing game. I have experienced it now three times—two of them vicariously—and whether the book sells or not, there is a satisfaction in a completed product that makes all the labor worth while.

Mandate for Change was published officially on November 9, 1963, and 125,000 volumes were produced at Berryville. The reviews began to pour in; and while some were a bit disappointing, they were generally good, considering the political temper of the times. The biggest disappointment involved the flounderings of the New York *Herald Tribune,* a newspaper that Dad had gone out of his way to try to keep in existence by writing articles without charge for its front page. (He wanted to help keep two morning newspapers in New York.) As I understand it, the *Tribune* had contracted for four reviews, one by Henry Steele Commager, known to be a "liberal" historian; a second by William F. Buckley, Jr., a conservative, of the *National Review;* a third by Dad's speech writer and my personal friend Dr. Malcolm ("Mac") Moos; and a fourth by Senator Hubert Humphrey. When it came time for publication, the *Tribune* backed off and published only the Commager piece. The feeble explanation was that while Mac's and Senator Humphrey's reviews were both highly favorable, they were offset by the vitriolic attack by Buckley. Therefore, the *Tribune* had supinely canceled the other three and settled for Commager, who anybody could have predicted would be adversely critical. The New York *Times,* much maligned among Republicans, did much better by the Boss in a reasoned, friendly lead review by James Reston.

The sale of *Mandate for Change* should have gone well. In fact I personally expected it to sell above the 125,000 copies that Doubleday had printed. It started out briskly, quickly reaching the second spot on the New York *Times* best-seller list. Less than two weeks after publication, on November 22, 1963, however, President John F. Kennedy was assassinated. The ensuing rash of books eulogizing the late President cut severely into the sales of *Mandate.* The public was no longer interested in the political opposition; it was now too absorbed in its grief over the tragic Kennedy episode. I have since been astonished when ostensibly knowledgeable people ask me questions which are more than adequately covered in *The White House Years.* The books, despite considerable worldwide sales, have simply not been read. But the facts, however one chooses to evaluate them, are there.

Shortly after the first of the year 1963 I was forced to make a major decision. A letter came in the mail from the Department of the Army, dated February 7, 1963:

SUBJECT: Amendment of Orders–PCS
TO: Indiv Concerned
     TC 370. Fol orders AMENDED.
SMO: LtrO AGPA-O 201 Eisenhower, John S. D. (9Jan 61), Hq
     DA, 4 Oct 1962
     Subj: "Orders" as amended
Pert to: EISENHOWER, JOHN S. D. 026607 LT COL INF AS
     USAWC Carlisle Barracks Pa
IATA: Rept date: NLT 3 Apr 63
Sp instr: Off to be util by Comdt USAWC pndg starting date of

crs 16 Aug 63. Prov of Para 4g AR 350-2 will apply for oblig svc

Translated into English, this bewildering language meant, "John, your leave without pay is over. Report to U.S. Army War College, Carlisle Barracks, for duty not later than April 3, 1963." I could not stall; I had to report by the specified date or resign from the Army.

I fully understood and agreed with the Army's position. The leave without pay could not be extended because I had now accumulated nearly nineteen years' service (including the two years leave without pay) and had my status been continued for another year, I could simply retire, with benefits, having been on active military duty only seventeen years.

Without much difficulty I decided to resign. Though the wrench of leaving the organization in which I had spent my life was strong, a couple of factors made it easier. For one thing, attendance at the War College meant signing an agreement to stay in the service for another four years after the end of the course. At this point, I was not prepared to sign up for five years of anything.[4] Furthermore, I was determined to finish my part in the writing project I was working on, regardless of the consequences.

I was a little chagrined, to be frank, at the lack of waves that my resignation caused. I expected to be on the carpet before at least a couple of general officers extolling the virtues of military service and asking me to stay on. No such thing happened. In late March I drove up to Carlisle Barracks to find that the secretary of the War College, happily, was an old friend from 1945. Colonel John H. ("Monk") Montgomery shook his head: "You've done all that's expected of you, John. Nobody will have the least objection. Just go see the Adjutant General and he'll take care of you."

At the Adjutant General's office I was quickly put in the hands of a sergeant with a couple of forms and a typewriter. I presumed

[4] There was always, of course, the option of going back into uniform but refusing the War College assignment. On this basis I could be a post exchange officer or something equally inconsequential for a year and then retire. However, my friends knew all too well of my situation, and to retire with half pay and full benefits on this basis would have caused more criticism than I was willing to accept, especially since I would have agreed that it was justified. Thus, resigning and keeping a commission in the Army Reserve seemed the best choice.

that the completion of the forms would take a long time. In fact, it took probably about a half hour. With this over, I was sent over to the hospital for my departure physical exam. This completed satisfactorily, I was told to return on March 27.

On the appointed day my records were given to me by an attractive WAC captain, who then proceeded on the spot to swear me in as a lieutenant colonel in the Army Reserve. All was finished, with no more ado.

As I was walking out of the personnel building at Carlisle Barracks, feeling a little peculiar, the sergeant who three days earlier had typed out my forms came running up behind me. "Colonel," he said, "I've been thinking a lot about your leaving. It seems crazy to get out after nineteen years! Don't you think you could pick up another year some place along the line?"

"Well, maybe I can some place, sergeant. Thanks a lot."

I laughed and walked back to the car and headed down the road toward Gettysburg and civilian life. I appreciated the sergeant's concern; sometimes I've thought he was right.

That evening I called the Boss at Palm Desert, California, and told him I had just resigned. Though vaguely aware that I had this problem coming up, I think he had presumed I would leave Gettysburg and return to uniform. At any rate, he seemed surprised. He paused for a couple of seconds and then he laughed, a little sadly. "Well, good luck," he said.

While we were in the process of working on *Waging Peace,* someone suggested to the Boss that he list the names of the handful of men he had known in government that he would call "great." He promised to try and then later reported that he had given up the effort. Completely by chance, however, when I was in his office one day, a paper sitting in plain view on the top of his wastebasket caught my eye. I fished it out and read it. The names contained thereon were (not necessarily in order) Churchill, Marshall, De Gaulle, John Foster Dulles, Portal (chief of the British Air Staff in World War II). I made a record of the list and put it away in my drawer.

A few months later, when I was visiting Dad and Mother at Palm Desert, I decided, on a whim, to put him to the test. I passed a sheet of paper down the dinner table and asked the Boss to make a list of the five "greats" he had known during his career. Somewhat amused but game, he furrowed his brow and began to write. At the same time I jotted down the names of those listed above and passed my sheet across the table to Freeman Gosden, one of the guests that evening. When Dad had completed his list, he handed it over to Freeman, who noted that Dad's and mine corresponded exactly.

Whether this evaluation of Dad's applied at all times during his later years I have no idea. Nevertheless, he seemed to have been fairly consistent during the time when he was writing his memoirs.

In 1964, as the second volume of *The White House Years, Waging Peace,* was going into its final manuscript stage, I had another decision to make. The question was what I should do for employment after *Waging Peace.* At this point, I had concluded that my work with Dad in helping him record his Administration for history was finished. The time had come—as I was now forty-two years of age—to establish myself in some other, independent profession. Coincidentally I learned that Admiral Felix B. Stump, executive officer of Freedoms Foundation at Valley Forge, was planning to retire. I contacted the foundation, offered my services, and was hired to begin work September 1, 1964. Barbara and I came over to Valley Forge and purchased a home nearby, just out of Phoenixville.

Between September of 1964 and October of 1965 my experience in the writing game took a holiday. As a matter of fact I had no intention, when I reported to the foundation, of ever going back. As executive vice president, my duties were almost exclusively administrative, involving, as it turned out, *money* above all. It would be less than candid, unfortunately, to say that I was content in my administrative function. The foundation lived from hand to mouth, on year-by-year contributions. Fund raising alone kept me so absorbed that the opportunities for study that I had expected never materialized. When an opportunity came in the late summer of 1965 to turn once again to writing, I was receptive.

The whole thing happened by chance. Even back in Gettysburg I had been aware that a company was embarking on a project to make a movie about the German counteroffensive of the winter of 1944–45, more commonly known as "Battle of the Bulge." I viewed the project at the time with casual interest. The Boss's policy, in which I enthusiastically concurred, was to give whatever aid we could to people who were honestly writing history. We gave what help we could to the Bulge movie. Later at Valley Forge the producer, Tony Lazzarino, asked if I would be a technical adviser on the movie; I agreed, but since I was employed at Freedoms Foundation, this arrangement could only be a hobby.

Then in late summer of 1965 Tony came by Phoenixville with a proposition: he would like me to write a book on the Battle of the Bulge to be associated with his projected movie. I was reluctant at first, but after a time, as I jotted down the titles of possible chapters, my interest grew. Matters were still extremely vague, however, and no concrete proposal was made.

Soon, at Tony's behest, I was visiting with Educational Resources Corporation (ERC) in New York City, the agent for the book. Since they were in the process of looking for an author—and I seemed to fill the bill—we went to G. P. Putnam's Sons to discuss the idea in serious terms. The editor-in-chief, John Dodds, was enthusiastic and specified the exact structure he desired. The book, Dodds said, should begin at the St. Lô breakthrough in Normandy, as the D-Day operation leading up to this breakthrough had already been adequately covered elsewhere. It should then build up to the day the German counteroffensive hit and treat the battle itself in depth. Dodds then specified that he would like some follow-up to cover the rest of the European Campaign.

Frankly, I was somewhat discomfited by this stringent, dictated organization. It seemed to me artistically incorrect to string out so many events, amounting, in fact, to a thumbnail account of the entire European Campaign. Nevertheless, these were the terms that Putnam's presented, and I could take them or leave them. I decided to take them. James Knox of ERC arranged adequate advances from Putnam's and from publishers in Britain, France, and Italy to make the project financially worthwhile for me.

Not surprisingly, this step gave me a certain hollow feeling in the stomach. While I had helped extensively on the Boss's books, I had never written a work of this size—150,000 words, the contract said—completely on my own. I was leaving a steady job to gamble on my own abilities to complete this work by June 30, 1967. I went ahead. On October 1, 1965, I rented an office on the edge of Phoenixville. I was fortunate in finding an excellent secretary, Mrs. Beverly Leeuwenburg. Moreover, the office was furnished; and with a few purchases such as a typewriter, a second-hand dictaphone, and a file cabinet, I planned to begin serious business the first week in November. To tide me over financially before receiving my first advance, I sold my airplane for $8,000.

I have no idea how other prospective writers approach a task of this size without going out of their minds. For my part, having made out a series of chapter headings, I broke the whole subject down to the point where I could define a decent day's work. Between November 1965 and July 1967 seemed like a short time. But I planned to do a first draft in a year. Computing on the basis of 150,000 words in 250 working days, I determined to do each daily task as if I were performing a routine job. A ten-thousand-word chapter in three weeks would, I calculated, represent an adequate rate.

Before I began work my father, who was vacationing in Augusta, suffered a second heart attack. I headed for Fort Gordon, Georgia, and remained there about ten days until assured that he was out of immediate danger. Then I settled down to writing toward the end of November.

From that time on I was able, with some success—not so much as I had hoped—to follow my schedule. With a portable dictaphone I went to Washington, where the members of the Office of the Chief of Military History (OCMH), under Brigadier General Hal D. Pattison, gave me full cooperation. OCMH introduced me to the World War II archives in Alexandria and the official U. S. Army histories, all of which were in the public domain. With the help of this material, so conveniently gathered in an area not too far from home, I found the research problem considerably easier than I had expected.

During the first phases I experienced the standard ups and downs of writers. It was something new to be doing this on my own. However, I received encouragement from the professional writers of OCMH; from my attorney, Bo Horkan, who checked the text for possible libel; and from Sam Vaughan of Doubleday who, on the basis of friendship (though I was writing for a competitor) repeatedly assured me that getting the "yips" in this type of business was completely normal. John Dodds from Putnam's came down to Phoenixville once to check on the first two or three chapters. His satisfaction with the progress of the work was more than welcome.

In the meantime, Tony Lazzarino continued on his film script, but it became obvious fairly early that we were engaged in two entirely different projects. We nevertheless conversed often on the subject, and Tony provided me with certain leads, not the least of which was the final title of the book, *The Bitter Woods.*

With the help of my friends in OCMH I was able, by New Year's, 1966, to scratch out a draft on all the background operations from COBRA (St. Lô breakthrough) to the point where the Allies were pounding on the borders of Germany. This material dealt with some sticky issues, principally the controversies that arose between Dad as Supreme Commander and his principal British subordinate, Field Marshal Sir Bernard Law Montgomery. To some extent their divergences were objective; to a larger extent, I am convinced, they fell along the lines of national attitudes, as Montgomery was backed up by the Chief of the British Imperial General Staff, Field Marshal Sir Alan Brooke; most of all, perhaps, they were occasioned by Montgomery's ego and ambition, a fearful combination. These controversial matters included the wisdom of the Allied landing in Southern France (Operation DRAGOON, in which for once Montgomery was not involved), the concept of an over-all land commander under the Boss, and the British-supported contention that all resources during the autumn of 1944 should be allocated almost solely to a single thrust under Monty across the North German Plain. There is no point in discussing these issues here. With no exception that I am aware of, the Boss's views, shared by nearly all Americans and by some of the British, prevailed. And the disagreements really centered around whether the Allies could have won the European Campaign more quickly and cheaply.

This part of the book, more than the story of the Bulge itself, turned out to be the object of greatest reader interest, partly because I, as the son of the Supreme Commander, was given credit for presenting a fairly balanced view. However, it was in many ways the easiest part of the book to write, as I had available the published accounts of all the principals concerned.

At the outset of researching I had considered applying for access to classified documents in the Army files. But when I learned that such a privilege would require me to submit a complete final manuscript for review, I backed off. It could easily have cost me three to six months of twiddling my thumbs, I feared, while some Intelligence genius would find the time to go through it. Therefore I waived all access to classified documents and determined simply to interview or correspond with the people who had written them. Verbally and by letter I learned all I needed. A remarkable number of the commanders and staff officers were still alive—and very helpful. I noted wryly that otherwise inaccessible generals were willing to talk with an author engaged in writing about their military exploits.

After the turn of the year I spent a good deal of time in Washington, going through combat reports, intelligence reports, and other documents which, although unclassified, had not been fully tapped. I have since learned that some writers find the research phase the easiest; I found it the most difficult, particularly since it required me to be away from home. On the other hand, there was always the occasional delight in discovering a real nugget of information. One that excited me, for example, was a hitherto unpublished letter in the archives, written by an unknown SS (Schutzstaffel) soldier, to his sister the night before the German attack:

> My daily letter will be very short today—short and sweet. I write during one of the great hours before an attack—full of unrest, full of expectation for what the next days will bring. Everyone who has been here for the last two days and nights (especially nights), who has witnessed hour after hour the assembly of our crack divisions, who has heard the constant rattling of panzers, knows that something is up and we are looking forward to a clear order to reduce the tension. We are still in the dark as to "where" and "how" but that cannot be helped!
>
> Some believe in big wonders, but that may be shortsighted! It is enough to know we attack, and will throw the enemy from our

homeland. That is a holy task! I do not want to talk or write much now—but wait and see what the hours ahead will bring!

Overhead is the terrific noise of V-1, of artillery—the voice of war. So long now—wish me luck and think of me. . . .[5]

The work ground on, and with every chapter I became more optimistic. Unfortunately, completeness required that I cover a certain amount of material, especially toward the end, that was less exciting than the suspenseful earlier portion.

In September and October of 1966, a draft finished, Barbara and I went to Europe to see the battleground and talk with some of the surviving principals. Our first stop was London, where I felt it exceedingly important to interview Field Marshal Montgomery. While the quality of Monty's friendship with the Boss had turned distinctly chilly after the publication of Monty's memoirs in 1958, he was still kind enough to agree to see me at his home, Isington Mill, in Hampshire. I approached the interview with a certain amount of trepidation. Monty's public statements had become increasingly vitriolic over the years; I was half expecting a scene. This did not turn out to be the case. Monty met Barbara and me at the door of his attractive house and, after assuring us that he had visitors coming and could not possibly pour us tea, he seemed to relax. Although we had met several times before, we were strangers to him; this I had come to expect.

While Barbara wandered around the grounds, Monty and I settled down in his upstairs living room. There was no need for preliminaries. "When you talk about the Battle of the Bulge," he began, "you have to realize that it need never have occurred in the first place." He then went on to reiterate his old arguments, with which I was so familiar, emphasizing once more that he could have driven into Germany during the fall of 1944 if only all the resources of the European theater had been allotted to him. One statement he made did surprise me. He considered the entire invasion of Europe, from D-Day on, as a completely foregone conclusion, no problem at all. "The Germans," he said, "were defeated by the beginning of 1944." Having been so imbued with the drama of D-Day, I could hardly swallow the idea that the invasion had

[5] *The Bitter Woods,* p. 179.

incurred no risks whatsoever. This statement was all the more surprising in the light of the major role that Monty had played, not
only on D-Day itself but in Operation COBRA. I could only surmise that by now, Monty, since he had been denied the ultimate
starring role in the invasion of Europe, had decided that his claim
to fame rested on the Battle of El Alamein in November 1942.
(Personally, I felt that Montgomery had been given undue credit
for that spectacular victory but held my thoughts to myself.) As to
the Ardennes in 1944, Monty brushed that battle off as a "piece of
cake."

In the course of the interview, Montgomery became more relaxed and amiable. He asked after the Boss's health and was particularly intrigued by the fact that "Brad" (General Omar Bradley),
who had been probably his chief rival among the Allied chiefs,
had recently remarried. He told me of the deficiencies of various
American generals, but with a light, humorous touch. In contrast
to the antagonism I found against Monty when talking to Americans, this strange, birdlike little man seemed to hold little resentment in return. The Americans weren't very good, of course, but
decent chaps.

I overstayed my time about fifteen minutes, not long considering
that our host really had nobody else coming for tea, and as we were
making our way down the narrow steps to the ground floor, I
asked him about something that had always puzzled me. "General,"
I said, "did you write your rather controversial memoirs in answer
to some of the unkind things that had been written about you by
American generals, Bradley in particular?"

"Oh, no," he tossed back over his shoulder. "Everyone else had
had his say and I just thought I would have mine."

So ended what turned out to be a surprisingly pleasant interview.
As with everyone else I saw, I promptly sent him a copy of my version of his remarks and he took the time to send me his comments
and corrections. I did not agree with Monty's various theses, and
so I wanted to be doubly careful not to misquote him.

While still in London I had the chance to lunch with Major
General Sir John Whiteley, who gave me an entirely different viewpoint. Jock Whiteley had been Deputy G-3 (operations) in Supreme Headquarters during the invasion. Although British, he, as

with nearly all of his countrymen who had served in SHAEF, disagreed completely with Monty's contentions. As to the idea of a single, narrow thrust across the North German Plain, he asked rhetorically, "Why should we have three quarters of our troops sitting on their fannies while Monty did all the fighting?"

Strictly an Eisenhower man, Whiteley provided invaluable inside stories about the personalities at SHAEF, particularly Dad's efficient but short-fused chief of staff, Lieutenant General Walter Bedell Smith. I was grateful for this visit and for the trouble that Whiteley had taken to travel to London. In only one respect was our talk a disappointment: he did not like to be quoted. A gentleman in the extreme, he was overly concerned about everybody's feelings. Thus when I sent him my version of his remarks, he struck out material that to me was painful indeed to lose. But I had no complaint; this was the rule of the game as I played it.

Our time in London finished, Barbara and I left for Brussels, where we rented a car and headed for a hotel at Spa, in the Ardennes. From that point I was able, by pushing hard, to cover every road of importance to the battle. Driving through the Ardennes was a strange experience. I had seen the ground only once, in 1945, and at that time had comprehended little. Now I felt as one feels on going home after a long absence. Having spent a year studying a triangle of ground about sixty miles on each side, I knew in my mind the location of every road junction and hamlet. In fact, I hardly looked at a map in all my racings from Ettelbruck in Luxembourg to Celles in Belgium, near the Meuse River.

While at Spa we were joined by a disabled American veteran of the Bulge, William James, of Port Chester, New York, who had taken an interest in this writing project. His platoon had by chance been swallowed up on the first day of the battle. Since all its members had been captured, they had never before told their story and it had heretofore been lost to the pages of history. In the course of time, however, certain members of the platoon had, on reading other histories of the battle, concluded that their small action had indeed been of critical importance. During their one day of combat they had held up the spearhead of a lead German division by a full day, when time was dear. The people of Port Chester had passed the hat and made it possible for Will to come on his own volition to Spa.

Will, who had lost a portion of his face in that first day's action, was an invaluable help. He bore no rancor toward the Germans, never forgetting that German doctors had operated on his face thirty-five times while he had been held in captivity. Will was obsessed with the importance of his own platoon, but he was completely reasonable on all other aspects of the battle.

From the Ardennes Barbara and I drove down the terrifying German *Autobahn*, headed for Munich. On this superhighway, uninhibited by speed limit, either maximum or minimum, we felt fortunate when we made it safely to our hotel in the center of the city. The purpose of the Munich stopover was to allow me a day with General (Baron) Hasso von Manteuffel. We met previously when he had visited Gettysburg with Tony Lazzarino. From an historian's point of view the Baron's position was nearly unique. He had been commander of the Fifth Panzer Army during the Bulge, the army which had broken through Allied lines from the Eifel and penetrated nearly to the Meuse River. He had been only forty-seven years old at the time and was now sixty-eight, rapidly becoming one of the few living high commanders of World War II.

Manteuffel's usefulness to historians was enhanced, moreover, by the fact that, though his experiences had exposed him to unusual situations, he was acknowledged by the Allies as completely clear of any taint of Nazism. He had, in fact, been a member of the German Bundestag for fourteen years after the war.

As we sat in the living room of his modest home in Diessen, south of Munich, Manteuffel spoke freely, even enthusiastically, of his experiences. His English was fair but, my German being nil, he had thoughtfully provided an interpreter. He described such personalities as the hard-driving but disturbed Panzer Field Marshal Walter Model; the stupid but rather decent General Joseph ("Sepp") Dietrich; General Fritz Bayerlein; and others. He outlined in detail the deception measures he personally had instituted to convince the Allies that the front along the Eifel was being used only as a German rest area. (Actually the entire Fifth Panzer Army was hidden only a few miles away.)

But the most intriguing tales Manteuffel had to tell were those about Hitler and the degeneration of his personality during the last year of his life. Manteuffel had been one of Hitler's favorite combat commanders, though strictly apolitical. Further, he had not been a member of the distrusted German General Staff. He had made his reputation in the successes of his 7th Panzer Division on the Russian front and as such had come to Hitler's attention. Elevated to army command, Manteuffel had been present at the planning sessions for the Ardennes offensive—when the time had become ripe for the participants to be let in on the secret. He described the glazed look in Hitler's eye, his apparent departure from reality, and the cleverness with which Hitler manipulated his limp and helpless left arm. At one point Manteuffel had stood up to the Führer regarding the tactics to be employed by his panzer army and had actually carried the day.

Manteuffel last saw Hitler about a month before the end of the war, when sent for to be given a new mission. His story of Hitler's screaming from across the room as he entered, of Hitler's weak effort to apologize, and of the Führer's physical feebleness held me fascinated.

Later Manteuffel, like the rest, cooperated in editing out any errors I made in taking notes of the interview.

From Munich Barbara and I drove to Vienna for a sentimental look at the place where we had met and courted. Thence home.

The next phase of this book project was the champagne. I now had a respectable draft and enough new material to enable me to rework not only my own material but also that of Dr. Woodrow ("Woody") Hansen, whose research on German planning had to be put in my own words.[6] During this more leisurely period, I took advantage of opportunities to interview such commanders as Generals Matthew B. Ridgway, Anthony C. McAuliffe, and Maxwell D. Taylor; Lieutenant General Troy Middleton; Major General Hal McCown; and Colonel William Dwight. All helped to enrich the material already on hand. I corresponded with Walter Cronkite,

---

[6] Jim Knox had brought me in contact with Dr. Woodrow W. Hansen, a friend of his father's, who, being on the loose at the time, was willing to research a couple of chapters on the German planning for the battle. Woody's research was a great help, releasing me to think in Allied terms, at least in the first stages.

Otto Skorzeny, and even the notorious *SS* Colonel Jochen Peiper (tried for perpetrating the "Malmédy massacre"). At the same time, as the publisher's advance money had run out, I took up professional public speaking. The subject of the standard talk was my experience in the White House during the Boss's Administration. I was astonished at the fees available, but they prevented a drastic deficit in the Eisenhower family's balance of payments.

Shortly after submission of manuscript—I made it on the exact date due—Arthur Fields, the new editor-in-chief at Putnam's, came to Phoenixville to discuss the text. As I have mentioned in connection with the Boss's books, the period in which the author is first faced with the editor's comments is difficult. Arthur wanted no really major changes but asked for a central theme, which we agreed on to be "a study in command," as in *Lee's Lieutenants* by Douglas Southall Freeman. As a result, I found myself back at work again, writing the introduction and revamping certain emphases in the text.

Once the new revision was in Putnam's hands I sat and stewed during what seemed an interminable delay. Winston Churchill, so a story goes, once described writing a book as an evolutionary process. It begins with great excitement, like acquiring a new mistress. It evolves into a marriage and progresses into a tired marriage. In the last stages it becomes a monster that has to be killed. In this instance, the "monster" stage, which began actually in June 1967, was excruciating, probably more so because I had no other book under way.[7]

In early December of 1968 I was sitting alone in a hotel room in West Baden, Indiana, where I was in the process of presenting a series of lectures at Northwood Institute. I had just received, through the thoughtfulness of Arthur Fields, the first copy of *The Bitter Woods*. I have rarely, if ever, experienced the thrill of satisfaction comparable to that of seeing my own first book come out between covers. That moment made three years of toil and frustration worth while. I sat up until all hours reading over my favorite passages and noting where I would write each a little differently,

[7] In a way, the necessary period of time after the galley proof phase was lucky; it allowed me to participate in the 1968 presidential political campaign.

given another chance. I fondled it like a doll and dozed off to sleep with the beloved monster lying on my chest.

It would be a happy thing, in a way, if the activities of an author terminated at the time when he received his first volume. Such, however, is hardly the case. The author still is faced with reading the reviews and then, if he is willing, with participating actively in promotion. The official publication date of the book comes weeks after the volumes have rolled off the presses. Time is necessary for distribution to the bookstores and advance copies to be sent out to reviewers. As a result, by the time one begins his activities to promote a book—that is, around publication date—the bulk of the reviews are appearing.

The general tenor of the reviews came as a happy surprise. Having been so close to the forest and conscious that *The Bitter Woods* was on a somewhat specialized military subject, I had not expected a great deal. But by and large, the comments were far more favorable than ones I would have written. Naturally, each contained at least one point of adverse criticism; this is desirable in order for a reviewer to maintain credibility. However, I was happy that the criticisms were far from uniform. One, for example, would say that I was at my best when describing the actions of American soldiers; another would say that I understood the generals but that my soldiers moved around like automatons. A couple mentioned somewhat plaintively the exhaustive research and detail I had gone into. (In these cases, I could at least feel confident that the reviewer had read the book.) On the other hand, I sometimes got the impression that a reviewer had merely scanned the book. One individual, for example, while highly complimentary, saying that I wrote "with power," mentioned a couple of important items that he felt I had omitted; actually I thought they had been covered quite adequately.

Only one review caused me irritation, although probably many other people who read it considered it favorable. This was the review in *Time* magazine. The headline read, "His Father's Voice." It included two severe criticisms: one, that I was merely speaking for the Boss and had no mind of my own; and two, that the text sounded as if it came from the blackboards of the War College. In this case, I gave in to an impulse to write a letter to the editor. I pointed out that my opinion of the Boss's conduct of the European Campaign—which was in contrast to Monty's criticisms—was based on my independent judgment. On the matter of my pedantry, I wrote (humorously, I thought) that if the text sounded like a lecture at the War College, all right; the book was not intended as a treatise on toilet training of infants. *Time*'s publication of the letter caused a certain mild shock among the women in my life, but most of the men who noticed it roared with laughter. However, as usual, *Time* got in the last lick. They entitled the letter "The Bitter Words."

As it turned out, my participation in the book's promotion began immediately after President Richard Nixon's inauguration in January 1969. This began with a radio program in New York and included a whirlwind of radio talk shows and at least four television appearances. None of these were too difficult, naturally, as I knew what I was talking about. Few of the interviewers had read the book, but a member of their staff always gave them a short, half-page summary with pertinent questions. The main problem in these television appearances was to stay on the subject. Public curiosity centered more around my relationship to the Nixon family and my possible role in the new Administration. Nevertheless, at the beginning and the end of each interview, the host would wave a copy in front of the television camera and mention its name. Personal promotion of this sort may have as much to do with the sale of a book as its intrinsic merits.

The final climax came while Barbara and I were on vacation in February. One day my secretary, Judy Tegethoff, managed to reach me in the Bahamas and said that *The Bitter Woods* had hit the best-seller list in both the New York *Times* and *Time*. Naturally, Barbara, our host and hostess, and I were delighted; and the news occasioned a celebration. But by now, my participation in the project completed, we were thinking of the future. My own reaction was somewhat similar to that of the American troops in Europe the day World War II ended. I was proud of this success—after all, 30,000 new titles are published in the United States yearly. But other things lay ahead, not the least of which would be to try another. After all, the unexpected success of *The Bitter Woods* had given me something to live up to.

12

Taps for a Soldier

In March 1968, while visiting Palm Desert, California, the Boss was struck with his third major heart attack. He had suffered two earlier ones, the first in September 1955 and a second one in November 1965.

At the time of his decision to run for a second term as President, after the first attack, the doctors had predicted that he could lead an active life for a period of as long as ten years. This indeed he had done. Not only had he completed his second term in office in excellent health but had, at the age of seventy, gone into a retirement at Gettysburg that most men would have considered a most active life. It seemed, before the second attack in November 1965, at Augusta, that he might never have another, although he had remarked just before the event that the ten years the doctors had prognosticated before were up. He had shown no marked further deterioration during the three years since 1965.

The role that psychological influence played in bringing on his long final illness can hardly be guessed at, even by the most competent specialist. But after the 1965 attack Dad showed signs of being aware that another attack might be his last. He began to simplify his estate by such measures as dispersing his magnificent herd of Angus cattle, and the doctors restricted his golfing, a real passion of his life. Dad showed no outward signs of worry, especially for himself. However, being a practical man, he realized that with every succeeding attack he had less heart reserve, and he simply made his plans, in the meantime following the doctors' instructions to the letter. He always had.

But isolated events disclosed that the recognition of mortality existed beneath the surface. When Dad and Mother arrived in Palm Desert in late 1967, for example, Mother called to say that the Boss was in bed with some sort of ailment, his spirits low. On the trip out, the train had stopped in Abilene, and Dad had made a special trip to the Meditation Chapel at the Eisenhower Center, his and Mother's future resting place. He had left, upset, an emotion brought on not by concern for himself but by the sight of the tiny plaque on the floor where the body of my older brother had been placed.[1] Icky's death had made an impact on both my parents that has been largely overlooked, principally because they rarely mentioned it, in private or in public. But in Dad's most personal book, *At Ease,* he wrote, "This was the greatest disappointment and disaster in my life, the one I have never been able to forget completely."

Happily, after a few days rest in the California sunshine, the Boss recovered from this low spot and was obviously the picture of elation when at the age of seventy-seven he shot his first hole in one on the par-three golf course he was allowed to play. "The thrill of a lifetime," he gloated, putting the presidency and World War II in the shade.

When Barbara and I received news in 1968 that Dad had been moved to March Air Force Base but that the situation was not acute, we waited until he was transferred to Walter Reed in Washington before we went to see him. In the meantime, however, the Boss had lost none of his flair for giving commands. Before departing from March, he had instructed the commanding officer of the hospital that the nurses accompanying him on the flight back East should be given a few days' leave in Washington before returning to California.

In Ward Eight at Walter Reed we found the Boss painfully thin but exuding his customary good cheer, at least in the presence of visitors. He continued to show slow improvement and managed to take an active interest in the 1968 presidential campaign. So keen was he for the election of Richard Nixon that he finally determined to break a lifetime precedent by coming out for a candidate before the national convention. With his age and detachment from the

---

[1] Doud Dwight Eisenhower—"Icky"—had died in 1921, age four. He had been buried at Fairmont Cemetery, Denver, but had recently been moved to Abilene in accordance with the Boss's wishes.

political arena, he decided he could afford to take the liberty, and he endorsed Nixon in a statement issued in the summer of 1968.

By late July the Boss seemed to be on the road to recovery. He was strong enough, the doctors decided, to make an address to the Republican convention. His attendance in Miami was, of course, out of the question, but he was able to put on a business suit and appear on television. That evening, August 5, I took the stage before the convention to accept a memento on his behalf. A few moments later he appeared on the screen, gaunt but alert, and gave a short speech of encouragement to the delegates present. Despite the normal confusion and clatter of a political convention, complete silence reigned until the Boss signed off. The next morning he suffered another heart attack.

On hearing of the Boss's condition I left Miami that Tuesday morning, August 6, to fly back to Washington.

This time Dad's difficulty took a new form. He suffered no additional muscle damage in the form of an "infarct," but the rhythm of the heart would periodically go out of control and "fibrillate," which means that instead of beating, it merely vibrated, pumping no blood. Any one of these attacks would have been fatal had they hit him on the street. But here in the hospital, sophisticated machinery could, by electrical impulses, restore the rhythmic beating. After the convention the rest of the family joined me at Walter Reed and we waited around for about a week, during which time Dad suffered these attacks periodically. When an attack occurred, the doctors would fly into action and the family would be relegated to a sitting room down the hall to await the outcome. I think it is safe to say that none of the doctors expected him to survive this period.

Strangely enough, between these attacks—which became less and less frequent—Dad seemed completely normal. Since each fibrillation was rectified quickly, no brain damage resulted. As a consequence, when the rest of the family arrived, he could visit with each one individually for short periods. His courage was inspiring and sometimes had shattering effects. When our daughter Susie, for example, was allowed to come into his room for a few moments, he forthwith admonished her lovingly about her current slimming diet. On leaving the room, Susie threw her arms around me and burst into tears of grief.

All families, in public life or not, face situations similar to this, in one form or another. We were utterly helpless to do anything and yet felt it necessary to be on hand. Barbara stayed with me in the Walter Reed guest house. The youngsters lived with friends around Washington. Mother was allowed to live in a room next door to Dad's in the hospital and naturally visited more frequently than the rest of us. She retained a remarkable spirit, sustained partly by many solicitous telephone calls from her friends and by the knowledge that the Boss was receiving the best medical attention possible. Further, the family was becoming inured to crises, all of which in the past had blown over. None of the other crises had appeared as serious as this one; still, the family retained hope, even expectation, of recovery, though given little encouragement by the doctors.

For my own part, the waiting was relieved somewhat by the fact that, as the son, I was saddled with certain responsibilities. These had begun some six years earlier when Colonel Paul Miller, of the Military District of Washington, had asked if I would assist him in his job of planning the Boss's state funeral, whenever that should occur. Such a request may seem morbid, but, as Paul pointed out, no man is immortal and *some* day this eventuality would have to be faced. Decisions made in a calm atmosphere, with the Boss in good health, would be easier to face than when made under the duress of bereavement. Accordingly, Paul and I spent hours in secret working out the details.

As a President's family is not accorded the privilege of a private funeral, these details are complicated. At the outset I convinced Paul that the length of time spent in ceremonies should be kept to a minimum in deference to Mother's frail health. Somehow Paul was able to cut off a day or two from his original plan, reducing everything to about six days. Further, since we could never subject Mother to the ordeal of flying under such conditions, plans had to be made for railroad transportation, even to the point of making a list of the people who would go along on the train to take care of her. With the basic plan agreed upon, then, we came to the touchy problem of who should be invited to attend each ceremony. Protocol dictated a good portion of these lists of "persons to be notified," but those to be invited on a personal basis had to be periodically brought up to date. Thus, for six years Paul Miller had been coming to see me to check over the names of persons who had died as well as those of new friends.

This prior planning of state and official funerals, to the best of my knowledge, had begun with General Marshall in 1959, and Paul had performed the same duties in other cases, such as those of General MacArthur and President Herbert Hoover. Now, in August 1968, with the possibility of the Boss's passing becoming hardly academic, Paul and I, in Walter Reed Hospital, were actively planning.

Furthermore, I was the member of the family responsible for making certain medical decisions, all of which were easy because they were recommended unanimously by the doctors. These dedicated people were being bombarded with medical advice from all over the world. The most frequent advice rendered at this time concerned a possible heart transplant. This, the doctors explained, was out of the question. Heart transplants had never been attempted on persons of the Boss's advanced age. The oldest patient on which a transplant had been attempted had been fifty-seven years old; there was no hope attempting the procedure with a man of seventy-seven. But the doctors needed, for their own records, my formal agreement with them, which of course I gave. This type of duty kept my mind at least partly off the fundamentals of the situation.

As time wore on, the fibrillations became less and less frequent and finally came to a complete halt. It now seemed safe to return to Phoenixville. Though the experience had, of course, been a difficult one, it at least pointed up certain administrative arrangements which we had previously not foreseen and which would be easier whenever they would be needed at a later time.

Again the Boss improved. Apparently undamaged by his week-long ordeal, he maintained the same acute consciousness of events in the outside world. On his birthday, October 14, he was able to receive a number of visitors at the hospital, including General William Westmoreland, who had just returned from Vietnam to be Chief of Staff of the Army. That afternoon Dad was serenaded by the Army Band and was wheeled to his bedroom window, where he acknowledged the tribute by smiling and waving a small five-star flag. The occasion was sentimental and touching. It was saddened by this formerly dynamic man's obvious physical weakness.

His outlook remained calm and cheerful. His mind had been eased, he told me, by the fact that a law had been passed which gave widows of former Presidents lifetime Secret Service coverage. "This last August," he said, "when it looked like I might cash in my chips, my only worry was about Mamie. This puts my mind at rest on that count at least." But other events absorbed his attention. He was elated, of course, by the election of Richard Nixon as President, and he felt confident that once again the country would be in the hands of a responsible administration. The President-elect visited with him several times, but the Boss went even further. As each future Cabinet member was named by Nixon, Dad would ask for him to come to Ward Eight. To the best of my knowledge, the Boss interviewed and advised each future member of the Nixon Cabinet, somewhat to everyone's amusement. He and Mother were sad, of course, that he was unable to attend the weddings of two of his grandchildren, Barbara Anne in November and David in December. But, at least in the case of David's wedding to Julie Nixon, arrangements were made for him to witness the proceedings on closed-circuit television. And Anne and Fernando Echavarria, after their wedding in November, visited him, Anne wearing her wedding dress.

The family missed having Christmas and New Year's with Dad and Mother, since at this time Mother herself had come down with a severe respiratory ailment. For a period of time, while Ward Eight was being renovated, Dad was moved temporarily to the so-called Pershing Suite nearby, where the commander of the American Expeditionary Force of World War I had spent his last years.

Shortly after New Year's, 1969, Mother was still sick. She seemed in no condition for me to break the news of my forthcoming appointment as ambassador to Belgium, even though Brussels was only a few hours' flying time away. I had no compunctions about telling Dad. As it turned out, he had known of this possibility for some time and was enthusiastic. "Don't worry," he assured me, "I won't tell Mamie."

Thus Dad's condition seemed always to improve, and the question concerning us most was that of his future after his presumed release from the hospital. It seemed possible that he might be able to walk again with help or at least be moved around in a wheel chair. In order to allow him to go to work, Bob Schulz was beginning to plan for an elevator at the Gettysburg office so that the Boss could reach his desk without having to climb stairs. However, we all realized that it would be some time before this would become an immediate problem.

Confident that things were stabilized, Barbara and I took a short vacation with friends in the Bahamas and returned by way of Gainesville, Florida, to visit with her parents, who were likewise in poor health. On a Sunday evening in late February 1969, we received a call at dinner advising us that Dad would now have to undergo a major abdominal operation. The Air Force aide in the White House, with the President's authority, dispatched a Jetstar to Gainesville, and that same night Barbara and I were once more in Washington.

On arrival we learned that complications had arisen from Dad's ileitis operation of twelve years before. Scar tissue had wrapped itself around his intestine and was causing blockage. The operation was delayed for a day, but the next night, cheerful as always, the Boss said not to worry, just to have a drink to him. As he was wheeled down the hall he gave us a "thumbs up" sign and broad grin.

A couple of hours later, General Leonard Heaton, who had performed the original operation and had been watching Dad's health over these many years, came in elated. Heaton had been seriously concerned that Dad's weakened heart would be unable to hold up through the present operation.

Barbara and I went back to Phoenixville, as no immediate danger seemed apparent and I remembered from the days after the ileitis operation that visitors were an annoyance right after surgery rather than a comfort. I continued with my schedule for public appearances in promoting *The Bitter Woods* and beginning preparations in the State Department to appear before the Senate Foreign Relations Committee for confirmation as ambassador.

After the hearing on March 7 I stopped by the hospital for a short visit. As he lay on his bed, Dad made a remark that jarred me. "It's an eerie feeling," he murmured, "to have them hit you with one thing and then another."

"Well," I stammered, "now that you've had that intestinal blockage taken out, you ought to start feeling better. Maybe now you can gain some weight."

"God, I hope so," he sighed, without a trace of a smile.

I left with a deep feeling of depression, not because I had been told anything disturbing by the doctors, but because this was the first time Dad had ever uttered anything bordering on despair.

About two weeks later, on the afternoon of Monday, March 24, having made my last "book-and-author" luncheon, I turned on the car radio as I drove home from New York.

"General Eisenhower" the announcement came, "has suffered a severe set-back. He is being given oxygen to combat a progressive heart failure." I knew this time that the end was really near. I pulled over to the Molly Pitcher refueling area on the New Jersey Turnpike and called Dr. Robert Hall at Walter Reed. Doc Hall obviously felt as I did but said there was no need to rush; tomorrow would be ample time to arrive. With this reassurance I went home for dinner but felt impelled to go on to Washington. I took my leave and continued to Walter Reed.

Everything at the hospital was quiet when I arrived at 1 A.M. After visiting briefly with Mother, I went to the guest quarters. Tomorrow would be another day.

The days dragged on, much as had the week during the previous August. David and Julie came, as did Barbara. Susie and Mary Jean were visiting Anne in Bogota; but despite the fact that they just arrived, they turned around almost immediately for Washington. The Boss lay with the oxygen tubes in his nose, suffering from a filling of the lungs and aware that this time he would not make it. Nor did he want to by now. He had called in the Reverend Billy Graham, I later learned, to talk of spiritual things. He had ordered a dozen copies of *The Bitter Woods* for me to sign for the doctors and nurses who had taken care of him. In our conversations he tried to be cheerful but would squeeze in what obviously were last-minute instructions, such as "Be good to Mamie." With his suffering, we could no longer give cheerful words of encouragement. We simply listened.

During all this time the family remained as before, in a state of suspended animation. But realizing that the situation was hopeless, viscerally we still refused to give up. Mother took every day as it came and as usual spent much time talking cheerfully to concerned friends on the telephone. The youngsters came and went, but generally we all stayed pretty close to Ward Eight.

On Thursday evening, March 27, I went as usual to the little hallway outside the Boss's bedroom. The electrocardiogram machine, which gave a visual picture of his heartbeat, showed just the slightest bit of improvement. But when I went into the room to say good night, the Boss indicated openly that this was the end and the sooner the better. He winced when I told him that his pattern on the cardiogram had slightly improved. I went to bed uncertain whether we had just been through another false alarm, but the sight of the Boss made me resolve to avoid ever being placed in a hospital where my life would be artificially prolonged.

The next morning Barbara and I were awakened at 8:20 by a telephone call from Dr. Frederic Hughes, commandant of the hospital. "The end will be coming pretty soon," he said. Barbara and I hastily dressed, alerted David, and headed for Ward Eight. As we tiptoed into Dad's room I turned to David and told him to stay out. "I've seen death many times," I said, "and this is not for you." David said nothing and merely followed me in.

At 9 A.M. the Boss began to make his final preparations. Mother, David, and I were at the bedside along with General Heaton, the doctors, and a nurse. Suddenly he barked out a fully intelligible command: "Lower the shades!" This being done with speed, the room became nearly dark, the gloom broken only by the streaks of bright sunlight that the venetian blinds could not completely blot out. The Boss then turned to Doc Hall and me. "Pull me up." We pulled him up on the bed to a point where we thought he was high enough. He looked from side to side at us. "Two big men," he growled. "Higher." We pulled him higher.

This done, Dad looked up at me and said softly, "I want to go; God take me." He then seemed to relax. One of the doctors gave him a shot of sedative. As it turned out, he never regained consciousness.

The moment had not yet come, however, and the family went across the hall to the dining room for a cup of coffee and a chat with James Rowley, head of the Secret Service. Shortly after twelve noon we were summoned back into the bedroom where, with Mother holding the Boss's hand, David and I standing stiffly at each corner of the bed, we watched the picture on the machine flutter and even out. Mother, David, and I began filing out of the room.

Something told me to go back. I stopped in the doorway and returned to the foot of the bed. On the machine the heart showed a final beat. General Heaton and I looked at our watches together. It was 12:35 P.M., March 28, 1969. Almost instantly bells began to toll all over the city.

13

Extraordinary and Plenipotentiary

On January 2, 1969, I was sitting in my Phoenixville office taking care of various odds and ends. The 1968 political campaign, in which I had been chairman of Pennsylvania Citizens for Nixon and Agnew, was now out of my mind, and the sting of losing the Pennsylvania vote was practically forgotten. The autumn had seen the weddings of two of our four children, Anne and David. Publication date for *The Bitter Woods* was only a few days off—January 9—and I was preparing to begin the series of radio and television appearances.

The telephone rang. On the other end was Andy Goodpaster, recently recalled from Vietnam to aid in the organization of the new Administration. "John," he said, "they have a job they'd like you to do. The President-elect would like you to go to Brussels as ambassador."

I was startled, to say the least. The prospect seemed exciting, but such an assignment would tear up the pattern of my rather settled life. Really, I had experienced enough excitement for a while. Furthermore, our personal financial situation, while not extensive, was complicated; we were still paying on the house we lived in and I had mentally adjusted to doing some more writing.

This was not, however, the first time that the prospect of an ambassadorial post had come up. At the end of the presidential campaign, various people had mentioned a position in the Nixon administration, but I had laughed it off. Once when pressed, I had said that I might consider going as ambassador to either Belgium or the Philippines, but I had never taken the prospect seriously.

When I regained my composure, I asked Andy the critical question: "General, do they really want me or do they feel indebted because of my participation in the campaign? If that's the case, let's forget it."

"No, they really want you."

"How soon do I have to make a decision?"

"Oh, no hurry—a few days."

"I'll call you tomorrow. Barbara will like it, but I don't know whether I can get my personal situation in order."

After we hung up, I began to pace the floor, fighting the problem of how things could be managed should I accept.

My secretary, Judy Tegethoff, looked up and laughed. "Well, you sure have committed yourself." I stopped and stared at her. She had read my mind.

"I have?"

"Yes, you have."

I gasped, realizing now that I really wanted to go. "Get me Goodpaster back on the phone right away."

Within fifteen minutes we had reached him. "General," I said, "I didn't mean to sound too reluctant a couple of minutes ago. I'll take the job and find some way to work out my own problems."

I then called Barbara at home. When I told her what had happened, she was startled but enthusiastic. Her reaction was not "if" but "when." If there was to be anyone dragging his feet, I knew it would be I; Barbara would always be willing to try something this exciting.

We heard nothing more for a couple of days, and I grew increasingly restive. Had I indeed sounded too reticent? Had I discouraged the approach? Early Saturday evening, January 4, I called Mr. Nixon at his New York apartment. The Nixons were out, but the butler, Minola Sanchez, promised that the President-elect would call back. At 10:30 the call came through. "Dick," I said, trying to sound appropriately casual, "Andy Goodpaster called me a couple of days ago and mentioned my going to Belgium as ambassador. I wanted to let you know directly that I would certainly like to do it."

"Well," he answered, "I think you'll like it. I've always felt that you wanted to get back into the foreign field anyway. That's so, isn't it?" It was so.

I have no idea whether this experience was typical. However, this was the way that at least one ambassadorial appointment was made.

After that conversation I heard nothing for a substantial period of time. Nearly forgetting Belgium, I threw myself into the business of book promotion. On January 20 came inauguration with its pageantry, splendor, confusion, and frazzled nerves. From now on, the man I had known as "Dick Nixon" would be addressed as "Mr. President."

On our return home from a short vacation to the Bahamas in late February, the announcement of my appointment had been made. I went to Washington for a two-phase briefing in the State Department. The first, a rather once-over-lightly affair, was designed simply to get me past the Senate Foreign Relations Committee; a second, later and far more detailed, would give me the background I'd need on arrival in Brussels.

Some years back an ambassadorial appointee—to Ceylon, I believe—had appeared before the Senate Foreign Relations Committee unable to name the Prime Minister of his future host country. Although the man had been confirmed and had gone on to do well, the case had become a sort of *cause célèbre,* still a subject of amused conversation—and a warning. In preparation, then, I was given a bundle of papers to study. Together in the car Barbara and I would go over them, searching for devices to memorize the names of the members of the Belgian Government. (Harmel rhymes with "Carmel"; Scheyven rhymes with "Say when!"; Segers, whose name we mispronounced as "Saygare," rhymed, we thought, with *c'est la guerre.*)[1] In addition, of course, I studied other material on Belgium in general.

I was called to appear before the Senate Foreign Relations Committee on March 7. Before we drove over to the Capitol, former Ambassador William B. Macomber, chief of legislative liaison for the State Department, gave a serious warning: "Answer all questions to the best of your knowledge but avoid volunteering anything; let the committee keep the ball." Good advice for new cadets and prospective ambassadors.

[1] Pierre Harmel, Belgian Foreign Minister; Louis Scheyven, ambassador to the United States; and Paul Segers, Minister of Defense.

Three of us were to be queried that morning in alphabetical order: Walter H. Annenberg to be ambassador to the Court of St. James's (Great Britain), Jacob D. Beam to be ambassador to Moscow, and me. This was my first encounter with a senatorial committee and at first, as I sat down in the front row, I saw the whole thing with detachment, as if I were on one side watching myself go through a new experience.

As the time wore on, however, our surroundings began to take effect. The hearing room was large, with high ceilings and ornate walls. About two hundred witnesses seemed to be crowding the room. The seating arrangement was ingeniously designed to give the committee every possible advantage—every inch of one-upmanship—over the person being interviewed. The members sat in a semicircle around the candidate's lone chair, the witness stand. Their seats were elevated by about two feet—it seemed like five or six—and lights blazed down from behind the members into the witness's eyes. The intensity of the light was not so severe as to make it impossible to see; however, the idea that one was being given the third degree could not be escaped.

Fortunately, I had known some of the senators before, among them Karl Mundt of South Dakota, John Sherman Cooper of Kentucky, Jacob Javits of New York, and Stuart Symington of Missouri. The presence of some old friends gave some feeling of assurance.

The first part of the proceedings consisted of a presentation by the senators whose states were represented by the three nominees. I was very appreciative, naturally, of the testimony given on my behalf by Pennsylvania Senators Hugh Scott and Richard Schweiker (who spoke for both Walter Annenberg and me), although I remember little of what was said. My attention focused on the battery of eyes looking down from the semicircle of desks above.

Following these presentations the committee chairman, Senator J. William Fulbright, of Arkansas, began to quiz Mr. Annenberg, who had taken his place on the stand. In advance, he assured everybody that all three nominees would be confirmed. It was the policy of the Senate, he said, to allow the President to have the people he wanted in his Administration. Fulbright went on, however, to say that some specific questions needed clarification. He wore a long slim visor; and that, together with the bright lights, gave him something of the appearance of a man running a roulette table.

Sitting approximately eight feet to Walter's right rear, I could feel the intensity of the physical and mental heat being engendered. Walter had obviously been well coached and knew his business. A former Philadelphia publishing tycoon, he had sold his Triangle Publications in order to take the position in London. His interrogation droned on and on, covering difficult personal questions going back as far as thirty-five years. Walter fielded these beautifully, I thought. Then he made the error of violating Bill Macomber's advice by volunteering that he intended, if confirmed, to refurbish the Embassy in London. Eyebrows were raised, especially by those who knew and admired his predecessor, Ambassador David Bruce. Walter thus came in for some petty criticisms which lasted for a few weeks, although the intensity was not noticeable to me at the moment. When Walter was finished—or rather when Fulbright was finished with him—I looked at my watch and noted that his questioning had required an hour and forty-five minutes. When, I wondered, would I ever get out of this place?

Jake Beam was next, and Senator Clifford Case of New Jersey spoke for him. Senator Javits, though from New York, seconded. Being a professional Foreign Service officer, Beam came in for little static. He had been the American ambassador in Prague when the Soviets had invaded in March of 1968, and he had previously developed stature as our unofficial link with the Red Chinese years back when ambassador to Poland. The questions put to him were substantive and respectful, pertaining to the situation in Eastern Europe and American-Soviet relations. His confirmation, especially, was a foregone conclusion.

My own interrogation proved to be an anticlimax. Most of the committee members, including my friends, had gotten up and wandered out of the room by the time I reached the stand. Senator Fulbright, whatever his attitude has been toward the Executive Branch since that time, was kind and considerate. He even welcomed me, saying, "Very glad to have you here this morning, Mr. Eisenhower." He asked about my background, which I described and asked if I meant to make the Foreign Service a career.

"No, sir," I answered. "I think that in view of the vagaries of politics, such would be rather impractical."

"Hmmph," Fulbright snorted. "In your case you could probably manage to do so." He then proceeded to ask me about *The Bitter Woods*. Somewhat apologetically he remarked that he had not read it, but he asked if it contained anything offensive to the Belgians. I said no.

Senator Claiborne Pell of Rhode Island, a former Foreign Service officer, endeared himself to me by asking a couple of substantive questions about Belgium itself. Having done so much homework, like a schoolboy, I wanted some chance to prove it. Pell asked about the existence of a third linguistic group within Belgium. I leapt on the question and explained that, in addition to the Flemings and Walloons,[2] a substantial German element existed in eastern Belgium. Three districts had been ceded from Germany to Belgium as the result of the Treaty of Versailles. Pell seemed satisfied.

The hearings over, I returned to my hotel to call Mother at Walter Reed. But somehow I felt inclined to stop in on the way home anyhow.

This was the moment, mentioned before, when the Boss showed his first sign of despondency.

From the period of the Boss's passing on March 28 to his burial, the events have been well reported. We bore the grueling events of the state funeral with remarkable ease, largely because of the relief we all felt that Dad's suffering was over. Mother was at her best. As soon as the bells began tolling that late day in March, President Nixon and a sizable entourage appeared at Ward Eight for a short call. Then the family moved to the Washington Hilton. Friends came and went that same night, and within a couple of days heads of state from all over the world began to pour in. President de Gaulle was particularly touching when he leaned over to Mother and said, *"Vous savez que le General était près de mon coeur."* Mother, while not understanding word for word, got the sentiment.

Before leaving for Abilene I was able to pay my respects to King

---

[2] "Walloon" is the term for Belgians from the French-speaking southern region of the country. "Francophone" pertains to all French-speakers, in both Wallonia and Brussels.

Baudouin, of the Belgians, one of those who had come for the funeral. From the outset I was much taken with his forthrightness and sincerity. He admonished me, "Whatever happens, always tell me the truth."

The subdued but impressive rail trip to Dad's home town of Abilene ended Friday morning, exactly one week after his death.

* * *

In mid-afternoon of May 13, 1969, Barbara and I stood on the bridge of the Dover-Ostend ferry which plied its way between the United Kingdom and the westernmost seaport of Belgium. At Ostend we were met by the U.S. deputy chief of mission, Melvin Manfull and his wife Suzie. We then boarded a train in the heat and soon were on our way to Brussels. Upon arrival at the railway station we were greeted by a distinguished group, which included Dr. Harlan Cleveland, outgoing U.S. ambassador to NATO and John Robert Schaetzel, U.S. ambassador to the Common Market.

Almost immediately Barbara and I were ushered to a black Cadillac limousine, which seemed about the length of a destroyer, and gratefully plunked ourselves down in the cool rear seat. An American flag flapped from the right fender and a blue ambassadorial flag from the left. "Boy, this is quite a car," I thought. "I wonder who it belongs to." It turned out that the car belonged to the U. S. Government and, with its chauffeur, was assigned to me for the length of my stay.

At the Embassy Residence we were greeted by the servants and a few members of the Embassy staff. As we walked slowly through the main hallway, observing its overstuffed French furniture and impressive brass staircase, I paused a second and gaped at two huge Belgian tapestries on the wall. "Somewhere in this house," I growled, "I'm going to have one room *strictly* American, with plain furniture and straight legs—and cowboys and Indians on the wall." I was obviously sustaining the first symptoms of mild cultural shock.

The big event, the presentation of credentials to the King, was scheduled for the next morning, May 14. This ceremony is tantamount, from an ambassador's point of view, to inauguration for a President. Ordinarily several days pass between an ambassador's arrival and his presentation of credentials, but in this case there was reason to hurry. The King was planning to leave for the United States in two days and remain there for two or three weeks. This hurry-up was essential, for only after the credentials are presented is an ambassador able to function in his job.

At 10 A.M., decked out in white tie, tails, and top hat, I met with the five Embassy counselors and the chief of the Military Assistance and Advisory Group (MAAG). Lieutenant General Georges Vivario, chairman of the Belgian Chiefs of Staff, joined us. At the appointed time, after a couple of other new ambassadors had gone before, General Vivario and I climbed into the car and slowly followed a spectacular troop of horse guards around the corner of the National Park to the Royal Palace. When ushered into the reception room at the palace where the King was waiting to receive us, I marched forward alone. In formal, prescribed words, I presented the departure papers of my predecessor, Ambassador Ridgway B. Knight, and then my own credentials. Following this ritual, I introduced the five Embassy officers to the King. I was surprised that I had a little difficulty—stage fright—but hoped that my awkwardness was not too apparent. After all, I was tired.

This short ceremony over, the King ushered me into the next room. After a brief conversation he made a little remark or gesture to indicate that the time had come to leave. I arose and the King walked me slowly to the door.

The champagne that day tasted especially good.

The traditional *vin d'honneur* at the Embassy completed, I joined Barbara for luncheon. We had hardly finished the soup when the telephone rang. I took the call in the kitchen and was startled when the voice on the other end said, "His Majesty would like to speak to you." The King immediately came on the line, totally dispensing with the formalities of the morning. When he went back to the United States, he said, he was anxious to view both the lift-off of Apollo X at Cape Kennedy and the splashdown in the Pacific several days later. Could I please arrange it? I returned to the luncheon table shaking my head. "They go into action pretty fast around this place," I thought.

I surmised, of course, that this call could not have been the King's first effort. Undoubtedly the Belgian Government had tried unsuccessfully to make the arrangements through "other" channels. Otherwise the King would never resort to such a direct approach. Possibly he believed I was in contact with the President continually by telephone. After a hurried meal, I called Charles Tanguy, my backstop in Washington, and laid the matter in his lap. If it was physically possible for NASA to comply with the King's request and it was still denied, I said, I would go to the White House myself, if necessary. I feared that the King might have been thwarted only by the lethargy of bureaucracy. That afternoon Charlie called back to explain that it was an impossibility: even the President couldn't see both lift-off and splashdown as the carrier that was to pick up the astronauts would leave port before the lift-off. I phoned my regrets to the King's residence and followed this up with a short note. My first flurry of activity in office ended with a whimper.

Next began the extensive rounds of prescribed calls. For the Belgians, they included at least a dozen or more important ministers, plus provincial governors and a few mayors. But traditionally a new ambassador also calls on members of the diplomatic corps who have presented credentials before him. If this criterion were to be observed literally in Brussels, that would mean some ninety-two calls on ambassadors alone! To find a reasonable compromise, I turned to the Belgian chief of protocol, Ambassador Carlos van Bellinghen, who set the tone for such things. The Belgian Government, Carlos said, requested only that I call on the ambassadors from NATO countries. I included more, countries of special interest to the United States. In retrospect, however, one of my regrets is that I did not expand the list even further. I later received word that a couple of ambassadors whose countries were friendly to the United States had remarked on the unintentional slight.

Belgium is a small country, but its importance in the world scheme far transcends its minuscule size—about one third that of Pennsylvania—and its population of nine million people. The reason for its significance lies partly in its geography. Normally, Americans, when thinking of Europe, place themselves in Paris and visualize Belgium as being in the North. Actually, Belgium is located centrally in Western Europe. Holland, Germany, Scandinavia, and Britain stretch far to the north of it.

When dealing with strictly bilateral issues between the United States and Belgium, one of the adjustments an American must make is to think small. Previously, as a major in Joint War Plans, Army General Staff, I used to study Navy's plans for fourteen or sixteen aircraft carriers (CVAs); now, as ambassador, I was urging the Belgians to maintain their NATO commitment, thinking in terms of a handful of mine sweepers.

Belgium is sound economically. When I arrived she boasted a gross national product of about $23.6 billion and per capita income of about $2,000. Lacking rich natural resources, she is basically a processing country, depending on the industry and skills of her people. Thus the mayor of Brugge (Bruges) could point good-humoredly at Russian logs sitting on one dock of his port, Zeebrugge, and then point in the other direction to indicate its end product, plywood, awaiting shipment to the United States. Through such manufacturing the Belgians maintain a slightly favorable balance of payments.

Industry is highly varied; it seems that a little bit of everything is manufactured in Belgium. The largest product is steel, produced by smelting iron ore from Northern France with coal imported from America. This industry probably should have gone by the board when Belgian coal became no longer competitive, but the Belgian Government, always concerned about unemployment, takes on the burden of subsidy, regardless of inefficiency. The government has been described as *laissez faire* economically and a welfare state socially.

The major problem that Belgium faces in the administration of its affairs is that of the cleft between the two major languages, Flemish and French. Outsiders tend to overlook the importance of Flemish in Belgium, as the Belgians conduct the bulk of their business with the other countries in French. However, internally, the feeling between the Francophones and the Flemings, who now comprise 60 per cent of the population, is strong.

The problem has arisen mostly during this century. The Flemings, formerly downtrodden, have become as well off as the Francophones economically and they are growing more rapidly. As a result, the Belgian Government has become highly structured to ensure equality between the two language groups. Nine of the eighteen ministers of government must be registered Flemings; nine, Francophones. (The Prime Minister is theoretically neutral.) The question of language has some bearing on nearly every problem faced by the Belgian Government.

Administratively, the country is divided into nine provinces, as established by Napoleon I. The governors are appointed for life by the King and exert no real power. To keep the balance, the four northern provinces are officially Flemish; the four southern provinces (Wallonia), French. The central province, Brabant, is divided, with the demarcation line running just between Brussels and Waterloo, twelve miles south. The fact that predominantly French-speaking Brussels continues to expand into the surrounding Flemish territory is one of the sore points in the linguistic issue.

Politically, the important unit of the country is the commune, a small political entity varying in population between 50 and 250,000. In a country of 12,000 square miles, 2,500 communes are recognized, for an average of less than five square miles apiece!

In common with most Western European countries, Belgium has a parliamentary government, in this case with a constitutional monarch and a parliament of two houses. In the Senate and Chamber of Deputies three major parties are each sufficiently strong that no single one will, in the foreseeable future, be able to form a government on its own. The largest and oldest of these, and commonly considered the center party, is the Social Christian, formerly known as the Catholic party. The party of the left is the Socialist, formed early in this century. Bourgeois despite its name, the Socialist party has been credited with preventing the Communists in Belgium from making significant progress. The party of the right is the Liberal party—"liberal" in the Jeffersonian sense. It is the party of the counts and barons and, more importantly, of the financial establishment.

Aside from the major parties, two splinter groups are just emerging. These, the Volksunie in Flanders and the Francophone Front in Wallonia and Brussels, share a common objective: to increase the linguistic split. Both contemplate a federation of two regions in place of the present unified government. Their influence is growing.

These are matters that the American ambassador in Brussels observes and reports on to Washington (largely through his staff). But he seldom discusses them with the Belgian Government. They are internal affairs; and while the Belgians are perfectly willing to supply us with all the facts, they are not matters for negotiation between the two countries.

The relations between Belgium and the United States were so cordial that rarely did a question come up—perhaps once a month—that required a serious discussion between an American ambassador and the Foreign Minister. And when they did, the subject was usually—not always—involved with economics. On the political side, the Belgian Foreign Minister (M. Pierre Harmel) was useful as a sounding board and bridge between the United States and others of the NATO Allies. Occasionally we asked for Belgian support in the United Nations. But on the whole one had to admit that a very large part of the ambassador's job was public relations, with much emphasis on ceremonies and social events.

Every year the American ambassador in Brussels traditionally talks to many organizations, American and Belgian. He reads the lesson at two American churches every Thanksgiving Day. At first, this dictation of the ambassador's traditional duties irritated me, particularly as I suspected that any activity once observed automatically attained "traditional" status.

I was honored, however, to speak on Memorial Day at the three American ceremonies. I probably shed more sweat per word on these speeches than on any other I have made. True, I had previously lectured professionally for a while and was pretty much at ease on my feet. But the solemnity of these Memorial Day services, coupled with the difficulty of finding anything original to say, required every scrap of imagination I could muster. Memorial Day of 1969 would be of particular significance; my father had died only two months earlier. And whether I liked it or not, the Belgians still regarded me more as the Boss's son than as the American ambassador.

These Memorial Day talks, difficult as they were, remain in my mind as the most worthwhile ceremonial activities in which I participated.

After Dad's death I had suggested that Mother come and take her ease with Barbara and me while she reoriented herself to a new life. We were delighted when she accepted.

Mother arrived late one rainy afternoon after a long trip from Le Havre to Brussels. She had rested up during her voyage on the *United States* and was excited to be in Europe. Milton Eisenhower, my uncle, made the trip with her. Also along, of course, was her normal Secret Service contingent and a volume of baggage so awesome that I irreverently named it the Second Invasion of Normandy. Without inhibition Mother unpacked two impressive paintings of herself and Dad, taken from the walls of the Gettysburg house, and had them hung on the walls of the Grand Salon. There they remained during our entire time in Brussels.

Mother's visit was particularly well timed, since Barbara's first trip to Brussels was short, just to examine her future home. Because Sue and Mary Jean were still in school back home, Barbara had returned ten days after arrival. Thus, for my first month in Brussels, I had Mother on hand to act as my hostess and as my companion. She renewed acquaintance with many of the people she had met in former days, when Dad had been Supreme Commander, Allied Powers in Europe. Others, such as the King, she had first met in Washington ten years before.

Mother and I were invited to the Royal Palace at Laeken where we spent a couple of delightful, informal hours with King Baudouin and Queen Fabiola. One evening, when a conflict of schedules made it impossible for me to be in two places at once, Mother stood in. While no longer a part of official protocol, she was indeed treated like a queen by all. For this I was particularly grateful.

In my years as a civilian I had been used to an easy informality with my friends, co-workers, and even strangers. While people occasionally addressed me as "Colonel"—a habit I did not encourage (I dealt with too many generals)—I was formally referred to as "Mr." but more often as "John." Now in Brussels the title was "Mr. Ambassador" to Americans and *"Son Excellence"* to the Europeans. (Actually, no American is properly addressed as "Excellency,"[3] but it was the local custom.) Being set off alone to such a degree required a bit of mental adjustment.

The attitude of the Foreign Service people toward the office of ambassador is fairly understandable since Foreign Service officers struggle up the bureaucratic ladder for twenty years, usually longer, to attain this position. And these struggles are not always in pleasant, comfortable, or even safe surroundings. Americans at home hardly share the Foreign Service's respect for the position; few American citizens can ever name more than a couple of their ambassadors, and the job is hardly a steppingstone to becoming known. We do call theaters, hotels, and clubs "Ambassador," as the word seems to have a ring of prestige. But it is only in the Foreign Service that it is spoken in hushed tones.

One day during this first month Patricia Saunders, my temporary secretary, brought me an "out" basket for my desk. When I thanked her casually, she hesitated a moment, apologized, and said she was going to replace it with another, a more finished variety with a rim around the base. I was a little surprised: "What's wrong with this one? It's deep; it'll hold lots of papers."

"Oh," she gasped, "that's a *junior* officer's 'out' basket!"

I howled but I also learned a lesson: don't fight it.

After I had been in Brussels about three weeks, the administrative counselor told me that former Ambassador Knight was having second thoughts regarding the magnificent tapestry he had donated to the Embassy, one of the two that hung over the brass staircase. Ridgway had been appointed to another post, Lisbon, and presumably had found use for the tapestry there if we didn't want it in Brussels. I shrugged—then confirmed that we did indeed need the tapestry.

At the middle of June, almost exactly a month after our arrival in Brussels, it was necessary to make a quick trip home. Barbara

[3] George Washington settled that matter for Americans when he was inaugurated President.

and the girls were packing; further, I had to close down my Phoenixville office, put the final touches on arrangements for my personal affairs, and visit Washington again, primarily to deliver an informal message from the King to the President.

When I visited the State Department, I found to my surprise that Ridgway Knight was still in Washington. Over a drink I soon realized that something was on his mind. Finally it came out. "John," he asked, "do you *really* want that tapestry hanging over the staircase in the Residence?"

"Hell, yes, Ridge. That thing really gives character to the staircase. The place would be naked without it."

"Oh, thank God!" he said, slumping back in his chair, "I was told you were going to redo the Residence in Early American."

My astonishment subsided after a few moments when I remembered my casual remark a month before. Something about a room with cowboys and Indians. The State Department underground was not only highly sensitive and active; it was also inventive.

Upon return to Brussels Barbara and I plunged once more into our schedules. We went with Mother to Casteau to see Andy Goodpaster take over as SACEUR; we went through the normal Fourth of July ceremonies; and we arranged two receptions in order to shake hands at least with every member of the Embassy, American and Belgian.[4]

The ambassadorial job has changed considerably in the course of the nation's history. No longer is the ambassador in substance the President's representative. Modern communications have deprived him of independent decision. In 1803 an American chief of mission, Robert R. Livingston (assisted by James Monroe) purchased the Louisiana Territory from Napoleon, committing

[4] There is some misconception on the part of many Americans regarding Embassy social functions of this type. There was indeed a "representation" fund of some $12,000 per year available to the Embassy in Brussels, from which the ambassador could draw, but this fund applied only to the entertainment of persons from outside the United States Government. Thus receptions such as the Fourth of July one were paid for strictly by the ambassador. Nevertheless, refreshments were inexpensive and occasions when the members of the Embassy staff could see the Residence were rare. These receptions were worth every cent we spent.

the United States to pay about $15 million, completely without authority from the government. Such action today would be unthinkable. Indeed, modern communications have now made it so that an ambassador now rarely, if ever, even corresponds with the President. If a problem of sufficient importance should arise he could go to the top, as I had threatened Charlie Tanguy two hours after presenting credentials. But it would be a radical act.

Considering that Belgium had few problems of emergency magnitude with the United States, I never found it necessary to write or call the President directly. To obtain authority for an action involving substantive decisions, I would normally send my recommendations to some selected person in the State Department—and hope that I had chosen the right one. Or, now and then, I might go directly to a White House staff officer or to a cabinet member. But even in doing that, it was only decent to inform Charlie, the so-called "country director" in State to minimize anguish when the problem would come back down to him. All this can be summed up simply: the ambassador today rarely, if ever, acts on his own in substantive matters.

The crux of the ambassadorial job in Brussels, nevertheless, still remained that of constituting the primary link between the United States government and the host country. This involved presenting the American government's views in such a way that they would be understood by the local government—at least to the extent that Washington wanted them understood. Further, I was to obtain the precise views of the host country—to the extent that they wanted them to be precise. Then, along with my own interpretations and recommendations, I made them known to the proper people at home.

Actually, the modern ambassador has become to a large degree a public relations officer. This function in a capital like Brussels is practically open-ended. Rare is the night that the ambassador and his wife are not invited to a reception, a recital, or a dinner. Many invitations are a potential waste of time; and the ambassador must be selective in how he dissipates his energies. Each one must develop some device for achieving occasional respite. One former American ambassador to Belgium filled at least one evening of his week with a private engagement involving a certain Belgian friend.

Only the ambassador and his close personal staff were aware that this friend was nonexistent. On my part, I felt I had little excuse for refusing any invitation for which there was no conflict—provided I was in town. Hence our frequent weekend trips to a house we rented in the Ardennes, the territory with which I was so familiar.

To me the easiest and most rewarding function on a day-to-day basis was administration of the American Embassy itself. Here, as ambassador and head of the so-called "country team," I supervised the activities not only of the State Department people but those of the Defense Department, United States Information Service, Department of Agriculture, and others. In Brussels the European headquarters of the Federal Aviation Agency (having jurisdiction from the East Coast of the United States to the Indian Ocean) and the European office of aerospace research came under my theoretical, though hardly close, supervision. With these agencies, which just happened to have their headquarters located in Brussels, my main function was to insure that their activities did nothing to injure the American presence locally.

During my first meetings with the "small staff"—the DCM, the political, economic, and administrative counselors; defense attaché, and others—I experienced a natural discomfiture. As the newcomer among a group of professionals, all of whom had been in Brussels for a couple of years (five years in the case of two of them), I realized that on any given subject I was the novice. At times I felt talked down to. Nobody committed this error on purpose. Loyalty was no problem. To these people an ambassador is an ambassador, regardless of background, with the future of his subordinates at least partially in his hands. The difficulty in communication stemmed from the fact that these men had been together so long that they had become a family among themselves. While they earnestly sought to be of as much help as possible, they could hardly avoid mentioning personalities and incidents unknown to me. As we sat comfortably in my long, narrow office, away from the desk and down at the "social" end, I sometimes had difficulty staying with the conversation. The first time someone blithely referred to the "L-O-C," I was taken aback. "The Yellow Sea!" I burst out. "What the hell do we have to do with that? It's between China and Korea!" (The LOC is the "line of communications" in Germany.)

Most of this chatter, I later realized, stemmed from a natural desire on the part of my officers to impress me; one counselor, for example, tended to become loquacious when tense and he monopolized the conversation at times. As a result, I directed that the meetings be made formal; we would meet in the conference room, each individual in a prescribed place. Mel Manfull would precede me, ascertain what each individual intended to cover, and then, on my arrival, would call on each to speak his piece. It was an artificial format that I disliked but it worked, and from then on we stuck much better to business. With the passage of time, after I had the opportunity to visit at some length with each officer outside of meetings, I became fond of all of them. The nervous talker, a true expert on Belgium, became a good friend, and I have since done everything in my power to further his career. But there is no question that at first I felt somewhat apart from the staff.

By the time I left Brussels I had cut back drastically on the number of small-staff meetings and had moved the location back to my more comfortable office. By then I enjoyed the informality, and after ordinary transfers of staff I had now been in Brussels longer than almost any of the others. Now I was in on the "in" jokes.

The running of the Embassy and the official chores, even the ceremonial ones, were functions in which I had some previous experience. The aspect of diplomatic life for which I was quite unprepared was the close relationship between normal business and one's private life. An ambassador has virtually no private life at all.

The most disturbing aspect of our family situation was the centrifugal effect our official life had on the individual members. Each was preoccupied with his own problems, each so busy that communication between us was difficult. One day in August 1969, after a difficult evening at home, I exercised one of my idiosyncrasies of writing out what was on my mind. The sequence, only slightly exaggerated, gives some idea of the strains that a diplomatic atmosphere can have on a family:

The cast of characters includes Barbara; our married daughter, Anne (planning to return home to Bogota, Colombia); Susan; Mary Jean; two butlers; and John. John at one end of the table, Barbara at the other, Mary on John's left, Anne and Sue on the other side facing kitchen. Table shined to a high polish and the $1000 chandelier hangs overhead. On Barbara's right is a large screen covering the kitchen door. It is baroque in design and the only interesting panel is one of Cupid and Psyche, Cupid obviously up to no good. Both parents have finished their cocktail and the children are hungry:

MARY: Why do you seat me on this side? I can't stand this side. You know it.

BARBARA: What difference does it make? You've got to learn to sit on both sides of the table.

JOHN: September sure is going to be the hell of a month. I'm stacked up already so there's not a free minute.

MARY: Guess what I just got—a letter from Jimmy Smith.

ANNE: Can you believe I'm a hundred pounds overweight in my baggage?

MARY: I should be getting one from Billy Jones too.

BARBARA: How do you like this cook we're trying out? He's new.

JOHN: It all tastes the same to me.

ANNE: Do you really suppose they will charge three dollars a pound overweight?

SUE: I think Albert is really cool. I hope that Henri doesn't find out about him.

JOHN: I think we'd better go to the Ardennes this weekend and get a last rest before September.

MARY: I think I had better do my hair before Terry gets back.

ANNE: Do you suppose I ought to send that hundred pounds air freight? The chances are only about seventy-five per cent of it would arrive.

JOHN: Damn it, I'll pay the whole overweight if I can just have some peace and quiet.

(All this while the two butlers do their jobs. Milano, a rather effeminate individual, who has just finished six weeks' unauthorized leave in Italy—and has had a breakup with his boy friend—is in a desolate state of mind.

Anton, a Spaniard whose French is as bad as John's, has a short career ahead of him, as he has been caught leering at the girls and going through a chest of drawers.

(Milano pours wine. The conversation continues.)

SUE: I don't want to go to the Ardennes, I can't stand the Ardennes.

MARY: I don't like it either.

(By this time John has given up on the conversation and is sitting gripping the table with white knuckles, spending half the time looking at the ceiling.)

BARBARA: I can't really talk about this house in here because we'll be overheard. Let's get together after dinner.

MARY: I think Terry is so cool.

SUE (*turning to Mary*): Yeah, we've heard about that. (*Turning to John.*) I don't see why you guys can't let me stay home from the Ardennes.

JOHN: I see no reason why you shouldn't.

MILANO (*to John*): Vin?

JOHN: Yes please, fill it up.

(By now dinner is over; Barbara looks perplexed.)

BARBARA: How many coffees?

JOHN: None for me.

BARBARA: How do you say "one coffee"?

JOHN: My God, Barbara, haven't you had that in class? *"Une tasse de café."*

BARBARA (*turning to Anton*): *"Une tasse de café."*

ANTON (*looking superior*): *"Un tasse."*

JOHN (*irritated*): *"UNE TASSE"! "Tasse"* is feminine!

SUE (*turning to John*): Don't be so tough on these people, Dad. (*Turning to Barbara.*) I'd like one, too.

(The family leaves.)

JOHN (*turning to Anton*): Deux tasses de café—aussi brandy grande, s'il vous plait.

(The family leaves the congenial dinner and each goes his own way.)

It soon became apparent that Barbara's chores as administrator of the household were every bit as difficult as were mine in the Chancery, if not more so. The Embassy Residence is a large and ornate establishment requiring a staff of some seven people. As local domestic help is nearly impossible to find in Belgium, the servants in the household consisted largely of Italians, Spanish, and Portuguese. At one time we calculated that the household consisted of two whose basic language was French, one Flemish, one German, one Italian, one Spanish, and one Spanish Basque. My efforts to communicate with a Spaniard in French, as illustrated above, often resulted in little less than disaster.

Another area in which Barbara assumed full responsibility was that of decorating the Embassy. The basic furniture of the Residence was magnificent—luxurious couches, beautiful woodwork, immaculate dining-room sets, ornate chandeliers—but, according to custom, the place was practically devoid of art. Barbara began by operating through "normal" channels—the State Department "Arts in the Embassies" program. This program had fallen into a condition of considerable disrepair. Among other difficulties, the paintings available were practically all modern impressionistic —hardly the thing to go with the formal, European ground floor.

As a result, Barbara turned to other sources. She wrote directly to various people. Andrew Wyeth in Chadds Ford, Pennsylvania, graciously agreed to send us two striking water colors; through Bo Horkan she obtained three magnificent paintings from the National Gallery of Art. The ground floor of the Embassy finally boasted the Wyeth water colors, two Canalettos, one huge painting by Arthur Devis, an Archipenko sculpture, "Josephine," and several pieces of Steuben glass from the Eisenhower Center at Abilene. Mrs. Floyd Gates of Philadelphia lent a personal family painting. With this assistance, Barbara was able to create an atmosphere in the reception area of which any ambassador and my country could be proud.

The summer and early fall of 1969 were active seasons. On July 21 (European time) the crew of Apollo XI made the first

landing on the surface of the moon. Along with millions everywhere, we in Brussels sat up through the night watching as the two
American astronauts took their first precarious steps. By the next
day the relief and joy of the Belgians was such that I honestly
believe it transcended our own.

This episode provided my first inkling of the degree to which
exploration of space can reach beyond national boundaries and
ideologies. The day the Apollo XI crew rested on the moon, July
22, 1969, I attended the Polish National Day reception. Here at
their Embassy I was greeted effusively by the ambassador and
cordially congratulated by the Soviet chargé d'affaires. As I was
preparing to leave, I felt a tap on my shoulder and a rather smallish
fellow with black curly hair threw his arms around me. After
bubbling forth his congratulations, he identified himself as the
president of the Belgian Communist party.

Perplexed, I returned to the American Embassy. Reporting the
incident briefly to Washington, I called in the political counselor,
George Moffitt, and told him what had happened. Looking over
his glasses and puffing on his pipe, George chuckled, "Well, that
rather makes sense, Mr. Ambassador. This Communist party here
in Belgium is the most bourgeois in Europe."

A complicating feature of the fall of 1969, which we should
have foreseen, was the twenty-fifth anniversary of the liberation
of Belgium by the Allies. This event was to be celebrated in great
cities and hamlets alike, each one on the day its own liberation
had occurred. Brussels celebrated this event on September 14 in
the Grand Place; Bastogne, on September 28. One of the high
points of these liberation ceremonies was the opportunity to renew
acquaintances with distinguished American generals, all of whom
had helped me in writing *The Bitter Woods*.[5]

At the Grand Place ceremony on September 14 I felt a little
chagrined about the appearance of the U.S. troops who were
placed next to the magnificent British Guardsmen. All of our
platoon-sized unit managed to make it out the same street, though
not noticeably in step. I could only lean over and congratulate
my friend Sir John Beith, the British ambassador, on the appearance of his guardsmen. It was an odd thing that the United States

[5] Generals Ridgway, McAuliffe, Taylor, and later, Mark Clark.

was spending approximately $80 billion a year on defense at that time, yet remained so parsimonious in matters of military representation.

The other major liberation ceremony in which I was involved was that held two weeks later at Bastogne, in the Ardennes. The King and General McAuliffe were in attendance. My role here was active, as this was an American show. I laid a wreath immediately following King Baudouin's and then proceeded to the rostrum to give a brief talk. Speaking before the King was another "Eisenhower first."

During this period, although I hardly realized it, I was continuing to undergo a somewhat extended, subconscious grieving period for the Boss. When he had died the previous March, the relief we all felt for him at the end of his suffering had made us artificially cheerful. Almost immediately after the end of the week of public ceremonies, I had plunged into action in preparation for Brussels. Being so occupied in the ensuing months, I had never had the chance to pause and endure the pain that accompanied the passing of a person who had been such an overpowering factor in my life. As a result, the residue remained for an inordinate length of time—the doctors told me to expect the effects for as long as a year. I felt the pangs only periodically, when my feelings would well up—fortunately always in private. One cartoon by Bill Mauldin, hardly known as a friend of the officer corps, got to me more than any other trigger. It depicted a World War II cemetery with a caption, "Pass the word; it's Ike himself." On seeing that cartoon in *National Geographic* one evening I went to my bedroom and sobbed. Barbara stuck her head in, took a look, and closed the door.

In the autumn of 1969 some Republicans in Pennsylvania were justifiably concerned regarding the upcoming 1970 gubernatorial election. Some—it is impossible to gauge the number—felt that I should come home immediately to be a candidate. Such a contention was manifestly ridiculous. My position as chairman of Citizens for Nixon-Agnew in Pennsylvania had not been sufficient to give me much political horsepower. But far more important was the fact that I could not, even had I desired, leave my post in Brussels so soon. The feelings of the Belgians would have been injured and the national interest would suffer; it would have been better never to have gone to Brussels in the first place. To anyone making inquiries as to my intentions, therefore, I would simply say that my place was in Brussels.

By circumstance—its central location, its hospitality, and its lack of position as a world power—Belgium has attracted organizations of sufficient importance for Brussels to be considered the "Capital of Europe." Besides the ninety-three foreign missions are also the political headquarters of the North Atlantic alliance (NATO), and the Common Market (EEC), each with its own American ambassador. Furthermore, because of Belgian hospitality to American business, our firms in Europe tend to locate their European headquarters in Brussels. Thus the American ambassador finds visitors in abundance flooding in from the United States every year. Very few of our governmental officials come on strictly Belgian business. Nevertheless, the ambassador, as the local representative of the President, is sought out, regardless of the purpose of the visitor's presence in Brussels.

One of the regrettable aspects of the ambassador's frantic schedule is the fact that the visitors from the United States are almost always intensely interesting people, people that one would wish he could spend hours with in conversation. The pace of life, especially during the fall season, is such that conversation with each is usually limited to a visit in the office, a drink at 6:30 P.M., or at the most a dinner. To name just a few we entertained in only a short period: Senator Karl Mundt; William Replogle, ambassador to Iceland; Daniel Patrick Moynihan, ecology expert on the White House Staff; Robert Duggan, a political cohort from 1968; Philip Crowe, ambassador to Norway; Secretary of Agriculture Clifford Hardin; Ambassador and Mrs. Walter Annenberg from London; the Reverend Billy Graham; Under Secretary of State Elliot Richardson; Secretary of State and Mrs. William P. Rogers; Secretary of Defense Melvin R. Laird; Arthur Turner, president of Northwood Institute; pianist Arthur Rubinstein; my predecessor, Ambassador Ridgway Knight; and former Secretary of the Treasury Robert Anderson.

On October 8 the astronauts of Apollo XI, Neil Armstrong, Michael Collins, and Edwin ("Buzz") Aldrin, the men we had all watched on television three months earlier, were scheduled to arrive in Brussels. The program, a major exercise in detailed planning, had been set up to occupy nearly all their waking moments—too much, I thought, though I deferred to their schedule, which had been set up in Washington.

The party arrived from Paris—the astronauts, their wives, and others, obviously showing the strain of their minute-by-minute program. A couple of them had been suffering from severe colds. "After all, Mrs. Eisenhower," said one of them to Barbara, "three Kings in one day is a little bit much!"[6]

The party called on King Baudouin first. As the five of us—the King, the astronauts, and I—sat in a circle, he asked in his very intense manner what the crew had been thinking about the universe and its significance while traveling through space. Mike Collins simply answered, "Your Majesty, on the next trip you'd better send a poet or a philosopher." I interjected that I doubted one could be found to volunteer. The King took this American levity in good stride.

The next group to arrive was a flood of high-level parliamentarians known as the North Atlantic Assembly (NAA). Soon thereafter the deputy foreign ministers of NATO arrived. At the same time as the NAA meeting, President Joseph Mobutu of the Congo arrived in Brussels for a state visit. During a reception at the Royal Palace I talked with him for a few moments. I found him, on the surface at least, to be a smooth and urbane man. Impressive in his military uniform, he inquired about the health of my mother and asked if she still lived in Gettysburg. Possibly Mobutu's ill-concealed ambition to substitute some American investment for Belgian in his country accounted for my being singled out for special attention, however brief.

During the first week of December came the regular meeting of the Foreign Ministers of NATO. The United States was represented by Secretary of State Rogers, with Secretary of Defense Laird and Secretary of Treasury David M. Kennedy in attendance. The presence of the three large delegations—State, Defense, and

---

[6] A slight inaccuracy, as France is a republic. Holland has a queen.

Treasury—was enough to tax the Administrative Section to its fullest. When we learned of the exact dates of the meeting, both Robert Ellsworth, U.S. ambassador to NATO, and I independently sent invitations to Secretary and Mrs. Rogers to stay in our respective residences.[7] We were notified that the Rogerses would stay in the Embassy Residence the first two nights and then pack up and move to the Ellsworths' home for the last two. Thus the whole arrangement worked out to the maximum inconvenience of the Rogerses.

Probably the Rogerses were just as happy to leave the Residence and move to the relative quiet of the Ellsworths' house. The one guest room in the Residence, unfortunately, is located on Rue Ducale, a popular thruway for speeding sports cars and Hondas. Mufflers are not required on European cars.[8] When Bill Rogers and I were driving to the airport on his departure, Bill asked me, rather diffidently, if the master bedroom was situated on the same street as the guest room. I hurriedly assured him that it was, in the forlorn hope that a country house for the American ambassador was in his mind. The only answer, however, was a low "Hmmmmmmmmm." The next year the Rogerses stayed at the Brussels-Hilton.

On December 20 a celebration was held in the Grand Place in Brussels, exactly twenty-five years after the Germans attacked Bastogne during the Battle of the Bulge. The ritual itself in front of the Hôtel de Ville was rather brief. A couple of short speeches were made in French. I then found myself on the balcony of the Hôtel de Ville with a sizable crowd staring up from the cobblestones below. Someone tapped me on the shoulder and handed me a double handful of large walnuts to be tossed down to the multitudes. I was embarrassed; something kept flashing in my mind, like "Let them eat cake." Nevertheless, I complied, only to glance back and discover that lined up behind me were six full

7 Rogers was there on NATO business—on the other hand, we were old friends; he had been Attorney General in the Boss's cabinet.

8 "It is absolutely impossible to sleep anywhere in the City. The perpetual traffic of wagons in the narrow winding streets . . . is sufficient to wake the dead." *The Satires of Juvenal*, A.D. 117.

sacks, each about the size of a twenty-pound bag of charcoal—and all waiting to be dropped.

I solved this dilemma when I discovered several young boys standing below with large open sacks. Here at least were youngsters willing to accept a scratch on the head in hopes of carrying home a few walnuts. I aimed for the open bags; no casualties resulted, to the best of my knowledge. Thus the medieval custom of throwing coins to the poor at Christmas had been brought up to date to commemorate the one-word message of defiance, "Nuts," issued a quarter century before by Anthony McAuliffe in reply to German demands for the surrender of Bastogne.

This was too good not to share with General McAuliffe. Accordingly, I wrote him a description of the incident:

> . . . I surmise that for decades to come walnuts will be dropped from the balcony of the Hôtel de Ville even after the significance of your terminology—"nuts"—exactly twenty-five years ago today, has been forgotten. Quite possibly tradition will dictate that walnuts have been dropped from said location since the tenth century.

The general's answer speaks for itself:

Helen and I were greatly amused by your report on the walnut dropping . . .

About fifteen years ago, some of my paratroopers stationed around Munich persuaded the American Nut Growers Association to provide many pounds of nuts to be dropped to the children of Bastogne. Our guys made parachute packages, somehow got a C-47, and did the job. It got a fine play in the press.

M. Henri Spaak was Prime Minister at the time. He told me that he received a letter from the Burgomaster of Waterloo saying that he had read with pleasure of the ceremony at Bastogne but hoped that it would not set a precedent which might be followed at Waterloo. (Le mot de Cambronne.)[9]

This is only one of hundreds of vulgar stories that have resulted from this one innocent word . . .

[9] The "mot," a terse term, translates into English as an earthy four-letter word. General Cambronne became famous for this outburst when, commanding Napoleon's Old Guard, he was commanded by the British to surrender after Waterloo. "Mot de Cambronne" has become a sort of substitute swear word in French.

Baudouin I, King of the Belgians, is a truly remarkable man. Together with his Queen Fabiola, he exerts a considerable force for good in his divided country. Through his tact, democratic demeanor, and masterful way of avoiding identification as *Wallon* or *Flamand,* he does all that can be expected of a modern monarch to bring those two disparate groups together. And the Belgians, always conscious of the small physical size of their country, can look to their King and Queen and say that their royal couple is the most attractive reigning pair in all Europe.

By nature King Baudouin is quiet, serious, and intense, prone to direct, personal observations. During one of our early encounters he looked me in the eye and asked, "Do you run a formal embassy?" He then took a second look and said thoughtfully, with only a faint touch of a smile, "No, you couldn't run a formal embassy." I took this as a compliment.

My encounters with him were frequent, considering that most ambassadors, even the American, rarely see him alone or even in a small company. We had, by the end of 1969, talked informally several times, including our meeting during his visit to Washington to attend my father's funeral. Once in June he sent for me to convey a personal message on the Congo to President Nixon; later I was granted a few minutes to present a gift from the President, a memento of the Apollo XI mission. In addition to these encounters, Barbara and I attended all the diplomatic receptions, including the rather restricted one in the summer when a score of newly arrived ambassadors formally presented their wives. In these large gatherings the King and Queen worked as a team, ensuring that each guest was afforded the opportunity of a few moments, at least, with one or the other. For each, the King had a special line of chatter; he would, for example, invariably ask Barbara how her French lessons were coming—then he would admonish her to keep trying and to avoid being bashful.

As a result of our visits I had, by the end of 1969, developed a truly warm feeling for the King. It could not really be called a friendship. With the number of diplomatic missions located in Brussels the King could never openly favor one ambassador or even a small group. Nevertheless, he always seemed to regard me with a touch of amusement, and my admiration for him eventually threatened my firm resolve never to develop a case of that disease known in diplomatic circles as "localitis."[10]

King Baudouin is the fifth monarch in Belgium's short history. His predecessors Leopold I, Leopold II, Albert, and Leopold III were all strong and distinctive personalities. Leopold I, the landless prince of the house of Saxe-Coburg was the elected monarch whose entrance into Belgium on July 21, 1831, established the Belgian National Day. Later, as uncle to Queen Victoria of England,[11] he exercised considerable influence on her, particularly after the death of Victoria's consort, Prince Albert (Leopold's kinsman). By his own marriage to Princess Louise, daughter of Louis Philippe of France, Leopold I succeeded in establishing France as an ally. Through his manipulations he gave a small, artificially created country a respectable place on the European map.

Leopold I was succeeded in 1865 by his son, the ambitious Leopold II. Whereas Leopold I had occupied himself with establishing Belgium as a nation of stature within Europe, Leopold II held wider designs. A master builder, and notorious throughout Europe for his greed, Leopold II participated in the slicing up of Black Africa for his own gain. Through the Association Internationale Africaine he obtained enough lands in 1876 to constitute the present Republic of Zaire, holding this vast territory as his own personal possession. As time went on he decided he could no longer afford to retain it as his own and late in his reign finally induced a reluctant Belgian parliament to accept national sovereignty. His impatience with his more cautious countrymen was summed up in one contemptuous outburst: "Small country, small minds."

Knowing Leopold's reputation, Kaiser William II of Germany felt that he could be bought and offered the Belgian King the former territories of Burgundy in exchange for allowing German troops to cross Belgian soil in the event of war with France. But

---

[10] A rather natural tendency to develop such an affinity for the host country as to lose one's perspective. If carried too far, an ambassador can tend to represent the host country rather than the United States.

[11] Leopold's sister was Victoria's mother.

for once Leopold drew the line. Unfortunately for Germany, as it turned out, the Kaiser never completely believed him.

The House of Coburg is one whose history has been beset by tragedy. Carlota, Empress of Mexico, the only daughter of Leopold I, went insane after her husband, Maximilian, was executed in Mexico. One daughter of Leopold II, Stephanie, became the wife of Rudolf of Hapsburg, who was later a presumed suicide at Mayerling. On the death of Leopold II in 1909, the throne passed to his nephew, the reticent but courageous Albert I.

Albert I remains today the national hero of Belgium. As Commander-in-Chief of the Belgian Armed Forces in World War I, he stubbornly resisted the Kaiser's violation of Belgian neutrality, finally withdrawing his forces to a patch of land in the northwest corner of Flanders. He and his army held a portion of the Allied line up to the end of the war and he commanded an army group in the last Allied offensive. Tragically Albert was killed in 1934 by a fall from a cliff in the Ardennes. His wife, Queen Elizabeth, who had been by his side during the trying days of World War I, survived him by thirty years.

Albert's son, Leopold III, turned out to be the most unfortunate of the Coburgs. His immensely popular Queen Astrid was killed in an auto accident in 1935, while Leopold was driving. In 1940, at the end of the "phony war,"[12] Leopold found himself in much the same position as had Albert in early 1914, but this time no "Miracle of the Marne" occurred, as in 1914. Instead, the Nazi armies broke through the Allied lines and dashed to the sea, cutting the British and Belgians in the north from the French in the south. Leopold was forced to surrender on May 28, 1940, only eighteen days after the beginning of the German offensive. The British and French, sorely in need of a scapegoat, raised their voices in his denunciation. Premier Paul Reynaud of France and even the Belgian ministers, who had fled to Paris, joined in the chorus. Not so the Belgian people; they sympathized with Leopold's plight and understood when the Nazis forced him to live in Laeken Palace till 1944. This shrewd move on Hitler's part made the hap-

---

[12] So named because no action took place on the Western front between September 1939 and May 1940, at the start of World War II.

less Leopold a tool of the Nazis by keeping him in the trappings of a monarch.

While at Laeken, Leopold's popularity with his own countrymen diminished, because of a controversial secret marriage to a commoner and two visits to Hitler. Public anger poured down upon his head. Exiled in Switzerland for five years after the war, Leopold finally submitted to a plebiscite to determine whether he should retain his throne. He won by a bare majority, 56 per cent, with a minority in Wallonia. On Leopold's return to Brussels in 1950, the disorder and rioting reached such proportion in Belgium that he was forced to abdicate the following year in favor of his son Baudouin.

The whole series of events left a deep imprint on Leopold and on his son Baudouin as well. It is no wonder that, with such a background of losing his mother, of being imprisoned by the Nazis as a child, and of seeing his father rejected by his subjects, King Baudouin was for some years an austere and distant young monarch. With experience and maturity, however—and with his extremely fortunate marriage to Fabiola, of the Spanish royal family —King Baudouin finally overcame his painful experiences to become the effective monarch that he is today.

During my stay in Belgium I had the privilege of meeting former King Leopold III only once. Most outsiders never see him at all. Sadly, our one meeting grew out of his unfortunate past.

One Saturday in mid-July 1970, I was sitting in my office wondering for once what I was going to do that afternoon. The duty secretary opened the door and informed me that I was wanted on the telephone by Leopold's aide-de-camp. I was not particularly surprised. Some months earlier, on the advice of Carlos van Bellinghen, I had requested an audience with Leopold to present Barbara to him and his wife, Princess de Rethy, as we all had presented our wives to Baudouin and Fabiola a year before. This, I had been informed, was the present King's desire.

When I answered the telephone, however, I was taken aback a little. The aide, Colonel Édouard de Vicq de Cumptich, informed me that Leopold would like to see me. "Oh, not in August, I hope; I plan to be away most of the month."

"No, His Majesty would like to see you as soon as possible."

I was puzzled. "How about this afternoon?"

"Very well, what time is convenient?"

Now I was truly confused; the protocol around royalty rarely give such options. "Is three o'clock all right?"

"Certainly."

"I'll be there."

I notified my driver François, dressed in my most conservative business suit, and arrived at the Domaine d'Argenteuil as scheduled.

I was ushered into Leopold's den, a large, cheerful, comfortable, but unpretentious room, with a desk at the far end and a sofa and easy chairs near the door. Leopold, tall, handsome, erect, spare, with high forehead and white hair, shook hands cordially and motioned me to the sofa. For a few moments he fixed me with a cool, steady, rather detached gaze. I was conscious of his clear blue eyes and of his youthful appearance despite his sixty-nine years. "You are a little young for an ambassador, aren't you?" he asked.

"I suppose so, Your Majesty. I'm forty-seven. But there are some who are younger." We then lapsed into casual conversation, mostly about my background and family.

Soon, however, Leopold produced a newspaper article from the New York *Times* dated June 29, 1970. The title was "Focal Point of Belgian Loyalties—Baudouin." The piece, by Clyde Farnsworth, was mostly accurate and quite favorable to King Baudouin. But a certain paragraph, which attempted to explain Baudouin's initial lack of enthusiasm for ascending the throne, included a statement that obviously hurt Leopold to the quick. Referring to the military campaign of 1940, Farnsworth had written, "Leopold waited for the Germans at Laeken in 1940 and remained there until 1944 and with his two sons and his daughter." This wording meant that Leopold had not even resisted Hitler, a far more serious accusation than mere criticism of his military skill. Leopold wanted me to have this statement "rectified."

On quick examination, I realized Farnsworth's error and promised to do what I could. Leopold was happy. Knowing that I was a writer, he offered to talk to me periodically. He promised to send me a copy of his book on the campaign, *Livre Blanc*—which he later did.

The former King walked me to the door, and we said farewell most cordially. I left a little shaken, feeling that I had been in the presence of one of the most tragic figures of modern history. It was particularly sad, I thought, that this regal man should still be concerned, thirty years after the fact, about a casual sentence in a newspaper article. And I was anxious to do what I could to see that he at least receive justice.

On returning to the Embassy I reached for my *West Point Atlas of American Wars,* which covered the 1940 campaign. This publication, not known for its charity toward unsuccessful commanders, indicated no criticism of Leopold. It confirmed what I already knew, that Leopold had notified the British of his impending collapse *after* the Dunkirk evacuation had been ordered; that the Belgians had covered the British withdrawal; and that Leopold had been taken prisoner by the Nazis in Brugge, not Brussels. I decided to write a letter to the editor of the *Times*.[13]

On Monday morning I called George Moffitt, doubling as political counselor and acting DCM, and told him what I intended to do. His reaction surprised me because George was a fairly free-wheeling officer, not always looking for a reason why something shouldn't be done. He shared my zest for an occasional turn of phrase when drafting our otherwise dreary telegrams. But George had been a junior officer in Brussels when Leopold had made his ill-fated entry in 1950 and the memory of the flying rocks was still etched in his mind. He stood on his hind legs. "Mr. Ambassador," he said, "you just can't write a letter to the *Times* in your position. If you were a private citizen, OK. But if you, as the American ambassador, took sides on this issue, eyebrows would be raised all over Belgium, even among the group that have always supported Leopold. You just can't do it!"

I argued for a while, as I really wanted to do something positive. "How," I demanded, "do you define 'raised eyebrows'?"

---

[13] My intention was simply to clear up the facts as I knew them about the military campaign. I have not done the research to take a position on the correctness of King Leopold's other actions.

"Well," he said, "you wouldn't be PNG'd[14] but you'd be doing injury to what you're here for." I gave in and settled for calling Farnsworth in Paris.

Clyde Farnsworth, known as a straight shooter, was more than cooperative when I reached him. He was chagrined at the injustice that had been done and freely admitted that he had not double-checked the work of his researchers on the particular point I had in mind. He volunteered to write a letter of apology to Leopold through his aide. I even gave him suggested wording, which he followed. In a realistic world, that was as far as I could expect Farnsworth or the *Times* to go.

On August 2 I received a letter from Colonel de Vicq de Cumptich expressing dissatisfaction with the extent of the "rectification." What His Majesty had in mind—I knew it before opening the letter—was a public retraction.

Sadly I set the letter aside. I could do nothing more and realized that I would not hear again from King Leopold III of the Belgians.

In preceding pages I have emphasized the close relationship between Belgium and the United States. On the political side of things the two countries today have very few problems or misunderstandings. But this happy situation is not necessarily permanent. A great deal of the affection the Belgians hold for the Americans stems from their gratitude for liberation nearly thirty years ago. The generation in charge still remembers the horrors of the Nazi occupation; not so the young people who will soon be taking over the reins of power. Thus we would be ill-advised to take this affectionate relationship for granted, an error that the United States is prone to fall prey to.

If relations between the two countries degenerate, the issues in all likelihood will be economic. The Belgians may tire of American influence in their economy—we have a thousand American businesses and subsidiaries in Belgium—or trouble could arise from the fact that economic issues considered trivial in the United States (and delegated to the lower echelons of government for decision) can become major problems to the Belgians, whose gross national product is about one fiftieth of ours. Thus far the types of bilat-

---

[14] Declared *persona non grata*.

eral issues that have arisen are those involving air routes, tariffs, and the effects of United States monetary policy. One which typifies them is that of the Belgian craving for us to grant their national airline, Sabena, rights to land in Chicago.

Sabena is owned and operated by the Belgian Government. It is a small airline and yet is overstaffed. When Sabena lost the bulk of its important runs to the Congo after 1960, nobody was laid off. As a result, Sabena today rates among the top with respect to employees per passenger mile. For this and other reasons, Sabena loses money.

This situation could be alleviated, according to the Belgian Government, if the United States would only grant a second landing right in continental United States—specifically, Chicago.

The United States Government, that is, the Civil Aeronautics Board, refused to grant this second landing right. Pan American and TWA were both losing far more money than was Sabena, though not proportionally. Further, the Belgian attitude made negotiations difficult by their refusal to consider any landing point other than Chicago. The negotiators from the two governments remained at an impasse during my entire stay in Belgium.

To Americans the Sabena question was a minor matter and it was difficult for our government as a whole to visualize its threatening to produce any deterioration in relationships. Further, in the early days of the Nixon administration, such a second landing right was granted to KLM, the Dutch-owned rival of Sabena. This error, typical of the early phases of any administration, made the Sabena issue an emotional one in Belgium, sufficiently so for the Foreign Minister to be called periodically to account to the parliament on the status of negotiations. And he mentioned it to me nearly every time we met.

Another economic cause for concern was the possibility of an increase in United States tariffs on flat glass. Belgian flat-glass exports to the U.S. amounted to $20 million a year, the equivalent, in terms of gross national products, of a billion dollars for America. In the summer of 1969 four American glass companies applied to the Tariff Commission for a "declaration of damage" resulting from Belgian flat-glass imports.

On this matter I think I might have had some influence. Immediately after learning of the problem, I visited with Bob Schaetzel, U.S. ambassador to the Common Market. We discovered that our views were the same: a raise in this tariff would be disastrous. Bob and I agreed for different reasons. He was thinking in economic terms; I was concerned primarily for the President's credibility in Europe. In my first speech in Brussels, before the Belgo-American Association in June of 1969, I had repeated the President's earlier words practically verbatim: that in our fight to rectify the United States balance of payments deficits, we would not resort to protectionism. With the President so clearly on record, any increase in flat-glass tariffs would run directly counter to that statement.

With the help of the economic counselor, Edwin Crowley, I began to bombard my friends in Washington. I wrote lengthy letters to special people in State, Commerce, and the White House. The replies were a bit of an education; from Commerce in particular I learned that not everyone admired "free trade" unreservedly There is at least an argument, whether one accepts it or not, on the other side.

This story turned out happily. The Tariff Commission, by a vote of four to two, declared certain varieties of flat glass to be "no damage"—the issue was dead for them. With other varieties the vote was three to three, and the President wisely decided the issue by postponing any raises in tariffs for at least a couple of years. This was all I could ask for. Some elements of the Belgian press complained that the tax had not been lowered, but in private their glass industry was delighted. They sent a representative to see me and urge that I should not take the press viewpoint seriously.

In March 1970 a mass of Belgian students were planning a demonstration through the center of Brussels to protest against the U.S. incursion into Cambodia. Accordingly, we in the Embassy put our full alert plan into effect. Doors were barred and the Marine guards, in civilian clothes, were retained on duty in the lobby.

The Belgians exercised every possible precaution. Besides surrounding the Embassy with dozens of *gendarmes,* they also assembled about two platoons of horse guards in the National Park behind the Residence for use as reserve.

One aspect of our defense, however, was annoying both to the marines and to me—the fact that Americans could take no measures to defend themselves until the lobby of the Chancery should be entered. This rule, though contrary to every military man's training, was logical. Inside the Embassy we were legally in United States territory; on the streets we were not. Should any Americans make a sortie outside to do battle, the victims of such a fracas would in all likelihood be innocent Belgians. Once intruders had broken in, however, we were authorized and prepared to use all the force necessary to eject them.

It so happened that our ambassador to The Netherlands, William Middendorf, was in for a visit. All afternoon Bill and I listened to reports from the police and periodically I would visit the marines in the lobby, reveling in my role as the local Supreme Commander of American Forces. Later in the afternoon we watched the horse guards trot out of the park and turn left down the street. By about 7 P.M. word came that the demonstration had been broken up at the Botanical Gardens, about a mile and a half to the north, and the alert was raised. While the matter fortunately turned out to be a false alarm, the episode gave us an opportunity for a realistic testing and perfecting of our defense plans.

Though we experienced occasional demonstration warnings and a couple of bomb threats during my tenure, our situation was, in the light of world events and the existence of small terrorist groups, remarkably placid. One night, however, some unknown persons managed to hang a Viet Cong flag under my office window. Fortunately, the flag was blown by a rainy wind up onto the ledge, out of sight from the street. Nevertheless, the culprits' ability to perform such a feat proved that the job was the work of professionals. Thereafter we supplemented our surveillance with an additional closed-circuit television.

The *gendarmes* in Brussels, incidentally, built around a hard core of toughened veterans, were serious about their business. Equipped with plastic shields and long, weighted billy clubs, they brooked no foolishness when disorder hit. One day a group of demonstrators chained themselves to the iron railings surrounding the Soviet Trade Mission, two doors away from the Embassy. By the time the *gendarmes* began to wield their nightsticks, keys rapidly came out of pockets and the group disappeared forthwith.

All in all, Brussels was one of the most orderly of the large cities of the world. Even lone women were safe on the streets at night. This fact helped make Brussels one of the more desirable of our diplomatic posts.

After the mad social month in May 1970, during the time when government personnel normally arrive and depart, I planned to go home on consultations and to give a commencement address at Northwood Institute in Midland, Michigan. Barbara and Mary were to join me after a week to see David, Julie, and Susie graduate from their respective schools. The trip back to the United States was noteworthy only for the emotion I felt at the first sight of United States soil. I have at this writing flown the Atlantic forty-three times and spent thirty months in Europe during and after World War II. But never yet on return have I felt quite such a depth of feeling as on coming back that time. I cannot explain why; perhaps it was simply fatigue.

Earlier that year David and Julie had decided, because of the vicious attitudes of a small minority of students at Amherst and Smith Colleges, which focused temporarily on the couple as symbols, that it would be wise to forego attendance at their respective graduations. Instead, President and Mrs. Nixon were kind enough to have a small group as houseguests at Camp David for a family party as a substitute.

The rest of the time at home was spent in consultations with the State Department and a week-long visit with Mother. Before the end of June we returned refreshed to Brussels.

On July 9, 1970, I went to the Foreign Ministry to sign the Double Taxation Treaty with Foreign Minister Harmel. In fact, I had not participated in its negotiation. It was one of those pieces of work that are slaved over by nameless government technicians for an extended period. Even though the treaty works to the benefit of citizens of both nations, it serves as an example of the fact that negotiations, no matter how reasonable, are usually tedious in execution. I mention the incident only because it is the one time I was able to exercise the "plenipotentiary" facet of my impressive title.

In early September Barbara's parents, Colonel and Mrs. Percy Thompson, arrived for a few months' stay in the Residence. Both had been suffering from ill health for some time, and one of the things that Colonel Thompson had been looking forward to as a patient in the Veterans Administration Hospital in Gainesville, Florida, had been this trip abroad. During their stay of five months they showed considerable improvement. Their presence lent life and interest for all of us when we were able to be at home to enjoy their company.

Then, the next month after the Thompsons' arrival, our daughter Sue arrived in Brussels one day all full of life and bounce. When the cocktail hour arrived, she and Barbara apparently felt the time had come to let the ogre of the castle in on a secret: Sue and Alexander Bradshaw, a British barrister and the son of Her Majesty's consul in Brussels, planned to be married the coming April. My permission was considered necessary and we went through the formality. But if I ever heard of a pure formality, this was it!

Nineteen-seventy went out with a whimper, but 1971 came in with a bang. That New Year's Day I went to bed at a fairly early hour, as Barbara and Sue were in the United States with Alexander. I was awakened by a transatlantic telephone call.

Our family is not given to casual long-distance calls, and I was concerned until I heard the news. Sue and Alexander, Barbara said, having gone through a successful International Ball in New York, had now decided not to wait; they wanted to get married the next week, January 8, in the United States.

I was delighted. The prospects of planning a huge diplomatic wedding reception in Brussels had been haunting me for some time. I was, I thought, getting off easy.

The next day, however, with memories of Gettysburg New Year's Eve parties still in my mind, I thought it best to double check with Barbara. The whole crowd could, after all, have been carried away by all the excitement. Not so: all were in dead earnest.

Alexander's parents, John and Joan Bradshaw, joined Mary Jean and me as we winged our way via Boeing 747 to Dulles International Airport four days later.

The wedding was beautiful, performed by candlelight at the altar, planned in detail by Sue and Alexander. John Bradshaw and I were each to read one of the lessons, favorite selections of the couple themselves. When it came my time to read, however, I ran into difficulty, as my part included passages from two places. On searching for the second, being color blind, I pulled the green marker instead of the red. Puzzled, I looked around the pages and found a chapter that I thought was a good guess. It turned out to be one castigating fornication rather than extolling the bliss of matrimony. I realized my mistake just as I finished the reading.

After the service, mortified by my blunder, I apologized to the officiating priest, Monsignor Alphonso T. Murcin Cavage. He simply smiled and said, "I didn't notice a thing." At Mother's house I also apologized to Sue and Alexander but they were unperturbed. "After all," Sue said, "the lesson had something to do with the subject. It could have been the story of the raising of Lazarus."

Once accustomed to the peripatetic life of an ambassador, one learns to take transatlantic travel in stride. In Brussels, on March 11, 1971, for example, I decided, in the course of about five minutes, to attend David's graduation from Naval Officer Candidate School at Newport, Rhode Island, the next day. David had entered this exacting school with some concern, principally over his lack of technical background from Exeter and Amherst, but he had applied himself and was now going to graduate near the top of the class.

Within a few hours of my decision, I arrived at David's and Julie's apartment in Newport. I checked in with the head of the Secret Service detail and with an air of mystery he asked me to wait a moment. David answered the door and the result was most rewarding. He looked as if he were seeing a ghost and gasped, "I don't believe it!" He staggered back a pace and said the same thing again. Julie had kept my plans a secret.

President Nixon was the principal speaker the next morning. The entire ceremony was brief and dignified, and I felt a surge of pride at the sight of the graduates. In the disorderly academic atmosphere of the moment their freshness and enthusiasm was a delight.

An unexpected bonanza of the trip was an invitation to David, Julie, and me to spend the weekend at the presidential retreat at Key Biscayne, Florida. In a beautiful environment the President's old friend Charles G. ("Bebe") Rebozo found swim suits and informal clothing to fit my size—we swam, played shuffleboard, toured Bay Biscayne under the steady hand of the newly commissioned ensign, hit old golf balls into the bay, and fished. We talked little business. One evening the President asked cautiously, "How are things in Belgium? Do you have problems?"

"We do, Mr. President, but nothing that needs to come to your level." This seemed to be the right answer, as my host visibly relaxed.

Two days later I boarded an overcrowded Boeing 747 for New York and thence to Brussels. The contrast between the quiet comfort of Key Biscayne and the conditions on the plane to New York were amusing; during the trip I sat next to a hirsute hippie who insisted on playing the harmonica the entire way.

In late June 1971 I formally submitted my resignation to the President as American ambassador to Belgium. There was nothing dramatic about this decision. A year earlier, when Bo Horkan had visited Brussels, we had discussed the length of time I should remain. (When I first went over, I had mentioned a possible stay of two years.) Bo and I were thinking much alike: if an ambassador is going to make any mark, that mark will probably have been made by the time two years are up. After that, the freshness wears off and the regular ceremonies become somewhat dreary repetition. What would Lincoln have said had he been required to dedicate the Gettysburg Cemetery four or five years in a row? Further, I had a writing career, I hoped, that had just been launched.

On top of these reasons was the fact that I could not make ends meet financially. Perhaps a better manager could have done so, but not I. Based on these considerations, the summer of 1971 had always seemed logical as the time to depart.

The decision as to length of my stay was one thing. Implementing this decision without giving the impression of leaving for some dire, hidden reason constituted another. I could only trust that the President would not take my departure personally. To guard against his misconstruing my reasons, I took steps to ensure that he not be surprised. In April I put in a call for Rose Mary Woods, the President's personal secretary, whom I had known through the days of the Boss's Administration. She promised to tell the President informally.

As time passed I heard nothing more. Although certain people in the Embassy were required to know my plans, the secret was kept until the day in June when I wrote my formal letter. It was intentionally brief and simply cited "personal reasons." There was no cause, I felt, to burden the President with a lengthy discourse. But when in August the White House announced my departure, one columnist, noting that I had been without Barbara at Tricia Nixon's wedding[15] in June, linked that fact with "personal reasons," saying that the combination of circumstances had people in Washington "excited." Others conjectured that my Mother's health was failing. I was happy to be able to provide Washington gossips with so much entertainment so cheaply.

In Brussels, during the summer of 1971 we sensed something of a diplomatic offensive on the part of the Warsaw Pact countries. Perhaps this was simply my imagination, but again, perhaps it was not. It had been apparent from the beginning that the Soviet diplomats in Brussels were of a high quality. Ambassador Fedor Molotchkov, who had arrived after me, seemed sick and troubled. However, the DCM and the political officer of the Soviet Embassy were both smooth and outgoing, speaking impeccable French, and cutting quite a swath socially around town.

The new Soviet ambassador, Vladimir Sobolev, presented a very

[15] Tricia Nixon's June wedding to Edward Finch Cox happened to coincide with a quick business trip to the United States I had long planned. I escorted Mother to the ceremonies.

different appearance from the conventional concept of the Russian diplomat; he was slim, rather handsome, and young. He had served as a company commander in the Red Army during World War II. Further, he had spent some years in Algeria, during which time he had perfected his French. He made humorous references to articles in the Belgian press that described him as a "mystery man," meaning that he was a relative unknown. He said he hoped to see me from time to time and volunteered that he hoped to live outside the Soviet Embassy compound, on the civilian economy, a drastic departure from previous policy. Of course, our talks were always discreet, and yet the atmosphere seemed easier than before.

One Saturday in September 1971, as I was lying on a couch reading a book, the major-domo of the Residence, Frans Vandenbrempt, came in from the kitchen to tell me that Nikita Khrushchev was dying. By Monday Khrushchev's death had been announced around the world.

Early that morning I called Alan Barr, the staff aide, and told him to telephone and inquire of the Soviet Embassy whether a condolence book would be available for signing. Khrushchev, we knew, was out of favor in Moscow, but I thought it might be worth while to ask.

On arrival at the Chancery I learned that the call had not been made. Alan, it seems, had consulted with the Political Section after having talked with me, and they advised against it. In a moment Alan was headed for the telephone.

Then I called in William Buell, the new political officer, to talk the matter over. The Russians, Bill thought, might consider such an inquiry an affront, since *they* knew that *we* knew of Khrushchev's status. I explained my own weariness with our apparent anxiety to cater to every trivial sensitivity of the Soviets. "Besides," I added, "the Russians know I had a special relationship with Khrushchev. I met him in 1955 and 1959 and came to sort of like him. If the Russians want to treat their former heads of government like dogs," I concluded, "let them admit it."

Within a few moments the Soviet Embassy had been contacted. There was no sympathy book planned at the moment, they said, but they would let us know should there be a change in plans. As it turned out, Bill was received with all cordiality when he called on his Soviet counterpart a few hours later. The chargé merely brushed off the Khrushchev matter. "After all, you know, Khrushchev did not deserve a state funeral because he was retired." The new suavity remained unruffled.

One learns, in diplomatic life, to live a day at a time—that is, if he hopes to survive. I never mastered the technique completely, especially with a calendar looking like a case of measles staring at me from the desk. Nevertheless I made considerable progress. Thus it was, when the month of September opened, signaling the rebirth of activity in Brussels, I re-entered the flurry, hardly giving a thought to the fact that we would be gone by the end of the month. Ironically, one of our more interesting discussions with the Belgians occurred during my last weeks, as we made efforts to get them to support us in keeping the Republic of China (Chiang Kai-shek) in the United Nations. The Belgians deserted us—after I had left, fortunately.

The timing of our departure, late September, had been calculated to provide me with the chance to be present during three Septembers—1969, 1970, and 1971—the opening of the Brussels seasons. It facilitated calls on Belgian officials who might otherwise be out of town. Any farewell receptions could be well attended, as they would not have been if given in July. The critical date of departure, for planning purposes, was geared to the call on the King, which should theoretically be the last official act. The King's schedule, however, was tight; he agreed that if we would give a last "official" day of presence, after which I would not show up at a public ceremony, he would try to see me as close as possible to that date. I chose Friday, September 24. Barbara and I were invited to dinner at the Palace the night of Sunday, the nineteenth, along with the astronauts of Apollo XV. This would be considered my farewell call, and the King would not be offended if I were to give receptions during the week following. Official calls were to be made on Premier Gaston Eyskens, Foreign Minister Pierre Harmel, President of the Senate Paul Struye, President of the Chamber Achille van Acker, and Archbishop Cardinale, who, as Papal Nuncio, represented the entire diplomatic corps.

Of these calls, one made me distinctly uncomfortable—the visit to Eyskens. Branded in my mind was the memory that the Premier had complained rather pointedly on my arrival about the brevity of the terms of American ambassadors. I anticipated a reprise and I was right. Leaning back in his chair, with feet hardly reaching the floor, Eyskens viewed me with that familiar look: half-closed eyes with the faintest twinkle. Not much of the twinkle was there today. *"Mis*ter Ambassador! I must tell you how sorry we are to see you go. We were so happy when you came, we now feel that leaving so soon, this is a great deception. Weren't you well received here?"

I was unhappy at the word "deception"[16] but tried to explain my situation as best I could, knowing that Eyskens could never conceive of a former President's son having to concern himself with earning a living. As we talked, the Prime Minister confided that when finished in his present post he hoped to go back to the University of Louvain and write. He also admitted that some ambassadors stay too long; one had remained twenty years and had become too Belgian for the interests of his own country. When he saw a faint grin starting on my face, he interrupted himself quickly. He pointed and blurted out, "But twenty years is *not* two and a half!"

I left feeling rather miserable, as Eyskens was one of my favorites. I suppose I should have been flattered; he could have said, "The Belgian Government will contribute to your plane fare—if you guarantee to leave." Finally, as he led me to the door, he said quietly, "You have made many friends here. Do not forget your Belgian friends."

The night of the King's farewell dinner was doubly eventful because of the presence of the American astronauts of Apollo XV, David R. Scott, Alfred M. Worden, and James B. Irwin, all Air Force colonels, who were in town for an international conference on space.

---

[16] Eyskens' excellent English failed him this time. *"Deception"* in French translates as "disappointment."

Before the dinner, the King and Queen asked Barbara and me to remain behind in the reception room for a few moments. He said little but presented me with a box containing the Grand Cross of the Order of the Crown. I was so touched as to be speechless and was relieved when, after a moment, we joined the group. I felt—and still do—a certain frustration that there was no way to reciprocate; and one does not write letters of thanks for decorations.

On Tuesday morning, September 28, the officers and many of the wives of the Embassy gathered in the reception room of Zaventem Airport to see Barbara and me off. Champagne flowed freely, and I was relieved that the group was large enough to preclude any intimate show of sentiment, as I had come to feel quite close to the dedicated members of the Embassy who had served so loyally with me. Barbara and I circulated around and said good-by to all. At the appointed time Louis Boochever, the new DCM, and his wife, Virginia, escorted us down the long corridors to the waiting aircraft.

As the plane headed for the English Channel toward London, my emotions were strong. We were leaving a host of fine friends— Americans, Belgians, and colleagues of other nationalities. And though I could point to no great achievements over the previous thirty months, I still felt an inward satisfaction. The events I had dealt with in Brussels had been less world-shaking than those in which I had participated a decade earlier in the White House; but this had been my own show. No matter how much benefit I had received from the assistance of others, the responsibility had been mine. I had been in charge, for better or for worse.

But ahead, as yet uncharted, lay a new life.

Appendix A

THE ENGINEER SCHOOL
The Engineer Center
Fort Belvoir, Virginia

19 January 1956

Dear Dad:

As so often happens with family visits, we really did not get a chance to finish our conversation the other night on the subject of the political decision facing you. I didn't want to pursue the matter further later in the evening for fear of appearing to be another "man with a message," of which you have an oversupply.

In her conversation with Mother today Barbara got the impression that you were at least casually interested in my opinions on the subject. I thought I would put them on paper for what they are worth. After all, there is nothing easier than throwing a letter in the waste basket.

I was quoted as having said, "That's your decision." If I used those very words, I meant them in the same sense that Milton did: that the decision belongs to you personally in the light of the national and your own interest, and not to a group who modestly take it upon themselves to dictate your duty to you. I shall try to analyze the matter as dispassionately as is possible under the circumstances. I have the advantages in this matter that due to our close and affectionate relationship I have developed many reactions, outlooks, and prejudices similar to your own, to say nothing of our similar training in the matter of duty; I have the disadvantage that I am incapable of completely understanding the burdens of the presidency; not having experienced those burdens myself. In addition, I have the disadvantage of lack of intimate knowledge of the intricacies of politics. With that by way of personal references, I begin my piece.

Assumptions:

(1) That if you choose not to run, you can arrange for the nomination of a man that you can support with a clear conscience. The list of such men would include probably Warren, Humphrey, Milton Eisenhower, Nixon, Adams, possibly Dewey, or others. Taken across the board, this man would have about a 45% chance of election, as things now stand.

(2) That the Democrats will nominate Stevenson, a man whom you have admired in the past but who has succumbed to ambition in his personal conduct. Looking back on the personal history and evolution of Lincoln, for example, this man might develop a lot of character under the responsibilities of office. His greatest weakness is probably a vacillation in his character; he would not be an all-out New or Fair Dealer. To sum up, his election would be a personal disappointment, and not for the *best* for the country; however, he is far from the *worst* the Democrats could put up. He has one virtue: Truman has not come out for him.

(3) That if you should run, your chances of winning would be about 75%. The Gallup polls showed your dropping only from 59% to 58% negligible. However, with the progress of the campaign hammering on the subject of your health, etc., this percentage would drop some more.

(4) That your experiments prove to *your* satisfaction that you can do the job as you think is essential. You have, of course, limited time to determine this, and it is a very critical matter.

(5) That the adverse effects of the office on your health can be minimized, and *will not materially affect your life expectancy.* Here the best judge in the world is Doc Snyder. He can balance the effects of the presidency against the effects of forced inactivity in the affairs of the government, with resulting frustration. If he is not willing to estimate (nobody can ever prove him wrong) that the office will not materially affect your life expectancy, then throw out this letter and tell all your well-meaning advisors to go to hell. This includes a limited campaign, which I would consider essential to insuring a reasonable political margin.

(6) That the existence of a competent, experienced working government with a vice president satisfactory to you, would more than overbalance the risk of changing presidents in mid-term due to your becoming a casualty in any degree. (This is viewed from a strictly cold-blooded angle, as an infantry unit commander ensures that the succession to command is established and the successor

trained for his own job before going into battle.) In my opinion, this is such a good assumption as to border on a fact.

Facts:

(1) Your reputation is unparalleled; a second term can add nothing to it other than the fact of being a "two-term" president, with the fact of re-election signifying contemporary approval of your administration. That is, in the big picture, a trifle.

(2) There is a chance of running and losing the election. This would have a slightly adverse effect on your long-term reputation; it would be fatal to your prestige as an "elder statesman" for a period of say five years, anyway. On this you would be taking on an assumed 25% risk.

(3) Your usefulness is not done when you leave office. Leaving under circumstances of health, your position as an elder statesman would be strong, especially if a Republican succeeds.

(4) Barbara and I have decided with little difficulty that whether you run again or not will have no material effect on the welfare of this family at Belvoir. There are advantages and disadvantages to your being in the White House, and they balance out nicely.

Discussion: Since the courses of action are only two, this can be discussed by merely comparing the advantages and disadvantages of running.

(1) Advantages:

(a) Increases the percentage of Republican victory in 1956 from 45% to 75%. This is an important matter for the following reasons:

1. The Democratic nominee will probably be a pretty weak fish as a president unless the Democratic party pulls a surprise at the convention. This is not anticipated.

2. Your government will have a chance, if you are elected, to continue its present work, which actually takes considerable time to organize. For example, the budget is just getting around to balancing right now.

(b) Gives a 75% chance that you can continue to lead the free world, inasmuch as it can be led. This is an extremely important item, and involves such intangibles as the fact that the Soviets fear and respect your judgment and military knowledge.

It is diluted by such imponderables as the French situation. In summary, however, there is no question that your personal leadership will improve whatever situation may transpire.

(2) Disadvantages:

(a) There is still a 45% chance of a Republican satisfactory to you of being elected. You might be able to raise this percentage by strong support on your part.

(b) By running you risk a lot: the chance of being an effective elder statesman, and a considerable amount of contemporary prestige. (By risk here I mean risk of political defeat, as with Mr. Hoover.)

(c) By election to a second term you risk:

1. Shortening of life expectancy (overriding if doctors feel that it may be severe).

2. Disrupting the government if you have to turn it over.

(d) Personal loss of prestige, in case something happens of a disastrous nature, over which you have no control.

(e) There is a limitation on how much one man can do, no matter how active and healthy he is. Personal example which you have practiced is almost stronger than the actual making of the decisions. This personal example can be continued from Gettysburg or from the presidency of some small university. As to the decisions themselves, too often they are decisions between two bad alternatives. If all the cards were in your hands, that would be one thing. But then there are the Mendes-France's, the McCarthy's, etc., whose existence somewhat nullifies advantage (b) in that St. Peter himself would also have to choose between bad alternatives when dealing with conditions brought on by these people.

Summary: While the advantages seem to lie in the direction of the unselfish course of action for the benefit of the US and the Free World and the disadvantages seem to lie in the direction of "playing it cool," this is *far* from clear-cut. You can still serve the nation well as a personal example (witness the case of General Lee) as a university president or as a writer and gentleman farmer. If you stay on, even a bridge expert can lose a hand if he gets no cards or inadequate cards to play with. At this point in the game the Eisenhower legend may be a more valuable national asset than Eisenhower the quarterback.

Recommendation: Don't run.

Final Comment: If assumptions (4) and (5) are valid, then this is an extremely close decision. If they are not valid, then writing (and reading) this letter is a waste of time; the decision is not close. At any rate, the edge goes to finding some other line of work, in my appraisal.

We are all fine and send our love to all. I hope that the above may at least focus attention on salient points where your viewpoint differs from mine and will help in your momentous decision. I do not need to point out that this analytical brain of mine managed to pull two "D's" on important exams at Leavenworth.

Devotedly,

JOHN

Appendix B

An Eisenhower Favorite

Sometime, when you're feeling important,
Sometime, when your ego's in bloom,
Sometime, when you take it for granted
You're the best qualified in the room;
Sometime, when you feel that your going
Would leave an unfillable hole,
Just try this simple experiment
And see how it humbles your soul.

Take a bucket, fill it with water,
Put your hand in—clear up to the wrist.
Now pull it out; the hole that remains
Is a measure of how you'll be missed;
You can splash all you please when you enter,
You can stir up the water galore.
Then stop; you'll find in a minute
That it looks just the same as before.

The moral in this quaint example:
To do just the best that you can,
Be proud of yourself; but remember,
There is no Indispensable Man!

Author Unknown

As recited by his friend General Alfred M. Gruenther
at the 83rd Eisenhower Birthday observance at
Gettysburg College, Gettysburg, Pa., October 18, 1973

Appendix C

JOHN J. MC CLOY
One Chase Manhattan Plaza
New York, N.Y. 10005

April 3, 1973

Dear John:

I have your letter of March 27th. It is quite true that on my visit to Khrushchev at Putzinda in 1961 Khrushchev talked to me about a possible visit of your father to the Soviet Union in spite of the effect the Powers' incident had on earlier plans for a visit.

We had been invited to a dacha on the Black Sea during an interval in our disarmament talks in Moscow. In the course of our visit there, Khrushchev came around several times to see us and we had some prolonged and interesting discussions. They were quite informal. In the course of these, he discussed a number of American personalities but seemed particularly interested in that of your father. He expressed regret that the plane incident had interfered with your father's contemplated visit to the Soviet Union.

Khrushchev rather fancied himself as a military strategist and he was commendatory of your father's handling of the many problems of the invasion, military as well as political. He told me that he had sensed your father's appreciation of the great contributions the Red Army had made in the defeat of Nazi Germany and his determination to avoid confrontations that could with less discretion have led to real trouble. This was the background against which he suggested that some time in the future if your father were so inclined, a visit to the Soviet Union could be still arranged. He was sure that it would bring forward a strong indication of the goodwill which the Soviet people and its leaders had toward your father. I gained the impression that this was more than a simple amenity on his part. The consequences of such a visit he had considered rather well. He seemed to be personally very much interested in having such a visit take place. I do not know now whether I incorporated all this in my cables home or whether I kept it to myself until I could return and talk to the Secretary of State and your father personally about it. My general recollection is that the spirit of the suggestion was appreciated by the leaders here with whom I talked and it was felt that in due course arrangements for such a visit might well be made. Before anything concrete in this direction could be effected, other events intervened and the opportunity passed.

Although I treated this informal invitation quite confidentially at the time, I do not feel there is any consideration now which would interfere with it appearing in any memoirs or reminiscences that you contemplate publishing. I have dictated this purely out of my recollections without any reference to notes or contemporary documents but you can rely upon its being generally accurate insofar as Khrushchev's attitude toward the matter was concerned —at least insofar as he conveyed his attitude to me. Whether Khrushchev had consulted with anyone else in the Soviet Union before suggesting the propriety of such a visit to me, I do not know. I gained the impression that the suggestion arose with him and was not contingent on approval by any other governmental authority.

Sincerely,

JOHN J. MC CLOY

Honorable John S. D. Eisenhower
Valley Forge, Pennsylvania   19481

Appendix D

En Route Atlanta,
September 2, 1952

PERSONAL AND CONFIDENTIAL

Dear Ed:

I understand and sympathize with the mental pain experienced by your young friends when they contemplate some of today's problems—including the one posed in your letter. Time and again I have condemned unfair and unjust practices against any human. Though I sincerely believe that, some years ago, subversion and communism had succeeded in penetrating dangerously into important regions of our government and our economic life, I still hold to the doctrine that every moral precept and law both condemn unjust accusation.

When such accusation is made from behind a curtain of immunity, the injustice is multiplied.

Our government—if it will use them—has the machinery and the power to rid itself of subversive elements without breaching, at any point, the protective wall that the Constitution erects around the individual's rights. However, there is plenty of evidence, in the field of financial responsibility, that the present administration has flatly refused to entertain and use evidence submitted to it by investigating bodies. (Some day I hope you will talk to Senator Williams of Delaware.) Moreover, before the Hiss case was finally broken, the government—including the President—had shouted "red herring."

What I am here saying is that no matter how bitterly we condemn un-American practices applied against the individual, we must not forget that governmental neglect, indifference, and arrogance gave to extremists an excuse to indulge in these practices.

In spite of this, I repeat that I do not condone such unfairness —and I'm astounded at the number of people who write to me applauding the "courage," "patriotism," and "devotion" of men who have employed them.

Now as to my own conclusion that I cannot fail to accord to all Republicans a pro-forma endorsement in the coming elections! I assume that none of us would, on the ground that an entire population was considered venal, oppose a decision reached by majority vote. If a Wisconsin primary names an individual as its Republican candidate and I should oppose him on the ground that he is morally unfit for office, I would be indirectly accusing the Republican electorate of stupidity, at the least, and of immorality, at the most.

Relative to this point I'd like to hear your conclusions on the distance we've covered in some one hundred and sixty-five years in justifying some of the most disturbing fears and doubts of our Founding Fathers. So concerned were they that popular sentiment or temporary majority would succeed in destroying state responsibility and local authority, that as one check on such a process, the Senate was established with equal representation from each state and with a six year term for each member. The discussions and arguments preceding adoption clearly show that a state's decision in such matters as these was to be final—the only concession to an overriding decision was the customary one of permitting the Senate itself to decide upon the fitness of its members.

For myself: Having consented to lead a crusade, based firmly on moral values—I want to carry my message to the people of Wisconsin. What do I do?

My own answer is that I shall never approve or condone methods that violate my own sense of decency and justice—but that I would accept the decision of Republican organizations in the naming of their candidates. Moreover, I feel that if there is to be a real two-party system in our country, then there should normally be single party responsibility in the Capital city. Here is the factor that crystallized the conclusion that I *could not* ask for the defeat of any duly nominated Republican, and this, stated backward, means that, politically, I want to see them elected.

Now there is the whole story! As you know, one of the reasons for my reluctance to enter politics was that I saw no real way of bridging the gap between clear judgments based solely on moral grounds, and the practical solutions that have to be developed in the field of politics. This observation is neither cynical nor is it any admission that spiritual values are not the foundation on which a free system of government must be built. In fact the farther I proceed in political life, the more I believe that I, as an individual, should have striven to be worthy of the pulpit as an avenue of public service instead of the political podium. But having yielded to the importunities and arguments of my friends in the first instance, I see no recourse for me except to hang on firmly to my own ideals and standards, and to remember that the friends who persuaded me agreed that, with my convictions I'd have *to declare as a Republican.* They were themselves aware of the existence of those paradoxical situations.

In this letter I am neither defending nor rationalizing. I'm faced with some stark realities—most of them are touched, at least, with unpleasant or perplexing considerations. I'm doing my best with them.

Perhaps what I am trying to say is this. To my young friends— possibly even to you—I may at times appear to be compromising certain values that I've constantly asserted were the guide posts of my life. My answer is:

(a) I'm not compromising them—I shall fight injustice as long as I live.

(b) Nothing I do is for myself—my own personal ambitions involve something far, far different from what I am now doing with all my mind and heart and strength.

(c) Political acceptance of an individual to establish party responsibility does not constitute endorsement of any view, practice or conduct.

(d) Faith of any man in another should not be lost on one seeming contradiction—or one tangled mass of conflicting considerations. Unless this were so—and if the opposite theory were carried to the extreme,—there would be 155,-000,000 political parties in the United States of America.

I hope, sincerely hope, that I can see you soon. I've written this (long hand) on my way to Atlanta. I'll have it typed before sending it to you.

With warm regard,

As ever,

DWIGHT D. EISENHOWER

Dr. Edward Mead Earle,
Institute of Higher Studies,
Princeton, New Jersey.

P.S. Personal. Of course—if a 3rd party had been started, and I had joined, then we could have excluded all with whom we did not agree on some major issue. I wonder how many we would have accepted???

DE.

Appendix E

REMARKS BY FRANK MC CARTHY
ANNUAL NATIONAL CONVENTION
JEWISH WAR VETERANS OF THE
UNITED STATES OF AMERICA
Friday, August 22, 1969

Thank you, General Klein. I am honored to receive such a generous introduction from a soldier and a gentleman of your attainments, which have been known to me for many years.

Commander Feuereisen, Past Commander Madison, veterans and your ladies, and distinguished guests:

If my remarks about General Eisenhower involve primarily his relationship with the Chief of Staff of the Army, General George C. Marshall, it is because during World War II I served as Assistant Secretary, later as Secretary, of the War Department General Staff, and thus as General Marshall's principal executive officer.

The General had no aide at that time. In fact, he seldom even used the word "aide" alone, but almost invariably referred to such officers as "gol-dern-coat-holding-aides," as though that were all one word, much in the manner that damn-Yankee was one word when I was growing up in Virginia. Fortunately the aide-type duties, the little personal attentions to the General and the very gracious Mrs. Marshall, fell to me, and I had opportunity to accompany the Chief of Staff to Casablanca, Cairo, Teheran, Yalta, Potsdam, and most of the other great meetings of the Chiefs of State, as well as to his headquarters and battlefield inspections at home and in the various theatres of operation. So when General Marshall saw General Eisenhower, I saw him also. I came to look at him pretty much through General Marshall's eyes and to admire him without reservation, just as General Marshall did.

I have never known of a more cordial relationship between two men, a greater mutual admiration society, than that which existed between these two Generals. In his fine book, *The Bitter Woods,* John Eisenhower says of his father's associates: "At the government level, the staunchness of two men shone through. . . . One of these was General Marshall, whose support of the Supreme Commander never faltered, no matter what the pressure. The other was Prime Minister Churchill . . ." General Eisenhower himself frequently referred to General Marshall as a true American patriot, as the most selfless man he had ever known in public life, and as one of the two most outstanding men of World War II.

As an aside on John, General Eisenhower came to the United States for final strategy conferences shortly before D-Day. The visit was secret since, if the General's presence in this country were known, the Germans would realize that the invasion was not immediately imminent and would be enabled to take a breather. He was of course eager to see his son, a cadet at West Point, but if John should show up in Washington, all sorts of suspicions would be aroused, both there and at the military academy. So I was assigned the job of smuggling General and Mrs. Eisenhower in a private railroad car from a siding in Washington to a siding at West Point.

For the purpose of surprise, I went unannounced to the Commandant and told him General Marshall had ordered that Cadet Eisenhower be assigned to me for several hours for a most important, top-secret Counterintelligence mission, and that we were not, under any circumstances, to be followed. John had lunch and a good visit with his parents aboard the private car, and I was able to accomplish my mission without prevarication, since Counterintelligence is defined as "an activity designed to deceive the enemy and to block his source of information."

General Marshall's reciprocation of General Eisenhower's high regard was best expressed in a personal radio which he sent General Eisenhower on V-E Day. It read:

"You have completed your mission with the greatest victory in the history of warfare. You have commanded with outstanding success the most powerful military force that has ever been assembled. You have met and successfully disposed of every conceivable difficulty incident to varied national interests and international political problems of unprecedented complications. You have triumphed over inconceivable logistical problems and military obstacles and you have played a major role in the complete destruction of German military power. Through all of this, since the day of your arrival in England three years ago, you have been selfless in your actions, always sound and tolerant in your judgments, and altogether admirable in the courage and wisdom of your military decisions. You have made history, great history for the good of all mankind, and you have stood for all we hope for and admire in an officer of the United States Army. These are my tributes and with them I send my personal thanks."

Despite all this, General Eisenhower enjoyed, in his latter years, being reassured as to General Marshall's personal feeling for him. Each time he visited Palm Springs, he would invite me down for lunch or an afternoon of reminiscences, mostly about General Marshall, and on one occasion he asked me why the General always called him "Eisenhower" and never "Ike," as almost everyone else did. When I explained that I had never heard him call any general officer by his first name, except one, General Eisenhower seemed pleased. Incidentally, General Marshall must have been a great joy to General Eisenhower's mother, who didn't like any nickname, particularly Ike, and who never even recognized it. On one occasion she wrote to the young bride, Mamie Eisenhower, "I am very glad you are having a fine motor trip, but who is this Ike you are traveling with?"

Also incidentally, the one and only officer whom General Marshall called by his first name was General Patton. He even called him Georgie. Since General Marshall never volunteered the reason for this, I didn't ask, but perhaps it had something to do with the old cliché that opposites attract.

I have been engaged for many years in developing a screenplay and producing a film called *Patton,* now happily completed and being edited for release. In one of our talks at Palm Springs, General Eisenhower asked me how I happened to pick General Patton instead of General Marshall or General Bradley, and similarly General Marshall asked me how I happened to pick General Patton instead of General Eisenhower or General Bradley. In his book, *At Ease,* published about two years later, General Eisenhower answered his own question with respect to General Bradley, and he could have been speaking just as easily about himself or General Marshall. He said:

"Of all the ground commanders I have known, and even of those of whom I have only read, I would put Omar Bradley in the highest classification. In every aspect of military command . . . Brad was outstanding . . . Patton was a master of fast and overwhelming pursuit. Headstrong by nature and fearlessly aggressive, Patton was the more colorful of the two, compelling attention by his mannerisms as much as by his deeds. Bradley, however, was master of every military maneuver, lacking only in the capacity—possibly in the willingness—to dramatize himself. This, I think, is to his credit."

You see, Marshall, Eisenhower, and Bradley were of such even temperament, so steady, so effective, so progressively excellent in everything they did, that the graph of each of their lives would be characterized by a line moving constantly upward. Despite his spectacular military successes, General Patton was sometimes so flamboyant, such a maverick, between battles that his line would look like the electrocardiogram of a man with serious heart trouble. That's what makes him ideal theatrical material.

Now, continuing to move his graph line upward after the war, General Eisenhower served as Chief of Staff of the United States Army, President of Columbia University, and Supreme Commander of the Allied Powers in Europe. He then returned to the United States to participate in the campaign which his friends had organized to secure for him the Republican nomination for the Presidency.

I have a memory of one rally, among many others, in this campaign. It was held in Denver in a vast enclosed arena which had a capacity of tens of thousands but which was inconveniently located well out of town. For some reason which escapes me, the rally had to be held at about 6:30 or seven o'clock in the evening, a time when most people are having dinner. Since the prospect of filling all the seats was dim, I was asked to round up some movie stars whose presence might help swell the crowd. Among those who readily consented to go were Humphrey Bogart and his wife, Lauren Bacall. All the stars and political celebrities rode about the hall in open automobiles, with General and Mrs. Eisenhower's own car the last in the procession. All received tremendous ovations, none greater than the Bogarts. After the rally the General thanked them warmly for their participation, as well as for their present and future support. On the way home, the Bogarts asked whether I could secure for them an autographed photograph of the General. Only a few days later Adlai Stevenson announced for the Democratic nomination. The Bogarts had already switched to him publicly and were out tub-thumping for him when General Eisenhower's handsome and warmly inscribed photograph arrived at their house.

General Eisenhower next visited Denver between the convention and the election. Senator Joseph R. McCarthy, a fellow Republican, to whom, parenthetically, I am not related, had recently been hurling vicious attacks against General Marshall, implying that he was a fellow traveler if not a Communist. At his Denver press conference, without calling McCarthy by name, General Eisenhower delivered a ringing defense of General Marshall as "a perfect example of patriotism and a loyal servant of the United States" and added "I have no patience with anyone who can find in his record of service to this country anything to criticize." Relman Morin, of the Associated Press, in his new, authoritative, and warm biography, *Dwight D. Eisenhower: A Gauge of Greatness,* includes this passage:

"Three times, while he was on this subject, reporters interrupted him with questions about other matters. And three times, Eisenhower brushed the questions aside and went on talking about Marshall's great services to the United States. He did not permit the press conference to move on to other topics until he had dealt thoroughly with the idiotic charges against Marshall."

General Eisenhower's campaign soon moved into Wisconsin. The news leaked out that, at the insistence of Senator McCarthy, the General had deleted from a major speech there a paragraph which once more praised General Marshall. Again, according to Morin:

"Next day front pages blazoned the report that McCarthy had bludgeoned Eisenhower into dropping the paragraph about Marshall. McCarthy himself denied it but . . . denials seldom fully squelch the original accusation, especially in a Presidential campaign where events swiftly crowd in on each other. The story remained a seven-day sensation. It filled liberal-minded persons, regardless of party, with despair and disgust. The Democrats, of course, expressed pious horror. Not only had Eisenhower tacitly endorsed McCarthy, they said, but he shrank from defending Marshall. The incident splotched an ugly smear on the knight's shining armor."

Now the truth of all this is that General Eisenhower held Senator McCarthy, later to become a painful thorn in his side, in low regard and campaigned in Wisconsin only on the advice of his political advisors and much against his own better judgment. Far from insisting or bludgeoning, McCarthy had nothing whatever to do with the deletion. In fact, it is my personal opinion that if McCarthy had seen it and had objected, General Eisenhower would have probably left the complimentary reference in his speech despite the counsel he had received.

Actually, he was simply persuaded by Sherman Adams, a campaign assistant, and Governor Kohler of Wisconsin to delete the reference, since he had only two weeks before lavished such high praise on the man who had served the opposition, the outgoing Democratic administration, as Secretary of State and Secretary of Defense. Further, they did not wish to provide McCarthy with more headlines garnered from another attack on General Marshall.

Two years later, with Eisenhower serving as President, Senator McCarthy was at it again. He read into the *Congressional Record* a letter from a disgruntled former government official saying that General Marshall "would sell out his grandmother for personal advantage." This disturbed me, so I sent President Eisenhower a telegram suggesting that he again come to General Marshall's defense in a press conference scheduled for the next day. When I arrived at my office the following morning, I was greeted by an Army major who, after inspecting my identification, delivered a confidential telegram from the President saying that he had accepted my suggestion enthusiastically. Again, for the benefit of the press and the public, General Eisenhower lauded General Marshall at great length, much as he had done at Denver, referring to his brilliant record, his patriotism, his selflessness, and his complete devotion to duty. He added:

"I think it is a sorry reward, at the end of at least fifty years of service to this country, to say that he is not a loyal, fine American and that he served only in order to advance his own personal ambition. I can't imagine anyone that I have known in my life of whom it is less so than it is in this case."

General Marshall was a soldier, a statesman, and a very practical man. His long and constant association with Presidents, Senators, Congressmen, and other government officials of the two parties, both elected and appointed, gave him a keen insight into politics. Out of this arose a complete understanding of the elimination of that one paragraph in Wisconsin which caused such a furore, and the legend of which still persists in some quarters today in distorted and apocryphal form. I hope my remarks tonight will help to stamp it out.

One thing I know: If General Marshall, a man of matchless integrity, had held anything against General Eisenhower, he would not have come out of retirement to accept the President's appointment as his ambassador and personal representative at the Coronation of the Queen of England. He would not have accepted in person a special award from the President on the tenth anniversary of the Marshall Plan. He would not have attended numerous White House functions, at each of which the President violated protocol by placing him next in order behind Vice President and the Secretary of State. And he would not have accepted the use of the Presidential Suite at Walter Reed General Hospital during several illnesses, including the one which culminated in his death.

I think it can be said of these two great men that both heeded the admonition of the poet, William Cullen Bryant, when he wrote:

> So live, that when thy summons comes to join
> The innumerable caravan which moves
> To that mysterious realm, where each shall take
> His chamber in the silent halls of death,
> Thou go not, like the quarry-slave at night,
> Scourged to his dungeon, but, sustained and soothed
> By an unfaltering trust, approach thy grave
> Like one who wraps the drapery of his couch
> About him, and lies down to pleasant dreams.

INDEX